THE MAD BOY, LORD BERNERS,
MY GRANDMOTHER AND ME

THE MAD BOY, LORD BERNERS, MY GRANDMOTHER AND ME

Sofka Zinovieff

JONATHAN CAPE

LONDON

Published by Jonathan Cape 2014

2 4 6 8 10 9 7 5 3 1

Extract from *Some People* by Harold Nicolson reproduced by permission of the Harold Nicolson Estate
Lines from 'The Green Eyed Monster', Words by Esther Duff, Music by Lord Berners © Copyright
1920 Chester Music Limited. All Rights Reserved. International Copyright Secured. Used by permission
of Chester Music Limited.

First published in Great Britain in 2014 by
Jonathan Cape
Random House, 20 Vauxhall Bridge Road,
London SW1V 2SA

www.vintage-books.co.uk

Addresses for companies within The Random House Group Limited can be found at:
www.randomhouse.co.uk/offices.htm

The Random House Group Limited Reg. No. 954009

A CIP catalogue record for this book is available from the British Library

ISBN 9780224096591

The Random House Group Limited supports the Forest Stewardship Council® (FSC®),
the leading international forest-certification organisation. Our books carrying the FSC label are printed
on FSC®-certified paper. FSC is the only forest-certification scheme supported by the leading
environmental organisations, including Greenpeace. Our paper procurement policy
can be found at www.randomhouse.co.uk/environment

Designed by Peter Ward

Printed and bound in Germany by APPL, apprinta Druck, Wemding

to Vassilis

CONTENTS

LIST OF ILLUSTRATIONS

CHAPTER ONE

A Fish-shaped Handbag

HEN I WAS SEVENTEEN, my mother took me to stay with her father for the first time. I knew that she didn't really like him, that he was homosexual, and that his house was remarkable. It took less than two hours to drive to Oxfordshire from London and I was full of anticipation as we arrived in the market town of Faringdon. Heading towards the church, we passed through an old stone gateway and into a driveway that began almost sinister, darkly hedged-in like a tunnel. Then an unexpectedly dramatic vista opened up between the trees; the town was left behind and an immense stretch of green countryside was revealed. Swinging to the right, we arrived in front of the house almost before we had seen it. A four-square, grey building, it was grand but not intimidating, handsome yet playfully gracious and as enticing as a Georgian doll's house.

As we came to a halt, the gravel crunched luxuriously and I watched in wonder as a flock of doves, coloured jubilant rainbow shades of blue, green, orange, pink and mauve, fluttered up like a hallucination. They swooped a couple of showy circuits around the roof of the house before landing nearby and picking matter-of-factly at dead insects on the wheels of our car. My mother explained that these dyed birds were a tradition, started by Gerald Berners many decades before. I had gleaned a little about Lord Berners – in particular that Robert, my grandfather, had been his boyfriend. I also knew that Berners had been an eccentric who

THE DRAWING ROOM AT FARINGDON: PORTRAIT OF THE YOUNG ROBERT HEBER-PERCY BY GERALD BERNERS; PORTRAIT OF BERNERS HOLDING A LOBSTER BY GREGORIO PRIETO; JENNIFER'S FISH-SHAPED HANDBAG ON THE CHAIR, AND ONE OF THE PINK DOVES ON THE TABLE composed music, wrote books and painted, and that he had left Faringdon House to Robert when he died. The 1930s had been their glory days together, when Gerald Berners created an aesthete's paradise at Faringdon. Exquisite food was served to many of the great minds, beauties and wits of the day. The place was awash with Mitfords, Sitwells and other visitors as diverse as Igor Stravinsky, Gertrude Stein, Salvador Dalí, H. G. Wells, Frederick Ashton and Evelyn Waugh. But my mother was not enthusiastic about the glamour or impressed by the famous old friends. She associated the place with snobbery, camp bad behaviour and a lack of love and affection. She had tried to get as far away as she could from this environment, and hadn't wanted to bring her three children into contact with it.

Robert was standing on the pillared porch under the crystal chandelier, a bullish boxer dog by his side. In his late sixties, my grandfather was wearing a well-cut dark blue suit and holding a drink and a lit cigarette in one hand. A wave of thick, metallic-grey hair swept off his forehead and unkempt eyebrows pitched at a rakish angle. I kissed him – he was my relation, even if I didn't know him. Nobody had told me then that his long-standing nickname was the Mad Boy, but his expression was obviously mischievous, his laugh a raucous bark. He must have been amused when Victoria, my thirty-five-year-old mother, and I introduced our boyfriends – hers much younger, mine much older; it was 1979. Robert turned our unlikely group into a joke for the next weekend's guests.

We were led through the hall filled with pictures and plants, and under a strange staircase that started double and then flew daringly overhead as a bridge to the first-floor landing. The drawing room ran the entire back length of the house, with one end pale, the other dark green. It was filled with light, as though we were very high up, and five tall windows gave on to an astounding view across the Thames Valley to the blurred horizon of the Cotswolds. To one side, a wooded valley led to a stone bridge and a lake, and to the other, cattle grazed in rough grass beyond the ha-ha.

Robert distributed champagne in pewter tankards and we took

in the long room, filled with things that had mostly been there since Lord Berners's day: ornate gilt mirrors, Aubusson rugs, a painted day-bed, a grand piano, antique globes, glass domes with stuffed birds and a collection of old wind-up mechanical toys. There were tall arrangements of flowers from the garden and the walls were covered with paintings – several by Corot, and some landscapes in a similarly muted style, which Robert said were by Gerald.

JENNIFER PAINTED BY GERALD

Lying on the seat of a gilded rococo chair was a white wicker handbag shaped like a fish and with a bamboo handle. 'That belonged to Jennifer – your grandmother,' Robert said to me, grinning. 'She forgot it when she left, and it's been there ever since.' Like so much in the house, it was hard to know whether this was a joke. A wooden sign on the front door said 'ALL HATS MUST BE REMOVED'; others in the gardens warned 'BEWARE OF THE AGAPANTHUS' and 'ANYONE THROWING STONES AT THIS NOTICE WILL BE PROSECUTED'. Robert also pointed out an unframed canvas propped on the top of the dado rail – an oil portrait of Jennifer by Gerald. She is gorgeous, with full red lips and brown hair swept away from rosy cheeks. Her eyes are dark and slightly protuberant, gazing inquisitively off to the side. Gerald made her pretty enough for a chocolate box, but you can tell that she is not necessarily happy. Maybe she really had left in such a hurry that she forgot her bag.

A Victorian music box in the hall tinkled a song to summon us for lunch and we were placed, slightly formally, at the round table in the dining room. I was introduced to Rosa, the Austrian housekeeper who had lived there for many years and was rumoured to celebrate Hitler's birthday. With dark grey hair pulled into a tight bun, and high-boned, florid cheeks, she seemed a bit flustered, though I quickly saw that the house was her realm almost as much as Robert's. Unmarried and utterly dedicated to her work, Rosa was last to bed, shutting up the wooden shutters in the drawing room after guests had retired, and first up, picking mushrooms at dawn, laying fires (lit at the slightest hint of summer chill) and preparing substantial breakfasts. Her hands were swollen and red, but they were capable of fine work and had produced an astonishingly elegant meal for us.

My memory of that first warm July day is of cold poached fillets of sole in a horseradish-and-cream sauce and tiny vegetables from the garden that could have fitted on dolls' plates – buttery new potatoes the size of quails' eggs and green-topped carrots no larger than babies' fingers. Afterwards, there was a dark crimson summer pudding, its fruity entrails swirling into the cream on our plates. Robert was master of ceremonies, pressing an electric bell under the table to summon the next course, and requesting that the ladies get up in order of seniority and serve themselves from the sideboard, followed, when they had returned, by the men. There was some sweetish white wine and Robert smoked between courses, filling his glass ashtray, carved with racing dogs, one of which was set at each place. My new-found grandfather was full of risqué humour and provocative remarks, but he evidently liked proper etiquette as a bedrock. I assumed it had always been like that; these manners felt long-established.

In the afternoon we walked in the gardens. The eighteenth-century orangery was filled with mirrors and large oil paintings – 'Gerald's ancestors,' said Robert, explaining that Lord Berners had not wanted too many of his haughty forebears in the house and had banished a number to the stables, from where some had ended up in here. There was mildew creeping up the crinoline of one of these unwanted ladies, but the general effect was so pretty it didn't seem wrong. The place was inundated with the intoxicating scent of pale Datura flowers – the angel trumpets that have long been used for hallucinogenic love potions and poisonous witches' brews. Outside, a small lily pond contained the bust of a whiskered Victorian gentleman submerged at the centre, 'As if he is the captain of a ship that has sunk in the pond, and he is alone on deck, at attention for ever, with the water up to his chin.'[1] 'General Havelock,' explained Robert, gesturing to the humiliated military man. A pattern was already emerging: the joy of pricking pomposity, of laying traps to surprise or delight.

Robert also took us to see the Folly in his Range Rover. He drove incredibly badly, taking no notice of other drivers, then careering off the road and onto a muddy track, banging carelessly over holes while smoking and talking. We arrived at the top of a hill and slithered to a halt in front of some surprised dog-walkers. Robert pointed through the clump of pine trees to a looming brick tower. 'Gerald built it for my twenty-first birthday,' he announced. 'I told him I'd have preferred a horse.' Robert produced a key and we ascended the rackety wooden steps to a small windowed room and then through a trap-door onto the crenellated observation platform. The 360-degree view above the treetops was astonishing. We gazed out over several counties, from the Cotswolds in the north to the Berkshire Downs in the south, where the chalky outline of a vast prehistoric creature is visible galloping across the green hills – the White Horse of Uffington.

In the early evening, we all changed for dinner. The unmarried couples were given separate quarters and I was put in the Crystal Room, which had a four-poster with glass columns and was hung with crystals and creamy chiffon. I lay on the velvet counterpane, taking in the strangeness of occupying a bed that had probably had people like Igor Stravinsky or Nancy Mitford sleeping in it. Mitford adored Gerald Berners and Faringdon, and fictionalised them in *The Pursuit of Love* as Lord Merlin and Merlinford. 'It was a house to live in,' she wrote, 'not to rush out from all day to kill enemies and animals. It was suitable for a bachelor, or a married couple with one, or at most two, beautiful, clever, delicate children.' My room was at the front of the house, looking onto swathes of green lawn, mown in perfect stripes, leading to the church. Rooks cawed from the spindly Scots pines as the light softened into evening. I had my own tiny bathroom covered in Rousseau-like murals and containing a pink bath and basin. When I lay in the scented bathwater, I seemed to be inside a bamboo hut,

looking out at a jungle fantasy of tropical flowers and birds, with a friendly black face peering in and a nineteenth-century lady-explorer making her way through the foliage.

At some point over that first weekend I saw the large photograph album that contained pictures from the 1930s and '40s stuck in somewhat haphazardly and without explanations or names. I didn't recognise most of the faces that stared out, though there were clearly many celebrities and beauties among them, some in bathing costumes on Italian beaches, others in evening dress at Faringdon, still more posed whimsically up ladders or behind plants. It was obvious that they were having an exceptionally good time. It was another photograph, however – one that wasn't in the album – that really struck me. By Cecil Beaton, a regular visitor, the black-and-white picture is a formal family portrait taken at the green end of the drawing room. Jennifer is moodily glamorous in a fitted summer dress, something like Ava Gardner, with dark, styled hair and painted lips. Robert is gazing past the photographer, casually handsome in sweater and gumboots, as though just in from the stables. He is holding a small lace-clad baby. A wedding ring shows on his finger. Over to one side in the shadows is a rounded, grandfatherly figure with a gnomic profile. Wearing a skullcap, suit and slippers, he sits on a sofa, apparently absorbed in a book. The impression is of a privileged family portrait: cut flowers, a portrait of Henry VIII, gilt-framed mirrors on dark walls, and a golden cockerel artfully placed in the foreground like a symbol of flamboyance, arrogance or perhaps infidelity.

It is a truism that photographs lie, but the extent to which this picture is misleading is staggering. It is 1943, though you wouldn't guess that it was wartime and that the house was occupied by the US Army. The 'grandfather' is Lord Berners and the father is the Mad Boy who had already been his lover for over ten years. Their differences were flagrant. Gerald was a stout, sensitive, intellectual older man with a monocle and spats, born in Victorian times. You can see he'd be at home in embassies, society salons and the creative world of theatre and ballet. Robert, on the other hand, was a wildly physical, unscholarly young hothead who was known to gallop about on his horse naked, and who preferred cocktails and nightclubs to cerebral activities. If the two men made an unlikely couple at a time when homosexuality was illegal, the addition to the household in 1942 of a pregnant Jennifer Fry was even more astounding. One of the high society *belles de nuit* who frequented Soho's Gargoyle Club, she was known for her style and charm. David

Niven said he never saw a better pair of legs among Hollywood's stars. I'd heard that once, when leaving the Ritz, her knicker elastic snapped and she simply stepped out of the underwear and left the silken scrap on the pavement. Like Robert, Jennifer was reckless and fond of sexual adventures. Even so, what could have brought her to marry a man who was wary of close relationships and evidently preferred men to women? What could it have been like to go to live in a *ménage à trois* with him and Gerald at Faringdon? In later years, Jennifer preferred not to speak about her short marriage or her time at Faringdon, though she said that Gerald was 'very kind'.

While I remember how dazzled I was by entering the strange and sparkling world my long-lost grandfather lived in, I now wonder what Robert made of me. Dressed in quirky vintage dresses and plimsolls, with waist-length hair, it must have been immediately obvious that I was from a very different background to him. After my parents' divorce when I was eleven, I lived with my father, who created the first British electronic music studio in our family house in Putney. I would get back from school to find famous pop groups of the 1970s or avant-garde composers from around Europe in our kitchen finishing a long lunch, or making their way to the basement studio. Amplified squawks and wailing sounds would emerge from computers the size of small cars and prototype synthesisers with hundreds of knobs and wires. All my childhood holidays, winter and summer, were spent on a remote Hebridean island in a house without electricity or telephone, where we read a lot, went on long walks, looked for fossils (my father had once been a geologist), and went camping on deserted islands. I was a funny mix – the kind of girl who got into trouble for being 'naughty' at school, who smoked behind the bike sheds and wore safety pins as earrings, but who also played Schubert on the piano, read Dostoevsky and could knock out any number of pies from my Russian grandmother's cookery book.

I had no experience of country estates or of Robert's life of horses, hunting and shooting. Nor was I impressed by the fact that my grandfather was rich and privileged, the Lord of the Manor with all the obscure rights and duties that went with that position. Nevertheless, I was deeply intrigued. Entering the gates at Faringdon took me into an unfamiliar yet hugely seductive realm. It was a version of passing through the fur-coat-filled wardrobe into Narnia; there were strange creatures and outlandish delights and preoccupations. At the end of my first stay, I signed my name in the visitors' book with no idea whether I would ever visit the place again. It would have been almost impossible to imagine that within eight years Robert would be dead and I would inherit his estate.

HEN ROBERT DIED, Faringdon seemed a place almost overwhelmed by the spirits of its past inhabitants; Gerald was its self-evident *genius loci*, but I was drawn to the mystery of what had happened to bring Robert and Jennifer together under his roof. And whether I like it or not, I have become part of their history. It has taken twenty-five years to reach the point where I wanted to tell this story, to get beyond the fish bag and the old photos. Gerald, Robert and Jennifer were all rebels of a sort, eager to escape and dismiss the old codes and expectations of their parents. None had a conventional education, but all were clever in different, sometimes surprising ways. Nevertheless, all three are in danger of being seen as caricatures. Playful and self-indulgent in ways that are no longer possible, it would be easy to dismiss them from our more egalitarian vantage point. Like the brittle Bright Young Things of the 1920s, the Faringdon crowd could be seen as deservedly extinct – irrelevant to today's preoccupations and values. Lord Berners is easily reduced by his tag as the wealthy dilettante, an eccentric in masks, a witty host surrounded by artifice, frivolity and famous friends. Yet he was also a sensitive, introverted, hard-working artist who was prone to depression, and a former diplomat who, at a time when it was illegal, chose as his life-companion a madly sexy, disastrously unreliable man less than half his age.

Robert is in even more danger of being seen as a clown. He had no obvious achievements to his name and was never a part of Gerald's cultivated, artistic milieu. On closer examination, however, Robert was steadfastly dedicated to the estate he inherited and deeply serious about preserving and improving Gerald Berners's extraordinary legacy. Jennifer is easiest to dismiss as the glamorous party girl who was only 'passing through' during her short time at Faringdon. But in reality, she was an intelligent, captivating woman. She brought a feminine (and family) element to a male-dominated world, and by producing a daughter and acquiring a granddaughter, she allowed this change to continue down the generations.

The crazy, pleasure-seeking world of Faringdon House in the middle part of the twentieth century sometimes looks like a wild, even farcical comedy. But somebody said that comedy is usually tragedy viewed at a distance, and the triangle my grandparents formed with Gerald Berners can be seen from either end of the telescope. Whichever way it goes, passing through the gates to Faringdon is still like stepping through the looking glass – the entry point to an extraordinary world where the unexpected is as fundamental as its beauty.

CHAPTER TWO

Behind the Rocking Horse

ERALD BERNERS met Robert Heber-Percy at a house party in 1931 or '32; nobody seems quite sure. At forty-eight, Gerald was already a well-established aesthete, known in high society for his witty charm, wide-ranging intelligence and his intriguing music. He was short and solidly built, his hair only barely there, and he sported a well-clipped moustache over a sensualist's lips. A monocle, a raised eyebrow and what he claimed were 'kind eyes'. His quietly observant gaze was contrasted with a mildly flustered fluttering of the hands that reminded one friend of Lewis Carroll's White Rabbit.[2] Robert was twenty and was only known for behaving badly. Slim and of medium height, his muscular grace was that of an athletic risk-taker. He had a long-jawed but handsome face, dark hair and eyes, and the unrestrained appeal of a gypsy, albeit with a public-school accent. He gave the impression that anything might happen. In an era where unusual pets were fashionable – lemurs or lions that might bite you or shred your curtains, but which were 'entertaining' – Robert had the allure and potential danger of a young leopard. Gerald liked to be amused, and this mad boy was irresistible.

The two men, so different in age, appearance and interests, were both staying with Sir Michael Duff in North Wales. Aged twenty-four, Michael had known Robert since childhood and, like him, was to marry twice, although he was believed to favour relationships with men. Unconventional, lanky and a stammerer, Michael was the owner of the huge Vaynol estate, which, despite its remoteness, was famous for its luxury and its outrageous parties. In the rhododendron-filled park, a collection of exotic animals, including a giraffe and a rhinoceros, gathered at the lake, miserable in the damp, Welsh cold. The house was decorated in eau de Nil, white, gold and pink by the fashionable Syrie Maugham, and the bedrooms, which slept thirty guests, all had the unusually lavish addition of their own bathroom.[3] Gerald had long been a friend of Lady Juliet Duff, Michael's tall, somewhat cold mother, and as a consequence Michael knew many of the younger men who formed part of Gerald's circle, such as Cecil Beaton and Peter Watson. A lifelong worshipper of the royal family, Michael's party piece was cross-dressing as Queen Mary, encouraging his butler to play along and address him as 'your Majesty'.

What passed between Gerald and Robert that first time at Vaynol is unknown. Robert somehow mistook the older man for a South African gold magnate. 'Then people told me he knew about art.'[4] Almost certainly he would have made him laugh with his knowing jokes and ruthless gossip. Though Gerald was a wonderful friend to many people, men and women, he had never been known to have an intimate relationship with anyone. He may, of course, have been skilful in his secrecy; certainly it would seem unlikely for an emotional, passionate man to have reached his age without a love affair of some sort. Robert, on the other hand, was highly sexual, and, though he preferred men, also had periodic involvements with women. Though there is no record of how the two men reacted to one another, it was clearly a catalytic point in both their lives. Those who knew Gerald described it as a *coup de foudre*. Not long after their meeting, they started living together.

ITLED, TALENTED AND RICH, Gerald risks being viewed only as Lord Berners, the eccentric joker, the 'versatile peer'. Like Nancy Mitford's minor though colourful character Lord Merlin, he can be blithely summed up by his facades and foibles, his glamorous parties and dyed doves. His image looks as managed as that of a contemporary celebrity, with a trademark style and the manipulation of publicity smoke and mirrors to create a personal myth. Hiding behind dark glasses and under hats, he went to parties in fantastical dress and posed for photographs wearing all sorts of masks, including a First World War gas mask; he was not afraid of the grotesque. He loved theatrical scenery, wind-up toys and decorated screens, and was well aware of the transformative and liberating nature of altering one's appearance and the power of creating the right surroundings.

Many of his famous and affluent friends mentioned Gerald in their memoirs and, though his artistic creativity is acknowledged, he tends to play a humorous cameo role, often as a generous, gourmand host. Harold Acton described him as bubbling over 'with private jokes and farcical inventions', but, more revealingly, that by 'constantly changing his skin, as it were, he revelled in mystification'.[5] Even friends like Siegfried Sassoon, who wanted to get beyond social niceties, were sometimes frustrated by 'the monocled peer, bowler-hatted, and imperturbable'. In his 1921 diary, Sassoon wrote, 'He wears the same mask (it *is* a mask, and is, to me, consistently inhuman and unfailingly agreeable).'[6] Sassoon later revised this opinion, but Gerald's disguises and superficiality became effective screens for the complex, thoughtful man behind them. Even his fascinating social circles and the good-looking women and men with whom he liked to surround himself sometimes appear like another protective layer. All the beauty and merriment make it harder to get through to the intimate sides of his character.

Given the decorative barricades that Gerald became increasingly expert at erecting around himself, it is important to uncover the thin-skinned, lonely boy and emotional, creative youth who made the man. *First Childhood* and his three other memoirs (*A Distant Prospect*, *The Château de Résenlieu* and *Dresden*) provide many clues, even if they sometimes sacrifice objective facts in favour of a good story. Additionally, two excellent books about Lord Berners have gone a long way to confounding the stereotypes and are fundamental reading for anyone wanting to know more about Gerald's life: Mark Amory's *Lord Berners: The Last Eccentric* and Peter Dickinson's *Lord Berners: Composer, Writer, Painter*.

Gerald embraced the twentieth century's iconoclasm and its love of experimental art forms, but he was a child of the nineteenth century. Throughout his life, he was characterised by a mixture of conformity and rebelliousness – a love of luxury and ease combined with a disciplined work ethic, an ability to play the fool while caring deeply about his creativity.

His early years bore many of the hallmarks of upper-class Victorian life that emerge in his novels and short stories, with critical or remote parents, nannies and servants at the heart of the household, and the oppressions of austere Christianity. It is an environment in which he pokes fun at vicars, well-heeled ladies and their pampered lapdogs, a contained world of rigid class barriers where everyone knows their place and where Gerald can do the subverting.

First Childhood manages to be both revealing and obfuscating: Gerald claims to be grateful for not having had childhood traumas, or if he did, 'they lie buried in my subconscious and I can only be thankful that they do not seem to have given rise to any very serious complexes, inhibitions or repressions'. However, his book paints a picture of an isolated little boy who suffered because of his parents' problems and was deeply unhappy at school. It is tempting to surmise that Gerald's lack of intimate relationships as an adult was linked to his parents' distance from one another and what he felt was their lack of warmth towards him.

Gerald Hugh Tyrwhitt was born in 1883, the only child of a marriage between two neighbouring Shropshire families. His mother,

Julia Foster, was thirty-one when she married a naval captain, Hugh Tyrwhitt (pronounced 'Tirrit'), who was four years younger. Julia's face is stern and, despite the heavy-lidded eyes, uncompromising. Gerald suspected it was her money rather than her charms that attracted his indebted father. Hugh might have been viewed as a catch on account of his titled ancestors; his mother inherited the Berners barony, an unusual title that could pass through the female line.

Julia and Hugh's ambitions were not enough to make a success of their marriage. According to their son, they were 'like two cog-wheels that for ever failed to engage'.[7] Gerald rarely saw his father, who was away at sea a great deal: Hugh was decorated for his part in the Nile Expedition of 1884–5 to relieve General Gordon at Khartoum. Admiring his father's wit and elegance, Gerald noted how, despite his small stature, he had the 'imposing swagger' of someone who could be taken for 'minor royalty'. Hugh was 'worldly, cynical, intolerant of any kind of inferiority, reserved and self-possessed'. He apparently took little interest in his son's education or well-being, to the extent that the young boy felt almost disappointed when, after some misdemeanour, his father said he could not be bothered to spank him.

Delving into his own subconscious, Gerald proposed that his father's *laissez-faire* approach had affected him in matters of religion. 'It is said', he wrote, 'that a child's idea of God is often based on the characteristics of its male parent.' Once, a nurse warned the young boy that if he was not careful, 'God will jump out from behind a cloud and catch you such a whack!' Gerald merely replied, 'Nonsense! God doesn't care WHAT we do.'[8] Gerald's mistrust of organised religion remained, though there were times when he wished he did have religious faith and regretted his lack of 'aptitude' for it, believing it to be something innate, like having a musical ear. Always keen to go against the grain, he liked to recall his hilarious misreadings of the Bible as a child, where he would automatically take the side of miscreants like Adam and Eve or Cain. Gerald used the language and trappings of Christianity to make it seem ridiculous: 'There is a legend that Our Lord said "Blessed are the Frivolous, for theirs is the Kingdom of Heaven" and that it was suppressed by St Paul!'[9] One of Gerald's fictional characters announces a sentiment that seems to characterise his own lack of piety: 'When I was a child I used to think that the Day of Judgement meant that we were all going to judge God, and I still don't see why not.'[10]

Underlying Gerald's witticism is the pain of a boy who is ignored and made to feel insignificant and unworthy by his grumpy, mostly absent father. And yet throughout his life, Gerald held one of his father's sayings almost as a mantra: 'Never trust a man with a grievance.' If the boy's achievements were not enough to bring paternal praise and love, then perhaps the only way was by doing things that would jar and annoy. Playing the fool can act not only as a way of attracting attention, but of subverting paternalistic authority; a symptom of pessimism as well as playfulness.[11] There remained a side of Gerald throughout his life that refused to be seen to take anything seriously; even his music was filled with jokes and parody, as though he could not risk appearing to try too hard and then be confronted with rejection. His love of disguises and fancy dress might also be linked to a fear of being himself – so much easier to put on another face and make people laugh. According to one friend, Gerald claimed to have dressed up as a wizard when he was young, so as to enthral other children. 'Robed, masked and bewigged', he burnt incense, rang bells and claimed as his familiar a huge white Belgian hare enthroned on a hassock.[12]

Gerald's friend Osbert Sitwell suggested that he was 'addicted to wit or humour as less gifted individuals are victims to drink or drugs'.[13] This implies that joking became a significant weapon against despair, tedium and frustration. It also hints that this trait was not always a positive element in his relations with others; some thought Gerald's teasing could stray into the realm of unkindness.

Julia was a more reliable presence in Gerald's early years, though he hardly appreciated her maternal skills when he wrote about her later. After her death, he accused her of being humourless, narrow-minded, conventional and, like so many in her family and social class, obsessed with country sports. There was shooting and fishing, but fox-hunting was her principal interest. She was an excellent horsewoman and Gerald claims that he 'never ventured to dispute the point of view that to ride well was the main object of life'. The boy tried to live up to his mother's ambitions, but to no avail. 'I grew to dislike riding more and more, but the ideal of "manliness" was constantly held up to me, and manfully I persevered.' He wondered why it was unmanly to cling to the pommel of the saddle when that was obviously helpful, or why it was manly to kill a rook or a rabbit but unmanly to hurt a dog.[14]

Like many creative people who come from dull or uninspiring families, Gerald was bemused by the banality of his own background. 'My ancestors, for several generations back, appear to have been country squires or business men with recreations of an exclusively sporting nature; although, of course, it is quite possible that there may have been among them a few artistic ladies who painted in water-colours, visited Italy or played on the harp.' Gerald felt himself to be the black sheep among his cousins and friends, living in fear and dread of humiliation because he could not ride well. While he was able to find refuge and inspiration in painting, literature and music, these were activities that counted for little among uncultured country grandees. He implies that he sprang, mysteriously creative, like Dionysus from Zeus's thigh and he attempted in later life to distance himself from his forebears – an irony for someone who inherited a title. He mentions a story of some long-gone gypsy blood in the family, hinting that these irregular genes might have surfaced in him. Indeed, others later noted his un-English appearance, with sallow skin and luminous black eyes; 'more Continental' or Jewish, some suggested.[15] Siegfried Sassoon described him to Virginia Woolf in 1924 as 'a Kilburn Jew', and she agreed – a strange indication of their snobbish anti-Semitism and a peculiarly inappropriate term to use when both knew he was nothing of the kind.[16]

The sense of being different makes a good story, but the truth about Gerald's family relations may be more hazy. Julia's diaries and letters show that while she was indeed a tough, critical woman who was more at home in the stables than the salon, she also painted and encouraged her son to do so. She and Gerald would set off on their bicycles armed with watercolour sets, and settle down to paint charming corners of the Shropshire landscape. Julia's diaries mention her only son frequently and she wrote to him with a tone of maternal affection and concern. She always made a note of when she heard from or saw her husband, so there are hints that the family was not as cold or uncultured as they were posthumously portrayed. Indeed, an affectionate letter from Captain Tyrwhitt to his son displays an easy amicability that does not fit Gerald's story.[17]

Whatever the parents themselves believed, and despite certain factual inaccuracies in Gerald's memoirs, the boy himself did not feel that he was appreciated and loved. This sense of being an outsider was later to be used by him to his advantage, but it may well have been at the root of some of his inherent sadness. The painful boredom associated with his paternal grandmother, Lady Berners (depicted as the ghastly Lady Bourchier in his memoirs), also left its mark. Her puritanical piety and narrow-mindedness surely contributed to Gerald's largesse, his love of luxury and, above all, his repugnance towards anything dull.

Gerald adored animals throughout his life. From school, he wrote to his mother, 'How are cat, dogs, birds, horses, pigs, poultry?' But his favourites were a different style from those favoured by his mother. Julia was inseparable from her horses and dogs, which included a spaniel, a collie, a fox terrier and a bloodhound, all of which were, according to her son, like her: loyal, rather dull and utterly predictable in their habits. When Gerald grew up, he would have dogs, but they would be decorative ones like Dalmatians, whose necks were hung not with practical leather collars but sparkling necklaces. Far more than dogs, however, Gerald loved birds, and these were the creatures that came to define his style and soothe his soul. 'At a very young age I became a bird bore,' he confessed, though as well as pretending to be a bird and making nests in the barn, he knew a great deal about ornithology. His idea of a childhood treat was poring over the weighty volumes of Gould's *Birds of Great Britain*, and in later life he told a friend how his purchase of a reproduction of Audubon's *Birds of America* had made his day.[18] He recommended it as 'an infallible cure for falling chins and wobbling upper lips' – symptoms of the melancholy and desolation which always lurked in his shadow. It is eminently appropriate that the Tyrwhitt family legend tells of a distant ancestor who was killed in battle, and how the mournful cries of three lapwings or peewits (also known as 'tyrwhits') drew searchers to find his body. The family took the noisy, gleaming-feathered tyrwhit's name and placed its image on their shield.

Among Gerald's earliest inspirations was the screen in his paternal grandmother's drawing room which, in his memory, was pasted with vivid pictures of unfamiliar, beautiful flowers, hummingbirds, doves of Siam and birds-of-paradise. Many years later he came across the screen in an old storeroom and was bewildered and disappointed to find that he had remembered it wrong. In reality, it was mostly country sporting scenes and political caricatures and the colourful flora and fauna were few and located far from a young child's viewpoint, near the top.

Another source for Gerald's youthful delight in birds and flowers was his beloved Aunt Constance. Handicapped after a riding accident, she had decorated her room with cages of birds, gaily coloured wallpaper and flowers all around. Gerald was transported by the atmosphere and loved helping her undo parcels of dresses and hats sent from Paris and London, and taking a look at her old Court dress and ageing ostrich feathers.

Like the many exotic birds he would later own, Gerald hoped to fly away from the place he came from and surround himself with beauty. His attraction to jewel-coloured tropical birds and flowers was in direct contrast to the sensible, earth-coloured dogs and dauntingly tall horses that he felt took first place in his family's heart. At Faringdon there would be birds-of-paradise strolling on the lawn and into the house. Another favourite would be the trumpeter bird, which he trained to leap from the ground to take titbits from his hand. A small, dumpy, dark-feathered thing from South America, like a hunched black chicken on tall, skinny legs, the trumpeter has stunning patches of iridescent plumage in purple, green and bronze on its chest and under its wings. It is something like Gerald himself – physically modest, without the showy beauty of other more obviously attractive creatures, but with flashes of brilliance, comic intelligence, flights of fancy, and a trumpeting call that could shock. Gerald appreciated an animal you could laugh with as well as admire, and one that could intrigue without being practical – like the eponymous camel in his 1936 novel, which arrives unexpectedly at a village vicarage one morning. Gerald liked to be surprised – anything but the practical, predictable animals of his childhood. As an adult, he didn't mind going for a ride on a horse, and it seems likely that his attitude to hunting was rather like Antonia's, the vicar's wife in *The Camel*. Due to her great love of animals, she was 'very much averse to blood sports, but she objected far less to fox-hunting than to the other forms of harrying wild beasts. Firstly because it gave pleasure to a large number of ladies and gentlemen, some of whom were her personal friends . . . And secondly because foxes very frequently made incursions into her hen coop.'

Although Gerald was wont to reject his family background, he adored his early home, Apley Park, which he calls Arley in his memoir. A romantic eighteenth-century edifice with turrets and Gothic flourishes, it was set in beautiful parkland in a valley through which the River Severn flowed. If the people surrounding him at Apley were not always caring or appealing, Gerald admitted that the place was particularly significant to him. 'When I hear cats spoken of slightingly as being "more attached to places than to people" I always feel a little conscience-stricken.' Wealth and luxury were taken for granted; there were twenty house servants within the crenellated walls, in addition to gardeners and estate workers.[19] But these privileges are not usually the source of happiness to a child, and Gerald had detested the 'long-drawn-out amusements enforced on me by my social position'.

When he was young, Gerald loved creating toy theatres, but he specified that he was 'more interested in the pageantry of fairyland than in the personality of its inhabitants . . . Rapunzel remained a vague and hazy figure while I could visualise clearly the tower from which she let down her hair.' He later admitted that 'A pretty house has the same effect on me as the sight of a pretty woman on the majority of people. Without any definite hopes or intention of acquisition, I like to have a good look at it.' This appreciation of place and ornamentation began early – Gerald decorated his room at Eton with fashionable Japanese fans and a large coloured photograph of a wisteria-covered tearoom – and it continued throughout his life. He was drawn to establishing spectacularly lovely and remarkable homes, the three main ones being in London, Faringdon and Rome. They were among his great creative works, comparable to his painting or writing, and he took pains to achieve the perfect *mise-en-scène* for himself and his favoured guests, who became the actors in Gerald's clever, stylish 'productions'. These homes were all extensions of the man – marvellous places to which he was deeply

GERALD AGED FIVE, 1889

connected and which he filled with an idiosyncratic mix of art and antiques, books and music, flowers and birds, and the best possible food. And when he could add something startling or surreal – a horse in the drawing room or guests dressed up as statues – so much the better.

Gerald's love of the aesthetically pleasing was dominated by the visual element, and yet his great passion was to be music. However, 'even to music I was at first attracted by its graphic symbolisation . . . My imagination was strangely moved by the sight of these black waves of notes undulating across the pages.'[20] As a young child, he quickly began to write imitation cadenzas on the page, creating make-believe music. His description of how he was first attracted to the aural charms of music is unusually precise. When a young female visitor played the piano, the romantic strains of Chopin's *Fantaisie-Impromptu* 'burst like a rocket in my imagination'. It was the beginning of a devotion that lasted all his life. The small boy tried to pick out the notes of the dauntingly fast piece and became fixated on it. Later, he was allowed to play the uncared-for upright piano in the billiard room – a gloomy, cold place away from the main house that 'bristled with antlers, wart-hogs, elephant tusks' and various barbarous weapons. Hardly the scenery this sensitive child would have chosen for his conversion to musician, but remote enough to give him the privacy he always appreciated.

For many years, Gerald remained largely self-taught as a pianist and he describes how his mother's reaction to his 'unexpected penchant for music' was 'an attitude of alarm, tempered with pride'. She was pleased enough to make him play to visitors, but his talent was not nurtured. Later, at prep school and then Eton, he was allowed lessons, but he felt the permission was given grudgingly and that his tuition was never enough to allow him to become a seriously trained pianist. At Eton, the older boys encouraged him to play light music at little private evening concerts, and his love of Chopin was replaced with a feverish passion for Wagner. Again, he recalled that it was the visual sense that came first; merely seeing the vocal score of *Das Rheingold* in a shop window made his heart beat furiously, while some years later, the sighting of a Richard Strauss score was as exciting as 'meeting the beloved one at a street corner'.[21] After much waiting, Gerald persuaded his father to buy the expensive item for him, and *The Rhine Gold* transported the teenager into his own Wagnerian legend. He would play the music every evening on the dining-room piano at school and his fervour for Wagner lasted many years. However, it was only after he had left school and was able to make more decisions for himself that he was able to pursue music more seriously.

 N SPITE OF his many advantages in life, Gerald was dogged from a young age by melancholy. Those who claimed that their childhood days were the best of their lives he suspected of having been particularly unfortunate later on, and he made it clear that he was not in that category: 'black care can sit behind us even on our rocking-horses.'[22] To an extent this was inherent in his character, and it appears that he was prone to misery as a child. However, it was also provoked by his experiences at school. At the age of nine, Gerald was sent to Cheam, a prep school to which his father and other male relations had preceded him. It is easy to believe Gerald's description of Cheam's horrible food, the lack of interest in the arts, and compulsory games. This was bad enough for a sensitive, creative, solitary child who didn't like sports. Worse, the headmaster was a sadist who terrorised the boys with caning and threats. Gerald's ironic depiction of the situation doesn't hide the fact that the psychological wounds never entirely closed. 'Nobody will deny that the majority of small boys between the ages of nine and fourteen are horrid little beasts and deserve to be frightened and bullied. But I find it difficult to believe that it is necessary for them to be tortured and terrorised to the extent that we were tortured and terrorised by Mr Gambril.'[23]

One punishment was recalled as even worse than the agony of the long wait before being caned. Gerald had thrown a copy of the Bible across the room for a bet with another boy that the irreverent act would not bring forth the wrath of God. Unfortunately, the headmaster entered the class just as 'God's Sacred Book' was hurtling through the air and Gerald saw it land at his feet. The punishment was peculiar but effective. Mr Gambril ordered all the boys in the class to hiss at the culprit. 'Surrounded, as it were by a roomful of infuriated vipers, it seemed to be the most terrible thing that had ever happened to anyone, and the suggestion of mass-hatred in a peculiarly venomous shape intensified my sense of guilt.' A beating was to follow, but it was the dreadful experience of ostracism that remained.

Later, at Eton, he was rejected by the boys in his house and the 'long hours of enforced solitude, spent in my room within earshot of the noisy companionship from which I was debarred brought with them an intolerable sense of inferiority and loneliness'.[24] The teenager was only too aware of his shortcomings and later wrote about how he developed a technique of self-preservation – 'the mixture of bluff and cunning that enables the physically weak to steer their way through dangers and difficulties'.

If Gerald felt wretched and isolated at school, he also experienced love. The first object of his desire was at prep school – a boy as different from him as he could imagine. Longworth was a tall, athletic, fair-haired youth, several years older. Captain of the 2nd XI, 'he seemed to me to embody every possible perfection', and it was his image that Gerald conjured in Greek lessons when learning about Homeric demi-gods. This yearning for someone apparently unattainable, combined with a deep appreciation of beauty, was to continue in Gerald's life.[25] Forty years later, the Mad Boy was just as unlikely and handsome a love, who would never be an equal soulmate and partner, and who had a way of keeping Gerald in a state of insecurity.

In *First Childhood*, there is an attempt to distance this type of adoration from clearly homosexual relationships. Gerald wrote that he was not aware of his longings for Longworth being sexual, though 'my infatuation for this boy-hero of my school-days was accompanied by all the usual symptoms connected with sexual attraction'. He suggests there was a purity 'in those innocent, pre-Freudian, pre-Havelock Ellis generations . . . [unlike in] these days of intense sex-sophistication'.[26] In *A Distant Prospect*, Gerald writes in an ostensibly open manner about the force of other passionate, youthful friendships, yet his discussion of homosexuality at Eton does nothing to elucidate his own experiences or his later life. He mentions the 'vices' which took place in the school and the hypocrisy that still existed on the subject, but then suggests that though a good deal of this sort of thing went on, 'to speak of it as homosexuality would be unduly ponderous. It was merely the ebullition of puberty.'[27] Gerald's soothing, avuncular tone was surely intended as a knowing wink to those who knew.

The Longworth episode did not end happily. Following a short if miraculous period of friendship, bestowed by Longworth *de haut en bas*, Gerald was dropped. His disgrace came after the two boys climbed onto the moonlit roof to smoke and Gerald vomited ignominiously. The misery of being rejected was overwhelming and the child fell into a state of deep depression. Whether this was the first time he experienced it is unknown, but it was a condition that recurred throughout his life. What he called *accidie* (a term originally used to describe the inability to work or pray among monks and other ascetics) made him feel that he 'might as well not exist'.[28] During these phases, he believed he was unloved, unworthy and that he would never do any good. The literary theorist Walter Benjamin described 'acedia' as an 'indolence of the heart' that ruins great men, and believed it was the key to understanding tragic figures such as Hamlet. This 'slothful inability to make decisions' leads to the hero passively accepting his fate rather than resisting it. Certainly, Gerald found that melancholia destroyed even his great love of music and literature, and what were normally such consolations brought no pleasure. There was 'that awful nervous sensation of a windmill going round in one's heart (known in later years as angst)'.[29] When struck by depression, nothing could comfort him and he re-experienced the hopeless disempowerment and torment he had known as a schoolboy. 'In this black nightmare all the old strictures of the headmaster . . . cropped up again and revived once more my self-consciousness at being bad at games'.[30] The triggers could be various, but the effect was deadening and familiar. Nevertheless, like many artists and writers who suffer depression, Gerald was able to spin creative gold from his disadvantages.

Gerald's unhappiness was not helped by a keen awareness that he was far from good-looking. At Eton, his contemporaries called him 'Newt' and Osbert Sitwell described his 'natural air of quiet, ugly distinction'. Even when he was an adult, some of his friends made unkind remarks. Beverley Nichols recalled, with cuttingly cruel, if inaccurate, comedy worthy of his subject, that 'he was remarkably ugly – short, swarthy, bald, dumpy and simian. There is a legend that nobody who has ever seen Gerald in his bath is ever quite the same again.'[31] In fact, Gerald's face is rather appealing in his photographs, with his evident intelligence and sensitivity taking precedence over his unremarkable features. He took care with his appearance and he was consistently well-dressed and groomed; striped socks or shiny white spats added a touch of elan to a dapper 'snuff coloured city suit'.[32] As a boy, he was always anxious to do the 'right thing', and it was not until later that he discovered the liberating effect of departing from conventions. Still, for someone who valued beauty so highly, it is likely that at least in his youth he was troubled by his lack of it. The frustration, even anger, Gerald must have felt was one of the roots of a humour that could be hurtful to others.

To make matters worse, Gerald's physical problems were not limited to his appearance and he often suffered from poor health – a bad case of rheumatic fever as a teenager may have had a lasting impact and his letters throughout his life are full of descriptions of illness. In a letter to Stravinsky written in 1918 when he was thirty-five, Gerald added a postscript: 'My illness was complicated: infection, inflammation, followed by an abscess – prelude, chorale, and fugue!'[33]

Gerald knew how to poke fun at himself, and he manipulated his sense of the absurd to entertain others. When still at prep school, he wrote to his mother: 'Why did you ask if I was ill? Because I have got insomnia in my leg very badly. Please come down to Cheam at once. I have also got Hooping-cough and measles and a slight inflammation of the bronchial tubes. Love to Everyone Gerald Tyrwhitt.' To this he added an accomplished and charmingly off-beat sketch of a barefoot girl in long skirt and military jacket.

ERALD IS SOMETIMES VIEWED as a quintessential English eccentric, but in fact he was highly cosmopolitan, spoke several languages and chose to spend much of his life outside England. Although his father travelled with the Navy, Gerald's affinity with foreign cultures did not seem to come from his family, whom he depicts as laughably parochial. When they had been in Italy, 'It rained in Venice, Uncle Luke caught sunstroke in Florence, my mother lost a bracelet at the opera in Milan, and my grandmother found a bug in her bed in Bologna. These mishaps were often referred to when anyone spoke too enthusiastically about foreign travel.'[34]

Gerald's love affair with 'abroad' began when he left Eton and, encouraged by his parents, decided to pursue a diplomatic career. Rather than go to university, it was deemed normal to go on a 'sort of protracted Grand Tour', to learn French, German and other languages.[35] In common with his friend and later colleague Harold Nicolson, as well as numerous other aspiring diplomats, the sixteen-year-old Gerald went to stay in various private establishments that took in young Englishmen.

The first exhilarating step towards leaving the straitjacket of his English upbringing was taken at the beautiful Château Résenlieu in Normandy, where the teenager was deposited by his mother. Under the tutelage of an impoverished aristocratic widow who had opened her home to young men wanting to learn French, Gerald did learn the language. But more important, conveniently separated from the narrow outlook of family, school and dreaded sports, his horizons opened up. Many of the seeds of his future existence were sown, from a love of Corot's art and a pursuit of this painting style himself, to an ability to converse on complex subjects with people from different backgrounds. Unlike so many of his compatriots who remained linguistically and culturally isolated, Gerald was brave enough to undergo the humiliation of being the vulnerable foreigner. He described the process of trying 'to be amiable in a foreign language' as like 'a dog trying to express its thoughts to a human being'.[36]

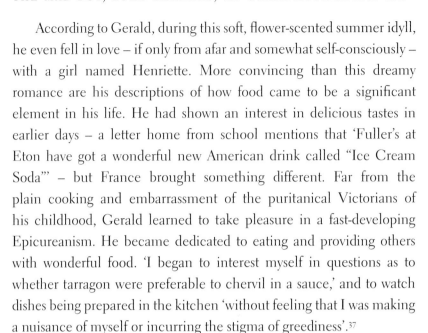

According to Gerald, during this soft, flower-scented summer idyll, he even fell in love – if only from afar and somewhat self-consciously – with a girl named Henriette. More convincing than this dreamy romance are his descriptions of how food came to be a significant element in his life. He had shown an interest in delicious tastes in earlier days – a letter home from school mentions that 'Fuller's at Eton have got a wonderful new American drink called "Ice Cream Soda"' – but France brought something different. Far from the plain cooking and embarrassment of the puritanical Victorians of his childhood, Gerald learned to take pleasure in a fast-developing Epicureanism. He became dedicated to eating and providing others with wonderful food. 'I began to interest myself in questions as to whether tarragon were preferable to chervil in a sauce,' and to watch dishes being prepared in the kitchen 'without feeling that I was making a nuisance of myself or incurring the stigma of greediness'.[37]

By 1901, Gerald was in Dresden attending a diplomatic crammer where geography, history and Latin were required as well as languages. Composition was becoming increasingly significant to him and he took lessons with the composer Edmund Kretschmer. His early love for Chopin had moved on to Wagner, but in Germany he became an ardent admirer of Richard Strauss. His peripatetic, informal studies continued over the next years in pursuit of passing the Foreign Office exams, but it was music that remained at the centre of his existence. Despite there being no evidence of any particularly close relationships at this time, what is clear is that he was an intensely emotional young man. Gerald later described how his moods swung from 'attacks of ecstasy almost orgiastic in their violence' to deep depression and despair.[38] It is tantalising to wonder whether these extremes of feeling were ever focused on people close to him, or whether (as some commentators have implied) he was too shy and diffident, and instead poured his passionate feelings into playing and composing music.

Despite Gerald's intelligence and years of studying, he failed the demanding Foreign Office exams in 1905, much to his distress. Two years later he failed again, and shortly afterwards his father,

Captain Tyrwhitt, died at sea – though he was convalescing on a cruise in the Mediterranean rather than on naval duty. Oddly, despite their alleged antipathy, his wife was on the boat too – her absence at the English memorial service was due to her being still at sea. Julia caused a family rumpus by remarrying the following year, confessing in a letter to her son, 'I do not feel so sad as I thought I would. After all I had not a very happy time with your Father, and as you say, one ought to live a little for oneself! I wonder if you will be very surprised to hear that Col. Ward Bennitt is very anxious to marry me. It seems so funny at my age to have anyone so wildly in love with me!'

GERALD IN 1905 AGED TWENTY-TWO, WHEN HE FIRST FAILED TO BECOME A DIPLOMAT

The ageing newly-weds rented a new home in Berkshire – Faringdon House – and Gerald often went to stay there when he was in England. Old photographs show the house and gardens at this time in its more conventional Edwardian guise: ornate flowerbeds on the lawns, potted ferns in the drawing room, and lace-draped ladies reclining on wicker chairs on the porch. Creepers sprawl across the facade, so it looks very different to Nancy Mitford's later description of the house as 'plain and grey and square and solid'.[39]

A CREEPER-CLAD
FARINGDON HOUSE
SOON AFTER GERALD'S
MOTHER MOVED IN WITH
HER NEW HUSBAND

So much had changed around him, but Gerald was still frustratingly without direction or achievement. His lack of musical training would appear to rule out a career in that direction and the Foreign Office evidently didn't want him. He was hardly on the look-out for a wealthy wife, as his father had been. The future must have looked quite bleak.

CHAPTER THREE

Russians, Radicals and Roman Catholics

GED TWENTY-SIX, Gerald finally entered the diplomatic service, albeit as an honorary (i.e. unpaid) attaché, and left for the British Embassy in Constantinople. This was one way of starting a diplomatic career if an applicant was not successful in the exams, and it allowed Gerald to establish an existence that was not pressured by too many professional duties and in which he could pursue his own interests and pleasures. He set off in February 1909, travelling on the fabled *belle époque* Orient Express, which moved slowly through deep snow after its stop at Vienna. Leaving the familiar environment of Europe, Gerald must have found Constantinople a different world. The exotic theatricality of the polyglot, multicultural 'Paris of the East' appealed to him, with its colourful, diverse inhabitants: sailors and merchants mixing with Jews, Greeks and Armenians; veiled women and hookah-smoking men in red fezes; and the Friday army parade when the Sultan went to prayers. Gerald visited the Old Seraglio palace, where he admired the jewels (an 'emerald the size of an orange') and the dazzling views from the Golden Horn. Much of this was about to change; his posting coincided with great political upheavals as the Ottoman Empire gave way under the pressures of war and the radical new republican movement of the Young Turks.

Gerald's contemporary Harold Nicolson overlapped with him as a junior diplomat, and though they were friendly, some have seen

Nicolson's unkind portrait of a mannered young diplomat, 'Titty', as being based on Gerald:

> A peaky face, a little grey face with blue-black shadows, two small unsparkling eyes, a wet and feeble little mouth, shapeless hair. He had the sickly and unwashed appearance of an El Greco page: he perked his head on one side towards a long black cigarette holder: his other claw-like hand clutched a grey woollen scarf; he looked infinitely childish; he looked preternaturally wizened and old.[40]

Much later, Gerald would exact his literary revenge, and annoy Nicolson with an absurd, puffed-up character largely based on him – 'Lollypop' Jenkins.[41]

Gerald may have been a shy young man, but he was safely buttressed by the embassy system; by this stage he was already giving dinner parties (some with mischievously arranged guest lists) and was remembered as dressing up in outrageous costumes. On one occasion he arrived at a large diplomatic party dressed in a black leotard and accompanied by two attendants playing pan pipes, and was tickled to see the ambassador's horror. '[He went] blue in the face with indignation. And little is so pleasing in the sight of God as a blue ambassador.'[42] Letters home describe sports more soothing to a mother's breast, like riding and even (following Byron's glamorous example) swimming across the Bosphorus.

In November 1911 – shortly before Mr and Mrs Heber-Percy of Hodnet Hall, Shropshire, were blessed with a fourth son they named Robert – Gerald was posted to Rome. Some of the joy he experienced living there comes out in his fiction, where he describes a city that still retained some of its relaxed nineteenth-century charm. 'The Forum and the Palatine had not yet been spoilt by archaeologists', and one could wander or paint at liberty. In the summer the embassy moved southwards to a villa on the Bay of Naples where magnificent terraced gardens filled with orange and lemon groves looked out towards Vesuvius. The British diplomats bathed each day at noon. 'It was almost too nostalgic. The days passed in a nirvana of delight and some of the happiest moments of my life were spent in a lazy amphibian existence, swimming in the sea or wandering about the hills with sketch book.'[43] Gerald's deepening devotion to Italy was reflected in the inspiration he found in the various intoxicatingly pungent scents: 'a mixture of drainage, orange blossom and the sea'. In his novel *Percy Wallingford*, he wrote, 'I have often thought of asking some chemist to concoct for me reproductions of certain mixed aromas evocative of places I have loved.'

Now almost thirty, Gerald established the sort of life he must have longed for. He lived in a series of beautiful houses until, in the 1920s, he finally bought 3 Foro Romano – an elegantly solid, wisteria-clad building on the less accessible side of the Roman Forum. Gerald created an entertaining, theatrical environment wherever

A PHOTOGRAPH FROM THE FARINGDON ALBUM SHOWING THE HOUSE IN ROME

he lived, and the impressive vaulted drawing room on the *piano nobile* made the perfect 'set'. Photographs show rooms decorated with a Renaissance elegance that was also playful: a large brass chandelier, heavy bookcases and impressive paintings were combined with a grand piano covered with *objets* (a mask, some portraits, a model galleon), and a leopard skin draped across the stool where Gerald sat to compose in the morning.

The arched loggia looked out across the spectacular sprawl of ancient columns and stone paths where, before the era of fences and tickets, Gerald and his friends could wander or sit in the sun. Gerald was later scathing about the burgeoning influence of archaeologists that made the Forum much less romantic and 'lost to poets and lovers'. Tito Mannini, Gerald's cook, bred canaries and once spent all day in the Forum trying to coax them home when they were somehow let out of their cages. Tito was temperamental and not universally loved, but he was a talented cook and made the most delicious chocolate cake with sour cream, rum, angelica and candied cherries. He took on the role of major-domo when Gerald let friends stay at the house in his absence, but there were rumours that he was spotted wearing his employer's clothes and using the house as a sales room for antiques.

Roman friends came from a variety of sources, including the British community and the Embassy, where the Ambassador was the Rt Hon. Sir Rennell Rodd and his domineering, party-loving wife, Lilias ('Lady Rude').* Gerald also got to know people in Italian high society, the most dashing of whom was the near-mythical Marchesa Casati, with her mesmerising, kohl-rimmed green eyes, white skin and Cleopatra fringe. A central figure in the European avant-garde that was flourishing in Rome, she was dressed by Fortuny, Erté and even Diaghilev's costume designer, Bakst, whose clashing colours and sensual clothes were thrilling audiences around Europe. The Marchesa's dramatic style and unusual looks made her a popular subject for artists of the day, and she was photographed by Man Ray, painted by Augustus John and sculpted by Jacob Epstein.

Like Gerald, Luisa Casati started life as a shy, plain child from a privileged family and later learned to use eccentricity (and her wealth) to create a successful, worldly persona. Certainly, her enthusiasm for her own celebrity was indefatigable compared to Gerald's, whose later use of publicity for his own purposes remained playful and low-key. The English diplomat and the Italian aristocrat also shared an unusual appreciation of animals, though La Casati had a

---

* Their son, Peter Rodd, would later marry Nancy Mitford.

menagerie that made anything Gerald would do look positively modest. Owning not only mauve monkeys, parrots and albino blackbirds, but also large and lethal snakes and felines, she became notorious for her appearances at parties, where she might walk in with a cheetah or a panther in a diamond-studded collar, or wearing a snake around her neck.

Italian life suited the young diplomat. There were dinners, rides around town, and expeditions into the stunning Roman Campagna to paint, or to the sulphur baths near Tivoli. Gerald helped found a 'quartette society', where members organised private concerts and gave poor but accomplished string players the opportunity to perform Mozart, Beethoven and early Italian music. Far more interesting, though, was his own composition, which he was now taking very seriously.

During these years, while much of Europe was plunged into the horrors of the First World War, Gerald's diplomatic status exempted him from fighting and he found himself at the centre of Europe's most excitingly innovative creative arts. Diaghilev's Ballets Russes, then at the height of its European success, was based in Rome during the war, and Gerald was pulled into the orbit of its thrilling, colourful, experimental combination of art forms. In 1915 he met Igor Stravinsky, possibly at the Italian premiere of *Petrushka*. The Russian was already well known for his daring, iconoclastic music, and the riotous reaction of the Parisian audience to the first performance of *The Rite of Spring* a couple of years earlier had only added to his fame. In the same year, Gerald wrote a piece for piano called 'Le Poisson d'or' and later dedicated it to Stravinsky after the Russian said he liked it. Gerald wrote words to accompany this experimental yet graceful musical picture, whose pretty glissandos, knowing dissonances and jokey repetitions and pauses seem to describe his own intimate feelings of sadness, tinged with a darkly humorous awareness of how small and isolated an individual life can be. In this piece, Gerald *is* the lonely fish, however much he makes others smile about it.

> Mournful and alone, the goldfish
> circles in his crystal bowl.
> He dreams of a little mate, beautiful and as shiny
> As a twenty franc piece . . .

A bright, modern cover for the score was commissioned from the Russian painter Natalia Goncharova, who designed marvellous costumes and sets for Diaghilev's ballets.

After the Russian Revolution in 1917, Stravinsky (who was a supporter) wanted to find a substitute for 'God Save the Tsar!' to play at his performances and to offer to the Bolsheviks. Though far from being politicised, let alone anybody's idea of a revolutionary, it was Gerald who worked through the night with Stravinsky to help orchestrate the 'Song of the Volga Boatmen'.[44] It was never used by the Soviets, but the exiled Russian composer went on playing it as a national anthem at his concerts.

Since the outbreak of the war, Stravinsky had been based with his family in Switzerland and in 1916 Gerald went to visit him there in the hope of musical advice. The thirty-four-year-old Russian was willing to act as a musical mentor to the thirty-three-year-old Englishman, and their correspondence illustrates their increasing familiarity, opening with, 'Dear Friend', 'Dear Friend Tyrwhitt', and Gerald signing off as 'Your devoted Gerald Tyrwhitt'. Gerald's penchant for pranks and jokes was already in evidence when he sent Stravinsky one of his characteristically doctored postcards – a painting of Brahms that was adjusted so he was surrounded by naked women and clouds. The caption reads: 'Why all of these nude women? I was always assured that Brahms was chaste.'

Stravinsky advised Gerald about composing, but the latter's style remained quite different from the former's, albeit displaying the odd Stravinskian fingerprint, such as the use of repeated rhythms and phrases, or surprising the listener with the sudden development of a melody in an unexpected direction.[45] Gerald tried to assist Stravinsky with practical issues concerning performances and even payments.

The letters show him to be more than willing to act as go-between in the famous composer's dealings with the Ballets Russes, the dauntingly demanding yet brilliant Diaghilev, and even government authorities. When Stravinsky had problems taking a Picasso portrait of himself back home from Rome to Switzerland, it was Gerald who arranged for the painting to be carried in the diplomatic bag and saw his friend off with delicious mandorlati figs.

While Gerald was mixing with the great artists and musicians of the day, an interest in popular theatre, pantomime and song had already taken root and would remain for life: years earlier, Gerald had admired Mozart's *The Magic Flute* for being 'just like a pantomime'. In 1917, Gerald wrote to Stravinsky: 'Near my house I have discovered a tiny, dirty little theatre-music hall, which I want you to see when you come. They have a variety programme and an orchestra *à tout crever* [that could raise the roof]. I took Picasso and Cocteau there the other night, and they were thrilled.'[46]

Jean Cocteau, like Gerald, was a man of varied talents who was in danger of being seen as a dandified dilettante. The apparent simplicity and succinctness of their work did not always endear them to cultural heavyweights. Gerald liked his compositions (and other people's) to be entertaining, even escapist; nothing too long or too serious was permitted. As he wrote in his novel *Far From the Madding War*, 'The English have a tendency to judge art by size and weight.' In his work, he always aimed for brevity, and frequently levity – not to mention parody. According to his future friend and collaborator, the composer Constant Lambert, Gerald 'was the first to introduce into music the Max Beerbohm type of sophisticated satire – a mordant wit combined with classicism of style'.[47]

Gerald's major influences were not English but European. His *Three Songs in the German Manner* are settings of poems by Heinrich Heine which sound like versions of conventional *lieder*, but subvert the traditional themes so that, for instance, one is addressed to a pig instead of a fair young maid. In his 1920 *Three English Songs*, the playful words of 'The Green-eyed Monster', by E. L. Duff, are just the sort of ironic take on an emotional theme that appealed to Lord Berners the composer.

> James gave Elizabeth a Dodo,
> He only *offered* one to me –
> The loveliest lemon-coloured Dodo,
> With the greenest eyes that you could wish to see.
>
> Now it isn't that I'm doubting if James loves me,
> And I know that he would ask me out to tea,
> But he *did* give Elizabeth a Dodo,
> And he never even *offered* one to me.

Nevertheless, there was feeling behind the flippancy. As Constant Lambert said in a BBC radio tribute to Lord Berners, 'though his tongue was often in his cheek, he could wear his heart on his sleeve'.[48] His clever, facetious wit did not undermine the deep emotions in his music, and while he did not create a huge body of work (thirty pieces in all), the composer Gavin Bryars describes him as one of the few truly original British composers of the twentieth century. 'In his music, Gerald Berners is true to himself. It is a key to his character and his emotions.'

The fact that this young, unknown English amateur was supported by leading professionals as dynamic as Stravinsky and the Italian composer Alfredo Casella was very encouraging. The former described him as 'an amateur, but in the best – literal – sense, I would not consider him amateurish, as we now use the word'.[49] And in 1917, the musical journal the *Chesterian* revealed that M. Igor Stravinsky had recently written to them saying that 'Mr Tyrwhitt is not only a composer of unique talent, but also a very typical and very representative character of his race.'[50]

Technically an amateur, Gerald was professional enough to have his Spanish parody, *Fantaisie Espagnole*, performed at the British premiere of *The Rite of Spring* in 1921, with Stravinsky present. And it was a major triumph that Diaghilev chose him as the composer for a ballet to be performed 'in accordance with Lord Rothermere's wish', in London in 1926.⁵¹ *The Triumph of Neptune* was choreographed by George Balanchine, had a story by Gerald's friend Sacheverell Sitwell, and took pantomime and a playful Victorian aesthetic as its inspiration. There are not only sailors, policemen and street-hawkers but also flying fairies, ogres and goddesses. Hornpipes and polkas are danced next to London Bridge and then in the Ogres' Palace and the Frozen Forest. Gerald's music combined charming dance pieces and comic burlesque with a characteristic hint of irony, and at one performance Diaghilev was said to have laughed 'till the tears ran down his face'.⁵² The first night was a great success; flowers were showered on the entire cast as well as Gerald and Sacheverell.⁵³

F GERALD HAD BEEN BROUGHT UP in the provinces, oppressed by the need to be manly and surrounded by horses and dogs and people who were traditional and conservative, he had left all that behind him. He had become a European: he spoke and read widely in French, German and Italian (even his music had foreign titles); and he was a modernist as interested in the 'free atonality' of Schoenberg as in the romance of Wagner or the immediacy of popular music. If not quite an *enfant terrible*, then he certainly knew a good number of them and used some of their techniques. In his memoir of childhood, he wrote, 'In those days the Three R's, Russians, Radicals and Roman Catholics, inspired many Victorians with an unholy terror.' His mother had opted for a Swiss governess to teach the young Gerald French, rather than 'confide a little protestant soul to a Papist'. He must have found it deeply satisfying to see how he had surrounded himself in Rome with these three Rs, with his friendships and collaborations with Stravinsky and Diaghilev, not to mention his innumerable Italian and French friends who belonged to the Catholic Church.

By the time *Gramophone* magazine surveyed some public figures

about their favourite music in 1926, Gerald was able to give witty
responses that showed the daring yet unpretentious breadth of his
interests and how far he had travelled from his childhood:

> My favourite song is 'The Last Rose of Summer'; my favourite composer
> Bach; my favourite tune is the third of Schoenberg's Six Pieces, because
> it is so obscure that one is never likely to grow tired of it (which you
> must admit is as good a reason for preferring a tune as any other); and
> if by 'singer' you mean any kind of singer then the one I prefer is Little
> Tich [a tiny comic music-hall performer]. But, on the other hand,
> if you mean merely concert singers, please substitute Clara Butt [an
> imposingly tall and loud contralto].[54]

Gerald's composition 'L'Uomo dai baffi' ('The Man with the
Moustache') was performed by Casella at a marionette show in the
Teatro dei Piccoli in Rome – perfect for Gerald's love of playfulness.
A somewhat provocative part of the puppet ballet was the 'Trois petites
marches funèbres', consisting of three marches for a statesman, a
canary, and an aunt leaving an inheritance. The humorous, even
subversive approach to death was daring. This was an era when lengthy
mourning periods and swathes of black crepe were still the rule, and
though the canary's march is genuinely sorrowful, the other two are
obstinately cheerful. But Gerald had long seen the potential in gallows
humour. As a child, he was said to have written a funeral dirge for
his mother, who had been amused enough to ask him to perform it
as a party piece.[55] Mixing the pathos of the small bird's demise with
the pomp of the politician's was typical of Gerald's naughty wit, and
while the statesman could be seen as representing his father's formality
and officialdom, the canary reflects both his and his mother's love of
birds.[56] Although Gerald was not sure of his own future inheritance, it
was a theme that had obvious humorous potential. Below the title of
'Pour une tante à héritage' (before music marked '*allegro giocoso*') is
the French tag, 'At last we can go and buy a car.'

It was not long before Gerald had his own windfall. In fact, it was
the death of his unmarried paternal uncle, not an aunt, and there was

a title as well as property and money. He liked to spin his own fanciful tales concerning his inheritance: a collection of uncles had all fallen off a bridge after a funeral, he wrote. But it was not actually such a surprise. Nevertheless, his letters suggest that he *was* unclear as to what his legacy would finally entail, and that he even wondered whether his uncle might have a hidden child or wife somewhere who would take precedence. Soon, however, Gerald was swanning around Rome in a large chauffeur-driven car. In 1918, just as the First World War was coming to an end, he became 14th Baron Berners, 5th Baronet. A year later, his surname was changed to Tyrwhitt-Wilson.

Gerald wrote to tell Stravinsky his news: 'Did you know that I had changed my name and am no longer Tyrwhitt? My aunt – or rather my uncle – *à héritage* died. Unfortunately I inherit only the title, with a lot of taxes to be paid. I would so much like to see you. I beg you to write me a little note and tell me what you are doing just now.' Gerald continued to compose music, pursue his painting and travel widely. Although his priorities did not change with his rise in social status, his circumstances did. He turned out to be much richer than he had first imagined – he sold houses, land and silver – and this eased Gerald's progress as an aesthete and allowed him to augment the degree of luxury and playful indulgence that already suited him so well and for which he became known. He gave up diplomacy (though remained technically attached to the embassy in Rome), and bought Faringdon House for his mother and stepfather, establishing two years later the Berners Estates Company to manage the property. He was delighted to notice how charming the Berners arms were. 'A Greyhound and an Eagle, symbolical of the two most admirable qualities – swiftness and clarity of vision.' Although Gerald was rather dismissive of his forebears for being dull, provincial types, he counted among them John Bourchier, the second baron and illustrious translator, whom Henry VIII appointed as Chancellor of the Exchequer, and as his diplomatic advisor at the Field of the Cloth of Gold.

Along with the new car, Gerald had hired a tall, handsome chauffeur, William Crack, who had 'gold hair and violet-coloured eyes' and wore a black suit and a cap with a shiny peak.[57] Universally liked for his quiet good manners, he later recalled leisurely drives across Europe with his employer. Mussolini was organising his first Fascist marches; Crack recalled that the blackshirts 'would pull you up in the street if you didn't wave your hat when they marched by'.[58] There was a Fiat, a Lancia and then a specially designed Rolls-Royce – a 'false cabriolet' with a top that could be lifted off and folded back if the weather was fine.[59] The car also had a space made under the front seats for a portable Dolmetsch clavichord (with no legs and decorated with flowers and butterflies), which Gerald took around with him and played when he stopped. This gave rise to one of the more lasting legends of his eccentricity – that Lord Berners kept and even played a piano in his car – but the reality was a clever way of keeping a small keyboard close at hand for composing and playing. Certain friends claimed that Gerald wore a hideous white mask made by Oliver Messel in the car, but his chauffeur denied it, admitting only that his employer donned a different hat when going through a town. Driving home from Rome, Gerald would allow up to two weeks for the journey, taking in the coast road past Genoa and Monte Carlo, and stopping to dine at appealing restaurants or to visit friends. In Paris, Gerald usually stayed at the Ritz,

WILLIAM CRACK DRIVING THE ROLLS-ROYCE

where Crack remembered delicious meals at a long table in a special courier's room.[60]

After staying with Gerald in Rome and then accompanying him on the long trip home, Rex Whistler wrote about outdoor painting sessions on the way, and 'a divine bathe in the river – with William the chauffeur!'[61] The attractive young artist was still in his early twenties but was making a name for himself with his beautifully delicate paintings and murals; his recent *trompe l'œil* mural in the Tate Gallery's restaurant had been a grand success, and Whistler's subsequent tent-like decorations for Sir Philip Sassoon's extravagant house in Kent, Port Lympne, include Gerald as a solitary child waiting by his coroneted trunk for a paddle-steamer, with Faringdon House in the distance. In 1929, he painted Gerald busy on a small canvas in the drawing room at Faringdon. Dressed in buttoned-up white shirt and striped tie, the balding, bespectacled Gerald has the awkwardness and careful deliberation of a bank manager at his first art class. Without his masks, hats and costumes and without the chance to speak or play music, he looks dull and rather gloomy.

During the stops for painting, Crack would unpack an easel, paint-box, camp chair and green-lined parasol for his employer. Once, when motoring in England, Crack was screwing together the easel as Gerald politely approached the ancient owner of an ancient cottage, who was tending his hollyhocks. 'Sir,' he enquired, 'have you any objection to my painting your cottage?' The old boy looked at Gerald with a suspicious eye, and said, 'Well, if I want me cottage painted I paint it myself and anyway it's barely six months done.'[62]

In London, Gerald lived in rooms or a shared house with other bachelors. There are some who wonder whether he might have been involved with one of his few close friends, Gerald Agar-Robartes (Viscount Clifden from 1930), though there is no solid evidence. Eventually he bought himself a more substantial townhouse in Belgravia – 3 Halkin Street – which became his London base until the Second World War. He made trips to the country to his mother and stepfather at Faringdon, visited Salzburg and Munich for their music festivals, and frequently went to Paris, where he met the members of *Les Six* (including Poulenc and Milhaud), composers who, like him, were influenced by the light, witty style of Satie. It was in this milieu that Gerald encountered the extraordinary musical patron Princess de Polignac. Born in America, Winnaretta (or 'Winnie', as her friends called her) was heiress to the Singer sewing-machine fortune and was known at the turn of the century as one of the 'Paris Lesbos', having affairs with many women, married and unmarried. Her husband was more interested in men and their *mariage blanc* was based on their love of music and the arts. Though the prince died in 1901, the princess developed the salon they had created together and which supported and performed the music of contemporary composers; Debussy, Fauré and Ravel had premieres of their works there.

Gerald met Winnaretta in 1923, the year she fell in love with Violet Trefusis, with whom she remained involved for the next decade. The daughter of Alice Keppel (Edward VII's mistress), Violet's marriage to the diplomat Denys Trefusis had been brief and unsuccessful, and she was notorious for her recent and scandalous liaison with Vita Sackville-West. Violet was twenty-nine and Winnie fifty-eight, but the attractive, amusing younger woman was fascinated by the older woman's intelligence, humour and her 'rocky profile . . . her face more like a landscape than a face'. She felt like a willow to Winnie's oak.[63] If some found Violet annoying for her fickle nature and gossipy ways, she was also fun and full of life. Virginia Woolf found her hugely seductive – as did many others: 'What a voice – lisping, faltering, what warmth, suppleness, and in her way – it's not mine . . . how lovely, like a squirrel among buck hares . . .'[64] And if Winnie could be daunting and formidable, she was also passionate and generous.

Gerald became close to both Winnie and Violet, and saw them at the princess's palazzo in Venice, where there was 'mad and constant music-making' and visits from Stravinsky, Cole Porter, Arthur Rubinstein and Diaghilev.[65] The tall American-born French princess and the short cosmopolitan English lord had more in common than might have been initially apparent and their interest in one another and in music developed into a lifelong friendship. Both were eccentric outsiders who managed to be at the centre of things, and though they were gay at a time when this was not widely acceptable, they were socially desirable because of their titles and their wealth. Above all, their love of music was the centre of their lives. There is an argument that music can be considered a conduit for ambiguous feelings that are 'different, irrational, unaccountable', and that it can provide the 'perfect field for the display of emotion' for those who have difficulty in expressing it or for whom there is disapproval.[66] Although this is speculative, it is an interesting theory that makes some sense in both cases.

If Gerald did not openly declare himself as homosexual and did not leave any evidence behind of relationships with men at this stage in his life, he did have many friends whose sexual preferences were more obviously expressed. Diaghilev was a significant lodestar for numerous men of similar inclinations – a powerful, successful artist who didn't hide his attraction to and liaisons with men. Another overtly gay friend was the young painter Christopher ('Kit') Wood, who had sat at the feet of Picasso in Paris and who took advice and opium from Cocteau. Gerald bought one of Wood's paintings, and saw him again in Rome, where they enjoyed 'painting trips . . . picnics, parties and dinners' and met frequently with Igor Stravinsky and the Marchesa Casati.[67] Kit Wood's pale good looks, his sexually ambiguous style (he also got involved with women), his polio-induced limp and his fierce dedication to his painting made him hugely attractive to many people, including Gerald. 'He was a painter who was at the same time naive and sophisticated. He saw directly with the eyes of a primitive and had that primitive sense of pure colour and elimination of the unnecessary,' wrote their mutual friend, the painter Francis Rose.[68] When Gerald wrote 'a fantastic ballet in one act', *Luna Park* – set in the freaks pavilion of a fairground and choreographed once more by Balanchine – it was Wood who designed the scenery and costumes for the show. The ballet was performed in 1930, the year the twenty-nine-year-old Wood, after a frenzied summer of painting and opium abuse, threw himself under a train.

It seems likely that Gerald introduced the young Kit Wood to Ronald Firbank in Rome. Tall, skinny, with white hands sporting long, carmine-coloured nails and Egyptian rings, Firbank stayed a good deal in Rome in the early 1920s, and constructed and cultivated even more masks and mysteries around himself than Gerald. His novels had already caused a stir, with their modern mix of unconventional sexuality, wittily malicious satire and experimental form, and while he often had to publish his own books, he is viewed by some as having written some of the most original fiction of the twentieth century.[69] Certainly his works were adored by the Bright Young Things of the 1920s and would continue to occupy a place in many of their hearts after they stopped being bright or young.

Gerald had become friends with Firbank during the strange, disorienting years after the war, when strikes, shortages and the ravages of the dreadful flu epidemic were ameliorated by the joys of Mediterranean life. Both men had found a refuge from the stifling restrictions of English society, culture and climate in travel and art and both were shy, clever, sensitive and sexually diffident. They met at the Ballets Russes, where the audience was understandably nonplussed by the lanky aesthete, whose favourite posture 'seemed to entail sitting with his head nearly touching the floor and with his feet in the air'.[70] Initially, Gerald found this degree of eccentricity embarrassing. Although he was three years older than Firbank, he did not embrace the decadent, lily-scented style redolent of the *fin de siècle*, *Yellow Book* days of Beardsley and Wilde. Firbank also drank too much and didn't always eat properly – when others ordered a meal, he might consume only peaches washed down with champagne.

Where Firbank was isolated and felt himself almost a social outcast, Gerald liked to be embraced by the society he also mocked, and was often surprisingly conventional in appearance and manners for someone known for eccentricity; he favoured a bowler hat and snug suits. Firbank, with his absurd behaviour, undulating walk and lonely isolation, might have seemed a warning to Gerald of the perils of taking unconventionality too far – a reflection in a warped mirror of his own characteristics. Firbank was not entirely devoted to Gerald, writing scathingly about Berners and 'the Sitwell set', whom he believed to be 'afraid of my "witty" pen!' In a letter to his mother, he compared Gerald to a great-uncle, 'only less distinguished! For his face has no cleverness to redeem it! He is fat and rather bald, but with a pleasant manner, although under the "flabbyness" of the surface there is certainly steel! He might be an unpleasant enemy, and he is, of course, not *at all* simple.'[71]

By the time Firbank died of alcohol and lung disease in 1926, aged forty, Gerald claimed to be his only friend in Rome; in charge of the funeral, he managed to make the kind of mistake that could have occurred in either man's novels. Having misinterpreted Firbank's disparaging remarks about the prejudices of the Catholic Church, Gerald had him buried in the verdant Protestant Cemetery behind the Pyramid of Cestius, where Shelley and Keats ended up. It was subsequently revealed that Firbank was a Roman Catholic and he was disinterred, but Gerald recalled the 'mistaken' burial on a summer morning with wry pleasure. Amid the cypresses and roses were nightingales 'whose vocal outpourings in Italy are not confined, as in Northern countries, to moonlit groves . . . The nightingales that attended Ronald's funeral were presumably Papists, for they did their utmost to drown the voice of the officiating clergyman.'[72]

HE YEAR 1931 might have looked unpromising to Gerald. Heading for fifty, he couldn't fail to notice the banking crisis that was leading inexorably to the Great Depression. Severe unemployment and a Labour government were hardly encouraging to the post-war era of excess, jazz clubs and fancy-dress parties so well satirised by Evelyn Waugh. In February, Gerald's seventy-nine-year-old mother Julia died. He was soon to write his first memoir, *First Childhood*, in which she would be caricatured as a hard-nosed yet parochial, country lady. These were some of the childhood feelings he retained and now felt free to express, but in reality Gerald was a loved and loyal son. His letters to his mother were warm and regular and he often visited, bringing friends with him for country weekends. He even had his own set of rooms at Faringdon, on the lower ground floor, where he worked.

Siegfried Sassoon's diary describes a stay at Faringdon in the 1920s: 'B's mother is a vague agreeable lady beautifully draped in old lace; probably a keen gardener; the drawing-room is full of freesias, and they are thinking of getting a new troop of goldfish for the lily-pond. In the dining-room are two glossy blue starlings in separate cages.' Colonel Ward Bennitt's ageing parrot, bought off a sailor many years before, was taken out for a bit of sunshine by the limestone pillars on the porch. It was presumably with this bird that Gerald tried to play tricks on his mother, persuading it to walk across the floor covered with a bowler hat. 'This strange sight of a self-moving hat didn't seem to surprise Gerald's mother, which did surprise Gerald: perhaps Gerald wasn't aware how well, even in old age, Gerald's mother understood her son.'[73] This was the woman, after all, who had welcomed the Marchesa Casati into her home when Gerald invited his Italian friend to stay, and was charmed. Despite the unusual appearance of the grandly eccentric Casati – unusually tall and slender, smoking cigarettes from a long, jewelled holder and sporting false lashes and tight, white satin trousers – Mrs Ward Bennitt later announced, 'I like her much better than your other foreign friends.'[74]

JULIA, GERALD'S MOTHER, SITS ON THE STEPS. HER SECOND HUSBAND, COLONEL WARD BENNITT, SITS ON THE WALL SMOKING A PIPE, HIS SAILOR'S PARROT TAKING THE AIR. THE LADY ON THE RIGHT CANNOT BE IDENTIFIED

Naturally, La Casati brought her python. Or was it an immense boa constrictor, as Osbert Sitwell remembered, packaged up in a large portmanteau with a glass top? 'It was neatly coiled for its journey, but showing that it was alive by an occasional glistening shudder of its scaly skin.'[75] Even this was accepted by Gerald's mother. Apparently the hostess asked the Marchesa if her pet was hungry. 'No, it had a goat this morning.'[76] The Italian signed herself in the visitors' book (an old hotel register) as *'Tempteuse de Serpents'*.

Julia's death was followed only three weeks later by her husband's, the now ninety-three-year-old Colonel. Both were among the first people to be cremated at Oxford's new crematorium and their tombstones are in the graveyard of Faringdon's All Saints' Church, just beyond the garden wall. Gerald decided to take over Faringdon as his own home (not relinquishing his others in London and Rome) and, freed from the beady maternal eye, the subsequent year would be a time of revealing and marvellous changes.

CHAPTER FOUR

A Delightful Youth

F GERALD AND THE MAD BOY were dramatically different in terms of appearance, age and character, their backgrounds were remarkably similar. Hodnet Hall, the home of the Heber-Percys, was only eleven miles from Apley Park, and both families were wealthy Shropshire landowners who might easily have visited one another's houses or ridden to hounds together. Though Robert was born twenty-eight years after Gerald, both experienced the same mixture of privilege and neglect as children, and both lived in households where horses were assumed to be as fundamental a species in daily life as humans. Throughout their lives, both retained a love of the rural English landscape, but they rejected the asphyxiating conventions of their childhoods and had a predilection for shocking the kind of people they had grown up with. They had different methods of achieving it, but in each case, *épater le bourgeois* was almost a creed.

Robert Vernon Heber-Percy was born on Guy Fawkes Day 1911. It is not recorded whether his mother was disappointed to have a fourth son, but she was a practical, no-nonsense sort of person who would not have made a fuss. By the time of his birth, Robert's older brothers were already of an age to be off by themselves, playing in the vast gardens of Hodnet Hall, but they were surely brought in by 'dear old Nannie Jones' and Dorothy Dodd the nursemaid to visit the new baby. The oldest brother, Algernon, was nine and the presumed heir to the estate. He was known as Algy, like so many of his forebears. (The family's ancestry could be traced all the way back to William de Percy, who came over with William the Conqueror and who had such fine moustaches that he was known as *aux* or *als gernons*, 'with the whiskers'.) The next was Cyril, who at seven was already a fanatical animal-lover, and, two years younger, Alan, who like Robert would turn out wild, unpredictable and dashingly attractive.

Their mother Gladys was by all accounts a dauntingly tough character, though early photographs indicate a classic Edwardian beauty with milky-skinned, sloping shoulders and lazy-lidded eyes. A strong nose and chin add a hint of the determination for which she was famed. Gladys was an elegant and gracious hostess in her evening dress and diamond tiara for the yearly hunt ball, but she was much happier on a horse. A brilliant rider who could break in the most troublesome young animals and who led the hunts that often met at Hodnet Hall, she rode an elegant side-saddle even in her old age. In pictures, she sits serious and poker-backed in her meticulous riding habit: glistening black boots and top hat and bright white gloves and stock. Gladys claimed happily to have survived numerous injuries from falls, and her reaction was no less carefree when her sons fell from their ponies. Once, a nanny took three of the young boys out for a ride, placing them in basket panniers, but the girths broke and the screaming children tumbled into a ditch. While the nanny was very distressed by the accident, Gladys showed no anxiety about the state of her offspring and merely laughed.[77]

The boys' father, another Algernon, was a semi-invalid, weakened by asthma and plagued by eczema to such a degree that he often had to be wrapped up in linen cloths to protect his flaking skin. Yet even he was more interested in his horses and dogs than in his children. A remote figure who criticised and scolded more than he encouraged, his greatest legacy to his sons was fostering a deep love and knowledge of estate life. His own parents had a large steam yacht, travelled extensively and were just as at home in London as at Hodnet, whereas Gladys's family, the Hulton-Harrops, were solid Shropshire gentry who tended not to stray too far from their estate. Nevertheless, Gladys proved to be the ideal partner in managing Hodnet. According to *Us Four*, the memoir by Robert's brother Cyril, 'Mummy ran the house, gardens, stables, and all of us,' giving instructions to each of the heads of departments: menus for the cook; lists of stores from Harrods that needed replenishing; orders for a sheep to be slaughtered or bacon cured; the stud-groom told which horses were required for riding or for breaking in; the head housemaid informed which rooms to prepare for guests; and the head gardener given requests for flowers, fruits and vegetables. Daddy, on the other hand, 'ran the estate through his agent, but what the agent told the men was often countermanded later in the day as Daddy rode round'.[78]

Hodnet Hall was a great rambling place of red sandstone and brick, with seventy-two rooms, enormous kitchens, a brewery, a dairy, a bakery and a laundry, not to mention extensive stables, kennels, a walled kitchen garden and a Home Farm. An Elizabethan-style great hall ran almost the whole length of the house and was filled with a terrifying array of stuffed animals. This included not just the normal range of heads severed from deer, foxes and other British fauna, but bounty from the big-game hunters among the Heber-Percys, who returned from their travels with lions, tigers, zebras, bison and even a baboon, which were duly dealt with and put on display. (Gerald would visit Hodnet only once; according to Heber-Percy lore, when he saw this phantasmagoria of taxidermy he had to be given smelling salts.)

Although the house was a Victorian pastiche designed by Salvin and finished in 1871, it was the third manor house built on one of the very few estates in England that have never been bought or sold. Related to the dukes of Northumberland, the family had lived there since 1200; the original half-timbered building was constructed in 1264. By occasionally allowing females to inherit, they claimed descent from the Norman lords of Vernon, and Odo of Hodnet, one of the Shropshire Knights. The motto on the coat of arms, with its Percy lion and Heber maiden, is *Esperance en Dieu* ('Hope in God'), but the old butler used to say that such was the family's sense of place and history, it should have been 'What I Have I Hold'.

In the 1960s, Hodnet Hall had its second floor, a wing, and the tower bearing the family's standard pulled down to make it more economically viable. The great hall was removed, the rooms reduced to about thirty-five, and the extensive old kitchens turned into garages. However, the essence of the place remains much the same, now cared for by another Algy – eldest son of Robert's eldest brother. You can tell by looking at the photograph albums that they nearly all retain the same lean, almost boyish frame throughout their lives, as Robert did too. And it is apparent that the latest Algy's dedication to Hodnet is just as strong as it was for his predecessors over so many centuries. He even has the same varieties of much-loved dogs that scamper in blurs across the Edwardian and Victorian photographs – Labradors and terriers. The gardens are still tended to the remarkable standards that the current Algy's grandfather and father kept them, and though thousands of visitors now walk around them each year, they continue to reflect the traditions and taste of the family. Tree-shaded driveways lead past perfectly clipped lawns and rose gardens, and paths lined by rhododendrons and camellias meander alongside a chain of ambitious cascading water gardens that were created by Robert's brother in the 1920s. The stuffed animals from the old hall, including a moth-eaten lion, were moved to the stables, now converted into a visitors' restaurant.

'By the time Robert came along, the parents had rather given up,' said Algy, remembering stories about his Mad Boy uncle. 'Nursery life had gone on so long and they'd said "No" so often. Nannie was retiring soon . . . so they probably said, "Come down for dinner" much sooner than they had with their other sons. Gladys was quite a harsh mother, but she spoilt Robert, and dressed him up as a girl. He was allowed to get away with things.' To what extent Gladys cross-dressed her youngest son is not known, and though there is a studio photograph of the four brothers where the oldest three are in short-trousered suits and ties and a two-year-old Robert wears a white pinafore, this sort of outfit was not unusual at the time.

There were tutors and governesses to give lessons up in the nursery and schoolrooms on the top floor. Footmen trudged up the seventy-odd

ALGY, CYRIL, ROBERT AND ALAN

steps from the kitchens to bring trays with the children's meals. None of the boys was particularly interested in their formal education and the focus at home was clearly on country pursuits, for which they were given a good deal of freedom. Cyril remembered Robert learning very quickly to stand up for himself. 'He was full of fun, up to every prank, could hoodwink most people, and developed a gift for repartee.' He was soon following his older brothers around in the grounds, tree-climbing, bird-nesting, or running down to the stables to ride. A favourite route was through the woods to the gamekeeper's hut, with its cages of stinking white ferrets and polecats. The gamekeeper, Holding, a tall ex-Coldstream sergeant, kept a macabre exhibition of dead animals he considered vermin. 'Strung on wire between two trees hung magpies, jays, crows, hawks, and a long row of stoats. Some had fallen to the ground rotten; others were skeletons except for their black-tipped tails. They were all maggoty; bluebottles buzzed around them.'[79]

Although the estate at Hodnet was a boys' heaven, the Heber-Percy parents were both severe in their dedication to tradition and regimentation. The morning began for all members of the household (including the servants and any guests) with prayers in the dining room. They were announced by Whitaker, the butler, who was a dab hand with the gong and made it resound in a crescendo around the house. Daddy read from the Bible and led the service. As they grew older, the boys found it an ideal opportunity to get a good look at any new or pretty housemaids, but once, after they succeeded in making a new maid giggle with their stares, Algy was flogged by his father and the younger boys were sent to their rooms without breakfast. According to Robert, his father would come into the bathroom when the boys were in the bath and lash out at them with a hunting crop. What this was for is not recorded, but certainly they were naughty, and cooked up mischievous schemes like hiding in the housemaids' cupboard to spy on their fat, whiskery governess as she bathed.

Despite his temper, Robert's father was also distant and uninterested – something that was exacerbated by his physical frailty. Cyril recalled that each evening the young boys were dolled up 'like Little Lord Fauntleroys' in frilled white shirts, dark velvet shorts, white socks and shiny buckled shoes and led by Nannie Jones into the library for an audience with their parents and any guests staying in the house. However, 'Daddy took little part in our amusements as he suffered from asthma. But occasionally he would recite *Hiawatha*, or continue a never-ending story about a Mr Snodgrass. He was a good story-teller. Usually he tired of the noise all too quickly, and would pull the bell-rope beside the fireplace several times to summon a footman, who would enter immediately, dressed in blue tailcoat with silver-crested buttons, and a blue-and-yellow striped waistcoat. '"Fetch Nannie," Daddy would say. "Sir." The door closed quietly. There would be a kiss for Daddy and Mummy, perhaps a reluctant peck at an aunt and a handshake for anyone else.'[80]

Religion didn't end with morning prayers; on Sundays the boys were trussed up in their best blue suits and caps before they trooped down the drive to the village church. The graveyard was filled with Heber-Percy tombs, and inside, the front two pews belonged to the Lords of the Manor of Hodnet. From the padded seats that were the squire's privilege, they could look across at the Victorian stained-glass window donated by their predecessors and the Heber-Percy chapel to the side. Hymns were sung, some of which were written by their illustrious ancestor Bishop Heber of Calcutta. A famous missionary who worked and died in India in the 1820s, Bishop Heber had been a brilliant young fellow of All Souls, Oxford. As vicar of Hodnet, he composed as he strolled around the grounds, leaving behind him many popular hymns, such as 'Holy, Holy, Holy' and the missionaries' favourite, 'From Greenland's Icy Mountains'.

During Robert's childhood, the house was almost teetotal. Even in the era of cocktails ('gut-rotting, a pernicious concoction'), Daddy only allowed a bit of sherry and port for guests and the whisky was kept locked up. Food was not adventurous but plentiful – especially breakfast, as Cyril's descriptions indicate.

> There were several hot dishes, always one of fish, eggs of one kind or another, thin crisp bacon – it had to break with the touch of a knife – and kidneys on toast with parsley butter, or home-made sausages, all in separate silver dishes. A ham on the sideboard . . . There would also be a large dish of cold partridge or pheasant when in season, a tongue, hot scones, toast, butter in small round pats and a flat glass dish of thick scalded cream, home-made marmalade, honey in the comb, and two sorts of jam.[81]

The boys had to eat this bounty in silence unless spoken to and, vocally critical of his sons' table manners, Daddy liked to sneak up if they had their elbows on the table and knock them off.

HE FIRST WORLD WAR broke out when Robert was three. His brothers were all away at preparatory schools by then, and Gladys opened up the house as a convalescent hospital with eighty beds. As 'commandant', she 'ruled with a rod of iron' and terrorised the patients and staff. Her husband was the recruiting officer for the district and travelled around in his Renault, a temperamental automobile that needed endless cranking to start and stalled on hills. Algernon took to treating it like the horses he knew much better, reining back on the steering wheel and murmuring 'Whoa' when he wanted to stop.[82]

Although his three brothers returned during holidays (the soldiers would give them surreptitious puffs on Woodbines if they were lucky), Robert was inevitably alone much more than before. With many of the male staff gone to fight and his parents extremely busy, the war gave Robert much more freedom and possibly neglect than before. It was easy for him to wander around the house, past the rows of taxidermists' glass eyes staring out from the walls and the distant gazes in the endless family portraits: Vernons, Hebers, Percys, a sixteenth-century countess, a bishop in his robes. One charming, full-length likeness depicted a flowing-haired young man holding a cricket bat – Richard Heber, the celebrated book collector who amassed over 150,000 volumes. He was, as the current Algy put it, 'more inclined to the males', though this would surely not have been spoken of by Robert's parents. Despite being the brother of the Calcutta bishop, Richard's good looks, intellect and charm could not save him when, at the age of fifty-two, he became involved with a twenty-three-year-old man. He was forced abroad and, when he returned to England, was ostracised by society, dying alone in 1835.

Despite his tricks and mischief, Robert showed a degree of sensitivity compared to his siblings. He didn't enjoy shooting or fishing like them, and Cyril recalled that he read and painted – apparently unusual pastimes in the family, despite their illustrious bibliophile ancestor and the library that was packed from floor to ceiling with books. Robert liked to pick bunches of flowers for his mother and visited her in her huge study on the first floor that looked out over the gardens and the lake to the undulating fields, where cows grazed by the sixteenth-century dovecot. Although Cyril claimed that his mother never showed that Robert was 'Mummy's darling', Robert himself recalled little secrets between them. When his mother returned to Hodnet from London and her youngest boy was asleep in bed, she would place a small bottle of scent under his pillow.[83] It is unclear whether this was a sign or a present, a phial of her own scent or some cologne for him, but it was clearly a small intimacy – unusual and delicate in the tough, physical environment where horse tackle and terriers, ferrets and pheasant shoots usually counted for more.

Hodnet was a version of Eden to Robert, yet he was surely aware from a young age that it was one from which he would be cast out. With so much emphasis on the line of inheritance and on preserving family names and traditions, he would have known early on that his eldest brother Algy would get everything. 'As a younger son, you are very low in the pecking order,' said Algy, Robert's nephew. 'If you're the youngest son, you know you are never going to inherit.' Given three older brothers, it was clear that Robert could envisage no future in the place that meant everything to his family. With the English system of primogeniture and 'the strict settlement of estates', the winner would take it all. And the same went for titles. As Nancy Mitford pointed out, 'The rule of primogeniture has kept together the huge fortunes of English lords; it has also formed our class system.'[84] It is the great distinction between the English aristocracy and any other; whereas abroad every member of a noble family is noble, in England none is except the head of the family. The sons and daughters may enjoy courtesy titles but as a rule the younger offspring of even the richest lords receive comparatively little money. Younger sons have thus habitually been left without money, property or title, often without the skills to acquire them and, above all, without belonging to the place they care most about. As clergymen, soldiers, sailors and resentful ne'er-do-wells, these high-born outcasts litter the pages of nineteenth-century English novels, with their hopeless attempts to make a way in the unfriendly world and their irresponsible sprees of adventuring.

Many of Robert's characteristics were formed by the early knowledge of his place in this scheme and the family hierarchy. Like all the Heber-Percys, he had an intense love of country life, but in becoming a daring show-off, he was demanding attention that was otherwise given elsewhere. A trickster and game-player, he lured people into giving him what he wanted. Easily bored, yet sensitive, he needed a protector who could care for him and get him out of trouble.

HEN ROBERT WAS THIRTEEN, a decision had to be made about his schooling. His older brothers had failed to get into Eton and ended up going to Harrow. Gladys was worried that her youngest child would not be able to follow in their footsteps. He was already renowned for his bad behaviour at Wixenford in Wokingham (a school that advertised itself as being for 'the sons of gentlemen and minor princes'). A couple of months before Robert was due to sit the exam for Eton, she approached a new school that must have seemed rather a novelty. Stowe was well known for its extraordinary gardens, landscaped in the eighteenth century into an Arcadian vision, complete with a triumphal arch, a Palladian bridge and any number of temples, sculptures and grottoes. The magnificent house had been sold and, in 1923, became a boarding school for ninety-nine teenage boys. Gladys wrote a somewhat grovelling letter to the bursar, revealing her anxieties about her undisciplined favourite. In the event, Stowe was desperate to recruit new pupils and Robert arrived in the summer term of 1925 – an exact contemporary of David Niven, who was already a popular boy, and whose talent for drawing sketches and caricatures amused his classmates. The two would meet again during the war under very different circumstances, but no evidence suggests they were friends at school.

There is a portrait of Robert at Faringdon that must have been painted at about the time he went to Stowe – a sugary confection that exaggerates his round brown eyes, bee-stung lips, high rosy cheekbones and golden-chestnut locks. A frilly-collared shirt completes the picture. He looks like the sort of new arrival the older boys would have pounced on, but from all accounts Robert was no victim. Accustomed to fending for himself in a large family with big brothers, he had no qualms about behaving just as he had at home, with jokes and an uninhibited air of *je m'en fous*. Only a year after he arrived, Robert's tutor wrote to Gladys, admitting that he had 'been thinking a great deal about Robert recently'. Young Heber-Percy had evidently been behaving badly and the family was already contemplating removing him, something the tutor warned against

> [as] one of the most unfortunate things that could happen to him . . .
> Mr Playford [his teacher] says that Robert is childish; that he asks foolish
> questions; that he does not retain even for a few moments what he has
> been told; and that he appears quite unashamed by public opinion, even
> when his failings do not pass un-noticed by the rest of the form; and
> from my own experience I am sure that all these indictments are true.
>
> In the House, too, he is so casual that he cannot be regarded
> otherwise than as a weak spot.
>
> However, in conjunction with all these, the fact that he has not as
> yet begun to develop must, in fairness, not be overlooked; nor must his
> praiseworthy efforts at improvement, which I am certain are genuine,
> even if spasmodic and undisciplined, be ignored.

Robert remembered his schooldays with affection and sometimes went back to visit. He also held fond memories of the legendary headmaster, J. F. Roxburgh (known as J.F.), who was unusually youthful and curiously humanitarian for someone in his position. Tall and well-built, J.F. was something of an intellectual dandy, but he was dedicated to his pupils who remembered him as a 'magnetically brilliant teacher to generations of boys'.[85] Evelyn Waugh, who was taught by J.F. at Lancing, described his sonorous voice as like 'a hot potato in the mouth', but also alleged that he had been caught *in flagrante* with a boy.[86] Roxburgh apparently allowed the boys to keep pets, something which escalated into a badly run zoo as boys grew out of rabbits and ferrets and allegedly acquired monkeys, bears and hyenas; it was eventually shut down.[87]

However, even J.F. found Robert a tricky proposition. In one report he wrote: 'He is a problem. Some people can't succeed, but he can't try – at least not for any length of time.' But J.F. was nothing if not an optimist, adding, 'Personally, I don't a bit despair of him, and I know that he has many virtues which will come out later, but I doubt if he will ever make any progress at school – probably not till he is about eighteen.'

Robert didn't make it to eighteen at Stowe, leaving for a crammer in Westgate-on-Sea in Kent when he was still sixteen. J.F. wrote to the director, urging him to take the boy and trying to mix honesty with hopefulness:

> Robert Heber-Percy is a delightful youth. Personally I have always been much attached to him, though he was at one time in a mild way something of a law breaker. Latterly he has enormously improved, and there has never been anything of the slightest seriousness against him. His great failing is that he cannot concentrate, and when he tries to do so for any time, or when he gets ill or tired, fatigue appears to make his mind go perfectly blank at intervals. You will find his work startlingly bad, but I shall be greatly surprised if you do not like the boy himself. Do take him if you can.

We don't know how long Robert stayed at the seaside crammer or what he got up to when he left. The three options listed by Stowe as 'possible career' when Gladys registered her son looked increasingly unlikely: 1. The University, 2. The Army or Navy, 3. The Medical Profession. To her credit, Gladys had even then written 'not settled'. Now, for this devilishly good-looking youth who took nothing seriously, matters looked even less settled. Sadly, there are no diaries or letters relating to this period of Robert's life; he was far too busy with escapades and adventures to write about them and putting pen to paper was never his strong point. He evidently started to spend a good deal of time in London, where life for a teenage 'mad boy' offered endless parties and the sparkling nightclubs that had opened up during the 1920s. Cyril recalled various of the madcap schemes that took place after his youngest brother left school and before he met Gerald Berners:

> He went abroad, here, there and everywhere. He worked his passage to America, where amongst other things, he acted as an extra in Hollywood and had a stand-in part falling off a horse at full gallop. He was a waiter at a Lyons Corner House, but was sacked for spilling soup all over a customer. Robert said, 'The man just complained too much.'[88]

Robert's older brothers had already pursued more conventional paths in the Army: Algy left Sandhurst and was commissioned into the Grenadier Guards, Cyril joined the Welsh Guards and Alan the Royal Scots Greys. Algy was the only one to stick with the military; Cyril had his heart with the horses and eventually left to become master and huntsman of a pack of hounds. Alan, like Robert, preferred dash and speed to discipline and duty. He bought a racehorse, drove fast cars and had a couple of black Alsatians, one of which had been trained as a police dog in Germany. He eventually gave them to Cyril, who took them everywhere, even to London on leave, where they could be relied upon to behave themselves in the theatre and tackle an enemy if necessary.

ROBERT'S BROTHERS CYRIL AND ALAN, CHANGING THE GUARD AT BUCKINGHAM PALACE, 1927

In March 1931, when Robert was nineteen, he tried to do the right thing and joined the 1st King's Dragoon Guards, a cavalry regiment established in the seventeenth century and based in Tidworth, on the edge of Salisbury Plain. Becoming a Guards officer was a well-trodden path for young men of his background, few of whom would end up as professional soldiers. There were all the trappings of an exclusive club – fancy, colourful uniforms and a variety of arcane rituals – and officers were given enough leave to allow a social life in London, albeit with rules about what they wore and carried: dark suits and bowler hats were de rigueur, a stick or umbrella was suggested, and parcels or a suitcase were forbidden.

Joining the Guards was the perfect occupation for the decorative, sociable male that Martin Green designated 'the Dandy' in his influential study of the post-war generation, *Children of the Sun*. Preoccupied with style, ornament and high manners, the dandy rejects the parents' seriousness and is 'dedicated solely to his own perfection through a ritual of taste'. At the root of the early twentieth-century cult of the dandy 'is the worship of the male adolescent by older men as expressed in the myths of Narcissus and Adonis'.[89] In the wake of the First World War, the circumstances were perfect for the expansion of this cult. The older generation appeared tainted with the blood of the golden youth: young men like Rupert Brooke, who had been sent to the slaughter by old men who were still alive. Elizabeth Bowen described this generation that grew up just after the First World War as one which was 'made to feel it had muffed the catch', but the other way of seeing it was that of Cyril Connolly: 'In those days whenever you didn't get on with your father, you had all the glorious dead on your side.'

Through the 1920s and into the 1930s, the pursuit of pleasure and beauty seemed some sort of reaction to the horrors of what had gone before. With a generation of young men wiped out, there is an easy psychoanalytical theory for the subsequent emphasis on masculine charms, and why it was that girls shingled their hair in short bobs and flattened their chests for flapper dresses. The excesses of partying – dressing up in costumes, drinking too much and ending up with unlikely bed partners – were methods of rejecting both the past and one's elders. And Robert was a perfect candidate for this existence.

Military entry papers report that Robert was admitted with the rank of second lieutenant. A few vital statistics make no mention of whether he was an Adonis, merely recording that he was of medium height and slim build: 'Height: 5ft 10½; Weight: 140 lb [10 stone]; Chest: max 36½ inches, min 33½ inches; Vision 6/6'. The short experiment with military discipline was not a success. Uninterested, disorderly and sloppy enough to commit a faux pas like taking off his military cap to a general, Robert was clearly not soldier material. At the end of the four months, the young officer's immediate commander wrote that duties were not carried out satisfactorily and that Robert was unfit for promotion. 'I do not consider that he was keen to learn his work whilst attached for instruction, he paid little attention to his instructors. He appeared to lack concentration and his proficiency after 4 months was very much below the average.' The multiple-choice answers that his superior underlined in a confidential 'Analysis of Personality' build up a picture of a young man who doesn't give a fig:

> Reliability: very reliable, average, <u>uncertain</u>
> Energy: hard-working, average, <u>lazy</u>
> Tact: very tactful, average, <u>tactless</u>
> Leadership: good, average, <u>indifferent</u>
> Loyalty : very loyal, <u>average</u>, poor
> Adaptability: most adaptable, <u>average</u>, unadaptable

'Intellectual Qualifications' are no better:

> Imagination: fertile, <u>average</u>, meagre
> General ability: brilliant, average, <u>poor</u>
> Tactical knowledge: excellent, average, <u>scanty</u>
> Common-sense: abundant, <u>average</u>, lacking
> Ability to teach: considerable, average, <u>small</u>

Even Robert's 'Physical and Athletic Qualifications' are called into question. After all those years on horses and chasing around the estate at Hodnet, he couldn't even be bothered to ride well, let alone join in team games:

> Physique: robust, <u>average</u>, poor
> Strength: powerful, <u>average</u>, weak
> Energy: untiring, average, <u>small</u>
> Horsemanship: excellent, <u>average</u>, indifferent
> Keenness at games: great, average, <u>small</u>

Cyril reports a somewhat different reason for Robert being

requested to resign his commission. After a London party, Robert arrived back at Tidworth the next morning, driving a hired Daimler and wearing evening dress. He was already late for the daily parade, known as Stables, which was obligatory for all but the most senior officers, so went straight to the dining room and ordered breakfast. As he ate his fry-up, the commanding officer and second-in-command came in. 'They halted, rooted to the ground. There before them sat a very junior officer, quite unperturbed, eating eggs and bacon. The meal was not finished, and his exit was speedy. Robert, they realised, would never make a soldier.'[90]

HE HEBER-PERCY PARENTS were reaching the end of their patience. Robert recalled feeling like the black sheep of the family, and was threatened with a sea passage to a rougher existence in Australia if he didn't shape up. No doubt Gladys went up to London and took her favoured boy for lunch at the Ritz for warnings and maternal advice. And one imagines Algernon senior summoning his youngest son to his tobacco-reeking study off the hall at Hodnet on his visits home. The horsewhip was no use now, but then nothing else seemed to be either.

In London, Robert was clearly maturing into the Mad Boy who would so captivate Gerald the following year. When he wrote his letter of resignation to his commanding officer, he was staying at the Jules Hotel in Jermyn Street, just next door to the Cavendish Hotel, a much-loved haunt of London high society that he surely frequented. The Cavendish was run by the legendary Rosa Lewis. Outspoken and fearless, she had worked her way up in life from a housemaid, then cook, to the owner of a hotel that reminded its clients of the splendours of the Edwardian era. Evelyn Waugh used her as a model for Lottie Crump in *Vile Bodies* – much to her annoyance. He described the Cavendish as being like a run-down but comfortable country house, where the head waiter was 'hard of hearing, partially blind, and tortured with gout', and there were 'innumerable old housemaids always trotting about with cans of hot water and clean towels'. Rosa had been there since 1904 and was favoured by the Bright Young Things; she had known their grandparents as well as their parents. She was a terrible snob, favouring the 'Three As' – Aristocrats, Americans and the affluent – and wouldn't hesitate to ban people she didn't like.

Rosa provided the perfect mix of decadence and familiarity for people in Robert's circle. Quick to flout the rules, she amused everyone with her gossip and propensity to break open 'cherrybums' – jeroboams of champagne. Food had declined since her days of cooking for Buckingham Palace, when recipes included quail wrapped in slices of beef and cooked in suet pudding, but it was solid English fare, even if Evelyn Waugh described the game pie as 'quite black inside and full of beaks and shot and inexplicable vertebrae'.[91] Rosa drove around in a decrepit Daimler that was 'even more old-fashioned and regal-looking than Queen Mary's'.[92] For a section of the well-heeled, well-connected London youth, the Cavendish was 'like the dream nursery they had never had, presided over by a nanny in turn forbidding and indulgent, ribald and stately, pickled in Edwardiana, peppering them with her fruity vernacular'.[93] Many of the people who would remain Robert's lifelong friends were Cavendish aficionados, including the glamorous Lygon siblings, the Betjemans and Daphne Fielding. Gerald too was no stranger to the place, and had chosen some years earlier to entertain the Ballets Russes under Rosa's eagle eye.

Robert had the confidence of a hedonist and the fearlessness of a wild sexual opportunist. He was a natural candidate for the mad, jazz-flavoured partying that had got going in the 1920s and never stopped, and certainly belonged to the category that was viewed with scorn by Evelyn Waugh, and labelled 'shrieking little poseurs' by George Orwell. Robert's older brother Alan was equally good-looking and disreputable. With an advantage of five years, he was 'the most wicked and the most attractive' of the four brothers and undoubtedly provided an example for his younger brother to follow. While the older two siblings remained lifelong devotees of rural activities and wildlife (particularly how to kill it), the younger two were just as dedicated to the wild life of the city. Robert later described how he had sometimes been so short of money during these times that he learned how to make one meal last three days – and if this sounded like the start of a sob story or a revelation about soup kitchens, it was not: 'I would get a rich man to take me out to Claridge's and order three large courses.'[94]

If Gerald was pushing the boundaries through his music and creative friendships, Robert was doing the same with his own body by testing his physical limits – the epitome of the *jeunesse dorée*. Both men fitted into what was known as 'High Bohemia', with its cosmopolitan, artistic aesthetic and irreverent exuberance. Despite the memories of Oscar Wilde's imprisonment and destruction, and the continuing threat of arrest for homosexuals, it was not such a bad time to be queer. Many of the old taboos were broken by the Bright Young Things, who refused to follow in the conventional footsteps of their parents, yet had (in the case of the men) gone to public schools where relationships between boys were the rule not the exception. A group of slightly older men had helped pave the way for Robert's generation – talented, mannered aesthetes who made it chic to prefer men. Cyril Connolly described the 'great homosexual trail-blazers in the arts in the early twentieth century who avenged on the bourgeoisie the latter's killing of Oscar Wilde', naming such inspirational spirits as Diaghilev, Proust, Cocteau and Gide. Even those who ended up marrying and loving women had often had liaisons with men when they were young: Connolly, John Betjeman and Evelyn Waugh were all part of the famous 1920s Oxford set who entered into the homoerotic spirit of their alma mater.

Robert probably didn't know much about these people – though he might have heard of the Russian Ballet – but he undoubtedly visited the Café Royal, Wilde's old haunt on Regent Street that was still going strong. And he surely made use of the Savoy Turkish Baths, which were just along from his hotel in Jermyn Street. Known as a safe haven for the sort of gentlemen who could afford the price of admission, the baths were filled with men eager for assignations in the changing rooms or dark corners.

He may have been a Mad Boy, but Robert was never one of the camp 'pansies', nor the painted and scented 'nancy-boys', 'West End poofs' or 'Dilly boys' who frequented the many public toilets without attendants that were helpfully identified in *For your Convenience: A Learned Dialogue Instructive to All Londoners and London Visitors*.[95] Whether or not he visited these conveniences – ironwork constructions that often had tiny holes so one could see who was approaching – is anyone's guess. But the locations of the more popular venues were well known – the spacious one off Wardour Street with two entrances, or 'Clarkson's Cottage' by Clarkson's theatrical costume shop. Naturally, there were risks involved and the so-called 'pretty police' (official *agents provocateurs*) were a source of fear to all who engaged in 'cottaging'. Robert at one point certainly worked in a Lyons Corner House, perhaps even the one on Coventry Street, by Leicester Square, 'the absolute Mecca of the gay scene' and one of queer London's landmarks. Quentin Crisp was a habitué of the Lily Pond, a tearoom on the first floor, where two old ladies served tea and toast and turned a blind eye to the flirtatious behaviour of their male guests.[96] It also seems likely that Robert would have made use of his Army contacts to meet willing young men, 'something in uniform', especially a red-coated Guardsman, who might be willing to go for 'a walk in the park'. As J. R. Ackerley wrote, 'It would be the blackest ingratitude to disparage the Guards. These brave soldiers are of incalculable use to a great many lonely bachelors in London.' In his day, 'A pound was the recognized tariff for the Foot Guards . . . The Horse Guards cost rather more.'[97]

It was perfectly acceptable to prefer boys in the circles in which Robert moved, but he was also interested in girls. At one point he was even engaged to the elegant and beautiful Kathleen Meyrick, four years his senior. She was already notorious, not for her own behaviour but for the sins of her mother. Kate Meyrick was an Irish-born mother of eight whose husband had left her and who became a hugely successful London nightclub owner in the 1920s. She believed that 'men will pay anything to be amused', and her post-war advocacy of the pursuit of 'pure pleasure' was still just as palatable for the young of the 1930s.[98] The 'Queen of Nightclubs' ran the Silver Slipper on Regent Street, where the glass dance floor was illuminated from beneath with coloured lights, and little slippers filled with sweeties and novelties were handed to guests on the opening night. 'Meyrick's Marvellous Maids' were the hostesses, carefully chosen for their good looks, their exquisite dancing and their charm.

According to Robert's family, he was not only engaged to Kathleen but lived in the Meyrick household and 'helped run a nightclub'. Although no details remain, it seems logical to surmise that the club was the 43, where many members and guests would have been his friends anyway. The 43 was Mrs Meyrick's greatest triumph. A large rambling place that occupied six floors at 43 Gerrard Street in Soho, it was depicted by Evelyn Waugh in A Handful of Dust as the Old Hundredth. It attracted the well-heeled types who were regulars at the Cavendish Hotel, and provided the glamour, pretty girls and flow of champagne that were prerequisites for dancing into the night. As at other exclusive clubs, there were membership lists, dress codes and the sort of prices that guarded against all but the most privileged becoming members; a bottle of champagne cost about 30 shillings, almost half the average working man's weekly wage.[99] Dressed in tall hats, white silk scarves, fur coats and long dresses, this 'animated gathering of toffs in toff's togs waiting to be raised up to the latest toff's paradise' was a familiar sight to Soho's locals.[100]

Mrs Meyrick managed to send her daughters to Roedean and her sons to Harrow, and they became part of the class to which she offered so much entertainment. Two daughters married into the aristocracy, becoming, respectively, Countess of Kinnoull and Lady de Clifford. But disaster was lurking. By the time Robert became involved with Kathleen, her mother had already been in prison several times. First, there had been raids on the club by 'ruffians' and by the police. Then, as part of a clean-up campaign, she was arrested for selling drinks after hours and jailed for six months. Kathleen was only seventeen. And then

KATHLEEN MEYRICK WITH ROBERT AT THE RACES. THE PAIR REMAINED
FRIENDS AFTER THEIR ENGAGEMENT, AND KATHLEEN OFTEN WENT TO
STAY AT FARINGDON. IN COUNTRY GET-UP, THEY BOTH LOOK AS THOUGH
THEY KNOW HOW TO PLAY BY THE RULES AND HOW TO BREAK THEM

the same thing happened all over again. Worse came when Mrs Meyrick was accused of bribing a certain Sergeant Goddard at Marylebone police station after his colleagues became suspicious about his sudden acquisition of a fancy Chrysler and an expensive Streatham home. Ten-pound notes were traced to Mrs Meyrick. The upshot was fifteen months of hard labour in Holloway and a reputation in the press as 'the most dangerous woman in London'. Although she survived, her health was wrecked. Her legal costs had been hugely damaging and it was not long before she died, aged fifty-seven, from pneumonia.

Gladys and Algernon Heber-Percy were appalled. Their youngest son didn't have a job and his life was filled with decadence and debt. There was little hope that the twenty-year-old would give up his life of metropolitan indulgence interspersed with a bit of careering around the countryside on a horse. According to Robert, his parents had already bought him a one-way ticket to Australia when he went to stay at his friend Michael Duff's estate, Vaynol, for the life-changing weekend. 'And he came back in a blue Rolls-Royce,' recounted one friend who heard the story later.[101]

It would be easy to presume that Gerald provided a way out for Robert: a sugar daddy for a spoilt young man. The story of the two men's meeting has developed all sorts of variations among people who knew them, including one that tells how Lord Berners came across the Mad Boy working in his Lyons Corner House, and another that has Gerald bowled over by him in Venice. The fact that they met on equal terms at the country house of a mutual friend who had known Robert since boyhood is interesting because the younger man was not at a disadvantage. A close friend of Gerald's, Diana Mosley, later wrote, 'Heber-Percy's high spirits, elegant appearance and uninhibited behaviour enchanted Gerald who no longer needed a drug to give him contentment.'[102]

Gerald did not write openly about his feelings for the Mad Boy, but a fair amount can be deduced from his light if bitingly satirical novel *The Girls of Radcliff Hall*. In this spoof girls'-boarding-school story, the schoolgirls are based on young men in his circle and Gerald himself is the headmistress, Miss Carfax. Robert is clearly Millie Roberts, a pupil who 'brought a new interest into Miss Carfax's life'. The tone appears confessional: the headmistress 'had become convinced that there could be nothing more in life that could arouse that wonderful sensation of ecstasy she had so often experienced in her youth . . . But now it seemed as though within her breast some strange unresolved chord had been struck that caused her whole being to vibrate.' Millie on the other hand, like the Mad Boy,

> was wild, unrestrained and a little crazy. You never knew what she was going to do next. Her movements were often violent but, although she was constantly breaking things, there was nothing clumsy about her movements. You felt that if things happened to get in her way and she was obliged to knock them over, it was their fault rather than hers, and everything she did was redeemed by a peculiar gracefulness. She was like a young panther.[103]

The attraction was not only one-way. The younger man was intrigued enough to take things a step further. Above all, Gerald was entertaining – a quality that each found essential to successful relationships. And although Robert made a point of portraying himself as uneducated and almost illiterate, he was intelligent enough to be interested in the stimulating world of the creative arts to which Gerald belonged. He also loved Gerald's iconoclasm, blended as it was with a deep understanding of the Shropshire boyhoods they had both enjoyed and endured.

Gerald had long left behind dun-coloured dogs and wearying blood sports and was now like the trumpeter bird: plain and plump at first sight, yet unusual, charming, iridescent, and free to fly in whichever direction he liked. That Robert seemed to him like a panther is revealing. Sleek, black and dangerous, the panther may threaten the trumpeter, but he cannot reach him: the bird can sit on the tree and tease as much as he likes. Gerald and the Mad Boy's relationship thus had the improbable and yet touching air of a partnership between the unpredictable, ebony feline and the shy, shimmering, inky-feathered bird. The pair were about to create a bizarre new life together, with Faringdon as the magical stage on which the public performances and private dramas were played out. In very different ways, each contributed to creating the captivating place that would enchant so many talented and remarkable people during the 1930s.

CHAPTER FIVE

Et in Arcadia Ego

ERALD'S FRIENDS WERE ASTOUNDED. They were used to the jokes and teasing, the stunts and parties, but there had never been a boyfriend. And here was a spectacular one. The Mad Boy could hardly be kept discreetly in the shadows, but this was part of the attraction. It was as though the death of his mother had freed Gerald to pursue love without fear or shame. There was also his age; forty-eight is a point when many start to ponder what time is left in which to taste the joys of life they have missed, or still desire. The younger man 'had a streak of pure fantasy in his make-up. With Robert about, Diaghilev's demand to Cocteau: "*Etonne moi!*" would not have been necessary, for he never failed to astonish.'[104] Life as part of an unlikely couple was not straightforward, but Gerald blossomed. In a letter to Cecil Beaton describing his travels and Robert's crazy escapades, he admitted, 'Far from being a strain on my system the incidents of the last month have acted as a <u>tonic</u> and I feel years younger.'[105]

The Mad Boy expressed aspects of Gerald's own character: a delight in the unconventional, in confounding expectations, and a tendency to what Nancy Mitford described as 'Neighbour-tease' – the pleasure in mischievously provoking the good burghers in the locality who could not see beyond their own parochialism. There was an element of savagery, even violence, in Robert that reflected Gerald's more hidden elements: an uninhibited, unashamed shout to the more suppressed aggression that emerged in his humour. Gerald kept himself buttoned up; friends recalled his laugh being like a sneeze, or 'a combination of a

GERALD IN PLAYFUL
HOLIDAY MODE

chuckle and clearing the throat'.[106] Even his eccentricity was described as 'a stately figure of nice madness; etiquette, and gracious manners were most important to this man who, physically, looked like a well-bred diplomat, a noble schoolmaster, a learned don.'[107]

If Gerald was struggling with his inner darkness and pessimism and transforming them into quirky jokes or artistic endeavour, Robert didn't appear to be struggling at all. Robert claimed that being with Gerald 'was the first time I had met civilised people. People thought

I was funny and didn't regard me as an outrageous child.'[108] He may have been wrong about the last point, but just as Gerald escaped his stultifying background by going abroad, so Robert cast off the circumscribed (if, as the youngest son, unavailable) environment of Hodnet Hall. He was pleased to expand his horizons by entering the often fantastical, cosmopolitan world surrounding Lord Berners.

The nature of this relationship was understood by their friends but the after-shocks from Oscar Wilde's trial still spread fear; the law had become no more lenient since the time of Wilde's imprisonment. Gerald and Robert were committing exactly the same 'crimes' and faced equally harsh punishments if caught. 'The love that dare not speak its name' remained just as risky as it had at the start of the century. It would be several decades before Wilde's eloquent testimony was heeded: 'There is nothing unnatural about it. It is intellectual, and it repeatedly exists between an elder and a younger man, when the elder man has intellect, and the younger man has all the joy, hope and glamour of life before him.'

It is undeniable that in addition to Gerald's intellect, wit and amusing character, Robert was offered the comforts and delights of his lifestyle. Life with Lord Berners incorporated London, travel abroad and, at Faringdon, the opportunity to pursue the riding and rural activities that he loved. Robert had scraped by with odd jobs and donations from his disapproving parents, but for how long could this have lasted? Gerald's life was nothing if not luxurious and he was a generous man. While Robert was hardly a penniless boy plucked from the unknown territories of other classes and cultures, there were obvious practical benefits to back up the relationship. He might have been too flighty and wild to be a docile kept boy, but there is little doubt that Gerald provided an extraordinarily alluring environment. At Faringdon, Robert lived the life of a favoured first son on a country estate, but with the indulgence of an older man who was in love with him.

A colourful, fictionalised impression of Robert at Faringdon is given by the person who introduced him to Gerald – Michael Duff:

Suddenly, down the double staircase, came a noise like a sack of coal being emptied, and in another minute a thunder-clap, in the shape of Robert Oddman, appeared in the room . . . He was dressed in brown corduroys, a yellow polo shirt, and round his neck, arranged in an untidy mass, was a blue and white spotted scarf; his eyes were hazel and very gentle, and he resembled an attractive ape with his protruding lower lip.[109]

Michael's camp novel, *The Power of a Parasol*, was published as a pretty, privately printed edition of 100, and gives a convincing if whimsical glimpse of some aspects of life at Faringdon after Robert moved in. The exhibitionism (he shows the Prime Minister's wife photographs of himself '*quite* naked', and picks his nose in public) is less than flattering. The Faringdon copy of the slim book is dedicated 'For Hebey, Whose character was never so endearing as in this book.' What Robert himself made of the portrait is anyone's guess. He probably didn't care.

Little is known about what went on behind the bedroom door between the trumpeter bird and the panther. There is a general assumption that it was not all that much. Gerald is presumed by some to have leaned towards the asexual or celibate. Other rumours said that Robert went for the weekend to Faringdon and his night with Gerald had been a flop. 'When on Monday he asked, "Shall I leave?" Berners replied, "Don't go. You make me laugh. I don't mind about the other."'[110] Some have suggested that Gerald's thrills were of the more vicarious kind, provoked by reports of, or even witnessing, the Mad Boy's exploits. Notwithstanding the guesswork, there was love and affection between the two, and also that frequently affiliated feature of sexual relationships, jealousy.

Gerald's letters from the early years of his relationship with Robert suggest a pitch of turmoil that normally accompanies the most intense emotional liaisons. When writing to 'Dearest Cecil' (Beaton), Gerald seems rather proud of how badly behaved his young lover is on their travels through Europe, though his remarks are unclear in their meaning: 'I have taken to adopting homeopathic (not homosexual) methods with the Mad Boy and making "scenes and situations" myself.' In spite of Gerald's efforts, Robert's 'scenes' continued.

> There was only one terrific fracas in the Hotel Santa Caterina at Amalfi where we went for the night. The Mad Boy woke up in a Neapolitan mood, put on a scarlet shirt, a blue jumper, green trousers and a yellow belt and then suggested that I should go down and have breakfast with him on the crowded terrace. I said No certainly not. Whereupon the creature flew into a rage and hit me over the head with a button-hook.[111]

Worse was to come, when 'the Mad Boy nearly killed a woman in the street at Salzburg by hurling down a glass tankard from that restaurant on the cliff'. And though Gerald makes light of it, things must have been pretty bad in Venice if the Mad Boy really tried to commit suicide as his letter describes:

> [Robert was] removed next morning by me in a heavily drugged condition. Our arrival at the Hotel Excelsior in Florence was, to say the least of it, sensational, as the Mad Boy had to be carried into the hotel in a semi conscious state still dressed in his Tyrolean costume and with his hair hanging all over his face to the amazement and stupefaction of Bobbie Casa Maury and the entire Dudley Ward family who I found seated in the hall. (It required some explaining away I can assure you!)

Gerald seems more concerned about the social implications than the fact that his boyfriend has tried to kill himself, which suggests that Robert was out of control rather than actually suicidal. The older man's tolerance of this degree of mayhem in a life that was normally orderly and determined by his own whims is surely an indication of the significance that the Mad Boy had taken in his life. Another guess about their relationship would be that while there was a sexual element, it was unlikely to have been the cornerstone of their bond, and doubtless created problems. Later in his life, Gerald admitted to his friend, the academic and writer A. L. Rowse, that 'all that sex business is over for me', and that this was a good thing as it was 'nothing but a nuisance'.[112]

FTER ALL THE TRAVELLING, the discovering
of other languages and cultures and the
metamorphosis from a shy, isolated Shropshire
boy into a cosmopolitan, artistically accomplished
baron, Gerald created the ultimate English
institution – the country house. Although Faringdon was compact compared to many such places
– no distant wings or chilly corridors – it came complete with all
the familiar accoutrements: kitchen gardens, parkland, stables and a
generous staff quota. Gerald had his mother's posthumous presence
to deal with in the form of her belongings and furnishings, which
had filled the place for nearly twenty years. The inherent elements of
tradition, stability and solidity were the opposite of Gerald's favoured
light-heartedness. How would he combine running a country estate
with the mood changes that took him touring, butterfly-like, from one
European beauty-spot or cultural centre to another? And yet, as Henry
James wrote, 'Of all the great things that the English have invented
and made part of the credit of the national character, the most perfect,
the most characteristic, the one they have mastered most completely
in all its details, so that it has become a compendious illustration of
their social genius and their manners, is the well-appointed, well-
administered, well-filled country-house.'[113]

Faringdon provided the solid canvas on which Gerald would paint
his own fantasy details, and Robert became part of that creation. On the
one hand, the Mad Boy can be viewed as Gerald's plaything – a human
version of the Marchesa Casati's cheetahs – but actually the younger
man found his own, complementary way of living at Faringdon. Osbert
Sitwell sent his love in letters to 'Robert *Le diable*', but in reality
the young devil was also building his own foundations, becoming
increasingly involved with running the estate. It came naturally to
Robert to take on certain responsibilities; he had been brought up
by his father to take an interest in all aspects of the countryside, and
it was not long before Gerald described him as the estate manager.
The house now resonated with Gerald calling 'Robert! Robert!' as he

required help and advice. There was evidently a dimension to the Mad Boy that was far from mad; indeed he had many practical abilities that his older partner lacked.

Robert brought his horses to Faringdon from Hodnet, and moved Gerald's ancestral portraits out of the stables where they had been languishing since he inherited them with his title. Robert went hunting and thus got to know the influential county set. They often met on the gravel at the front of Faringdon House on frosty mornings, and trays of stirrup cups were handed up to the riders in their scarlet-and-black finery. Photographs show Robert in immaculate hunting gear – tightly fitted jacket, top hat and shiny black boots, ready to speed away on his thoroughbred Arab hunter. Although Gerald was never a keen rider, there was a quiet old horse kept for him, and sometimes he would don his jodhpurs and go out for a gentle ride around the farmland with Robert. Admittedly, the Mad Boy was also known to ride into the grounds naked and bareback, and then return, like a living statue, to the house.

Both Gerald and the Mad Boy bore the legacy of their Shropshire gentry backgrounds; they could both dress impeccably and liked a well-run house and good manners. It would be easy to assume that the Mad Boy was the one who brought an anarchic streak to their cohabitation, but actually it was sometimes Robert who introduced the county conventionality that bored Gerald. After all, it was Gerald who had a lifelong fascination with masks and fancy dress and who wrote modern music and cultivated artistic, avant-garde friends. While Robert loved fine clothes and would often mismatch his colours to produce a clownish, dandy effect, he was not intrigued by the grotesque and the peculiar like Gerald. Once, when Robert was entertaining some dull hunting friends in the drawing room, Gerald made himself scarce so he would not have to talk to them. Then, realising he needed a book from the shelves, he pulled a large hearth-rug over himself and, as if disguised as a strange animal, crawled into the room, proceeded to the bookcase, reached up a hand to take the required volume and crawled out again.[114] One can only imagine the guests' conversations after they had departed. When Robert later asked Gerald why he had done this, he replied, 'I didn't want to draw attention to myself.'[115]

'LL BE ACCUSED of dropping names if I admitted to having spent the weekend at Lord Berners, so I deny absolutely that practically everybody was there.' Thus wrote Tom Driberg, journalist, socialist and later Labour MP. Yet another Oxford contemporary of Harold Acton and his circle, Driberg was unusual at Faringdon for his Communist leanings, if not for his open homosexuality or his penchant for rough trade. Clever and witty, he had long used and been used by his extensive social network to fuel his *Daily Express* gossip column, which he believed 'described the absurdities and extravagancies of the ruling class', and into which he tried to smuggle as much social conscience as possible.[116] Driberg invented or confirmed people's social rise and demise, revealing the artificial tinsel shine of the Bright Young Things and their endless, madcap parties, while also enjoying himself with them. But he was careful to remain loyal to old friends and avoided biting too hard on the many hands that fed his column. While his height, deep voice and authoritative bearing were those of a bishop, his scandalous sex life and links to Aleister Crowley led people to call him 'satanic' and 'evil'.[117]

There was a steady parade of friends to Faringdon, especially at the weekends. Gerald was busy with his composing, writing or painting in the mornings, and Robert might have been out and about on a horse, but standards for visitors were high. One friend claimed that when listening to Lord Berners's music, 'I can always tell when Gerald's weekend guests arrive. There's a sudden cymbal crash!'[118] All reports are of spectacular food, dazzling surroundings and company that included many of the wittiest, most attractive people to be found in English and European drawing rooms. Although the house was comfortable, it was not overly formal; there were worn chair covers and piles of books lying around. Gerald's easel and typewriter were left with on-going endeavours, and music books and manuscript paper were out on the Bechstein baby grand. Gerald didn't need to try too hard. The magic was there.

GERALD PLAYING THE PIANO AT FARINGDON, THE TRAVELLING
CLAVICHORD VISIBLE TO THE RIGHT

The airy eighteenth-century elegance of Faringdon House made it the perfect architectural style for the times. There were various campaigners for the celebration and re-invention of the Georgian aesthetic, from Lytton Strachey and Edith Sitwell to the Georgian Group, a charity that worked to protect and preserve eighteenth-century buildings and gardens. Gerald's young friend Cecil Beaton dressed up his friends in Georgian costumes, but he was also serious about the visual strength of classical proportions. Gerald added effortlessly to the vogue, simply by taking over his mother's place and then making it his own.

Faringdon House had been built around 1780 by the Poet Laureate who is most famous for being the worst – Henry James Pye. So poor a verse-maker was he that the nursery rhyme *Sing a Song of Sixpence* (with its blackbirds baked in a pie) was supposedly some kind of tease, and Sir Walter Scott quipped that Pye was 'eminently respectable in everything but his poetry'. Since the 1620s, Pye's forebears had lived in a much larger Elizabethan house, a long, gabled affair nearer to the church. Earlier still, the Manor of Faringdon had belonged to the medieval Beaulieu Abbey that was to the north, by Grove Wood. During the Civil War, the old Faringdon House was garrisoned by the Royalists, where they remained, despite Cromwell's attempts to break in with 500 soldiers. During the fighting, the solid, thirteenth-century stone church near the house got its spire knocked off and it was never put back.

When Henry Pye decided to build another manor house, it was to replace the charred remains of the previous one after it burned down. He moved away from the church and closer to the edge of the Golden Ridge on which the town is situated. This gave an ideal vantage point, looking north-west across the Thames Valley, and the grounds and lake that would also be landscaped. As Pye put it in one of his poems, 'Through aromatic heaps of ripening hay, / There silver Isis wins her winding way.'[119] The house was to be what people then called a 'neat villa', constructed using material from the old manor, as well as some creamy, newly cut Bath stone that livened up the dove-grey rendering. In addition to the two main storeys, there was a useful semi-basement level and an attic floor that was hidden by a parapet. The architect remains unknown, and although some have said that Wood the Younger of Bath was associated with it (he designed nearby Buckland House in the 1750s), there is no evidence to support this. But whoever it was, his collaboration with the mediocre poet was inspired. As a 1930s architectural guide put it, 'The house is as charming an eighteenth-century stone house as may be seen in England.'

During the nineteenth century, the house passed through various hands, including that of the Cunard family. (Their legacy was a number of massive cast-iron cauldrons that had been used to melt down blubber on a fleet of whaling boats that formed part of their enormous shipping empire.) Not all that much had changed by the time Gerald and Robert lived there during the 1930s. By all accounts, the small market town of Faringdon was a charming Berkshire backwater (until later county restructuring brought it within Oxfordshire). Most of its buildings were made from local limestone and its streets were still lit by nineteenth-century gaslights. Visitors usually arrived at Faringdon by train, disembarking at the end of the branch line into the Victorian mock-Tudor station. London had been left far behind. This was deep countryside. A car would be sent from the house to collect the guest for the short drive through the centre of Faringdon, past the old town hall (like a Wendy house perched on stone pillars), up the sloping market place and through the main gate by the church. Parking on the gravel in front of the porch, the visitor would leave the footman to deal with the luggage and was shown into the house by Lambert, the butler.

The hall was filled with exotic plants and flowers brought in from the greenhouses or orangery and emanating a powerful scent. The guest would proceed through to the drawing room, with its ceiling-high windows flooding the place with light. It was always warm – not something associated with English country houses, which were frequently cold, uncomfortable places with a temperature in inverse proportion to the social standing of the owner. The painter Adrian Daintrey nicknamed the place 'Faringdonheit' for its luxurious heat, and Nancy Mitford too memorialised this unusual lavishness in *The Pursuit of Love*. When Aunt Sadie and Louisa go to dine with Lord Merlin at Merlinford, they come home 'with their eyes popping out of their heads. The house, they said, had been boiling hot, so hot that one never felt cold for a single moment, not even getting out of one's coat in the hall.'[120]

Gerald decorated his home with a characteristically eclectic, magpie-like approach, and was not interested in the designs of trend-setters like Syrie Maugham, with her fashionable layering of white on white, mirrored screens, white leather furniture and books covered in white vellum. Gerald threw in whatever pleased him. He had the confidence to combine furniture inherited from his mother or the previous Lord Berners with pieces he picked up on his travels, ancestral portraits and French landscapes with small oils painted by himself and friends, ornate antique mirrors draped with Woolworth's pearl necklaces, busts crowned with animal masks and marble tables topped with mechanical toys.[121] An appreciation of the strange, monstrous and kitsch combined with an educated degree of good taste made for a fascinating interior. A wry affection for Victoriana was thrown into the mix. Anything linked to the grumpy old monarch who had reigned during Gerald's boyhood was fodder for fun: small figurines of the plump Queen sat on mantelpieces and her portraits were scattered unceremoniously.

The drawing room was divided into two parts with the larger section papered white and filled with gilded French and Italian furniture. The other, smaller end was olive green, 'providing a perfect background for a riot of tropical birds, some alive and hopping about, some stuffed in cases, some pressed, like flowers in a screen, some modelled in china, one jumping with a song out of a gold box, and hundreds between the green morocco covers of Mr Gould'.[122] There could never be enough birds for Gerald, and he introduced flamingos, storks and other gaudy-feathered creatures that strutted around the gardens and into the house. Guests were amused to find that 'odd, large-beaked birds wandered through the Georgian silver on the Chippendale dining-table, pecked in one's plate or left squarking horribly on some guest's head'. Plumed birds-of-paradise brought flashes of unfamiliar colours to the subdued palette of the English countryside as they patrolled the house or sat, preserved in fixed poses, beneath glass domes. One of Gerald's favourite pets was a flashy green member of the Paradisaeidae family who he named John Knox, honouring the sixteenth-century Scottish Protestant in a way that would have appalled him. Gerald claimed that once, when he was laid up in bed with lumbago, he entertained himself by teaching the bird to turn somersaults. When the pet died, Gerald placed a notice in *The Times* personal column: 'Died of jealousy, aged fifteen, John Knox, emerald bird-of-paradise belonging to Lord Berners. His guests are asked to wear half-mourning.'[123]

It was an inspired day when Gerald decided to help nature along in the decoration department. According to Robert, Gerald read about dyeing doves in a Chinese book. 'They should have whistles on their wings too, but we never got round to that. We thought up some of the ideas together but I always did them.'[124] Colours were acquired and the effect was stunning: turquoise, emerald, ruby and sapphire fantailed pigeons swept over the plain stone town like a bizarre daydream of gems thrown into the air. It was just the sort of alchemy that pleased Gerald: aesthetically surprising; a challenge to the humdrum; a sophisticated tease to the English, the conventional and the rural. And it involved birds. After a visit in 1937, Stravinsky's mistress, Vera Sudeikina, sent some new dyes, and Gerald wrote to thank her, calling them 'magnificent' and saying that they 'add a tropical touch to this wintry country'. There were suggestions that all sorts of animals (even the grazing cattle) might go the way of the pigeons and improve their natural colouring, but it doesn't seem to have happened. Later, in a novel, Gerald would describe another version of this trick. A papyrus box is filled with flies that have had tiny streamers of coloured silk attached to them and when it is opened, 'Like miniature birds of paradise they filled the air with swirling colour as they flew out into the

THE COLOURED
DOVES AT FARINGDON

courtyard and settled on the trees.'[125]

The weekend guest at Faringdon might have been surprised by the degree of warmth, the number of flowers and birds and even, beside the bedside biscuit tin, the pornographic books disguised inside a copy of the Bible, or the Bible inside a dust-jacket reading 'This is the hottest thing written in the last 20 years – sex, crime, violence . . .'[126] He or she was never one of an overly large group; it was not like Vaynol, where vast numbers made up the house parties. At Faringdon, there were only five main bedrooms on the first floor, two of which were taken up by Gerald and Robert, so three couples would normally be the maximum number that could stay the night. Helping run the place were two housemaids, a footman and a kitchen maid, in addition to the butler and the cook. Dairy produce was brought from the farm and there were six men under Mr Morris, the head gardener, to provide vegetables and fruit for the table: peaches and grapes from the glasshouses, and raspberries, strawberries and all manner of other summer produce from the fruit cages. Later, when wartime austerity would decimate culinary standards, Cyril Connolly said that 'when every sort of luxury has been forever banned in England, Lord Berners will somehow manage to maintain a secret melon house'.[127]

Additional guests were often invited over at weekends for the famously marvellous meals. Gerald had learned to take food seriously as a sixteen-year-old in Normandy, but what was viewed as culture and pleasurable Epicureanism on the Continent was often seen as gluttony, or even an 'improper' subject for conversation in England. 'I don't mind owning up to being greedy,' he wrote. 'Greediness is among the more amiable of the Vices: it does less harm in the world than, for instance, Vulgarity or Priggishness.' Fond of wine and cigars, but not excessively so, Gerald was not ashamed to like rich food, claiming that delicacies like caviar or plovers' eggs 'have the additional merit of not being exposed to the danger of being spoilt by bad cooking'. Elsewhere he wrote, 'It was a happy moment in my life when I discovered that, in the Diet my Doctor had prescribed for me, he had omitted to mention both Caviare and Foie Gras among the forbidden foods.'[128]

Faringdon's dining room acquired a reputation for the bizarre, and some recalled further experiments with colour. Stravinsky mentioned meals 'in which all the food was of one colour pedigree; i.e. if Lord Berners's mood was pink, lunch might consist of beet soup, lobster, tomatoes, strawberries . . .'[129] But most close friends recalled the consistent quality rather than the games. Naturally, the table was laid with attention to the linen, silverware and china. Gerald loved gaily coloured geraniums, which were planted out in pots and urns for the summer months, and he sometimes filled a silver basket with pink and red geranium flowers as a pretty centrepiece; at other times he preferred to create an entertaining arrangement of tiny cuckoo clocks or swathes of Venetian beads.[130]

'What food does Lord Berners dislike?' asked the *Daily Express* in 1937. 'Hotel food,' was the reply; 'Especially the kind of hotel food which you get in some private houses, with watery soup at its beginning and indifferent ice which brings it to an equally watery close.' His preferred cuisine was French, and his partiality to rich sauces and extravagant puddings evokes the recipes of his childhood housekeeper, most of which began with instructions like: 'Take two pints of cream, two dozen eggs and one pint of old liqueur brandy.'[131] Another cherished Faringdon dessert was pudding Louise, with boiled *marrons glacés* and raspberry jam, topped with ice-cream, although Gerald once listed his 'favourite dish' as *pouding Nesselrode* – a cream-filled, custardy ice, made with chestnut purée, candied fruits and maraschino liqueur, invented by the eponymous Russian diplomat.[132]

Gerald tempted his guests by describing the enticing food they were about to eat, and had daily discussions with the cook. As the *Daily Express* reported, 'Lord Berners believes in conversing with his cooks. He thinks that a cook who is hardly ever spoken to becomes a bored cook. And a bored cook soon becomes a bad cook.' His four tests of cooking were 'the making of coffee, soufflés and pastry, and the roasting of a joint. A cook who can do these four things well, he thinks, can cook anything well.' An accompanying photograph of Mrs Dora Nelson, the cook from Gerald's London house at Halkin Street, smiles out from the page – a dark-haired, wholesome-looking woman. She had apparently been to America and offers recipes for a couple of her favourite dishes from there: 'Johnny Cake', the American breakfast dish made with yellow cornmeal, eggs and butter, baked in a Yorkshire pudding tin; and an apple tart sprinkled with cheese. 'Apple tart without cheese is like a kiss without a squeeze,' said Mrs Nelson roguishly. She also mentions *soufflé de Berners*, which sounds like the *Nesselrode*, with cream, rum and mixed crystallised fruits previously soaked in brandy. 'Put into a charged ice cave and freeze for 2–3 hours.' Heaven.

HE MAD BOY was finally getting an education. He might have been fictionalised by his friend Michael Duff as someone who was continually flinging off his clothes, but he was becoming a part of Faringdon life. He was increasingly involved in the practical aspects of the estate as Gerald appreciated home-grown flowers and fruits but was not interested in the details of how they were produced. And it was usually Robert who dyed the doves and kept the grounds in order. More important, he was absorbing the cultural world that Gerald had created. He couldn't help finding out about food and he became attentive to what was served at Faringdon in a way that must have pleased his teacher. On their travels, the Mad Boy didn't have to try in order to learn about architecture or landscape – it was laid out before him, discussed and written about by others, painted by Gerald and their friends. He gradually started to use this knowledge, bringing home ideas about how to improve the house and grounds that would continue over a lifetime.

Robert observed Gerald's routines: his tea brought at eight in the morning, breakfast downstairs at nine and then some concentrated hours of writing, painting or composing before lunch and more leisurely activities, often with friends. It is possible that some of the conversations were above Robert's head – he claimed he barely read books, though he exaggerated the degree of his illiteracy, an easy way of contrasting himself with all the highly literary people he was now surrounded by. The truth was not quite so simple. Gerald mentioned in the early days that Robert was writing poetry. Playing the fool or the daredevil was an obvious method of not competing and one which could easily be picturesque enough to appeal to Gerald and his friends. According to one friend, the Mad Boy would use words incorrectly, leading to much hilarity. Once, when he was annoyed, he said he had 'taken unction'.[133] When Gerald published *First Childhood* in 1934, he dedicated it, jokily ironic, to 'Robert Heber-Percy[,] whose knowledge of orthography and literary style has proved invaluable'.

Gerald and Robert began to make friends together, some of whom lived nearby. Perhaps the most significant were the newly married Betjemans, John and Penelope, who were close in age to Robert. John had published his first poems (supported by Gerald's friend Edward James) as well as a book about architecture, and worked for the *Architectural Review* and the *Evening Standard*. Penelope was the daughter of Field Marshal Lord Chetwode, a former Commander-in-Chief of India, and the great loves of her life were India and horses. Together, the young couple embraced local life in the little village of Uffington, where they had recently moved, going as far as founding the Uffington Parochial Youth Fellowship, which offered music, talks and various entertainments to locals.[134] John and Penelope were clever and fun, with the determined yet impish and impulsive air of characters out of one of Gerald's novels. Indeed, he dedicated his strangely surreal book *The Camel* to them, hinting that they had similarities to the two main characters, the Rev. Aloysius Hussey and his wife Antonia, who adopt a mysteriously psychic camel. Unaffected and adventurous, Antonia has spent her youth in the Orient and takes to riding the camel around the parish. More like a fable than a novel, the atmosphere is intensely English, mannered and provincial, while bringing in a gay organist romping with his choirboys, a verger called Beaton, murder, suicide and a finale where Antonia rides off on her camel into the sunset.

The Betjemans were unlike some of the older, more eminent visitors, but Gerald was unafraid to mix his friends and was charmed by the young couple's unaffected energy. Penelope became so at home that she would sit down for dinner and say, 'Gerald, what's the pud?'[135] and took to darning John's underclothes in the drawing room. She was simple, even tomboyish, in her appearance, but ambitious in her way. Shortly after their wedding, she went to Germany to improve her German because she wanted to learn Sanskrit and most scholarly works about India were in German. Penelope soon became very close to Robert, bonding over their love of horses. The two of them often rode out together, while John and Gerald stayed at home discussing poetry or the delights of some obscure stone carvings in a tiny Berkshire church.

Like Gerald, John understood how silliness and joking could be ways of dealing with the misery of the world and of subverting authority. Both men were able to take things seriously, but their creative output and their social personas relied on lightness and playfulness – characteristics that belied their dark insecurities and even despair. In common with Firbank and many other humorists since, they recognised 'frivolity as the most insolent refinement of satire'.[136] Gerald still had dramatic mood-swings, so he could be 'talkative and gay at lunch, keeping everybody happy, then he'd be very down the whole afternoon probably. Then if somebody came to dinner he'd whizz up again.'[137] This was a pattern that had started at school, where he described himself as not being 'what the Americans call "a good mixer"'. John recognised Gerald's shyness and self-doubt and appreciated his 'remarkable gift for making friends and a loyalty to them which no reverses in their fortunes would shake. He was a man of few words and nearly all of those were extremely amusing.'[138]

John also had the outsider's sympathy with the predicament of the outlawed homosexual in England. While it is unlikely that anything would ever have been discussed openly with Gerald about his relationship with Robert, John's marvellous poem 'The Arrest of Oscar Wilde at the Cadogan Hotel' is a beautiful attack on the absurd cruelty of the law:

'. . . Do fetch my morocco portmanteau,
And bring them on later, dear boy.'
A thump, and a murmur of voices –
('Oh why must they make such a din?')
As the door of the bedroom swung open
And TWO PLAIN CLOTHES POLICEMEN came in.

John had an enormous love of Englishness, and was a great defender of architecture that was deeply unfashionable; his 1933 book, *Ghastly Good Taste*, is a celebration of the much maligned Victorian and Edwardian styles. Later, he became editor of the celebrated Shell County Guides, which brought in excellent writers to explore aspects of the English countryside that had been neglected.

Although Gerald had turned himself into a European and collected books, friends and paintings from the Continent as much as from within Britain, he now became increasingly involved in local country life. As Alexandra Harris has pointed out, if there was a Domesday Book for the 1930s, it would show that almost all the major figures of English art and letters lived in the countryside, including Evelyn Waugh, E. M. Forster, Stanley Spencer, Vita Sackville-West, Cecil Beaton, Eric Ravilious and many more. While it might seem counter-intuitive, given the long-held ideas that 'modernism was cosmopolitan' while English art was pastoral, in fact there was a huge amount of creative energy emerging in rural England.[139]

It was John and Penelope's influence that brought Gerald and Robert into their orbit of village fetes and church concerts – an unlikely milieu for the eccentric lord and the Mad Boy. Penelope persuaded Gerald to write the overture for a mystery play she organised at her village church. He even played the organ, while Penelope played God the Father, chasing the children out of the church on the grounds that they were Adam and Eve and the church was the Garden of Eden.[140] Gerald said he'd tried in the music 'to express the fact that the expulsion from paradise was very unfair'. And while Penelope became ever more devout, Gerald could not escape the conviction that you had to have a talent for God in order to believe. Yet it niggled; sometimes he longed to have the comfort religion evidently gave others, especially when the dark moods of his dreaded *accidie* descended.

We have no record of what Robert thought of all this, though church services were naturally familiar after the schooling he had had and his childhood at Hodnet Hall. According to Penelope herself, not only did Gerald play the harmonium when she sang in a Methodist choir, but 'Robert used to come, and I think he even preached a sermon at one of the Methodist things once.'[141] These local gatherings were not limited to churches. Osbert Lancaster did a charming drawing of the Betjemans and friends putting on a performance of 'Sumer Is Icumen In' at a village hall, presumably in Uffington. Gerald is at the piano, Penelope holds a guitar, Lancaster plays a flute and John and Maurice Bowra (the famous Oxford don) are singing.

The Betjemans' house was just under the Downs and the legendary White Horse of Uffington, whose strangely modern lines visitors flocked to admire; Penelope stood on its eye to pray for a baby, much as others do at the Giant of Cerne Abbas. In Penelope's case it was hardly surprising that she preferred the horse's blessing. Moti, her beloved snow-white 'grey', had been shipped back from India and was the centre of her life. His name was Hindi for 'pearl' and he had been her hunter with the Delhi Foxhounds. Maurice Bowra reported that 'there were generally marks of lipstick on its neck'.[142] Although John was not interested in horses, they were Penelope's passion; John's biographer named Moti as 'a third in the marriage from the start'.[143] Penelope would harness him to a dog-cart and drive over to Faringdon, where she'd take Gerald and Robert for slow rides along local roads, during which they'd gossip wickedly about the neighbours or dreaded 'dry blankets' who bored them with their pomposity or expertise. At other times, Penelope and Robert would set off on wild bareback rides or chase boldly at the head of the local hunts. Most famously of all, Penelope would show off Moti's marvellous character by bringing him inside the house. A photograph of the white horse taking tea in the drawing room at Faringdon has become emblematic of this era of Gerald's life, the hallmark of his brand of eccentricity. In fact, the eccentricity in this case was surely Penelope's. She is shown dressed in checked shirt and tie, with a page-boy haircut, holding a saucer from which Moti is slurping tea. Gerald, Robert and another friend sit around a dainty, lace-clothed table. Gerald was delighted by Moti's perfect manners, and inspired by the beautiful incongruity of this elegant animal to set up his easel and oils to paint him *in situ*. There is a photograph showing Gerald perched on an ornate stool, buttoned up and penguin-like in co-respondent shoes, while Moti poses, calm and proud. If there were multi-coloured doves outside the house, then there could be a white horse inside; both caught the imagination in exactly the way that Gerald loved.

It is fitting that Gerald's 'English period' should produce more writing and painting than music. While some of his music

GERALD PAINTING
MOTI, HELD BY
PENELOPE BETJEMAN

is unconventional, harmonically modern and must have been challenging to many of his more conservative contemporaries, his books are light and funny and his paintings mostly peaceful landscapes, with the occasional portrait of a friend.[144] He had started young, with his watercolour outings with his mother and producing sketchbooks full of competent and charming impressions of his early travels. In one of his many notebooks, Gerald described his youthful passion for watercolour painting that incorporated his great admiration for Turner:

I produced a sunset that outdid Turner's most lurid efforts in almost every respect. I was very proud of my sunsets but my father, when I showed him one of them, rather dampened my pride by saying that, although he was sure it was very nicely painted, he was not sufficiently fond of either poached eggs or tomato soup for the picture to have any very strong appeal for him. This chilling appreciation of my work rather put me off sunsets and I turned my attention to other less flamboyant aspects of nature.

Gerald then describes how a 'particular hue of green stirred my fancy in a strange and violent manner'. Finding out the name of the colour led to a very liberal use of oxide of chromium for a while, and Gerald playfully quotes Havelock Ellis's theory 'that a partiality for green is one of the things that denote unnatural tendencies so perhaps this is a dangerous admission; however this mania for green on my part was only a passing phase . . .'

In adulthood, Gerald took the lead from Jean-Baptiste-Camille Corot, the painter he most admired, and created gentle, mild-coloured oils that are pleasing but hardly unexpected or strange. According to Gerald himself, he liked 'the directness and simplicity' of Corot's early paintings and found his style 'the perfect method of dealing with landscape'. He was an avid collector of the nineteenth-century French artist, picking up many early pictures at bargain prices and later trying them out at home before buying them from London's Reid & Lefevre Gallery. He eventually amassed the largest collection outside the Louvre, as well as acquiring paintings by Matisse, Sisley and Degas.[145]

Gerald's friend Harold Acton saw his conventional approach to the visual arts as 'the residue of his very conventional ancestry – the aunts and people who went sketching. A sort of compulsive thing.'[146] It is interesting that Gerald didn't feel the need to live up to his reputation as full of surprises, and was willing to study and follow in the well-trodden footsteps of the masters. It has been suggested that Gerald wasted his efforts by spreading his creativity so widely and not concentrating on music, where his real talent lay. Nevertheless, his paintings were good enough to be exhibited, and they sold. The mealier-mouthed cited his social standing as a contributing factor – 'It just goes to show the advantages of being a Baron,' sneered Evelyn Waugh – but the pictures continue to be admired and to sell today. Gerald had his first exhibition in 1931 at Reid & Lefevre. It included many Roman scenes, some Venetian views and some lush English landscapes. When Gerald had his second exhibition at the Lefevre, he received a positive review in *The Times*: 'He appears to see instinctively and naturally with Corot's eyes . . . And he can also see without the help of Corot, so that nearly all his landscapes are sedate and satisfactory in their organization and observed with quiet and unpretentious precision.'

FARINGDON HOUSE
PAINTED BY GERALD

Although his landscapes are well executed and charming, it is often Gerald's portraits that are the most memorable. He managed to get Robert to sit still long enough to paint several pictures of him – though he did work from photographs as well. Gerald also encouraged the Mad Boy to develop his own strengths and was delighted when Robert rode his horse, Passing Fancy, in the Grand National, sporting the Berners colours of red and green with a black cap. Deborah Mitford wrote to her sister Jessica: 'Lord Berners had a horse in for the first time in his life and the Mad Boy said to us before the race "If it falls at the first fence Gerald will be broken hearted." And it did! Wasn't it *awful*. But luckily he is very short-sighted and he thinks it was the second fence so all is ok.'147

There is no evidence of any fall-out from this disappointment, but both Gerald and Robert were superstitious. According to Robert, if

Gerald saw a white horse he would stamp, even if he was in the car. Then he might add, 'You can't talk now. When I've stamped 100 white horses I get my wish.'[148] Gerald later admitted that this was useful for when there were bores in the car. However, he also considered it bad luck if you neglected to pick up a fallen white feather and 'plant' it upright in the ground.

Robert had been unhurt in the Grand National fall, but his equally daredevil older brother Alan was less fortunate. In 1934, he rode in a National Hunt steeplechase at Cheltenham, where he was thrown to the ground and killed after his horse hit a fence.* It was particularly hard for the Heber-Percy parents, as Gladys had recently forbidden him from returning to Hodnet Hall after a scandal involving a married woman. Robert was devastated. He never forgot that before the race he had driven under a railway bridge while a train was crossing – something he considered bad luck – and he connected it with witnessing his brother's death. He retained a lifelong superstition and would stop the car rather than pass below a bridge if a train was coming.

* Alan's neck was broken. The coroner's verdict was accidental death.

CHAPTER SIX

Boys and Girls

I<small>T WAS NATURAL</small> that a more youthful group of friends should accumulate after Gerald and Robert started living together, but this was not just because of Robert. Many entered the Faringdon orbit as friends of Gerald; their reactions to Robert varied from delight to antipathy. Among the most frequent visitors to Faringdon in the early 1930s were the dazzling Lady Mary Lygon ('Maimie') and her sister Lady Dorothy, known as 'Coote'. Two years younger than the Mad Boy, Coote was the youngest daughter of Earl Beauchamp. She was plumper and plainer than her three beautiful sisters, her pudding face hidden behind thick glasses, but they were all known as 'the Beauchamp Belles'. Coote was intelligent, kind and discreet and quickly became a close and lifelong friend to Robert and Gerald. Nobody would have been more surprised than the participants if destiny had been revealed – that many decades later, the elderly Coote and the Mad Boy would do something that might have been the young woman's wildest dream. But we are jumping ahead of the story.

Coote and her six siblings had been brought up at Madresfield Court in Worcestershire, which had been home to Lygons for almost a thousand years. Gerald and Robert became familiar with the remarkable house that boasted a moat, twelfth-century oak doors and a Tudor great hall combined with Georgian fireplaces and Arts and Crafts murals. The Lygons also had a house in Belgrave Square and a castle in Kent to which they travelled by private train. The Lygon children's existence

Coote (Lady Dorothy Lygon), Robert, Penelope Betjeman and Gerald, ready to ride

had been one of extreme luxury combined with an extraordinary set of problems. Their father, known as 'Boom' for his voice, took snobbery and etiquette to their limits: guests would go into the dining room for meals in order of precedence (royals, then dukes, then earls and so on); he referred to his children by their titles ('Lady Lettice' or 'Lady Dorothy'); champagne was decanted into jugs so as not to be 'middle class'; and the numerous servants were dressed in gleaming livery of black tailcoats with silver buttons.[149] Nevertheless, Lord Beauchamp was a member of the Liberal Party and was informal enough to invite his children to visit him during his bath time for chats (and sometimes a cocktail), and to take them swimming in the freezing Kentish seas. His wife was less popular. Her children found her strict, cold and mean – she dressed her daughters in embarrassingly shabby clothes – and she was ultimately behind the disaster that befell the family.

Though the Lygon family was actively Catholic, with household prayers held twice a day in the family chapel, the morals at 'Mad', as the house was known, were notorious. Robert must have been amused if he was ever among the young male guests that Coote and her sisters advised to lock their bedroom doors at night in case their father had taken a fancy to them. And while Gerald was never known to act inappropriately with his employees, he probably enjoyed the evident fact that Lord Beauchamp took on his male servants according to their looks – footmen were dressed in the Beauchamp colours of maroon and cream and were observed to sport an impressive array of rings and bracelets.[150] Harold Nicolson was once at dinner at Madresfield when a fellow guest asked him, 'Did I hear Beauchamp whisper to the butler, *"Je t'adore"*? 'Nonsense,' replied Nicolson. 'He said, "Shut the door."' Nicolson (the bisexual husband of the bisexual Vita Sackville-West) knew that the other guest had heard quite well and observed that the butler was most handsome.[151] It was hardly a secret that Lord Beauchamp took his footmen and grooms as lovers, but when he went on a tour of Australia in 1930 and lived openly with his nineteen-year-old valet as his 'joy-boy', it became something of a scandal. Lady Beauchamp's brother, the Duke of Westminster, hired private detectives to collect evidence, reported it to the King, and organised an attack.

One summer day in 1931, as Lord Beauchamp sat doing his embroidery in the Moat Garden, several cars drew up and a number of severe and important-looking men, including the Liberal Chief Whip Lord Stanmore, got out. They had been sent by 'the highest authority in the land' and announced that there was evidence of 'criminal acts of indecency' between Beauchamp and a number of men. He was told he must leave the country and never return, or expect to be arrested. Coote was only nineteen, at home with her twenty-three-year-old sister, Sibell, and a friend. Their mother had already moved out and their other siblings were either married, living in London or at school. Boom's first reaction was that his only option was suicide, but after his rapid departure to a German spa, his children took it in turns to stay with him and make sure that he didn't manage this.[152] Only the oldest son and heir, William, Viscount Elmley, took his mother's side; all the other children stayed loyal to their father, travelling with him and helping him bear the humiliation and isolation.

With their father 'gone to have mud baths' (as the euphemism had been for Wilde and others in their exile), the young Lygons had the run of Madresfield, inviting their own friends for weekends, and continuing to hunt and serve champagne in jugs. They now had to cope with the fact that they were simultaneously highly attractive, privileged people, and almost like orphans. To some extent, they became social outcasts because of their father – unwelcome in certain circles and tainted as prospective wives, even if Sibell had persuaded her lover, Lord Beaverbrook, not to let the story get into the press. Nevertheless, there were enough open-minded people and the Lygons' Madresfield friends overlapped to a large extent with the Faringdon set. Gerald and Robert went to stay there, as did Michael Duff, the Mitfords, Cecil Beaton and many more. The Lygons were always welcome at Faringdon. Coote remembered this phase as being rather fun: 'We were young and foolish and just enjoyed ourselves very much.'[153]

Gerald was loyal to the entire Lygon family, inviting the nomadic, exiled Lord Beauchamp to stay with him and Robert on his travels. Beauchamp tended to move between cities that were more tolerant to homosexuals – Sydney, San Francisco, Paris and Venice – often accompanied by one or more of his children. Supporting friends in trouble was a high priority for Gerald, who was fearless of public opinion. Evelyn Waugh joined them in the Holy City and Boom organised intensive sightseeing, including visits to St Peter's, while Tito, Gerald's factotum, cooked and kept house.

Evelyn Waugh had become a fixture at Madresfield after his first stay in 1932. Recently separated from his first wife, he had been at Oxford with Coote's brother Hugh, who would later become the model for Lord Sebastian Flyte in *Brideshead Revisited*: handsome, boyish, drunken and homosexual. It is believed that Waugh had a fling with him during their student days. Though Coote loyally denied that the book had been modelled on her family, there were enough parallels for most people to draw a different conclusion. Coote certainly had overlapping qualities with Cordelia, the youngest daughter of Lord Marchmain (not to mention *King Lear*), and the dazzling Maimie, whom Waugh adored, was not unlike the unavailable and compelling Julia Flyte, with whom she shared a wild, uncontrolled streak and a tendency to depression. The Lygons represented all the romance of youth, grandeur and indulgence that Waugh had not experienced at home.

Waugh took on the role of naughty, flirtatious older brother to the sisters. He defaced young Coote's diary of humdrum routines and spiced them up with orgies and incest. And he liked to play the game of 'marrying off Coote', so that every man they encountered would be inspected to see if he was suitable: 'Would he do?'[154] His letters to Coote ('Pollen' or 'Poll') and Maimie ('Blondy') are intimately bawdy, insulting Coote jokily as a 'Filthy Bitch', and using the fashionable expressions of the day to express how much his stays at Madresfield meant to him: 'It would just be too lovely for any words to join in your Christmas cheer. Deevy [divine], in fact hot stuff. Oh, but you can't really mean it . . .'[155] He dedicated *Black Mischief* to Coote and Maimie in 1932. Waugh was also intrigued by 'the wicked Lord Berners's and later, when house-hunting, he wrote, 'I wouldn't mind the Berners Betjeman country.'

Faringdon became an ever more significant refuge for Coote and Maimie as disaster continued to dog their family. After the death of Lady Beauchamp, Hugh, who had become increasingly dissolute, went on a driving trip to Bavaria, fell on a pavement and fractured his skull. He died in 1936, aged thirty-one. Within two years, Boom would also die, attended in New York by Coote – now more of an orphan than ever. At the age of twenty-five, there were increasing indications that she might remain a lifelong spinster; Waugh's old teasing about prospective grooms must have worn very thin. To make matters worse, she and Maimie felt unwelcome at their beloved

Madresfield, now dominated by the new Earl, their formal older brother, and his frosty Danish wife. They didn't return for fifty years.

MAIMIE AND ROBERT
IN ITALY

The old album at Faringdon shows photographs of Maimie and the Mad Boy sprawled in skimpy bathing costumes on the beach at Ostia. They look like something out of an unsuitable Hollywood movie; in one, someone has taken a lipstick and written SHIT in large letters across Robert's muscular back. It would be hard to believe that they were not physically involved, even if it was under Gerald's watchful eye. Like his friend Derek Jackson, Robert liked to 'ride under both rules'.[156]

Though it was Maimie whose sex appeal was tangible, it was Coote who stayed more often at Faringdon. Maimie was a beauty, but she drank too much, suffered from melancholy and insomnia and had a succession of Pekingese (including Grainger, whom Evelyn Waugh called 'the lascivious beast') that piddled on the Aubusson rugs, rather as Gerald's fictional dog, Mr Pidger, would do in the eponymous story. No doubt Maimie and Gerald discussed diets and sleeping pills and fashionable cures. Coote, on the other hand, rode an elegant side-saddle out with Robert, was interested and informed about books and travel, and her independent mind made her a valued friend. She was there at the party given for the opening of the Faringdon Cinema, where Gerald made what might have been the only public speech in his life – and even that was only three sentences long.[157] There was also an element of the 'Jagger' about her – an expression that Waugh and the Lygons used to describe a helpful, dependable, good-hearted friend who doesn't make too many demands.[158] Certainly Coote was tactful and steadfast; even her nickname emerged from her secretive ways that reminded her siblings of the

MAIMIE WITH HER PEKINGESE GRAINGER AND ROBERT AT FARINGDON

hymn 'God Moves in a Mysterious Way', which they thought was by a Mrs Coote but in fact turned out to be by William Cowper. It was nothing to do with the feathered variety, and she could never have been said to be 'queer as a coot'. However, as a daughter who had doted on her disgraced father, she was always unobtrusively sympathetic to the ways of men who preferred men.

HEN CECIL BEATON had first met Gerald in the mid-1920s, he didn't take to him. 'A ridiculous-looking man – like a silly tailor's dummy', he wrote.[159] But he soon longed to be part of Gerald's inner coterie. A contemporary and enemy since school days of Evelyn Waugh, he shared the novelist's intelligence, ambition and sense of being an outsider. Both men began as middle-class boys who longed to be part of the smart set and Waugh later claimed Cecil's diaries revealed him as a man 'unashamedly on the make'.[160] The latter never denied this – in fact he admitted to being a 'scheming snob' – and there were others who levelled remarkably similar accusations at Waugh. Cecil was close to Michael Duff and even without the manifest talents that endeared him to Gerald, the willowy, mannered young man was soon a member of the privileged set of creative types and party-goers who surrounded Gerald and Robert.

Cecil was seven years older than Robert but their loathing was mutual. Robert didn't like Cecil's spiky calculating ambition, and Cecil despised Robert as a waster. There was an obvious incompatibility between the effete, artistic photographer and the chaotic, sometimes aggressive country boy, but there was also jealousy over the Mad Boy's honoured position in Lord Berners's life. In Cecil's private photograph albums there are two pictures of Robert from the mid-1930s, dressed in scruffy corduroys and adorably handsome and boyish, a flop of hair curling over his forehead. In one, he is carrying a billycan beside what looks like a campfire. The caption, in Cecil's hand, reads 'Horrid Madboy'.

Robert spread a story that Cecil initially thought him 'divine'. Once, when they and Gerald were at a country-house party together (possibly at Madresfield), the Mad Boy led Cecil on and explained exactly where his bedroom was situated. That night, Cecil tiptoed along the corridor and crept quietly into Robert's room, at which point the light went on. Gerald, rotund in pyjamas, a grin on his face, was sitting up in bed. 'Cecil, I never knew you cared!'[161] Although Cecil stood for this teasing because he appreciated Gerald, he also considered him quite cruel in his humour. This was a running theme in their relationship. Gerald, for instance, took great delight in defacing Cecil's 1930 *The Book of Beauty*. While Cecil was known to doctor his pictures to make people slimmer or prettier, in this case milky-skinned debs with pearls were transformed into moustachioed hunchbacks, and satin-clad hostesses underwent skilful metamorphoses into hags and harridans, their teeth blackened.

Cecil was delighted to be in Gerald's inner circle, but thought him 'a very odd character with very little heart'.[162] Nevertheless, the two men shared many interests and appreciated one another's talents. When Cecil moved into Ashcombe, the beautiful Georgian house in Wiltshire that he leased from 1930, Gerald joined the guests in decorating the bedroom walls in the 'circus room'; his panel had a Columbine and performing dogs, with an ugly mastiff jumping through a paper hoop. And later Gerald would gamely dress up as the fictional King Boris to be photographed for Cecil's spoof book, *My Royal Past*, where friends took the parts of various royals in absurd Edwardian tableaux. Cecil

PHOTOGRAPH OF ROBERT FROM CECIL BEATON'S PERSONAL ALBUM: 'HORRID MADBOY'

was becoming an increasingly significant element in fashionable society, photographing beauties, the famous and royalty so much that his particular, mannered style came to symbolise the decade before the war. Working his way up as a portraitist, he was invited to photograph the Queen and became the preferred royal photographer, contributing substantially to creating their public image. He was also thriving in the world of fashion and design, working for *Vogue* and making trips to America to photograph Hollywood celebrities and New York socialites and models.

Though Cecil seemed to triumph in every sphere he entered, the same was not true of his love life. The great passion of these years was Peter Watson, the immensely rich young man who would later be a connoisseur of the arts and co-founder (with Cyril Connolly) of the literary magazine *Horizon*. Slim and dark-haired, Peter had a black-and-orange Rolls-Royce, dressed in the finest suits and had the face of 'the frog just as he is turning into a prince: a face lit by inner amusement and a kind of reluctant practicality'.[163] Tragically for Cecil, Peter was never quite available. He was involved with the stage designer Oliver Messel, and drove Cecil into paroxysms of jealousy when he took up with Robert. Peter gave Robert a golden retriever named Pansy Lamb despite the dog being clearly male.* Far worse was when he bought the Mad Boy a car. Robert raced around in it, getting charged for speeding, driving without a licence and driving without due care and attention. 'This young man will have to mend his ways if he is to continue to be in charge of a motor-car,' said the Mayor of Evesham after Robert was convicted and fined in his court. 'He seems to be a dangerous man on the road.' Cecil was outraged. He insisted Peter buy a car for him too – which he did. Money was no object, even if love was. A cheque for £1,000 was handed over and Cecil was briefly soothed. Notwithstanding the present, Peter told Cecil, 'I'd be delighted if you had an affair.' Wracked with years of miserable anxiety, Cecil took his advice. But imagine everyone's surprise when he chose a woman.

Doris Castlerosse was a remarkable person. Vivacious, sexy and boldly ambitious, she had begun life as Doris Delavigne from Beckenham, determined to do well for herself. As a 'balcony girl' at the Café de Paris, she acquired a series of lovers who kept her in the style she came to demand, until she achieved her aim of marrying a lord and became Viscountess Castlerosse. A frequent and popular guest at Faringdon, she would arrive in her Rolls with coroneted luggage and weighty jewel case, and provide much amusement with her unabashed talk, her extravagant elegance and her overt, very un-English physicality that some attributed to her Dutch heritage. According to a close friend, Daphne Fielding, 'Hers were the prettiest legs that ever stepped into a punt or danced a fox-trot at Skindles. She had hair the colour of ripe corn and a flower-petal complexion. Deep-set blue eyes were fringed with enormously long dark lashes. Although her features were far from perfect, they were infinitely more intriguing than those of

* Named after their mutual friend Lady Pansy Lamb, writer and wife of the painter Henry Lamb.

most classical beauties.' Her two front teeth had a small gap between them, but she didn't care. '"Wouldn't have them changed for anything, darling, shows I'm lucky and sexy . . . and *how*," she would say, with a hoot of raucous laughter.'[164]

Gerald was particularly fond of Doris. '"Let's dish the dirt," she would say as she curled up on a Faringdon sofa stroking her gazelle-like ankles.'[165] And Gerald, sitting at the piano, 'would listen fascinated to her tales of rascality and violence, striking an occasional chord and making some Puckish suggestion for a happy solution to her marital dramas.'[166] She would complain about her lack of money and such was Gerald's affection for her that he even offered to help her out. According to Robert, 'She came over and kissed him, which was very surprising, because he didn't like being kissed, and said: "Dear Gerald, anything you could do wouldn't last me two days!"'[167] Doris was unrepentant about her approach to taking lovers and allowing them to fund her extravagant lifestyle – one that even Lord Castlerosse could not afford to support. She had stunning clothes from Worth and Reville and favoured shorts to reveal her finest features. Her collection of jewels was impressive and when making a promise she would mischievously touch her forehead, breast and two collar-bones, murmuring 'Tiara, brooch, clip, clip'.[168] Described as 'the enchantress of the Thirties', Doris was said to be the inspiration behind Amanda in Noel Coward's *Private Lives*.[169] Certainly she was a performer, which suited Gerald. Doris was also a sexual performer, with a similar hard-nosed rumbustiousness to the Mad Boy. Robert described a night with Doris in Paris, where, for his birthday, she hired a young woman for him to 'whip to death'. When he gave a couple of unenthusiastic taps, Doris lashed out herself, leaving an unpleasant welt on the prostitute's skin, and saying, 'I haven't wasted my money just for this.' This was too strong even for the Mad Boy's daring taste. 'Doris, any more of that and I'll be sick.'[170]

Doris planned her seduction of Beaton with care – tuberose were strewn on Cecil's bed – and she was confident of her well-tested love-making techniques. Curious, if not flabbergasted, guests at

Gerald; Doris, Lady Castlerosse; Daphne, Viscountess Weymouth (later Fielding); Robert

Faringdon crept to eavesdrop outside the new lovers' bedroom, only to hear Cecil squeal, 'Oh goody, goody.' Cecil saw himself as a 'terrible homosexualist', but Doris claimed to believe that 'There's no such thing as an impotent man, just an incompetent woman.'[171] Daphne Fielding quipped, 'He wouldn't have had to do a thing.'[172] Many years later, Cecil described how Doris had helped him delay his orgasm by ordering him to 'Think of your sister's wedding!' According to Robert, Doris was the proud possessor of the Cleopatra Grip, a natural vaginal feature that made sexual activity particularly pleasurable for the man. 'If you come across one of those, you sign away your kingdom,' Robert later told Hugo Vickers.[173] This was also something that Mrs Simpson was rumoured to possess, possibly adding another factor to the King's obsession with the married American.

Lord Castlerosse, however, was not amused. Coming across his wife dining with Cecil in a restaurant, he said to his companion, 'I never knew Doris was a lesbian.'[174] Portly and charismatic, Valentine Castlerosse was no fool to be swept off his feet by a grasping courtesan. A dedicated bachelor until he married Doris, he was a man of the world. He dressed in velvet jackets and fur-lined coats, and kept a big cigar in the corner of his mouth in the Churchillian manner. His *Daily Express* column, 'The Londoner's Log', was a portrait of interwar society, with photographs of beauties of the day and descriptions of his friends, travels and escapades within a 'small glittering world – Mayfair, Monte Carlo, Deauville . . .'[175] Lord Castlerosse was initially intrigued by Doris's shameless ways, her earthy language and humour mixed with an appreciation of beauty and pleasure, and they were both extravagant and hot-tempered, with a tendency to jealousy. They also cared about one another, though they tried not to show it.[176] Their infidelities were legion and as legendary as their fierce rows: once, after Lord Castlerosse hit Doris and was reprimanded for it by a friend, he pulled up his trousers to show bite marks on his leg: 'She did it with her teeth!'[177]

And yet, as with so many hilarious stories that get passed on, the comedy is only the veneer; the emotions beneath were complex and often painful. Not only was Lord Castlerosse miserable, but Doris developed a perverse and unrequited passion for Cecil. In his diary, Cecil wrote: 'Peter loves people that are not in love with him and I in my turn am now worshipped and adored by Doritzins for whom I hold no emotion whatsoever. It seems so terribly unfair that there cannot be a great straightening out and saving of waste.' For a time, Cecil played along, if only to soothe the ache produced by years of rejection by Peter Watson. By the time Lord and Lady Castlerosse finally got divorced in 1938, it was Robert and not Cecil who was listed as the co-respondent. And Castlerosse was closer to the truth than he suspected when he had quipped about his wife being a lesbian. Doris took up with an immensely wealthy American, Mrs Eleonor Hoffman (or 'Margot', as she signed herself in at Faringdon), who bought her a palazzo in Venice. The unfinished Palazzo Venier dei Leoni passed through many extraordinary female hands in the twentieth century, having been formerly the Marchesa Casati's (when its drawing room was lined with gold leaf) and later Peggy Guggenheim's. Doris made the most of it, ferried about by liveried gondoliers and showered with hefty jewels by her girlfriend.[178]

ERALD WAS SO AMUSED by the youthful shenanigans unfolding before him that he wrote a book about them, a parody of a lesbian school story: *The Girls of Radcliff Hall* by 'Adela Quebec'. This playful skit mocked Gerald's young male friends, who were transmogrified into schoolgirls, but their characters and involvements were barely disguised. It also cocked a snook at the lesbian writer Radclyffe Hall, whose confessional book, *The Well of Loneliness*, had been banned in England following an obscenity trial in 1928. Gerald wrote the slim, wicked volume in Rome in 1934, and each morning he would read the latest chapter aloud to his guest, Diana Guinness (later Mosley), stopping frequently for fits of laughter.

Miss Carfax, the headmistress – like her creator – was melancholic. 'In spite of a superficial gaiety of spirit she often felt unhappy and tormented.' Robert's wildly shambolic, unreliable yet adorable character, Millie Roberts, 'was growing into a very pretty girl', with 'a decided talent for "chic"', though she 'was at heart a simple, country girl, who liked games and country pursuits'. Miss Carfax asks Millie to go and live with her in the country on her chicken farm, but only on condition that Millie should have nothing more to do with Lizzie Johnson, who keeps giving her presents, including a car. It was obvious to anyone who knew all the characters that Lizzie was Peter Watson. Predictably beside herself with jealousy is young Cecily Seymour –

Cecil Beaton. Poor Cecily; Lizzie 'has never even thought of giving her a bicycle'.

'"Supper!"' cries Cecily. '"Bags I sitting next to the Head!"' And all the girls scamper into the dining room. The headmistress is impressed by Cecily, who was 'so temperamental, her wit so exuberant, and she was, above all things, so versatile. Miss Carfax felt that there was nothing that Cecily could not do if she set her mind to it. She was certain that one day Cecily would make a name for herself in some branch of art.' Other characters include Miss MacRogers, the teacher who introduces Millie to Miss Carfax and who is surely Michael Duff. There is also the exotic Madame Yoshiwara, a 'Japanese lady artist' who is a feminised version of the Russian surrealist painter and theatre designer Pavel Tchelitchew. He was a friend of Peter Watson and, through Gertrude Stein, became a part of the Sitwell circle. Gerald acquired an exuberant watercolour sketch by the Russian of a leggy dame sporting a vast hat and transparent skirt, riding in a carriage. Underneath, someone has written: 'A design by Tchelitchew for Cecil Beaton to wear at King George and Queen Mary's Jubilee.' So Gerald wasn't the only one to have fun at Cecil's expense in 1935.

'Next term there was a great deal of excitement over the arrival of the mysterious new dancing master, Mr Vivian Dorrick' – quite evidently Doris Castlerosse. 'He was blond, slim, debonair and delightful, and it was not surprising that many of the girls' hearts were fluttered by the appearance in their midst of such an Adonis.' Mr Dorrick was 'extremely soigné; he was always beautifully turned out', but he didn't seem to want to get closer to his pupils. '"I expect he only does it for money," remarked one of his disappointed admirers.' But then Mr Dorrick is spotted by Olive Mason (the stage designer Oliver Messel) 'trying to kiss Cecily behind a screen', and Cecily cries out, '"No, no, Mr Dorrick, my heart belongs to another."' But Cecily soon changes her mind, and, smiling coyly, admits, '"Strange as it may seem, I really do believe that I've fallen for him . . . just a little."'

Poor Cecil was mortified when he went to stay with Gerald in Rome in 1935. He had had no idea about the novel, which had already

A PAGE OF THE FARINGDON HOUSE VISITORS' BOOK FROM DECEMBER 1934 TO JANUARY 1935. NAMES INCLUDE: DAISY FELLOWES ('AMATEUR SANS DISTINCTION'); REX WHISTLER ('PEINTRE DE LUXE'); COOTE AND LATER HER TWO SISTERS, LADY SIBELL AND MAIMIE, BOTH OVER FROM MADRESFIELD; GERALD WELLESLEY, LATER THE DUKE OF WELLINGTON, AND THE ARCHITECT OF THE FOLLY, CLAIMS TO BE A 'WORKER', AND IS STAYING WITH HIS SON VALERIAN, A STUDENT AT OXFORD; CECIL BEATON PUTS HIS BUSINESS ADDRESS AS 'HAMAM BATHS' AND HIS PROFESSION AS 'MASSEUR'; DORIS, LADY CASTLEROSSE, IS A 'PROCUREUSE DE LUXE'; LADY JULIET DUFF IS THE MOTHER OF SIR MICHAEL DUFF, WHO INTRODUCED GERALD AND ROBERT TO ONE ANOTHER

been privately published and passed around the ranks to much hilarity. Cecil now observed that Gerald couldn't resist 'joking about one's softest spot and prodding one's Achilles heel'. And none of the 'girls' can have been too pleased. 'I absolutely adored Les Girls,' wrote Noël Coward to Gerald. 'Oh dear! What a beastly little book.'[179] According to Hugo Vickers, Cecil attempted to destroy as many copies as possible of *The Girls of Radcliff Hall*. John Byrne, who reissued the extremely rare satire in 2000, wonders whether it was actually more likely to have been Robert. After all, he is treated almost as harshly and he was certainly well placed to 'diminish the stock' and then spread rumours about

Cecil. After decades of searching, Byrne only ever located four copies of the very plain, inconspicuous little book – once in a US bookseller's catalogue under 'Lesbian Literature', with the author taken at face value as Adela Quebec.[180] Gerald would have been most gleeful.

CHAPTER SEVEN

Fiends

URING THE EARLY 1930s, one of Gerald's closest friends was Diana Guinness. One of the six already famous Mitford sisters, she was remarkable for her beauty: endowed with a fashionably willowy build, she had perfect features, a soignée golden bob and ice-blue eyes. According to her youngest sister, Deborah, 'without make-up or artifice, and often in clothes that she wore till they were threadbare, she was always the best-looking woman at any gathering'.[181] She was also sharply intelligent and humorous, although none of the six Mitford girls received much formal education as their father, Lord Redesdale, didn't think it necessary. Although the Mitfords were less privileged than the Lygons, there were parallels between these two large families that became close to Gerald and Robert.

Aged eighteen, Diana had married the poet, writer and Irish brewing heir Bryan Guinness (later Lord Moyne), thus escaping the stifling home environment of the sort that Gerald and Robert knew only too well. As two of the youngest, richest, most glamorous and good-looking Bright Young Things of the late 1920s and early '30s, Diana and Bryan lived a dazzling existence. There was a country estate, and their fashionable parties in London attracted many of the most interesting, creative people of the day. Two blond baby boys were born.

Diana's parents had not initially approved of the engagement, but they were horrified when only three years later she threw everything away. Leaving Bryan, she set herself up in a flat in London, waiting for visits from the married man she had fallen in love with: Oswald Mosley, future leader of the British Union of Fascists. Rejected by her parents and ostracised by many, Diana was turning herself into a rebel, increasingly disgraced and despised but always adored as well.

When Diana first knew Gerald, it was before she and her five sisters took their paths in extreme and varied political directions. They were not yet stereotyped as 'Diana the Fascist, Jessica the Communist, Unity the Hitler-lover, Nancy the Novelist, Deborah the Duchess and Pamela the unobtrusive poultry connoisseur'.[182] Now they have been so well documented in countless memoirs, biographies and films that a Mitford mythology has grown up. Their private expressions and nicknames have long become public: the absurdities of 'Farve' and 'Muv' are as familiar to readers as the gatherings of 'the Hons' in the linen cupboard. Both their jokes and their seriousness can seem ridiculous, even horrifying, yet they still fascinate.

It was while Diana was in a vulnerable phase, kept away from her younger sisters and known as a home-wrecker, that Gerald came to her rescue. He had a penchant for outsider-insiders, who knew the rules but could also break them. Throughout his life he displayed a tenderness towards friends who were vulnerable, irrespective of whether – or perhaps particularly when – this flew in the face of public opinion. Certainly Gerald provided Diana with a haven, both at Faringdon and in Rome. 'He never failed me,' she wrote. 'It is impossible to exaggerate how much I owed him.'[183] She was charmed by the older man, and wrote with warm affection about her time with him. Diana first met the Mad Boy at Gerald's house in Rome, and she liked the crazy youth who was a year younger than her, and who shared her uncompromising refusal to take any prisoners. They remained lifelong friends.

The charged chaos of Diana's scandalous love life and Gerald's newly ensconced Mad Boy did not alter the daily routine at via Foro Romano. Gerald got up early to work at his music, sitting at the piano to compose, or going out with an easel and paints. In the afternoon there was sightseeing. Social life remained of utmost importance and both luncheon and dinner appointments were made with Romans and visiting foreigners, whose own gossip and scandals would be discussed at length. 'Half way through the morning Gerald would telephone from the landing outside my room, making plans for parties and expeditions,' wrote Diana. '"*Pronto, pronto, e Lord Berners,*" he began. His Italian was fluent but he made no concessions, he pronounced it as though it were English. He never embarrassed with a good accent like some of one's compatriots.'[184] Gerald's fictional character Percy Wallingford remarks, 'An Englishman should not speak French too well.' This, claims the narrator, is absolutely true: 'Except for purposes of secret service, a too perfect French accent is inadvisable and is apt to disconcert the English and the French alike.'

Diana may have been in love with Oswald Mosley, but she was not the only person to be enamoured with his new brand of politics in the 1930s. Fresh ideas and extreme political tendencies were a natural product of the combustible post-war combination of too much partying, disillusionment with democracy and economic decline. Mosley was attracted by Mussolini's brand of Fascism, and although he supported the King (Edward VIII was viewed as a representative of new ways), he rejected the old ruling class, which, he declared, was not to be trusted any more. The 'spineless' politicians who didn't dare confront the problems, the 'old muttons' who had sent a generation of young men to their death in the war, had to be got rid of.[185]

Mosley's New Party attracted all sorts of people when it was founded. It appealed to the young, rather as Communism did, with its loathing of lukewarm liberalism, its patricidal tendencies and its romantic talk of new beginnings and ridding society of 'parasites'. There was an emphasis on athletics, fighting and uniforms, and with its military comradeship and the veneration of young male heroes, there were many in Gerald's circle who were seduced, at least initially. These included Osbert and Sacheverell Sitwell, Cecil Beaton and Harold Nicolson, who wrote in his diary, 'I find myself having daydreams of power and youth.'[186] The *Daily Mail* and the *Daily Mirror* also gave their support to this movement in its early days: 'Hurrah for the Blackshirts!' trumpeted Lord Rothermere's *Daily Mail*. Most

DIANA GUINNESS
(NÉE MITFORD, LATER
MOSLEY) ON A TRIP
OUTSIDE ROME WITH
GERALD

of these people fell away when Mosley's views became increasingly objectionable and extreme after the founding of the British Union of Fascists in 1932; Diana only became more convinced of the righteous cause of the love of her life.

It was not long before Diana began visiting her sister Unity in Munich. They attended the first Nuremberg rally and the 1936 Olympic Games, and Diana became almost as enthusiastic as Unity about 'Wolf' – the nickname Hitler's friends used. She read *Mein Kampf* and declared Hitler 'the kindest man in the world', a position she hardly retracted during a lifetime of rejection, criticism, imprisonment and, ultimately, exile. Diana and Mosley were married in secret in October 1936 in Goebbels's Berlin drawing room, with 'Wolf' as the guest of honour. The bride wore a gold dress and the Führer's gift was a photograph of himself in a silver frame. Later, Diana wrote to Unity about the occasion:

Darling

I am sitting in a bower of orchids envying you, because I expect you are still in the Fuhrer's train . . .

The wedding itself was so beautiful and the blick [sight] out of Magda [Goebbels]'s window of the Fuhrer walking across the sunny garden from the Reichskanzlei was the happiest moment of my life. I felt everything was perfect, Kit [Mosley], you, the Fuhrer, the weather, my dress . . .

With hindsight, Diana seems a beautiful monster. It is now almost inconceivable that she could have stubbornly maintained her dreadful and dangerous opinion of Hitler. Even the Holocaust did little to alter her beliefs and her anti-Semitism. She became as fanatical as her increasingly rabid husband and never changed. According to her youngest sister, Deborah, Duchess of Devonshire, 'Her rigid views on race were partly influenced by Grandfather Redesdale, an advocate of Teutonic supremacy, and were hardened by the experience of war and her unyielding nature.' The unyielding nature also seemed to apply to Jessica ('Decca'), who became a Communist and moved to America, and Unity, who was infatuated with Hitler and shot herself (but survived as an invalid) when war was declared. 'Once Diana had decided on a course of action there was no deviating or turning back and, like them, she was drawn to extreme politics.'[187] Yet in spite of her revolting views, even Diana's detractors often agreed that she was one of the most charming people, who could win over those who thought they'd hate her.

It is unsettling to think about Diana's enormous charisma combined with such poisonous attitudes, particularly because, at least in the early years, she was far from being alone in holding them. The question of where Gerald and Robert stood politically is much less clear, although neither of them ever seemed to take politics seriously; entertainment, excitement and the pleasure principle were much more important. Gerald detested pomposity and posturing and was much too pessimistic to believe in the grand ideals of extremist politics – he had moved in both Fascist and anti-Fascist circles in Rome. Neither was he interested in attending the House of Lords after he took his seat in 1923; when Diana asked him if he'd ever been, he said, 'Yes I did go once but a bishop stole my umbrella and I never went there again.' Robert was too undisciplined and flighty for the paramilitary element of the Blackshirts and could not have taken his place in such an authoritarian system.

Whatever Gerald and Robert's reservations about politics, their social circle was overwhelmingly one that leaned to conservatism or further to the right, even if this was largely due to social circumstances rather than design. They also had friends of other political convictions, including the journalist Tom Driberg and their neighbour at Buscot Park, Lord Faringdon. The latter was a socialist who supported the Republicans in the Spanish Civil War, and while he was known as a 'roaring pansy', he was serious about his Labour Party politics and was a pacifist during the Second World War. He commissioned murals at Buscot that depicted dinner parties with Gerald, Robert and a surprisingly demure-looking Marchesa Casati at his table. A friendly rivalry existed between the two bachelor peers, though Gavin Faringdon was accused of being both a 'champagne socialist' and parsimonious, especially with the alcohol. Robert was known to announce to friends, 'We've got to go for drinks at Buscot, so we'd better start now.'[188]

Gerald had Jewish friends, but anti-Semitism was not only acceptable in his milieu, it existed throughout European society. A 1930s survey suggested that up to three-quarters of the British population harboured unfavourable attitudes towards Jews.[189] Robert may have been too disorderly for politics, but he was certainly anti-Semitic. At a time before the Holocaust changed everything, the concept of Jews as money-grubbing, vulgar and ostentatious was only too prevalent. T. S. Eliot's implied comparison of Jews to rats ('money in furs') was far from unique.[190]

As Mosley's Fascists gained strength their message became increasingly anti-Jewish, and there was an increased reaction from their opponents. In June 1934, the huge Olympia stadium was hired for a

Blackshirts' rally and Gerald and Robert went along, driven by William Crack. It seems likely that they went out of curiosity, though all the muscular young men in uniform were an added attraction; this feature of Mosley's movement did not go unobserved. Certainly, Gerald and Robert also wanted to support Diana by going, though in the event she had a temperature and was unable to attend. Nevertheless, they dined with her beforehand, along with their mutual friend Vivian Jackson, a young and brilliant astrophysicist and beloved twin brother of the equally intelligent, rich, small-built, fearless scientist Derek (who married Diana's sister Pamela).[191] Both brothers were extremely right-wing and favoured Mosley, but their true love was horses; Derek's greatest compliment was 'As perfect as someone on two legs can be.' It was Vivian who accompanied Gerald and Robert to the rally.

The violence that erupted at Olympia is well documented, with each side blaming the other. Groups of anti-Fascists, including Communists and Jews, arrived with the intention of heckling Mosley and disrupting the event. Soon there were vicious fights going on between the uniformed Blackshirts patrolling the stadium and their unwelcome guests. Hecklers were set upon by Mosley's 'Biff Boys' and the numerous casualties on both sides were taken to hospital. The police made many arrests, among them the twenty-seven-year-old Vivian. Gerald rang Diana at midnight to say that Robert had just bailed him out and that he was charged with obstructing the police. The next day, the two men gave evidence in Jackson's defence at the West London Police Court before Sir Gervais Rentoul, KC, something that was reported in *The Times*. Robert described himself as a horse-trainer and gave a Shropshire address. He said that a policeman knocked Lord Berners against the railings and Jackson had shouted, 'You can't do that.' Gerald claimed a policeman spoke to him very rudely and then hit him on the head with 'a weapon like a sword' and that Jackson had gone to his defence. The crowd was not rioting, he said, but was singing 'a very dreary song' which he believed was called 'The Internationale'.

Jackson was fined twenty shillings and acquired a good story on which to dine out, but public distaste for what had happened at Olympia resulted in a backlash against Mosley. The *Daily Mail* withdrew its support and many people began to realise what odious views British Fascists held. As a result, Mosley dropped the word 'Fascist', but the British Union only became further entrenched in its anti-Semitism, and there were marches through the East End of London resulting in street-fighting such as the infamous 'Battle of Cable Street', where East Enders tried to stop the Fascists passing through. In 1937, the Public Order Act banned political uniforms and made these marches increasingly difficult to stage. Hitler already appeared threatening, war was in the air, and Fascists were not looked upon kindly by most people.

Earlier in 1934, Gerald had written 'A Fascist March' for the piano; apparently Diana thought he might come up with something nice for the Blackshirts to march to. The first eight bars were published in the *Daily Express* – and nothing more is known of it. It is hard to imagine that Gerald could have done this with an entirely straight face, as his music nearly always contained jokes, parody and a lightness that is inimical to the tenets of Fascism. But what with Mussolini's boys strutting about all over Rome (where Gerald wrote the piece) and Mosley being flavour of the year in England, perhaps he really did do his little bit. After all, plenty of political thinkers took Mosley seriously at the start. What does appear to have been a joke was Gerald's claim to have had lunch with Hitler, though the evidence is highly contradictory. It is true is that Gerald and Robert were in Munich in the late summer of 1935, where they spent most days with Diana and Unity, whose growing obsession with the Führer was most amusing to Gerald. William Crack said he drove Gerald to a restaurant where Hitler was dining, and Robert (whose version is probably less reliable) claimed that Gerald dined with Hitler and that *he* was invited for coffee. According to the Mad Boy, the English lord and the German dictator discussed composition. Hitler mentioned 'his own composer' (never identified) who was not in favour, and said: 'I thought of sending him up in an aeroplane,' presumably with the implication that he would not be coming back.[192] Robert then returned alone to Faringdon and

Gerald sent him a postcard, giving various practical details: 'Did you find any visiting cards? If so please post <u>here</u> as soon as possible. Sorry you had such a lousy journey back. Lucky you had a little Ham to keep you company. It was lovely meeting Hitler. Will write you a nice letter shortly. Love Gerald.'

Diana later claimed that Gerald didn't meet the dictator and that she would have known, as they were constantly together. Diana was less of a joker than Gerald and more in the know than the chauffeur, so she may well have been right. John Betjeman wrote to Penelope, 'Apparently it is all rot about Robert and Gerald lunching with Hitler.' So maybe, in this open postcard, Gerald just wanted naughtily to set the gossip mills spinning. He was certainly no supporter of Nazism. In a notebook he wrote that he had been put off Wagner's music (that he had loved so much in his youth) because it had been taken up by the Nazis, and he claimed that it was their banning of the poet Heine that first led him to execrate them.[193] In 1935, when Diana brought Mosley to stay at Faringdon, Oliver Messel added a satisfying provocation under Mosley's signature in the visitors' book: 'F.S.P.M.B.W.N.R. Founder of The Society for the Propagation of Marriages between the White and Negro Races.' Other old friends confirmed that Gerald was not interested in politics. 'He'd only have been intrigued because it was intriguing,' said one.[194]

Nancy Mitford, Diana's eldest sister, had a brief flirtation with Mosley's movement, but soon took against it and leaned leftwards, or merely in the direction of satire, ever after. Diana accused her of being 'synthetic cochineal' – unlike Decca, whose dedication to Communism was almost as unwavering as Diana's to Fascism. But Nancy despised both extremes. In 1939, she wrote to a friend, 'There isn't a pin to put between Nazis & Bolshies. If one is a Jew one prefers one and if an aristocrat the other, that's all as far as I can see. Fiends!' Nancy's approach was far more in line with Gerald's, and he became an increasingly important friend to her. Like him, she preferred humour and thoughtfulness to the bombast and grand plans of Mosley. Both Diana and Mosley were appalled when Nancy satirised their movement in her 1935 novel *Wigs on the Green*. Unity (who was over six foot tall) is portrayed as 'England's largest heiress', Eugenia Malmains. Mosley is the Captain, who must be obeyed in all things. The innocent, passionate Eugenia stands on a washtub on a village green, calling 'in thrilling tones . . . "Britons, awake! Arise! Oh, British lion! . . . [the] Union Jack Movement is a youth movement . . . we are tired of the old."' Eugenia has a dog called the Reichshund, after Bismarck's dog, and a horse named Vivian Jackson. Diana was outraged, Mosley furious and Nancy was banned from their house for years.

ERALD MAY HAVE BEEN running around with a younger set and getting caught up in politics more than was his natural inclination, but he didn't neglect his long-standing friends. He continued to visit the famous London hostesses Lady Cunard and Lady Colefax, who skimmed off the cream of society for their gatherings. Robert might stay in the country or see his own pals; he was not generally interested in finely wrought soirées, where everybody was 'somebody'. Gerald could catch up with worldly, cultured people like the Princesse de Polignac, Harold Nicolson or Lady Diana Cooper, the celebrated society beauty and actress who might be found there with her husband, Duff, politician and diplomat. People tended to speak of the two hostesses in one breath, and there were many who found them tiresome. 'Coarse and usual and dull these Cunards and Colefaxes are,' wrote Virginia Woolf, though there were many who adored one or the other and remained their supporters and friends.[195] Gerald was far from being a Bloomsbury bohemian type ('not for him the rufty-tufty Bloomsbury clothes with their unpressed trousers', wrote Diana Mosley), but he was interested in meeting certain members of this influential group and a few cropped up at these parties. He had friendly relations with Virginia Woolf, who mentions him in the preface to *Orlando*, her 1928 novel that created a transsexual, time-hopping hero based partly on the life of her lover Vita Sackville-West. Woolf thanks Lord Berners, 'whose knowledge of Elizabethan music has proved invaluable'. It sounds like a friendly little tease – a wink from one cerebral, creative, depressive type with an unconventional love life to another.

Gerald himself joked that while the tea parties of Sibyl Colefax were 'a party of lunatics presided over by an efficient, trained hospital nurse', those of Emerald Cunard were 'a party of lunatics presided over by a lunatic'.[196] Of course, there were those who claimed that Gerald himself offered more to this type of gathering than he took. Osbert Sitwell wrote, 'In the years between the wars, Berners did more to civilise the wealthy than anyone in England. Through London's darkest drawing rooms, as well as through the lightest, he moved, dedicated to their conversion, a sort of missionary of the arts, bringing a touch of unwanted fun into many a dreary life – fun perhaps all the more funny for its being unwanted.'[197] Gerald was the perfect guest for these ladies – accomplished, titled and witty. His increasingly notorious eccentricity only added a dash of welcome spice to the mix.

Certain commentators claimed there was no comparing the two *grandes dames*. While Lady Cunard's witty intelligence sparked off truly interesting conversations, her rival, Lady Colefax (the 'Coal Box'), was merely fixated with collecting famous names and didn't know what to do with them when she got them.[198] Harold Nicolson wrote of her formidable energy: 'While London still slept round her, she would have written and addressed some sixty postcards and the telephone would start shrilling before the postman dared . . .'[199]

About ten years older than Gerald, Emerald Cunard had started off life in America as Maud Burke. After marrying into the Cunard shipping family, she changed her name to the more sparkling Emerald, and managed through intelligence, charm and ambition to create an immensely successful salon at her home in Grosvenor Square. Her great talent was to mix writers, musicians and painters with politicians, soldiers and members of the British and European aristocracy. Small-built, with birdy eyes and a small mouth, she had many lovers, including the conductor Sir Thomas Beecham and the writer George Moore, both of whose work she promoted and inspired. Harold Nicolson caustically described her in later years as 'looking like a third-dynasty mummy painted pink by amateurs', and many said she neglected her skinny, kohl-eyed daughter Nancy, who made a name for herself as a provocative anti-racist and civil-rights activist, taking up with a Harlem-based jazz musician.

Though the Ladies Cunard and Colefax were always pleased to catch the biggest social fish, the Coal Box was an easier target for teasing. Sibyl Colefax was an interior decorator, founding Colefax and Fowler and adopting the traditional Georgian country house as her style. 'Dark, sharp-featured, beady-eyed',[200] she was an inveterate snob: 'Like a bunch of glossy red cherries on a hard straw hat,' said Virginia Woolf.[201] She had less money and panache than her American rival, and she was a notorious social climber, who would go to great lengths to 'acquire' the famous and the rich. But as Beverley Nichols admitted, 'a woman who is neither nobly born, nor very rich, nor very beautiful, does not create a brilliant salon unless she has herself some brilliant qualities.'[202]

Gerald quipped that when Sybil Colefax visited him in Rome and was given the room next to him, he got no sleep as 'she never stopped climbing all night'.[203] In a thank-you letter following a 1945 weekend at Faringdon, the playwright Terence Rattigan continued the theme, imagining Sibyl's social activities continuing beyond death, something, he joked, he himself could soon be responsible for if her hand turned gangrenous from a cut she had sustained when he helped her through a barbed-wire fence on a walk.* 'By the way,' he asked Gerald, 'who do you think will be at her first dinner party in Paradise? Would she begin with Shakespeare, Disraeli, Mrs Sidders and a member of The Divine Family, or start lower down and work her way up?' Easy to caricature, the Coal Box provided inspiration for various

---

* The same age as Robert, and gay, Rattigan wrote *Flare Path*, based on his experiences as a rear-gunner in the RAF, and would become celebrated for *The Winslow Boy* and *The Browning Version*.

writers of fiction, including Evelyn Waugh, Aldous Huxley and Osbert Sitwell.[204]

Gerald is said to have once sent Sibyl a postcard asking her to a lunch to meet the P. of W., knowing only too well that the Coal Box would assume he meant the Prince of Wales. The entire country was gripped by the future king's dalliance with the married Wallis Simpson. Imagine Sibyl Colefax's disappointment when the guest turned out to be the Provost of Worcester (College, Oxford). It might have been apocryphal, but Lady Colefax trumped Gerald by inviting him to an evening at her King's Road address where the newly crowned King Edward VIII turned up with Wallis Simpson. The fashionable couple's preference for glitzy clubs was well known, so it was a triumph for the ambitious Coal Box. However, the evening nearly ended in disaster when the after-dinner entertainment was provided by Arthur Rubinstein, the world-famous Polish-American pianist, who performed several pieces by Chopin. The King became increasingly restive and got up, plainly intending to leave. In desperation, Sibyl begged Gerald to play something instead. Gerald refused, claiming that he had only come as a guest, at which the Coal Box threatened, 'I'll never ask you here again!' Gerald's teasingly nonchalant response was, 'I rather think you will.'[205] The impending calamity was narrowly averted when Noël Coward, who had just arrived, charmed the King with 'Mad Dogs and Englishmen' and '(Don't Put Your Daughter on the Stage,) Mrs Worthington'. Rubinstein had meanwhile left with the Princesse de Polignac, both no doubt appalled by the musical taste of the English upper classes.

Gerald himself developed friendly relations with Wallis Simpson – another person whose well-known Fascist tendencies were not an impediment to adulation from vast numbers of people, though this was probably more a reflection of the gilded allure of 'Majesty Divine', as Lady Cunard called the King. (The diminutive hostess had snapped up her fellow American and was a great supporter of the woman she hoped would be the next queen.) Letters remain from Mrs Simpson to Gerald, written in a flowing, rather elegant hand. Though they are mostly apologising for cancelling engagements, they give a small taste of their intersecting lives:

Dear Lord Berners

I am so very sorry about last night – but I suddenly developed a pain around my heart. I'm afraid I'm very tired – the doctor has put me to bed for a week – no telephone calls. No visitors. It was disappointing to have my <u>first</u> party postponed. However I shall try again and hope to be fortunate enough to find you free to come. I did so enjoy my lunch with you both conversationally and gastronomically.

Yours Sincerely
Wallis Simpson

Gerald liked the pleasures of fashion and high society, but he was not seduced by their superficial glitziness. Sometimes he bridged the gap between his higher aspirations and his partiality to the social whirl by teasing, which took everything down a peg or two. Once, he was dining in the Ritz when a woman friend came in. She was well known to have had many lovers, who were getting younger and younger. On the day in question, she arrived with her eleven-year-old son, and Gerald said: 'This time you're going too far!'[206]

Sometimes, Gerald himself went too far. One prank involved placing an advertisement in a national newspaper: 'Lord Berners wishes to dispose of two elephants and one small rhinoceros (latter house-trained). Would make delightful Christmas present. Apply R. Heber-Percy, Faringdon House, Berkshire.' When a 'special correspondent' from the *Daily Mirror* rang up to enquire, R. Heber-Percy reported that 'Harold Nicolson and Lady Colefax had snapped up the elephants.' Several newspapers followed up the joke with articles, and both of Gerald's old friends were mortified. Nicolson responded to the press with little of his usual *jeu d'esprit*: 'It is just Lord Berners adding to the Christmas merriment. I have known him for twenty-five years but I do not feel friendly towards him today. I do not want an elephant, have never wanted one, and I have not bought one.'[207] The endless teasing of 'Harold Nickers' (as one friend called him) and his wife, 'Rye Vita' (Vita Sackville-West), had worn rather thin.

No doubt Gerald revelled in the po-faced responses to his mischief. Although he was often gloomy and certainly valued time alone, he tried to make himself entertaining, if sometimes startling, to those around him. According to one friend, Gerald worked out a trick for keeping his train compartment to himself: wearing dark glasses, he would beckon to fellow passengers from within, with a sinister expression on his face, while holding a newspaper upside down.[208] The story became legendary, and while it is unknown whether this approach was taken more than once, it became assumed by some that this was what Lord Berners always did if he was travelling by train.

Far worse than these more puerile japes, in fact positively sadistic, was the trick that Gerald played on some house guests to whom he had been speaking about suicide, well aware that they knew about his depression. Once his friends had gone to bed, he blew up a paper bag and popped it, making a bang that sounded disconcertingly like a gun. People rushed from their bedrooms to find Gerald sitting disingenuously downstairs, greeting their sudden appearance with an enquiring expression. Although Gerald was mocking his own vulnerability, it was a pitiless way to laugh at people who cared for him. Cecil Beaton's assessment that Gerald had 'very little heart' sometimes seemed to be true. His jokes could be a form of self-defence, but they could also cross over into calculated aggression.

Flashes of psychological brutality had been a feature since the young Gerald worked out how to make a plank swing up under the outside lavatory to spank his governess's bottom. But it was sometimes more chilling than practical jokes. It was as though the empathy that made him such a loyal friend could occasionally evaporate. When he was a boy, Gerald claimed to have thrown his mother's fat spaniel out of the window. This was not, he wrote, from 'innate cruelty', hatred for dogs or because this particular one resembled Elizabeth Barrett Browning with its ringlets. It was merely because he had wondered whether the dog would fly, just as it swam when thrown into water.[209] In Gerald's story *Mr Pidger*, an angry husband throws his wife's beloved, if infuriating, little lapdog out of the train window after it unwittingly destroys a large inheritance. There is drama and humour in the scene – rather as there was when Gerald popped the paper bag – but the overwhelming atmosphere that remains is one of isolation (the couple divorces) and sadness.

Despite Gerald's declared dedication to frivolity and social life, there was a lurking doubt that made him mock, tease and sometimes hurt the people he cared for. Evelyn Waugh viewed Gerald's milieu as fundamentally flawed, marked by a sort of original sin. 'The friends of Berners were so agreeable, so loyal, so charming, but they were aboriginally corrupt. Their tiny relative advantages of intelligence, taste, good looks, and good manners . . . were quite insignificant.'[210] Gerald himself did not articulate this, but his pitiless satires on the sorts of people he surrounded himself with reflect a layer of doubt. Even the companionship of the Mad Boy, with his inspiringly bad behaviour and refusal to toe the line, could not get rid of the darkness that lay at Gerald's core.

CHAPTER EIGHT

Follies and Fur-lined Wombs

OBERT CLAIMED THAT THE TOWER on the hill overlooking Faringdon was built for him by Gerald as a twenty-first birthday present. Although his flippant follow-up was usually 'I'd have preferred a horse,' there was a gleeful pride in showing off the gargantuan gift. And perhaps there was an idea of constructing a 100-foot folly as a phallic tribute to the Mad Boy around the time of Robert's formal coming-of-age. It would have been not long after the two men met in 1932 – maybe some kind of ludicrous honeymoon fantasy? Various people are unconvinced. Some suggest that Lord Berners wanted to provide employment for local builders who were having a hard time during the Depression, or that it was celebrating George V's jubilee. Others have seen it, more convincingly, as a flight of fancy – the last great folly to be built in England. By its very nature it should have no purpose, though celebrating forbidden love is hardly functional.

Predictably, the authorities were unhappy with the idea of this pointless eyesore that would poke up above the treetops on what was already known as Folly Hill, its name possibly deriving from the French 'feuilles', 'leaves'. The place was a 'well-known landmark of historical interest' and the site of an old fort. There was a running argument with curmudgeonly neighbours, and the Rural District Council rejected Lord Berners's plans in 1934: 'High Words over Lord Berners's Tower', reported the *Oxford Mail*. This was followed by a Ministry of Health inquiry, and ultimately compromise, with an agreement to stop the tower going too high above the trees.

Gerald had chosen as architect Lord Gerald 'Gerry' Wellesley, the future 7th Duke of Wellington. He had been a colleague at the British Embassy in Rome during the First World War and the two men remained friends; in the 1920s, Gerry had returned to stay with Gerald in Rome along with their mutual friend Harold Nicolson, and the two men's wives, Dorothy 'Dottie' Wellesley and Vita Sackville-West, had had an affair. It is unknown to what degree Vita played a part in the break-up of the Wellesleys' marriage, but while her romantic interest quickly moved on, Dottie (a poet) remained devoted to Vita, waiting to collect her from the station in her Rolls after a trip abroad and feeding her champagne. It was Dottie Wellesley who first discovered the ruined Sissinghurst Castle that became the Nicolsons' celebrated home.[211] In the 1920s, Vita and Dottie had gone together to stay at Faringdon, something Harold Nicolson approved of at the time as it kept his wife away from Violet Trefusis, her great and scandalous love (who had previously been engaged to Gerry). All of this kept the gossips busy, what with the titles and the imposing, literary Englishwomen behaving more like the French.

Gerry Wellesley's plans for the tower were somewhat plainer than the folly Nancy Mitford describes in *The Pursuit of Love* – a confection of marble and semi-precious stones with a gold angel on the summit that blew a trumpet every evening at the hour of Lord Merlin's birth. In reality, it was built of red brick and was proceeding squarely upwards when apparently Gerald returned from a trip abroad and was appalled to find that the style was austere Classical rather than the Gothic he had desired. Known by some as 'the Iron Duchess',[212] John Betjeman joked that Wellesley was the only modern architect with a style named after him – the 'Gerry-built style'. Everyone's honour was saved when Gerry conceded the final section to something fancier, adding a pinnacled, crown-like viewing platform at the 140-foot summit and, below that, an airy belvedere room with arched windows. Gerald hoped to have a grand piano up there, but presumably the narrow wooden staircase that snaked up the interior walls prevented that. A notice was put up stating: 'MEMBERS OF THE PUBLIC COMMITTING SUICIDE FROM

THIS TOWER DO SO AT THEIR OWN RISK.' Both building and creator shared the characteristics of charm and gaiety tempered by undertones of gloom. Solidly impressive yet light and witty, traditional yet rebellious, generous-spirited yet private, Lord Berners and his Folly had much in common.

The Folly had its grand opening on Robert's twenty-fourth birthday, 5 November 1935. Gerald was the maestro, laying on a marvellous party, with fireworks shooting like comets and exploding above the looming dark outline of the tower. The *Express* reported that Lord Berners's guests were invited to 'bring effigies of their enemies for the bonfire. No guest may bring more than six effigies.' Gerald claimed to have always been more interested in settings rather than their inhabitants, but he liked to bring people to admire his creations, whether they were musical, artistic or architectural. A natural host and master of ceremonies, he himself opined that 'humanity may be roughly divided into hosts and guests.

LORD BERNERS' TOWER, FARINGDON.

A POSTCARD
DOCTORED BY GERALD

A psychologist has explained the types as representing two kinds of will, the will to power and the will to subjection.'[213] And although he was not obviously dominating, it was through giving and exhibiting that he established his influence. Yet Gerald could also identify with the vulnerable. His 1930 ballet, *Luna Park*, is set in a fairground, where the showman displays a one-legged ballerina, a man with six arms and a three-legged juggler. The performers all turn out to be fakes, and eventually escape their master as normal people.

It is possible that some sort of rift occurred between Gerald and Robert that November. On the last day of the month, the Mad Boy signed himself into the visitors' book, giving his address as Hodnet Hall and writing in the 'Profession' column 'unwanted'. And yet, only one week before this, Gerald had contacted his London solicitor to confirm

that he wished to leave his entire estate to Robert in his will. According to a letter from Winter & Co., Gerald had already made Robert the heir to his freehold and leasehold properties. This would now be extended to cover absolutely everything apart from a few annuities and legacies to faithful servants. Gerald also added another new clause: 'I desire that I shall be buried at the base of the Tower which I have lately caused to be erected on the site known as Faringdon Folly.' The two men had only been together a few, tumultuous years, but Gerald was making it clear to Robert that he was no plaything to be discarded, but the love of his life who would inherit as though he were his son or his spouse.

GERALD'S PAINTING OF THE FOLLY FOR THE SHELL GUIDE POSTER, COMMISSIONED BY JOHN BETJEMAN

The Folly became immensely popular; it was opened to the public on certain days and became a local landmark. When John Betjeman published his influential Shell Guides to the English countryside, he also commissioned some of Britain's best artists and designers to produce posters. They included Rex Whistler, Eric Ravilious, Duncan Grant, Vanessa Bell and Paul Nash. Lord Berners's contribution was a rolling Berkshire idyll, with his Folly protruding proudly from the circular tree canopy on Folly Hill.

Salvador Dalí must have been thrilled by the Folly when he came to stay with his wife Gala in the summer of 1936. Gerald had met them in Paris with Winnie de Polignac and was intrigued enough by the rising surrealist star to invite him to Faringdon. Though Gerald might have sensed that, like him, Dalí was sexually anxious and even timid, he probably did not know about the increasingly famous artist's obsession with towers. Intense insecurity about the size of his penis and in particular a terror of the 'lion's jaws' of female genitalia, had led Dalí to take a compulsive refuge in masturbation – a recurring theme in his paintings. According to Dalí's biographer, his onanistic fantasies were usually connected to towers, with a preference for church belfries that reminded him of his adolescent frenzies. It was often by fantasising the exact position of the three belfries of Sant Pere, his baptismal church, that he could achieve an orgasm.[214] One can only imagine the effect on Dalí as he climbed to the top of Lord Berners's impressive brick erection and, gazing out over four or five verdant English counties, pictured the extraordinary ejaculation of fireworks that had taken place there only months earlier.

It was still years before Dalí would start churning out the clichés of surrealism for American commercials, when his soft watches and lobsters would become old hat. In the mid-1930s he was at the height of his creative powers and on the cusp of great fame. Though plagued by strange phobias (locusts terrified him) and preeningly unpredictable, he was certainly entertaining, which never stopped being high on the list of requirements for guests at Faringdon. Gala, Dalí's Russian wife, was a decade older than him, though her slim, supple body and flirtatiousness belied her forty-two years. She was as sexually uninhibited as he was awkward, and while she was probably his first female lover, he was certainly neither the first nor the last of her male conquests. Like her husband, she was obsessed with physical beauty and couldn't bear ugliness. Always ready to fling her clothes off and jump into bed with someone handsome enough, Gala must surely have taken a shine to the Mad Boy. Some years later, when Robert acquired a daughter, she was given the middle name Gala. Though many would agree 'that to know her was to loathe her', Gala was undeniably powerful, elegant and impressive.[215] Penelope Betjeman recalled having dinner with the Dalís at Faringdon, and noted how attractive Gala was. As to Dalí himself, 'I remember sitting next to him at dinner. He liked to shock you, and never stopped talking about fur-lined wombs!'[216]

Robert remembered the Dalís coming to stay for several months 'solidly'[217] – they returned again in 1938, and also had a long stay at the house in Rome. But he claimed to have been very fond of the crazy pair. Dalí gave him a beautiful ink drawing of a horse and rider, dedicated 'A Robert Heber-Percy, son ami Salvador Dalí'. The muscular

SALVADOR DALÍ'S DRAWING DEDICATED TO ROBERT, 1938

horse is filled with coloured starbursts, while the naked bareback rider's red scarf flies in the wind, both creatures clearly expressions of sexual energy and freedom.

Gerald undoubtedly recognised another successful self-publicist, who loved annoying the bourgeoisie and whose partner caused consternation. 'When I paint, the sea roars. The others splash about in the bath,' was Dalí's opinion of his place in the world. In the visitors' book, the Spaniard wrote his profession as '*artiste, peintre et philosophe*', while Gala put '*sans profession*'. In comparison, Gerald's attempts to startle the neighbours look quite gentle. But as he admitted of his fictional alter ego, Lord Fitzcricket, 'He was astute enough to realise that, in Anglo-Saxon countries, art is more highly appreciated if accompanied by a certain measure of eccentric publicity.' Dalí clearly put his own myth-making and success above all else, and in this he was encouraged by Gala, who was ruthlessly ambitious, especially when it came to financial arrangements. Dalí's hard-heartedness stands in stark contrast to Gerald's milder approach to creativity and his differing style of life. These divergences are nowhere more apparent than in the two men's treatment of animals. Gerald took a genuine interest in animals, with a characteristically English concern for their welfare, and was fascinated by their beauty and exoticism; he once left in the middle of one of his London lunch parties to visit the zoo with the leopard-loving Marchesa Casati.[218] Dalí, on the other hand, would daub frogs and octopuses with ink to see what drawings they produced and throw cats in the pool for fun.[219] When asked his favourite animal, he replied, 'Fillet of sole.'

Though man and wife, Salvador and Gala made just as unlikely a couple as Gerald and Robert. But there were various common meeting points, including the emphasis on beauty and the love of the unexpected. Gerald was intrigued enough by the unpredictable spins of the psyche in Dalí's art to dedicate his poem 'Surrealist Landscape' to him. Although you can't help feeling he's teasing (especially in the last line), it is marvellously evocative of the insane juxtapositions and beauty of Dalí's paintings:

On the pale yellow sands
Where the Unicorn stands
And the Eggs are preparing for Tea
Sing Thirty
Sing Forty
Sing Three.

On the pale yellow sands
There's a pair of Clasped Hands
And an eyeball entangled with string.
(Sing Forty
Sing Fifty
Sing Three.)
And a Bicycle Seat
And a Plate of Raw Meat
And a Thing that is hardly a Thing.

On the pale yellow sands
There stands
A Commode
That has nothing to do with the case.
Sing Eighty
Sing Ninety
Sing Three.

On the pale yellow sands
There's a Dorian Mode
And a Temple all covered with Lace
And a Gothic Erection of Urgent Demands
On the patience of You and of Me.

If Gerald was just the sort of rich aristocratic type that Dalí liked to cultivate, their mutual friend Edward James proved an even more fruitful contact. Sexually ambivalent and emotionally unstable, James had inherited a fortune and was the godson of Edward VII, who some said was his father. He had, like Gerald, been a diplomat in Rome, where he sped about in an open-top Alfa Romeo. He was asked to leave for muddling up the dispatches, although he had also caused a minor scandal after he protested to Mussolini about the plight of the depressed eagles and mangy wolves that were kept caged on the Capitoline Hill. Displayed as symbols of the Eternal City, they kept on dying and the English animal-lover was outraged by their cramped conditions.

James had been briefly married to the gorgeous cat-faced Viennese prima ballerina and actress Tilly Losch. Fascinated by the surrealist movement and its anarchic escapism, he had an impressive collection of art and was painted twice by Magritte, whom he had to stay in London. He was also a generous sponsor and host to Dalí, supporting him financially and inspiring some of his most iconic work. At West Dean, James's Sussex home, the two men came up with the famous *Lobster Telephone* (also known as the *Aphrodisiac Telephone* – the speaker's mouth is carefully aligned with the lobster's genitalia) and the *Mae West Lips Sofa*. In happier days, James had ordered a stair carpet woven with the imprint of Tilly Losch's footprints, to recall the marks she made with wet feet after a bath. Their very public divorce provoked a huge scandal: she accused him of being homosexual (her close friend Adele Astaire caused a stir with her evidence), and he accused her of adultery with Prince Sergei Obolensky. Following the separation, James got another carpet made with the paw-prints of his Irish wolfhound.

Somewhere in his house was a moth-eaten polar bear shot by some forebear in Greenland. James had it shipped to Dalí in Paris, where the artist dyed it mauve (did he already know about the Faringdon doves?) and had drawers put in the bear's chest to keep his cutlery in.[220] Some years later, James would create Las Pozas (The Pools), an astonishing surrealist Eden of waterfalls and sculptures high in the Mexican rainforest.

In July 1936, the International Surrealist Exhibition was held in London. The great names of surrealism attended, André Breton gave the opening speech and thousands came to see what all the fuss was about. At this point, Dalí was seen as 'an incarnation of the Surrealist spirit' who 'made it shine with all its brilliance'.[221] Several hundred people came to the New Burlington Galleries to hear him give a lecture in French, 'Fantômes paranoïaques authentiques' ('Authentic Paranoiac Fantasies'). He was accompanied by two white Russian wolfhounds and was dressed in a lead-weighted deep-sea diver's suit. It was Gerald who had obtained this equipment for his guest – to enable him to dive 'to the depth of his subconscious'. Nobody had thought he might require some oxygen equipment on this plunge into his psyche; after the bulky helmet was bolted on by a mechanic and Dalí went on stage, he soon realised that he was running out of air. As he grappled, increasingly terrified, with the metal globe, his face visibly panic-stricken behind its thick glass window, Gerald banged at the bolts with a hammer. Witness accounts vary as to whether the hero of the hour was Gerald, Edward James with a billiard cue or a spanner-wielding workman. The audience assumed it was all part of the mad pantomime, which was a great success.

The fun did not end with the exhibition. Even if Edward James was right when he said 'All the stories about orgies at Faringdon are untrue,'[222] there were certainly games of other kinds. Dalí managed to get Gerald to put the grand piano in an ornamental pool on the lawn, and then placed chocolate eclairs on the black notes.[223] This was the kind of surrealism that suited Gerald; his interest in the shocking, subversive qualities of the movement was purely from the sidelines. He dabbled in the same way that he might dress up in some peculiar clothes or appreciate some escapade, and he went along for the fun of the stunt. While Dalí wrestled with sexual images linked to masturbation or the now famously homoerotic figure of St Sebastian, pierced by phallic arrows, Gerald preferred to find absurd subjects with innuendo, where he could pierce pretension and provoke laughter. Rather than bloodied, penetrated saints, he went for large or engorged noses – for example, in his 1941 novel *The Romance of a Nose*, Cleopatra is transformed into a beauty after having a 'nose job by a Theban physician'. His comic song 'Red Roses and Red Noses' is dedicated 'To a Young Lady who wished

Red Roses to be strewn on her tomb'. The cover of the manuscript has goofily picturesque red noses with cupids' wings fluttering down the page.

Some people praise red roses:
But I beg leave to say
That I prefer red noses –
I think they are so gay.

A Kempis says we must not cling
To things that pass away:
Red Noses last a lifetime –
Red Roses but a day.

Red Roses blow but thrice a year –
In June, July or May:
But owners of Red Noses
Can blow them every day.

It was only weeks after the diving-suit fiasco that Dalí's first great love, Federico García Lorca, was shot by a Fascist firing squad. The painter and the poet had been friends and lovers as art students in Madrid, at a time when it was risky and difficult to be gay and when both longed to push cultural boundaries. They had shared artistic ambition and a horror of intimacy with women; Lorca's metaphor for sexual intercourse was the 'jungle of blood'. And though they had not remained close, it must have been shocking, even for an egotist like Dalí, to learn of Lorca's death. Still, it was not enough to stop him from showing support for Franco, and it was only a few years before the surrealists, under Breton, would expel Dalí from their movement as 'the ex-apologist of Hitler, the Fascist, clerical and racist painter and the friend of Franco, who opened Spain as a drilling field for the worst barbarism ever known'.[224] When Max Ernst refused to shake Dalí's hand, saying, 'I don't shake the hand of a Fascist,' Dalí replied, 'I am not a Fascist, I am only an opportunist.'

In England, Dalí's encounters were of the more light-hearted sort, though they often boosted his career. With Edward James and Gerald, he got to know many influential people of the day, including Cecil

ELSA SCHIAPARELLI
ON TOP OF THE FOLLY
WITH GERALD

Beaton. He also collaborated with the famous Italian couturier Elsa Schiaparelli, who became friends with Gerald and stayed at Faringdon. Some years younger than Gerald, she had been a philosophy student in Rome when he was a diplomat, during the giddy days of futurism. 'Schiap', as she liked to call herself, was just as keen to shock with her clothes as Dalí was with his paintings. Working with great names like Jean Cocteau and Man Ray, she made sweaters with patterns of skeleton ribs or tattoo-like pierced hearts, suits with pockets like a chest of drawers, and introduced zips (specially coloured), wedge-heeled shoes, culottes and simple 'smalls' to replace elaborate silk underwear.

Influenced by Dalí, she made hats that looked like upside-down shoes, and dressed Wallis Simpson in a lobster-print dress for a photograph by Beaton just before her marriage to the Duke of Windsor.

Although based in Paris, Schiap was an Anglophile. She had a place in London and adored roaming around the countryside picking up bargains in antique shops. John Betjeman recalled how Gerald once took her to a jumble sale in the vicarage garden at the little village of Baulking, where she was pressed into buying something at the second-hand clothes stall. 'People came to stay at Faringdon not as the famous men and women they often were, but to be themselves.'[225]

Schiap was just the sort of person that Gerald liked to throw into the mix at his extraordinarily eclectic weekends, and she was there in June 1938 at a glamorous house party that included H. G. Wells, Baroness Budberg (Wells's dashing Russian mistress who had famously been involved with Gorky and was suspected of being a double agent) and Tom Driberg. In the visitors' book, Schiap enters her profession as 'Hopeless job' and 'Cosmopolitan', while H. G. Wells writes 'Lighting and Hot Water Expert'.

One of Gerald and Robert's closest friends, who lived close to Faringdon, was Daisy Fellowes, a woman famous for being spectacularly well-dressed, even 'the best dressed woman in the world', favouring outsize jewels and exotic creations by Schiaparelli. Daisy was the glamorous niece of Winnie de Polignac, who had brought her up after Daisy's mother had killed herself. Like her aunt Winnie, she had first married a French prince who seemed to prefer the company of men. Her second husband was Reginald Fellowes, a cousin of Winston Churchill, and they set up home at beautiful Compton Beauchamp House. Some years younger than Gerald, The Hon. Mrs Reginald Fellowes was the first person to wear the Schiaparelli–Dalí Shoe Hat, with its inverted velvet heel, and was said to have 'the elegance of the damned'. Described by Francis Rose as 'the beautiful Madame de Pompadour of the period, dangerous as an albatross',[226] Daisy had a villa at Cap Martin and a fabulous yacht, took lovers with impunity and, predictably enough, was photographed in glamorous poses by Cecil

Beaton. Some have remarked that in Gerald's novel *The Romance of a Nose*, the well-dressed, independent heroine has much in common with Daisy. Diana Mosley wrote that Gerald loved Daisy's elegance and 'her malicious remarks made in silky tones', while Evelyn Waugh gossiped that Daisy had 'taught Gerald B to take cocaine'. Like him, she loved practical jokes – you never knew what she might do next.[227] Placing a statue of St Joseph in front of her house, Daisy claimed she was honouring the patron saint of cuckolds. She represented a worldly, fashionable side of Gerald's life that he admitted enjoying despite its obvious limitations.[228] And if Daisy was old enough to be Robert's mother, she was playful and charming enough to appeal to him too.

ARGE PORTIONS OF LIFE at Faringdon were given over to the delights of entertaining, and though Gerald was more confident and contented, his music was no longer given such single-minded priority. Some have contended that he squandered his greatest talent by dispersing his energies across other arts for which he had less flair. Later Robert and others would say that Gerald was too keen on having a pleasant life to be really ambitious about his musical career. Nevertheless, Gerald's most successful and lasting piece was composed during this glittering and sociable time. *A Wedding Bouquet* is a satirical, merry yet also melancholy ballet with orchestra and, unusually, chorus. The subject is a French provincial wedding, based on the initial part of Gertrude Stein's 1931 play, *They Must. Be Wedded. To Their Wife*. The plot has the sort of messy emotional tangles that visitors to Faringdon were only too familiar with: amusing on the surface and deeply painful underneath. There is a wistful bride, a disreputable groom (who dances with his mistresses), and a Mexican terrier called Pépé (like Stein's own), who fends off her mistress's suitors and is played by a child ballerina.

A *Wedding Bouquet* was first performed at Sadler's Wells in 1937, and the production brought together some of the most significant names of the time. Gerald himself designed the sets and costumes; there are backdrops with scenes from Faringdon and from his travels abroad. The young Frederick Ashton was the choreographer, and the cast included Margot Fonteyn, Ninette de Valois and Robert Helpmann. Constant Lambert had just become musical director of Sadler's Wells and conducted the piece that he had encouraged. Like Gerald, he was a composer who loved bringing the freedom and fun of more popular musical forms to serious music and who detested pomposity and the insularity of some English music. Constant and Gerald were the only two English composers whom Diaghilev commissioned to write for the Ballets Russes. Both men were influenced by Stravinsky and appreciated popular music – Constant was a fan of The Blackbirds, the famous black jazz musicians who were such a success in London during the 1920s. He also championed Gerald's music; in America, he had to explain that far from being another stage name like Duke Ellington or Count Basie, Lord Berners was actually an English lord.[229] In A *Wedding Bouquet*, the brassy fanfares of jazz and the song tunes of the music hall merge with the more classical lyricism of orchestral ballet. Underneath, the darkness is lurking; like Gerald's depression, it was one aspect of the whole. The inherent satire and parody do not exclude true emotions. Gertrude Stein said of the ballet (as she might have said of its composer), 'They all say it is very sad and everybody has to laugh and that is very nice.'[230]

Many have remarked on how Gerald was at his most genuine and exposed in his music. Hearing him play in the 1920s, Beverley Nichols wrote:

As soon as he is at the piano, the mask drops, and the revelation
through music begins. It is curiously personal music, distinguished by
a Rabelaisian humour. I shall never forget his playing to me a passage
for horns which occurs in his ballet. There had been a theme which
galloped and sparkled; up and down, in and out, like a scamper of wild
horses over the plains. And then suddenly, in an unexpected key, there

came a regular cackle of fifths – loud and broken, staggering and absurd. It was as good an example of a musical guffaw as I can imagine.[231]

Frederick Ashton, too, admired Gerald for his professional approach to collaborating on the production. 'He was very good at constructing a ballet. He could do a very good *pas de deux* in rather a Tchaikovsky/ Delibes way. And he understood about lengths . . . If I said, "That's too long," he would cut it. With Benjamin Britten, every note was sacred . . . Gerald was much more realistic.'[232] With his lifelong dread of boredom, Gerald strongly believed that small, or at least short, was beautiful in music: 'The symphonies of Schumann and Schubert, beautiful as they are, contain passages one feels might conveniently have been shorter, while in Bruckner and Mahler there are moments that even an audience of tortoises might find tedious.'[233]

Although extremely different in character, Gerald and Lambert became close, and remained friends until they died within a year of one another. They shared a playfulness, though Constant was a far more chaotic personality, with a tendency to drink too much and lose control. Like Gerald, Constant had worked with Christopher Wood, who painted a memorable portrait of the young composer. Despite his youth (Constant was in his thirties), he was plagued by worsening health and was already running to fat, but he had immense charm and his charisma worked on both men and women. Lambert had his own wounds stemming from his family (his father, a portrait painter from Australia, was hardly doting), but his fresh, unabashed hedonism combined with originality and talent was appreciated by his older friends. With his Chelsea pub crawls, scruffy appearance and casual flings with girls who were much too young, he lived a version of the Swinging Sixties three decades earlier than the baby boomers. Constant had originally been picked up as a friend by the Sitwell siblings when he was still a teenager in the early 1920s, and he frequented Edith Sitwell's literary gatherings and tea parties at her Bayswater flat. His talents were manifest. Osbert Sitwell described the seventeen-year-old as 'a prodigy of intelligence and learning, and gifted with that particularly individual outlook and sense of humour which, surely, were born in him and are impossible to acquire'.[234]

It was also Lambert's lack of respect for boundaries that appealed to this older generation of eccentric artists who had been brought up in the confining Victorian era, and who had broken the chains through creativity and through their personalities. If Gerald had felt oppressed by the narrow horizons of his childhood, Edith Sitwell's had wounded her far more deeply. Born only a few years after Gerald, she shared the isolating, emotionally desiccated environment of a wealthy, upper-class family and the misfortune of lacking good looks. She had grown to six foot by the time she reached puberty and was extremely thin with a crooked nose. Having been forced by her parents to wear vile and hated 'Bastille of steel' contraptions to correct the problems with her spine and legs, she ended up accentuating her own peculiarities.[235] Later, she used unusual clothes and unconventional jewellery to create her own peculiar beauty. But like Gerald, with his masks, costumes and mockery, these external coverings provided a sort of emotional armour for someone already injured.

Having become a Sitwell protégé, Lambert became a legendary speaker at performances of *Façade*, in which Edith Sitwell's bizarre poems were recited to what was initially considered very daring music by William Walton – another *enfant terrible*. Walton was both friend and rival to Constant, and the two young composers shared Gerald's appreciation of continental composition as well as his rejection of the patriotically English music of compatriots like Elgar. In *Façade*, Sitwell's experimental, nonsensical words were declaimed through a megaphone from behind a screen. Constant proved to be 'the perfect instrument of this performance, a speaker *sans pareil* of the verse, clear, rapid, incisive, tireless, and commanding vocally an extraordinary range of inflection, from menace and the threat of doom to the most debonair and jaunty inconsequence'.[236]

By the time Constant became a frequent visitor to Faringdon, he was already at crisis point in his marriage. He had married the seventeen-year-old Florence Kaye ('Mouse') in 1931, following several years of admiring her extraordinarily lovely oriental features and her feline, adolescent figure. Mouse's father had been a sailor from Java or Malaya, nobody was quite sure, and she was brought up in an orphanage.[237] After their marriage, a son, Christopher (called 'Kit', after Christopher Wood), was born, but Constant proved as neglectful a parent as his own father. (Robert would later describe himself as Kit's godfather and the ageing Mad Boy would become close to this younger mad boy as he went through his own creative yet self-destructive adventures.) Mouse worked as a model and tried to bridge the gap between herself and her husband by improving herself culturally. Constant merely retreated, taking to serious boozing and philandering, and absenting himself from domestic life.

When in 1935 he came across the fifteen-year-old Margot Fonteyn at Sadler's Wells he must have seemed to her old and disreputable – he was already becoming burnt-out, limping around with a stick, and he had many physical problems (including diabetes) that remained undiagnosed until his premature death. But Constant fell in love, and eventually Fonteyn in turn fell for this magnetic and fascinating man. The details of their relationship remain hazy; neither ever talked about their involvement, though it lasted for many years. They often stayed at Faringdon, where irregular couples were more the norm than the exception, and nobody was going to make a fuss.

Robert Helpmann, one of the star dancers in *A Wedding Bouquet*, described a visit to Faringdon when another of the more unusual and interesting couples to visit was there: Gertrude Stein and Alice B. Toklas. Helpmann recalled entering the drawing room at teatime and having to wait while a horse was fed buttered scones before being introduced to his fellow guests. Stein was dressed in tweeds and a deerstalker hat, while Toklas 'was equipped with a growth between her eyebrows that suggested the unicorn but did her best to conceal the fact so that she resembled an old English sheepdog instead.'[238] The two women had been living together for decades in Paris, where Stein had discovered and supported artists including Picasso, Matisse and Cézanne. Her art collection was astonishing and the couple hosted a

Saturday evening salon at rue de Fleurus – with Toklas's *petits fours* and drinks – for painters and writers such as Hemingway and Fitzgerald, and where Picasso might drop by. Cecil Beaton described the beauty and solidity of their apartment: 'The Misses Stein and Toklas live like Biblical royalty: simply, yet in complete luxury.'[239] Stein's admiring protégé Francis Rose wrote that such was her 'majestic presence that everyone rose at her entrance as though to greet a princely Cardinal instead of America's great spinster writer'.[240]

Stein's *The Autobiography of Alice B. Toklas* had recently brought her the fame and commercial success both she and Toklas believed she deserved as 'a genius'. Gerald was not necessarily convinced that Stein's experimental writing was as good as she and Toklas made out; Diana Mosley claimed he thought her writings were 'real rubbish'. But he was intrigued. 'A Rose is a Rose is a Rose' was playful and provocative in a way he could relate to, though Gerald might have chuckled at Hemingway's addition to *his* copy (in a magic circle similar to that on the cover): 'A Bitch is a Bitch is a Bitch'.[241] Gerald was impressed by Stein's art collection and evidently liked her playful freedom with words – enough at least to want to use her play for his ballet. Doubtless it helped that she was highly fashionable among the avant-garde. And at a personal level, Stein and Toklas were extremely intriguing: two Jewish-American lesbians who had lived together openly since before the First World War and who were a magnetic force for the best emerging art in Europe. While there was gossip about the pair once they'd left, they were honoured guests at Faringdon.

Gerald went to stay with the couple at their house in Bilignin, near Lyons, and liked it so much he returned several times. Toklas picked wild strawberries at dawn for breakfast and Basket, the large poodle, ran wild in the fields.[242] Stein got up late and in the afternoons would take Gerald out for wild drives in the Ford along the dusty country roads. Unlike other women in Gerald's circle, Stein cropped her hair like a man and experimented with gender issues in a way that was far ahead of her time – something that probably intrigued him. She was also warm, gregarious and very good company, and his letters to her are full of genuine affection and the signs of mutual friendship: 'Thank you <u>so</u> much for sending the corn seeds. My first lot is coming up well. Also the hibiscus . . . Give my love to Alice and lots for yourself.' Gerald even honoured the American with a parody of her writing in his poem 'Portrait of a Society Hostess', probably based on Lady Colefax.

> Give a canary champagne and it spins. Chandelier drops glitter and drops glitter and are conversation. Bohemian glass is cracked in Mayfair. Mayfair-weather friends come and go come and go come and go. The house is always full full full full.

> Are you there? Are you there? There! Are you not all there? Many are not quite all there but royalty are there and lots and lots and lots. Glitter is more than kind hearts and coronets are more than comfort. She praises and embarrasses she praises and embarrasses she confuses cabinet ministers. Some will not go.

> What with one thing and another. What with another and one thing. What with what with what what wit and what not.

> Squashed bosh is her favourite meringue.

There are various photographs documenting the stay of Stein and Toklas at Faringdon, but none so revealing as the one picturing them with their hosts and several other guests posing on the front porch one cold February day. Gerald and Stein sit perched opposite one another on the curved, low walls that flank the steps: solid and confident in their hats and coats, each has the small hint of a smile. They are the oldest in the company (Stein was almost a decade older than Gerald), and they emanate the power of two creative forces, politically conservative but radical in their art; people who know what they are searching for. Stein brings to mind the comments that Toklas made when they met in 1907: her 'beautifully modelled and unique head' like a Roman emperor's, and her voice, 'deep, full, velvety like a great contralto's'.[243] Toklas claimed to have heard bells in her head at this meeting; a sure sign that she was in the presence of genius. Toklas herself is sitting tiny and hunched on the steps at Stein's feet. She is frowning, clutching her dark coat around her as if she is not happy to be there. But surely, as the woman who was not only lover but ambitious manager for her partner, she must have been pleased that Stein's name was now associated with Lord Berners, Sadler's Wells, and some of the most exciting, up-and-coming names in English dance? Stein described meeting Frederick Ashton, the choreographer for A *Wedding Bouquet,* who was also friends with Gerald. 'I am always asking Alice Toklas do you think he is a genius, she does have something happen when he is a genius so I always ask her is he a genius, being one it is natural that I should think a great deal about that thing in any other one. He and I talked a great deal on meeting, and I think he is one . . .'[244]

Toklas took care of all the practical aspects of Stein's, or 'Lovey's' life, organising where she should go and whom she should meet. Toklas looks mousey, with her pale, pointy face and her dark moustache, though Stein called her 'Pussy'. Nevertheless, it would be wrong to think that Pussy was dominated by Lovey; if anything, Toklas knew how to wield the upper hand. Hemingway described a visit to rue de Fleurus shortly before his friendship with Stein evaporated. He was told to wait by the maidservant, and overheard someone speaking to Miss Stein 'as I had never heard one person speak to another; never, anywhere, ever. Then Miss Stein's voice came pleading and begging, saying, "Don't, pussy. Don't. Don't, please don't. I'll do anything, pussy, but please don't do it. Please don't. Please don't, pussy."'[245]

Sitting next to Toklas on the steps is the Mad Boy, who doesn't look very mad at all. Nattily clad in jodhpurs, riding jacket and tie, with hair as brilliantined as Valentino's, he has a shotgun across his knee and a dead rabbit at his feet. He has evidently been up since dawn, while some of the other guests clutch a glass that is presumably the first cocktail of the morning. Robert was increasingly in charge of estate matters, and he looks the part. Gerald was busy with his creative concerns and uninterested in this aspect of Faringdon, which Robert approached with mixed success. It was at around this time that he came up with a disastrous scheme to save money by sacking all the garden

GERALD AND GERTRUDE STEIN SIT OPPOSITE ONE ANOTHER, WHILE ROBERT SITS NEXT TO ALICE B. TOKLAS ON THE STEPS. OTHER GUESTS INCLUDE LADY DIANE ABDY (FRONT WITH GLASS) AND HER HUSBAND, SIR ROBERT ABDY, BEHIND HER.

and woods staff and then rehiring them at a reduced wage. At a time when the rural working class were often extremely badly paid, this was deeply distressing, and several of the men didn't want to return. One long-standing estate employee remarked, 'Robert was a queer man. One minute he was as good as gold, and he'd give you anything. And then he'd bury you in the earth.'[246]

Toklas claimed that frequently, when Stein met with various geniuses of the art world, she would end up in a room with the wives. She considered writing *Wives of Geniuses I Have Sat With*. Though Stein and Gerald clearly look like the husbands and geniuses in the group photograph, it is hard to imagine Robert as the 'wife' having

IGOR STRAVINSKY
WITH GERALD AT
FARINGDON

cosy chats with Toklas. But perhaps he talked with this notoriously grumpy, if highly intelligent woman about food; the hunter and the cook bonding over game. The legendary *Alice B. Toklas Cook Book* (published in 1954) has recipes for jugged hare, and her 'Rabbit with Dumpling' has a touch of Stein's spirited prose style: 'Cut your Belgian hare!! In pieces. Roll in flour and brown in an iron pot in which you have slightly cooked 4 or 5 slices of bacon . . .' The reader is warned that 'when cooked the meat should have the consistency of chicken, and not slimy restaurant rabbit.' There is also a recipe attributed to 'The Late Lord Berners's for 'Roast chicken in cream' – using plenty of Gerald's favourite ingredient plus sherry and lemon juice – and 'Filet de Sole à la Ritz', poached sole served cold, in a sauce of whipped cream and grated horseradish – an exquisite summer dish that was passed on through the decades at Faringdon.[247]

In 1937, the visitors' book at Faringdon shows a remarkably busy year: in addition to everyone connected to *A Wedding Bouquet*, Gerald and Robert welcomed Igor Stravinsky and his mistress Vera Sudeikina, Malcolm Sargent, Osbert Sitwell, Emerald Cunard, Winnie de

Polignac and Robert's mother, Gladys. Among the younger guests were Lygon sisters, Mitford sisters, Kathleen Meyrick – Robert's old flame – and Cyril Connolly. And there are two visits recorded by someone who has not been seen before – a twenty-one-year-old woman with dark hair, captivating eyes and marvellous clothes. Her signature is tidy and plain, though an angled dash underscores the surname. She doesn't fill in her profession or nationality with jokes like many others. On her second visit in November, she puts her address as Sloane House, Church St, sw3 – a Georgian mansion in Chelsea. Her name is Jennifer Fry.

CHAPTER NINE

The Orphan on the Top Floor

HEN JENNIFER FRY first visited Faringdon, it was as a friend of Robert's. He was five years older than her, but their sets overlapped and their backgrounds were not dissimilar. The Mad Boy was an ideal playmate – 'fast', good-looking, roguish. They were both without any fixed employment or education and like most of their friends spent an inordinate amount of time and effort on enjoying themselves. Jennifer would surely have got on with Gerald too. Like him, she could be shy – an insecure only child from a wealthy family, she too had been both over-protected and disregarded. She might have appeared a giddy nightclub butterfly, but she was also a thoughtful, widely read person who loved the arts; she would have been interested in Lord Berners the composer, writer and painter. And he would have liked her spirit.

Jennifer was born in the middle of the First World War, in 1916, exactly nine months after her parents' wedding. Her mother, Alathea Gardner, had been a lovely bride with the preferred looks of the age: only twenty-one, she was ethereally pale, with long, elegant hands, auburn hair and dauntingly large, melancholy blue eyes. Both of Alathea's parents had unusual genealogies. Her father, Herbert Gardner, was the illegitimate son of Lord Gardner and the actress Julia Fortescue. He was thus far from being a conventional product of the English upper classes, despite his parents ultimately marrying. He became a Liberal MP and was later made a baron in his own right, as Lord Burghclere. Alathea's mother was Lady Winifred Herbert, daughter of the 4th Earl of Carnarvon. It was Lady Winifred's brother, the 5th Earl, who funded many of Howard Carter's Egyptian expeditions, and who was there to unearth the astonishing tomb of Tutankhamun in 1922. Jennifer was six when she learned about the world-famous discovery by her great-uncle; it must have been tremendously exciting for a child. Sadly, it was only a year later that Lord Carnarvon died – from the 'Curse of Tutankhamun' (as the popular press declared) or an infected mosquito bite, as his nieces, including Alathea, believed.

Alathea and her three sisters were brought up to be cultured, literary women, learning languages and reading politics and history as well as all the regular lessons. Yet they were only too aware of the disaster of their gender – the family's wealth was tied up with the Burghclere title and the lack of a son meant that both the barony and the money would disappear. (When an uncle famed for magic tricks came to visit, the young Gardner girls would beg him to turn them into boys.) Given these family tensions, it was a relief to Alathea's parents when their second daughter agreed to marry twenty-seven-year-old Geoffrey Fry.

Geoffrey was a member of the Bristol-based family that had made its fortune in the nineteenth century with the popular drink Fry's Cocoa. As 'Manufacturers to H. M. The King', Fry's produced the famous Five Boys chocolate bar that was moulded to show five versions of a little boy's face, moving from 'desperation' through 'pacification' to 'Realisation "It's Fry's."' Geoffrey's wealth came from the chocolate factories but he was no swaggering industrialist. He didn't have as many titles as the Gardners and Herberts, but he was an educated, sensitive man – a contradictory mix of *belle époque* aesthete with a Quaker background. His father had been Sheriff of Bristol and he counted among his ancestors Elizabeth Fry, the ground-breaking campaigner for prison reform.

Geoffrey studied Classics at King's College, Cambridge, where he was close to Rupert Brooke; he was not the only man or woman in love with the alluring poet whom Yeats described as 'the handsomest young man in England'. The two men had a long correspondence that Geoffrey later donated to the university library. It was a terrible loss for him when Brooke died en route to Gallipoli in 1915; Jennifer remembered the poet's photograph in an oval, silver frame by her father's bed throughout her childhood. Tragedy continued when Geoffrey's only brother, Harold, was killed in France the following year, months after Jennifer's birth. Geoffrey did not serve in the war, probably because of delicate health, but he became involved in politics, serving as (unpaid) private secretary to the Conservative Prime Minister, Andrew Bonar Law, and then between 1923 and 1937 to Stanley Baldwin, throughout his three periods as Prime Minister.

The few photographs of Alathea and Geoffrey together show an appealing couple, with furs, fine clothes and self-absorbed, sensitive intelligence. Geoffrey was quite a dandy, with superb tailored suits topped by debonair cloaks and hats, and his favoured oval Turkish cigarettes. He was, however, a prickly and critical husband and father, and the household was not a happy one. Alathea's sisters told the story that when, on her wedding night, the bride had knelt to say her prayers by the bed as she always did, the groom laughed. Alathea's piety, inherited from her mother, was only one element of difference in a marriage that was strained.

According to Jennifer, her father used to tell her how disappointed he had been when she was born and he discovered that she was not a boy. 'I wanted to put you in a bucket and drown you like a kitten,' he joked cruelly. Jennifer was left-handed, something Geoffrey had suffered with as a child, when pedagogical practice encouraged tying his left hand to his high chair so he would use the right. But this shared trait did not endear his daughter to him. And by the time Jennifer was old enough to be taunted and rejected by her father, her mother had become a reclusive semi-invalid and was also largely unavailable to her daughter. Still beautiful and dressed exquisitely, Alathea spent much of her time in bed, attended to by the best doctors and nurses, staying in clinics and convalescence homes and taking therapeutic trips to warmer climes.

During their many years of marriage, both Geoffrey and Alathea took their breakfast in bed, but in separate rooms. Impatient and nervy,

ALATHEA FRY GAZING
AT A BUST OF DANTE

Geoffrey hated dawdling. Chafing to get on with the day's endeavours, he would down his breakfast tea and hurriedly gobble a boiled egg and brown toast with honey. Alathea, on the other hand, followed her 'tea and bath ceremony', with hours in her spacious bathroom, followed by dressing, applying delicate make-up and choosing her jewellery, which usually included a long string of pearls. She read in her room, answered letters, and if it was a good day she'd be ready in time for lunch. Her movements were slow and when she stood up, she leaned back slightly, one slender hand placed lightly on her chest. She was always late.

When Geoffrey commissioned Walter Sickert to paint Alathea's portrait in 1934, the celebrated avant-garde artist sent a photographer to snap the Hon. Lady Fry in bed as she took breakfast. When Sickert had completed the work, Geoffrey was instructed to 'meet his wife's portrait off the train' and found an unconventional depiction of his wife staring wide-eyed from a mass of pillows and bedding – a pose which truly captured her in the place she came to inhabit most, and was thus closer to her essence than the many more graceful, highly stylised, photographic portraits that exist.[248]

As with so many children of her milieu, Jennifer was largely cared for by nannies. By the age of five she had already been through nine, several of whom had been unkind and violent. She was hit and shut in the cupboard, and at the age of three was smacked for dancing on the grass in her white boots. It seemed wrong to worry her fragile mother with these things; 'Don't disturb Mummy' was the watchword of the house. Even a peep around the door to see the bedside table covered with potions, pills and a jug of home-made barley water was discouraged. Decades afterwards, Jennifer wrote part of an autobiographical short story about 'Miss Jane' being summoned to say goodnight to her mother. The young girl dreaded the darkened room, the smell of scent, the lack of response.

> Mummy was everything. Beautiful, frail, dressed in satin negligées, sometimes a yellow Spanish shawl. A nurse in a white uniform stood like a sergeant by the door. In her hand was a syringe, negligently but obviously held. 'Do come in, dear, Mummy wants to say good night.' On the pink draped bed, swathed in lace and satin, her mother lay. Jane sat on the bed as near as she dared and gazed at the beautiful lost face. She tentatively put her hand on her mother's arm and then kissed it, where the veins were blue. The arm was swiftly withdrawn and Jane felt she had committed some unknown sin.

Like countless mothers of the time, Alathea was denied the opportunity to look after her child and had little else to occupy her. The figure of the sick mother, neurotic, fainting, depressed and 'ill' on a couch or in her bedroom is a staple of the reality and fiction of the time and was often linked to 'a profound sense of uselessness'.[249] Alathea's reliance on various drugs was only increasing. Many later surmised that it was Geoffrey who contributed more than the nannies to his wife's malaise. His unkindness was never of the noisy or physical variety, but there was an unhappy vacuum left by his criticism and undermining emotional absence.

The family had been based in a large apartment near Berkeley Square in London, but when Jennifer was four, they acquired a Queen Anne house in Wiltshire. Built of ornamental black and red brick and surrounded by walled gardens, Oare House is tucked below the Downs near Marlborough. Set high enough to have stunning views of the undulating Vale of Pewsey, it is still low enough to feel intimately connected to the avenues of old trees and lush meadows of grazing sheep that surround it. The square eighteenth-century building was wonderful, but not quite big enough for the Frys, who wanted a drawing room 'large enough for dancing', a substantial library for all their books, good-sized bedrooms and a modern kitchen to replace the old one in the basement. Geoffrey called in the fashionable Welsh architect Clough Williams-Ellis, who added two new brick wings in two phases. A 1928 *Country Life* article shows that the collaboration was a great success. There was an atmosphere of almost austere elegance to the new neoclassical drawing room and Ionic-columned library that contained 'a handsome set of Empire chairs covered in rose and wine coloured velvet'. Huge windows flooded the rooms with light. Alathea's spacious bedroom was a shrine to her delicate tendencies – a place it was tempting never to leave. There was 'an amusing bed of her own designing', hung with Shantung silks which 'combine mauves, yellows and black'. The walls and ceiling were 'sunlight' painted and the effect was both 'restful and bright'.[250] In contrast, Geoffrey's dressing room was a modest room along the corridor, where he slept in an austere single

OARE HOUSE TODAY.
JENNIFER'S NURSERY
AND BEDROOM WERE
ON THE TOP FLOOR
OF THE MAIN PART OF
THE HOUSE, WHILE
ALATHEA'S BEDROOM
WAS AT THE END OF
THE RIGHT-HAND
WING, ADDED (WITH
THE LEFT) BY CLOUGH
WILLIAMS-ELLIS IN
1925

bed. It always smelt of aftershave. Clough Williams-Ellis designed new gardens, loggias and walkways, a swimming pool gleaming turquoise amidst swathes of bright greens, and even wooden garden furniture and a lead gutter hopper that commemorates the Frys' creation with their initials: 'AF, GF, 1925'.

Jennifer and her nanny were kept far away from the airy new wings, on the attic floor of the main house. A steep, narrow staircase wound up to the low-ceilinged nursery and bedrooms for employee and offspring – a child-sized realm looking down to the gardens and across to the chalk swellings of the Downs. It was much too far to shout and be heard by either parent, let alone envisage going to visit them in the night, though as Jennifer grew older she appreciated the expanses of roof terrace above the recent extensions that were perfect for hiding or sunbathing. The child was miserable with her various nannies, and saw herself as 'the orphan on the top floor', but she loved rural life. Later she recalled in a stream of consciousness 'the lanes and hedgerows on the way to Huish. The wild garlic and wild flowers – vetch, scabious. The mystery and sinister atmosphere of the village ... Biblical names – Zebedee. The white road to the church past Mr Strong's farm. Elderberries, slightly dusty. Gophin Wood with King John's treasure buried nearby . . . the Post office with sweets in glass jars and liquorice bootlaces.'

Geoffrey was often away for his work, but when he was at Oare he strode about the grounds organising the gardens, planting rare shrubs (never with variegated leaves – terribly vulgar), putting in avenues, and saddening his wife and daughter by cutting down trees to open up some vista or other. When she wasn't in bed, Alathea was frequently absent, as testified by the many letters Jennifer wrote to various European spas and hotels to her 'Darlingest Darling Mummy' with 'very best love' from 'Baby Mink' or 'your loving Black-Panther'. Their relationship was one of pure adoration from a distance, unsullied by bad moods or temper, which never got an opportunity to be expressed. 'I wish I was on the ship with you,' wrote Jennifer aged about seven. 'Thank you for your lovely letter. I love porpoises they salute so beautifully . . . Harvey has put my swing on a different branch and it goes much better and higher.'

When Jennifer was seven or eight, Alathea missed her daughter's birthday celebrations.

> My Sweetest Mummy
> Thank you so much for the watch and book, it looks so interesting. I had lots of presents. A baby doll and books, a Hymn book, some little knifes and forks and spoons. A little case with a thimble and knife and scissors. A post card album. Some chocs from Mr and Mrs Baldwin, a toy theatre. The Birthday cake was lovely. We had a treasure hunt.
> Tons and Tons of love and kisses from
> Jennifer

As Jennifer became more aware of herself physically, she felt very insecure about her looks; round-faced and more curvaceous than her wafting mother, she felt galumphing and unattractive. Even worse was the wretchedness brought on by her father, whose criticism and impatience – 'drumming and snapping at us' for being slow – could make meals a particular misery. If a child ate toast with two hands,

Geoffrey would snap, 'One hand, not two, like the monkeys at the zoo.' In later life, Jennifer described the tensions associated with the dining room.

> There was so much to eat in those days, and no choice not to eat it unless you were a rebel. If you were an unconfident only child you ate too much, too quickly, especially on Sundays, after church, when you were cross questioned on the sermon, often in the midst of a luncheon party of elderly but not entirely unsympathetic politicians and the occasional local writer. It was a nerve-wracking and silencing experience, and one which has had a lasting effect on my feelings and behaviour.

One autumn evening when Jennifer was about six, she was in the hall having tea – the house was still unfinished and this was the most convenient place to sit by a fire. 'We were awaiting the arrival of the new governess,' she wrote. 'I was very nervous as I'd been warned by the last nanny she'd give me "what for". "You wait," she said as she stomped out.' With the arrival of Miss Beatrix Smith, soon to be known by all as 'Pixie', Jennifer's life changed unrecognisably. 'It was instantaneous love,' she wrote. When Pixie's cases were carried up to her bedroom near Jennifer's in the attic, the young charge helped her unpack. Although Pixie was not beautiful, and would never compare to Alathea for elegance or style, she had an open face and clear blue eyes and she loved nice clothes. Jennifer was delighted at all the outfits that emerged, and was allowed to try on the new governess's different hats.

'Happy times started, and soon reading and writing and walks under the lime trees where she would find fairies in the roots and tell stories.' The nursery room became a cosy haven rather than a lonely exile. There was a blackboard, a wooden table and shelves of books: E. Nesbit, Frances Hodgson Burnett (Pixie read *The Secret Garden* aloud and *The Little Princess* was a firm favourite) and the *Red*, *Blue* and other coloured *Fairy Books*, whose illustrations Jennifer tinted with watercolours where her mother had not already done so at the turn of the century.

Gentle, kind and exuding Christian goodwill to all, Pixie was to remain Jennifer's doting and unmarried fairy godmother for the rest of her long life (she died aged a hundred). She became a substitute for an inadequate mother, a cold father and the lack of any siblings. Jennifer always claimed that 'Pixie saved me.' Certainly, she gave her the love and security previously missing in a life that otherwise looked fortunate and privileged.

PIXIE, JENNIFER'S ADORED GOVERNESS, READING ALOUD TO HER SEVEN-YEAR-OLD CHARGE AT OARE

Pixie became a trusted and capable part of the family, so much so that Geoffrey sometimes even asked her to perform some small task for him. Naturally, she became acquainted with the Prime Minister, Stanley Baldwin, who was not only Geoffrey's employer but a frequent visitor to Oare. One day (as the story goes), Baldwin fell ill, and Geoffrey took over, probably asking Pixie to help him with a few letters or phone calls. Then Geoffrey succumbed and took to his bed. And so it fell to the only available person to take over; plump-cheeked, pastel-clothed and always sweet-natured, Pixie suddenly found herself responsible not only for Britain, but for the vast areas of pink on the world map that she pointed out to young Jennifer – the Empire. 'The Day Pixie Ran the Country' became a favourite Fry family fable, and Pixie was always happy to laugh along with them. Later, when Jennifer was grown up, Pixie worked as a companion-secretary for Alathea's maternal aunt, Lady Victoria Herbert. A god-daughter of Queen Victoria, Aunt Vera (as she was known) disliked men, never marrying and employing only female servants. She wore floor-length lilac dresses, matching stockings and ermine tippets well into the 1950s. Pixie reported that once a vicar came for tea who was known for having an affair with a local farmer's wife. Afterwards Aunt Vera asked that all the sofa covers be removed: 'A bad man has been sitting on them!'

hen Jennifer was about ten, she was sent to Miss Wolff's Girls' School in London to bump up her education a bit and prepare for senior school. She also received elocution lessons. Pixie remained as her governess and constant companion. Located just off Park Lane, Miss Wolff's was rather smart and scholastically exacting. Vita Sackville-West had been a pupil there twenty years earlier, as had her future lover, Violet Keppel (later Trefusis). Jennifer won the English literature prize (a copy of *Poems from Kingsley*), as she wrote to tell her mother from Oare, where she spent weekends and holidays. At about this time, the Frys bought Sloane House in Old Church Street, Chelsea, an elegant Georgian house with a ballroom and a spacious walled garden. Peaceful and light, it had been an asylum for ladies 'suffering from the milder forms of mental disease' in the mid-nineteenth century – eminently suitable for a lady with a delicate disposition like Alathea.

N 1928, JENNIFER was kitted out in gymslip, navy coat and gloves and driven each day from Sloane House to St Paul's Girls' School in Hammersmith. She family's chauffeur to let her out of the Rolls Royce before they arrived, so she would not be seen as different by her fellow pupils. St Paul's was a highly academic school, where girls were expected to study Latin, the three sciences and scripture as well as French and the more usual subjects. The future actress Celia Johnson had just left the school when Jennifer arrived and the music master was Gustav Holst – a shy, retiring man, who had already written *The Planets* during the First World War, but who preferred the anonymity of teaching to celebrity and public exposure. Jennifer neither enjoyed nor excelled at her school life, provoking her father even more by failing to live up to his hope that, even if she were not a boy, she might succeed at her studies. She was acutely aware that he considered her stupid.

It was just before Jennifer started at St Paul's that her beloved Aunt Evelyn got married to Evelyn Waugh. Evelyn was Alathea's youngest sister who had borne the brunt of not being a boy – the last hope for the Burghclere title. Given a name that would have done for a son, she was neglected by her parents even more than her sisters, and as she grew up she flung herself into the post-war party scene, often dressed as a version of the son her parents desired. The ideal female figure of the times was anyway veering to the androgynous – corset-less, flat-chested and lean, with 'naked legs', sleek swimming costumes and cross-dressing tendencies. With her 'Eton crop' haircut, exquisite choirboy's snub nose and petite frame, Evelyn was the perfect 1920s girl. She used lipstick, smoked shamelessly and liked sailors' clothes; her attempts to remove herself from parental control had led to her making and then breaking nine previous engagements. Some saw her as annoying, with her whimsical ways and cute slang, though the fact that she called Proust 'Prousty-Wousty' said something about her reading habits as well as her manner. Her mother was not amused when her youngest

'SHE-EVELYN' WAUGH,
JENNIFER'S AUNT

took up with the emerging 'middle-class' writer who shared her first name. After an investigation into his Oxford past, she declared that Waugh would drag his wife 'down into the abysmal depths of Sodom and Gomorrah'.[251] Waugh himself declared that he had always believed himself a gentleman until he met his future mother-in-law.[252]

The two Evelyns, whom Nancy Mitford described as looking like a pair of fresh-faced schoolboys, got married in secret. The bride wore a black-and-yellow jumper suit, Harold Acton was best man, Robert Byron gave the bride away, and they drank champagne cocktails at the 500 Club afterwards. When Lady Burghclere did find out she was 'quite inexpressibly pained'.

The newly-weds were known by their friends as She-Evelyn and He-Evelyn and they dashed about to the sort of parties that Waugh would dissect with loathing in *Vile Bodies* and were written about in all the fashionable gossip columns. She-Evelyn had several bouts of bad health, as He-Evelyn described to Harold Acton, writing from Oare. 'The last 3 weeks have been very distracting with Evelyn in bed and my flat in possession of nurses and doctors. We have got away at last and we are staying in my brother in law's house in the downs near Marlborough in great peace and luxury.'

In his diary Waugh noted his amusement at finding Marie Stopes's *Married Love* fallen down behind the architecture books in a small study. He also commented on the atmosphere of the house: 'There is an epicene preciosity or nicety about everything that goes better with cigarettes and London clothes than my tweeds and pipe.'[253] Some months later, when She-Evelyn got double pneumonia and was critically ill on a Mediterranean cruise, it was Alathea who wired them money.

Two of Evelyn's sisters had already made disastrous marriages (Juliet's had lasted twenty-four hours and Alathea's relationship with Geoffrey was hardly contented), but Waugh was devastated when only fourteen months after the wedding, he announced the shocking news 'that Evelyn has been pleased to make a cuckold of me with Heygate* and that I have filed a petition for divorce'.[254] Waugh confided in the writer Henry Green, 'There is some odd hereditary *tic* in all those Gardner girls – I think it is an intellectual failing more than anything else.'[255]

The separation lost She-Evelyn many friends, including Nancy Mitford, to whom she had been close and who had stayed at Oare with her. The other 'Gardner girls' took their sister's part, and when Jennifer gradually learned the details, she believed that her youthful aunt had come out badly from the scandal. Evelyn claimed that she had married Waugh believing he would help her get away from the depressing restrictions of upper-class life – the 'huntin'-shootin'-fishin'' brigade with their snobbish cliques and narrow obsessions. In reality, her husband appeared to be mesmerised by the aristocratic environment she disdained, and wanted nothing more than to belong to these circles – something even his friends teased him about, and that emerged in his subsequent alliance and fascination with the Lygons at Madresfield, not to mention his penchant for the grandest London clubs.

---

* John Heygate, BBC News editor and later novelist, 1903–76.

 S A TEENAGER, Jennifer continued to feel the physical and emotional awkwardness that had dogged her childhood. She had fabulous legs that she was proud to show off and what she considered an embarrassingly large bosom that she tried to disguise. As she developed a sexual awareness of her own, she also began to understand more about her parents' complex relationship. In Jennifer's unfinished short story about Jane, there are strong clues as to how she discovered Geoffrey's secret: 'When Jane was fourteen, her mother started confiding unsuitable stories about her love affairs, her husband's homosexuality. It explained the presence of certain ambiguous young men in the house, her mother retiring to her room.'

Geoffrey's rejection of his daughter and his lack of interest in his wife reflected not just a cruel and misogynistic streak, but a fundamental attraction to men. Jennifer began to notice how many young men came to visit and to stay – some of them students from Oxford, others involved in the political world. Eventually, she deduced that some were his lovers. Jennifer's Aunt Evelyn later claimed that on one occasion Alathea had 'walked in and found Geoffrey in bed with a boy'. Although Evelyn was unspecific about the age of the boy, the shock of witnessing what was, after all, a criminal act was inevitably severe. It can only have served to make Alathea feel even more unwanted and unhappy.

Geoffrey's work as private secretary to Stanley Baldwin meant that he aligned himself with the highly conventional Conservative leader, whose influence in the decades after World War I was such that some called it the Baldwin Age. First cousin to Kipling, Baldwin was a generation older than Geoffrey – a representative of the old, rural England that had been rejected by many of Geoffrey's blood-spattered contemporaries, disillusioned by war and its aftermath. Significantly, however, Baldwin's elder son, Oliver, was homosexual, and Baldwin was a close and loyal friend to Lord Beauchamp (Coote's father) and lived close to Madresfield, where he was a frequent visitor.

GEOFFREY FRY:
BOOKISH, BISEXUAL
AND COLDLY CRITICAL
OF HIS WIFE AND
DAUGHTER

It was Baldwin who made Geoffrey 1st Baronet Fry of Oare in 1929 for his contribution to politics. Nevertheless, Geoffrey was cut from different cloth to his employer; a sensitive man who was interested in the arts and who had a strong sense of classical elegance. While his work propped up an old-school political system and social world, his personal leanings were influenced by his homoerotic impulses and his love of the ancient world and poetry. His obsession with Rupert Brooke was only one indication of this. Sir Geoffrey also invited a stream of cultured literary and artistic people to Oare, and commissioned work from Eric Ravilious, who painted some beautiful watercolours of the gardens and some fashionable murals of tennis players for their London house. Jennifer remembered that Ravilious had taken quite a shine to her and her mother, which annoyed Geoffrey.

Jennifer realised she would never live up to her father's expectations. His love of the ascetic and of classically orientated young men only emphasised her girlish frivolity and her increasingly feminine figure. While Geoffrey hoped she'd be studying Latin verbs in the library, she would be sunbathing on the roof terrace, and if he hoped she might at least take after her mother in terms of wafting, delicate sophistication, she'd be bursting out of a sexy frock, ready to go to a party. Jennifer's closest friend was Primula Rollo – a blue-eyed, fair-haired classic English rose. Prim lived near to Oare, in a house called 'Cold Blow'. Geoffrey had commissioned the building from Clough Williams-Ellis for Prim's parents, who were his friends – her father was a solicitor and worked for Geoffrey. Although Prim was two years younger than Jennifer, she often joined schoolroom lessons with Pixie. As they got older, the two girls would go to dances together, sometimes chaperoned by Pixie, whom they would shamelessly mislead so they could get up to mischief – although Prim was not as naughty as Jennifer. If not exactly prim, she was the kind of teenager who was chosen to be head girl at her boarding school. Jennifer did not get anywhere near being head girl. 'I had Latin verbs drummed into me, as well as Mathematics at St Paul's Girls' School. All I longed for was to learn Italian, study Ballet and lead my own life,' she wrote. After less than four years at the school, she left just after her sixteenth birthday.

When she asked her father if she could study Italian, he replied, 'Whatever language you learn you will speak stupidities, as you do now, in your own language.' Instead, Jennifer was sent to Vienna to learn German, accompanied by a toothy young governess – a vicar's daughter – to keep bashing on with the Latin lessons. If Geoffrey hoped that this trip would drum some sense into his flighty daughter, he had misjudged her capacity for adventure. Jennifer's frank and witty description of her experiences gives a picture of how she blossomed away from home.

JENNIFER AGED ABOUT
SIXTEEN

I stayed in a family who took me to their hearts as my parents were incapable of doing. We sat round their Biedermeier table drinking china tea with lemon and a dash of rum, ate Sacher Torte and filling Austrian meals. Wiener Schnitzel, sauerkraut, the best potato purée. They took me to concerts and the opera – my first introduction to Wagner – The Ring in its entirety – where I met my first lover . . . He was a Hochgeboren [highborn] count – a painter – and he asked if he could draw me. I was a pretty dark girl with slender legs, and wore flat red shoes with ankle straps which were unusual and admired. He painted me half naked in a kimono and re-christened me Kotoro. He saw me as a Geisha, and I was flattered and enchanted by his attentions. As I had never been allowed so much as a sip of wine at home, I was easily seduced. Also by the elderly uncle of the family, a kindly roué who put an arm round my waist on the one occasion I was alone in the salon, kissed me, gave me a glass of Liebfraumilch, and there I was on the Biedermeier chaise longue, my knickers skilfully removed, being really made love to for the first time.

. . . I floated from cathedral to café, on to a gallery and then to my rendezvous as a Geisha. There in his studio, my kimono hung on the side of an Art Deco screen, I was soon in it – at first primly draped as a Japanese virgin, then one breast exposed and then taken on the floor in various positions.

Escaping the governess was easy – Jennifer just said she was going to a museum or a shop, and the new-found freedom was intoxicating. When the Viennese sojourn drew to an end, she begged her new family to keep her on, weeping each night with dread of returning to England. Like Gerald many years earlier, she had begun to discover new pleasures far from home, released from her family's expectations and repressions. Gerald had also been sixteen when he went to France and began to develop into the person he wished to be. Although Jennifer's experiences might have been more daring, they both shared a powerful sense of awakening. Such was Jennifer's misery when she left that she became sick and feverish on the journey home. On her arrival in London she was put to bed 'without seeing my parents, who had unexpectedly gone to the south of France'. When Geoffrey and Alathea returned, the governess was dismissed for neglecting to supervise her charge, although Jennifer never learned what they found out.

OT LONG AFTER Jennifer's catalytic trip, she fell in love again – this time with a young man her father had met on his way to a conference in Canada.

He was a regular soldier, an Olympic athlete and very handsome. I tossed and turned in my bed, fantasising, but he was too correct and my father seemed to disapprove of my schwerm as it was called in Vienna.

Innocently one day, as I was sitting on my mother's bed, I said, 'Why is father so irritable and disapproving when I look at John or speak about him?' She turned her immense blue eyes on me, slightly twisted her star sapphire ring and said, 'Men sometimes love each other.'

Jennifer was also discovering more about Alathea's secrets.

My mother's only pleasure in life was visits from the doctor, new clothes and jewellery and occasional escapades of which I was made aware by servants' gossip and glances in the other direction when I came into the room. Dim young men came and went . . . Once a very attractive young man with red hair came to stay. He was a nephew of a Cambridge friend of my father's, and this was the excuse, as he had no money or room. He had a brief romance with my mother – Her Last Attachment she called it, and they went to New York together. I hope she was happy. He told me years later he had been in love with me.

Pixie had sustained Jennifer through her childhood and continued to give her the affection and stability her parents were unable to offer, but her natural innocence prevented Jennifer confiding in her about what were increasingly daring adventures. Pixie still acted as chaperone, and Jennifer continued to run circles around her adoring governess. Fortunately she found the perfect friend in Violet Wyndham. Violet was old enough to be Jennifer's mother, but understood all about problematic families, and offered a perfect haven of fun, sympathy and intelligence to Jennifer at Parliament Piece, her home not far from Oare. Violet's mother was the novelist and literary hostess Ada Leverson, famous for being a supporter and friend – 'The Sphinx' – to Oscar Wilde before and after his disgrace. Though sought after in her salon, the Sphinx was less of a success as a mother, which doubtless gave Violet insight into Jennifer's problems at home.

Photographs from the time show Violet tall and willowy in chic outfits, draped with fox furs and accompanied by dachshunds. Nobody quite knew her age; like Jennifer when she got older, Violet forged the date of birth on her passports. She was, according to her son, Francis Wyndham, 'social but not snobbish'. Married to a much older man who 'only wanted to play bridge', she provided dinners and weekend house parties for a range of interesting, attractive and often younger people. Her house was the only place in the vicinity that Jennifer's parents approved of her visiting, and the teenager started to spend a great deal of time there. More significant for Jennifer than the social gatherings was the fact that Violet was a wise older woman – almost a substitute mother – who was a sympathetic, dependable and crucially non-judgemental confidante. If she gave advice, it was likely to be: 'You should always go to a party, even if you don't feel like it.' And Jennifer tried to follow that. As a Jew living among a class of English people who were easily anti-Semitic (even her friend Diana Cooper called her 'Auntie Nose' behind her back), Violet probably also knew what it was to feel different – an outsider within an elite. Gradually, as Jennifer came to trust Violet, she arranged to meet her boyfriends at her house, and started to invite along her own friends.

If her Aunt Evelyn had been the perfect 1920s party girl, Jennifer's more voluptuous figure, feminine dresses and flirtatious ways made her the ideal version for the 1930s. With her penchant for sunbathing and easily tanned skin, she followed the fashion for sun worship that marked the decade: sun baths for their 'health-giving rays' and the use of new-fangled suntan oils were all the rage. One of her favourite songs was Cole Porter's 'Experiment', its promotion of curiosity and personal rebellion perfect for this stage of her life. Some saw Jennifer as giddy and superficial: 'She had a throw-away manner. Passing herself off as frivolous was her way of managing her life. But it was deceptive, and covered somebody much more thoughtful,' said one friend who knew her for decades.[256]

In 1934, Alathea managed to get out of bed to ensure that her daughter went through the traditional rite of passage for girls of her background and had a London season. Like Jessica Mitford, who described it as 'the specific, upper-class version of a puberty rite', Jennifer was not excited by the idea of being a deb. Her coming of age was closely allied with creating a distance between her parents and herself, but she went along with the convention of 'coming out'. There were interminable balls, dinners and race meetings, and in May, the

JENNIFER, 1930S PARTY GIRL. SHE WAS VERY LIBERATED AND ENLIGHTENED ON SEX AND WAS ATTRACTED TO MEN WHO WERE 'QUEER'

eighteen-year-old was presented at Buckingham Palace. Along with a crowd of other young women in long white dresses and evening gloves, virginal in their lack of jewellery, she queued up to make the deep curtsey to the sovereign that they had all been practising. In July, *The Times* reported 'Lady Fry's small dance' for her daughter, where the 'decorations consisted of roses, sweet peas, carnations, delphiniums and clarkia'. Jack Harris's band played the latest fashionable dance tunes, like the slow foxtrot 'You Forgot Your Gloves': 'You forgot your gloves / When you kissed me and said goodnight, / So I've brought them, you see, / But don't thank me, it's quite all right.'

As she changed from girl to woman, Jennifer remained close to Prim, her childhood friend, but also fell in with a crowd of young people who were more decadent – beautiful and mostly upper-class, they had been to good schools and had their photographs in *Tatler*. She was particularly attracted to men who were 'queer', as she put it – not

PRIM AND JENNIFER ON A SHIP HEADED FOR HOLIDAYS

necessarily the 'roaring pansies', but those who could play it either way, using ambiguity to their advantage. She was often attracted to the same men as those that caught the eye of her gay friends. Good looks were important to her and smooth-skinned, limber youth was preferable to the macho style of the alpha male. Jennifer's notebooks from when she was undergoing psychoanalysis in her sixties describe her sexual development at this time. In one passage, she turns from the first person to a note-form in the third person to depict how she deliberately encouraged an admirer to make love with her, 'and has first real violent orgasm. Has never known of the clitoris or that form of pleasure, but from then on uses it to full advantage, alone, with girls, but not with great success with men though enjoys love making and thinks herself in love with one or another.'

If Robert had occasional flings with women but was basically gay, Jennifer had occasional flings with women but was basically heterosexual. Jennifer 'had a gay sensibility', said one friend, 'and on the whole, she liked beautiful boys. She could be quite explicit and quite camp.'[257] Another friend recalled that 'She was very liberated and enlightened on sex – rather as people are now. She would have casual sex as well as love affairs. She might go down to the docks in the East End after a party – sometimes her men friends would use her as bait. She liked to peep into that world, and sometimes she'd pick someone up too. She liked the idea of "rough trade", even if it wasn't something she did very much. She wasn't sordid.'[258]

Treading a delicate line between sexual ambiguity and getting involved with men who were never going to end up with a woman, Jennifer fell in love with Hamish St Clair Erskine. A dark-haired, finely built dandy and the son of the Earl of Rosslyn, he was described by Harold Acton as 'an elegant and amiable young social butterfly'.[259] Hamish preferred boys but was happy to string girls along. He had already made Nancy Mitford miserable for years, with their engagement that everyone except Nancy seemed to realise was hopeless. Despite Nancy's perspicacity, she entertained the common but often erroneous belief that Hamish's dalliances with men were youthful peccadilloes, and as in many similar cases, they would surely be replaced in the long term by marriage, children and family life. Whether or not Jennifer had the same illusions is unknown, but she was certainly involved with him.

One of the aesthetes who had been at Oxford in the 1920s with Nancy's brother Tom, Hamish had been sent down for his behaviour. Foppish, frivolous and dedicated to drink, he was pinned to the page as Albert Gates in Nancy's first novel, *Highland Fling*, where he is depicted as wearing crêpe de Chine shirts, taffeta wraps and tartan trousers, while trailing wafts of gardenia perfume. He calls his friends 'Darling', quaffs sidecars at the Ritz and is enamoured of the Victorian era in the fashionably semi-ironic manner of the times. 'Albert disliked women, his views on the sex coinciding with those of Weininger – he regarded them as stupid and unprincipled; but certain ones that he had met in Paris made up for this by a sort of worldly wisdom which amused him, and a talent for clothes, food and *maquillage* which commanded his real and ungrudging admiration.'

Hamish was friends with Gerald and Robert, and he introduced Jennifer to many people who were racy, clever and determined to keep things fun. 'Hamish was a little king in that world depicted by Nancy Mitford and Evelyn Waugh,' remembered Francis Wyndham.[260] Their language and expressions defined them almost as much as the invitations to their parties: 'Darling, how divine' and 'I could-dern't care less.'[261] And they liked to use the word 'Miss' in a camp or ridiculous way: 'Where's Miss Taxi? She's late.' Or 'I just can't get on with Miss Proust.'[262] Never mind if it was all a bit light-hearted and giddy – anything to be amused. Hamish may have found Jennifer amusing in certain similar ways to Nancy. Both had an intelligent wit and dressed with elegance. Yet their astuteness apparently deserted them when it came to getting involved with Hamish. Nancy once admitted, 'Hamish said to me in tones of the deepest satisfaction "You haven't known a single happy moment since we met, have you."' She even made light of an attempt to kill herself: 'I tried to commit suicide by gas, it is a lovely sensation just like taking anaesthetic so I shan't be sorry any more for schoolmistresses who are found dead in that way.'[263] And ultimately, Jennifer would probably have agreed with Nancy's comments in a letter to her brother, Tom. 'How is one to find the perfect young man, either they seem to be half-witted, or half-baked, or absolute sinks of vice or else actively dirty . . . All *very* difficult.'[264]

If Jennifer felt doomed to be a misfit and a failure in the eyes of Sir Geoffrey and Lady Fry, she threw herself even deeper into the hedonistic circles of her new friends that she knew would not please them. In addition to Hamish, there was another unsuitable man called Peter, whose surname remains unknown.

> I had made friends and was also attracted to an amusing young man, also homosexual, who wanted to marry me for my expectations. My father disapproved and feared that Peter knew they shared the same inclinations. He tried to break up our friendship but I followed him to New York, where I received short shrift, as he had got into café society, where I felt I was a fish out of water. I stayed with a friend of my mother's who knew little of the Harlem nights, the clubs and the wild dancing and drinking, though no harm came to me. I lied to her, and said I was going to stay with a respectable couple in Jamaica, but set off with Peter and his raffish friends and generous keeper, on a tour of the islands, then by boat to British Guyana, train to Guatemala, by car through the forests and lakelands and another train to Mexico City.

Photographs from this time show Jennifer tanned and gorgeous, beaming for the camera, arm-in-arm with her fellow travellers. She got drunk on tequila, hardly noticed an earthquake that up-ended the table in a bar, and acquired a pet squirrel that drowned in the lavatory. When a handsome Mexican serenaded her with a guitar under her window, she let him in and took off her clothes, only to find that 'Peter opened my bedroom door and sent him packing and we moved on the next day. He was yet another governess, but more successful as I never made love with the Mexican.' Meanwhile, Sir Geoffrey was sending telegrams to every port they visited, demanding that his errant daughter come home. Eventually she left, travelling alone by boat and returning 'to an icy welcome'.

By the late 1930s, Jennifer was an elegant, cultivated young woman. Her hair was styled, her clothes were chic, and she had a strong sense of how to create beauty around her. Like many of her aesthete friends, she had picked up on the kitsch appeal of Victoriana, and dug around in antique shops for what were still the unfashionable relics of her grandparents' generation: decorated boxes, vases in the shape of hands, and dainty bracelets and rings studded with seed pearls and turquoise. But she was also something of a dandy – a category that might primarily apply to men, but that included a few women such as Nancy Mitford, Edith Sitwell or Nancy Cunard. Jennifer's interests went further than a narcissistic dedication to style, but she was developing something of a reputation: 'Where would it get her, all of this running around with queers?' Certainly not the right sort of husband, murmured the older, more experienced society types.[265]

Life was not unpleasant; there were certainly thrills, even if they were within the tightly drawn boundaries of Jennifer's particular world. While she still lived with her parents in Sloane House and at Oare, she was increasingly independent, if necessarily reliant on her father for financial support. Her parents may have sensed that their daughter understood about their more shameful secrets and they were unable to exert much pressure on her to conform. There were parties, weekends away, and trips to the South of France or Majorca, where she sported a daring two-piece swimming suit. She continued to read voraciously and to attend the ballet whenever she could – she was a great fan of the Ballet Russe de Monte Carlo.

Many years after the first generation of Bright Young Things, Jennifer was taking on their mantle, drinking late into the night at the Cavendish, where Gerald had entertained the original Russian Ballet and where Cyril Connolly was still gossiping with the irrepressible owner, Rosa Lewis, just as he had when he came down from Oxford in the 1920s. By 1937, Jennifer was included on one of Cyril Connolly's many and frequently changing lists of significant friends, which also included the Betjemans, 'Wiz' (W. H. Auden), 'Pierre' (Peter Watson, who would fund *Horizon* magazine) and the writer Peter Quennell. Although many of the names left the lists over the years, Jennifer's remained: Cyril adored her for the rest of his life, and their *amitié amoureuse* sustained them both. Thirteen years older than Jennifer, Cyril was already a successful literary critic – a romantic cynic, a melancholic wit and a chubby, snub-nosed dandy who almost made a profession of depicting himself as a failure. It is easy to understand his attraction to Jennifer on physical grounds; years later he wrote to her recalling 'the brown-gold evening dress you had in the War and those lovely hands and tiny feet'.[266] Continuing the colour scheme that he adored, he also eulogised her voice, that some found 'actress-y' or affected; Cyril said it was 'like a brown sunny stream with a smell of pine needles as one finds in the Lande'.

But their friendship went much further than Cyril's romantic admiration. Both wanted the shifting excitements of nightclubs and parties and the indulgent giggling and gossiping of intimate friendship combined with periods of retreat into reading and solitary introspection. They loved luxury and beautiful things while abhorring snobbery, and had as strong a depressive streak as a sense of fun. 'If Jennifer had been an actress,' said Cyril's daughter, Cressida Connolly, 'she'd have been a light comedienne – with the intelligence to carry it. A funny person with a tragic side; melancholy but loving life.'[267]

Cyril had been at Oxford with the group of men who already

formed a distinguished generation of writers, and who mythologised their student years: Evelyn Waugh, Graham Greene, Anthony Powell, Henry Yorke (who wrote as 'Henry Green') and Robert Byron. He was confident enough to produce the highly influential and original *Enemies of Promise*, but he claimed he couldn't fit into 'smart Bohemia' and that he hated 'the metallic voguey London', even though many of his friends belonged to these milieux.[268] Like Jennifer, Cyril was at ease with homosexuals; both he and Jennifer were often spotted at the Gargoyle Club or the Café Royal, drinking cocktails with Brian Howard, Cyril's notorious Oxford contemporary. The 'Brightest of the Bright Young Things' in the 1920s, Howard was later thought by some to be de trop, and overly drunk. His early literary promise was never fulfilled and W. H. Auden called him 'the most desperately unhappy person I have ever known'. But Howard was marvellously witty and clever, if mannered, and Waugh scarcely disguised him as the *outré* Anthony Blanche in *Brideshead Revisited*. He dressed impeccably and wafted about in a cloud of delicious perfume, applied from a small bottle he kept in his pocket, given by the celebrated perfumer Mary Chess – his American aunt.

Cyril was already friends with Gerald; their circles overlapped extensively and their shared interests were not only in the arts. Cyril had a similar predilection for unusual pets, favouring lemurs (which he'd allow in his bed and take around in his jacket), a ferret, and once (bought with wedding-present money), a racoon. Like Gerald, Cyril saw himself with a critical eye: each felt he had not used his artistic talents to the full extent, being too fond of the art of living – particularly the high life. Each admitted to being overly concerned with his food to the detriment of his figure, and each could veer swiftly between gloom and gaiety. Like Gerald, Cyril loved travel and spoke several European languages, but he was not an intellectual snob.

Cyril also became friends with Robert, doubtless admiring him for the attributes that he himself lacked, such as physical daring and impressive looks. On one of Cyril's lists for 'A sexy party', he included Robert alongside Jean Harlow and Joan Crawford. It appears that

Robert.

JENNIFER'S RECORD
OF HER STAY AT
FARINGDON IN 1938.
ROBERT MANAGES
TO TAKE ALL THE
INNOCENCE OUT OF
EATING GRAPES

Jennifer shared his opinion. In her photograph album from this period, there are several photographs of Robert. Smooth-skinned and shirtless on a daisy-sprinkled lawn, he looks moody and sexy, his luxuriant dark hair slightly wet from a swim, a stray lock naughtily curled in the middle of his forehead. Next to him in the album is Jennifer in a summer frock, sprawled on what looks like the same grass. She is peeping out mysteriously from behind her hair that tumbles over her face. They both look relaxed and very attractive – as if they have secrets. Jennifer took him to the Wyndhams' at Parliament Piece, and there are pictures of him with Prim, who accompanied Jennifer on her first visit to Faringdon.

One page in the album is titled 'Faringdon House, Berks. June 27th 1938' – the first time Jennifer stayed there unaccompanied. There are a couple of photographs of the house, and one of the Mad Boy in a greenhouse. He is straining his body upwards so he can eat grapes straight off the vine without using his hands – a wickedly provocative, Dionysian pose for Jennifer, who was presumably the photographer and who remembered the exact date of that

Ingrid Wyndham

Ingrid

Robert Heber Percy + Prin

Elspeth Villiers Stewart & Ingrid

weekend. Did they have some kind of fling? Probably – though there is no hard evidence apart from the expressions on their faces and the fact that both were sexual buccaneers whose bodies were their boats.

Robert would surely have taken Jennifer to the stables to meet his adored horse Passing Fancy, which he had ridden in the Grand National. The racer was a beautiful animal, and so swift that Robert tended to find himself alone and ahead with the hounds when out hunting with the Old Berks. Robert's tall, thin groom, Fred Shury, lived over the stables with his short, plump wife. Shury claimed the animal was so intelligent that it 'nearly talks to you', coming up to him and trying to say, 'Where's the apples?'[269]

Of course, life was about to change irrevocably. The following year was 1939, and much of what was taken for granted would soon look like elements of a lost, distant civilisation.

CHAPTER TEN

In the City
of the Dreaming Dons

'HE SUMMER OF 1939 SHONE with a halcyon light,' recalled Daphne Fielding. People were giving more parties than ever, fearing they might be the last. 'The atmosphere was tense and feverish, no one dared to pause and the music went round and around.'[270] You could get dizzy, wrote another young party-goer, watching them 'all swivelling round, powder, rouge, & tulle, & crepe – the black cloth, the red carnations, the pearl & onyx studs, the smell of expensive hair oil & Chanel *numéro cinq*'.[271] Hitler's tanks had entered Prague in March, Neville Chamberlain was making desperate attempts to avert war, and in July Mosley held a huge rally at Earls Court, trying to whip up anger: 'A million Britons shall not die in your Jews' quarrel.' Mosley's wild-eyed ranting was making his fanaticism clearer than ever.

At Faringdon, all the old friends were still turning up for the indulgent, piquant weekends they had come to expect. Doubtless they 'howled with laughter' (as the Mitfords often put it) over reports of Cecil Beaton's latest project, *My Royal Past* – a spoof memoir of a Baroness von Bülop that parodied the reminiscences of European royals. The book would be published at the end of the year and contained photographs of numerous old friends who had gathered for elaborate photographic sessions, dressing up in *belle époque* costumes as the Baroness and her ghastly titled relations. Gerald appeared as King Boris, with fake beard and pompously swathed in ermine, Michael Duff as a ramrod-straight

FREDERICK ASHTON, ROBERT, MAIMIE, CONSTANT LAMBERT, GERALD,
VSEVOLODE, 'PRINCE OF RUSSIA', AT FARINGDON, EASTER 1939

military man with a sash, epaulettes and medals, and Frederick Ashton
posed in convincingly aristocratic dowager drag.

In April, Gerald's ballet *Cupid and Psyche* was premiered at
Sadler's Wells, with musical direction by an increasingly drunken and
unwell Constant Lambert, and choreography by Ashton. The original
myth was turned into a frivolous, sometimes farcical performance
that divided audiences: Juno was a pantomime dame, Venus 'a rather
shop-soiled floozy', and Jupiter gave Fascist salutes and strutted with
goose-steps – more chilling than amusing given the political climate
in Europe.[272] The production was generally judged a failure – the
audience booed and the whole thing felt more like a private joke than a
fully fledged creation. In these worrying times, 'the cult of frivolity had
backfired'; *Cupid and Psyche* folded after only three performances.[273]

Not long after this theatrical flop, Maimie Lygon got married to

Prince Vsevolode, a nephew of the last Tsar who had fled Russia after the revolution and ended up in England, where he attended Eton and Oxford. Although 'Vsev' was penniless and could not compete with Maimie on looks, his background added to his glamour and Maimie was happy to become Princess Romanovsky-Pavlovsky, though some thought it sounded like a stage name.[274] Maimie's old friend Evelyn Waugh disliked the 'intolerable Russian', but he was generally welcomed into her social circle, though he drank as much as she did and didn't make her happy. The couple stayed at Faringdon several times during 1939, including a couple of weeks after their wedding, where they posed for photographs and signed the visitors' book as 'Vsevolode, Prince of Russia' and 'Mary Pavlovsky'.

One August weekend, the sole guest was Gerald de Gaury, a forty-two-year-old explorer, orientalist and diplomat. Suave and scholarly, he had fought at Gallipoli, been wounded several times, and awarded the Military Cross. During his extensive travels in Arabia, he not only learned fluent Arabic, but came to deeply love the people and the region, which he photographed, painted and later wrote about in several books. The British government sent him to Kuwait as political agent in the 1930s, and he was a special emissary to King Ibn Sa'ud, who liked him and allowed him to stay in the royal household. With conflict looming, the War Office had just appointed de Gaury to manage intelligence and counter-intelligence in Arabia. Petroleum had been discovered there the previous year and the British were keen to keep things sweet with the King.

It seems likely it was over this August weekend that de Gaury decided to take the Mad Boy with him to the Arabian peninsula. The former soldier knew what was coming and Robert would surely have feared that his call-up papers might arrive at any time, as they would for nearly all the male staff at Faringdon. De Gaury must have told Gerald and Robert about the romance of the desert: fine horses, hunting gazelles with falcons, and the legendary, warm-hearted generosity of the King, who had forty-five sons. 'He gives away motor-cars as European royalties used to give tie-pins and Negro servants as they gave boxes of cigars. Gold daggers and watches are frequently sent to visitors at their departure. The *kiswa*, a camel-hair cloak, head-kerchief, and gown, or set of clothes, is sent to every guest leaving the Court.'[275] Robert was probably intrigued by the prospect of an exotic journey; if he had already experienced the gift of a motor-car from Peter Watson, he certainly had not been given a Negro servant or ventured into the wilderness. De Gaury's motive in taking such a notoriously unpredictable companion on a delicate intelligence mission is less obvious. Still, the experienced traveller knew how much the Arabs valued good looks ('they are more readily affected by human beauty of face and form than are Europeans, who add other qualities to the list when making up the sum of appeal in fellow beings'), and de Gaury was far from immune to the charms of male youth and beauty himself.[276] Add to this the Arabian appreciation of good breeding, courage and manliness, and the Mad Boy began to look like a useful weapon in the spy's armoury.

F ROBERT WAS PREPARING for a *Boy's Own* adventure, Gerald felt himself on the brink of an abyss that would end everything worthwhile and beautiful about his life. He had been planning a trip to Rome, but that was obviously now impossible. Faringdon would have to be closed up; without staff to run the place and without his Mad Boy, it would not be feasible to stay there. The warnings of what this conflict could bring were horrifying. Bombs would soon be raining down on England and a generation of young men who had been too late for the First World War would now be annihilated. Although Gerald had lived a protected and privileged life far from trenches, bloodshed and grieving, he knew enough about the devastation wrought by one world war to be appalled by the prospect of another.

When Robert left in September, Gerald was almost beside himself with anxiety. But he had to take some decisions: London was too risky and his Halkin Street house was shut up (to be sold by the end of the war); travel abroad was almost impossible; and he tried to rent out Faringdon, though a tenant was never found. Deciding to go to Oxford, he moved in with his old friend Maurice Bowra at the Warden's Lodgings of Wadham College.

A classicist with a devotion to Greece, Bowra was well known in Oxford for his waspish wit, his love of young men, and his exhilarating, audacious conversation that could leave the listener shocked, horrified and thrilled all at once. Anthony Powell described him as 'Noticeably small, this lack of stature emphasized by a massive head and tiny feet', resulting in a Humpty-Dumpty appearance (something that was also said of Gerald). Bowra's humour easily slid over into cruelty; his 'passionate praise and unbridled denunciation of enemies produced an intoxicating effect', and 'he dared say things which others thought or felt, but were prevented from uttering by rules or convention or personal inhibitions'.[277] He wrote outrageously scatological poems about his friends.[278]

A generation of young men in the 1920s and '30s had gathered around Bowra, including Evelyn Waugh, Graham Greene, Harold Acton and Kenneth Clark. John Betjeman claimed to have 'met my friends for life' within Bowra's rooms. Cyril Connolly called him 'Mr Bowra the boarer', though it was clear that the older man 'had developed a mocking, cynical way of treating events because it prevented them from being too painful'.[279] Seen by some as a 'dandified sodomite',[280] Bowra actually appears to have had much less experience in seduction than some supposed. Fearful of blackmail, he claimed that for him, sex was 'inescapably in the head', and that his lust was stirred by fetishism – the white shorts, grey flannel trousers and plimsolls he admired in the student population.[281]

Gerald and Bowra had many things in common, from their stocky physique and love of fine living to their remarkable intellect and razor-sharp humour. Both men were also dogged by insecurity and had troubled sex lives, while revelling in handsome, talented youth. They should have made perfect bachelor companions as the Phoney War dragged on through the autumn of 1939. But Gerald was descending into deep despondency. Everything that provided the foundations for his life appeared to be vanishing, swallowed up by the miserable mix of bureaucratic restrictions and fear that would now dominate everyone's lives. Rationing and petty rules would replace the colourful, luxurious life before the war.

In a notebook of this time, Gerald identified himself with the character of the hedonistic grasshopper, which finds itself dying of hunger when winter arrives in Aesop's fable *The Grasshopper and the Ant*. 'The ant never stops doing its duty. I am not saying anything against doing one's duty as a principle, but one can have too much of it. People who never stop doing their duty are seldom very agreeable people and generally end by doing more harm than good.' Unlike the people who threw themselves into war work, Gerald saw only the quagmire that was enveloping him. Characteristically, though, even at a time of such gloom, his fear of war was evaluated in terms of amusement: 'I can face the idea of annihilation with a certain amount of complacency but there is no doubt that it is an awfully dull idea.'[282]

According to Diana Mosley, Gerald's two greatest anxieties were being cut off from all his friends (he imagined no telephone, post or petrol) and that he would be hurt, not killed, in an air raid. 'He did not fear death, but he greatly dreaded the idea that he might agonize untended, and he wished for a pill which would kill instantly.'[283] There was widespread conversation about what citizens should do on encountering a German parachutist or how to behave in the not unlikely case of invasion. Certain people believed that death would be more welcome than life under the Nazis. Cyril Connolly openly discussed which sleeping draughts might be taken in overdose in the case of a German victory, while Harold Nicolson and Vita Sackville-West agreed to find a 'bare bodkin' for their 'quietus', putting their plans in Hamlet's terms.[284] 'Gerald keeps on asking what is the best form of committing suicide just as if he was asking for a cold-cure,' wrote one friend.[285] For a less dramatic solution, another friend recommended an unusual tranquilliser for general use and discovered by Frederick

Ashton – 'A splendid drug given to dogs to prevent them barking during air raids, it is called "Calm Doggie" and you can buy them in any chemists.'[286]

In his subsequent novel, *Far From the Madding War*, Gerald fictionalised himself as Lord FitzCricket – perhaps a reference to the musical, improvident grasshopper he identified with. He is merciless in his depiction of the bald, stout man whom gossip columnists referred to as 'the versatile peer'. 'When he was annoyed he looked like a diabolical egg', due to the 'peculiar slant of the eyebrows.' Lord FitzCricket admits that for a time, 'the war knocked me out. I felt as if I had been pole-axed. I was unable to do anything at all . . . I couldn't compose music, I couldn't write or paint. It all seemed to have become so pointless. I believed it was the end of everything and certainly of people like me.'

Although Gerald felt his creativity had been sapped, he managed to stay active, taking on a part-time job at the Taylor Institution Library in St Giles'. 'The war has set me back mentally a bit,' he admitted in a letter to Cecil Beaton, 'and cataloguing books is about all I'm good for at the present moment. One must have something to do every minute of the day. Otherwise it's hell.' Over the first winter of the war, Gerald helped catalogue two collections of books recently acquired by the Institution – the Montgomery collection of German books and the Moore collection of volumes of Dante. Transcribing the authors and titles onto index cards, Gerald had plenty of time to think about Germany and Italy, the two European countries whose cultures and languages he treasured and whose citizens were now enemies. His old friends were now 'Krauts' or 'Fascist Wops'. 'I like everything to be nice and jolly and I hate to think of people hating one another,' confessed Lord FitzCricket.

Things didn't work out with Bowra – some suspected the don might have been too boisterous for Gerald in his nervy state – and by mid-1940 Gerald had found lodgings in a small house at 22 St Giles'. His rooms looked out at the memorial commemorating the dead from the First World War and the gloomy graveyard of the twelfth-century

church after which the road is named. Even the irrepressible John
Betjeman wrote:

> Intolerably sad, profound
> St Giles' bells are ringing round,
> They bring the slanting summer rain
> To tap the chestnut boughs again . . .

Miss Alden, Gerald's tall, bony landlady, brought austerity food
to his dim, ground-floor rooms. She was kind to her unusual and
distinguished tenant, even if some did see her as a 'dragonish' bully.[287]
Given Gerald's miserable mood, she appears to have been useful as a
guard-dog to stop unwanted visitors; 'Miss Alden wouldn't like that'
precluded all sorts of meetings. Apparently, on Robert's return from
Arabia, she never refused him, on the assumption that he must be
Gerald's illegitimate son.[288]

The slide into *accidie* was not unfamiliar to Gerald, but this time
it was more severe and lasted longer. With so little in which to find
hope or joy, it was hard to return to normality. To make matters worse,
Gerald's habitual (and groundless) worries about money increased due
to his psychological state. 'Like some other rich men, when depressed
he had an odd conviction that he was on his way to the work-house.'[289]
He believed, like one of the characters in his story *Mr Pidger*, that one
of the chief advantages of being rich was that it enabled one 'to ignore
the follies and wickedness of the human race'. This no longer looked
possible, money or not. 'If only all this were just a nightmare!' he wrote
to Gertrude Stein in December. He even confessed to Cecil Beaton
that he wished he could find God: 'I think it might help – but He
seems so very far off just now.' Penelope Betjeman had a mass said for
him at Uffington, but it didn't bring Him any closer.

In the desperation and self-loathing of a serious depression, Gerald
decided to undergo psychoanalysis, something that had been gaining
popularity since the 1920s. 'Four times a week I visited an amiable
Viennese Jewess, a pupil of Freud, and lay on a sofa in a small room
in the Woodstock Road and was invited to say anything that came into

my head (free association), evoke early memories and recount my dreams.' It was significant that while birds brought an enormous degree of pleasure to Gerald's existence, he announced: 'The first discovery I had was that I had a dead bird inside me . . . Walking with my nurse in the fields I came across a dead swallow. It was my first sight of death.'

Gerald began to keep a dream notebook and the intensity is remarkable. Birds crop up frequently, sometimes horrifically: 'Dark courtyard in the snow. I slip and fall. Near me what I take to be two large birds fighting. One of the combatants is a raven the other an evil looking little man. The raven is getting the worst of it. The little man says it will make a good stew.' Friends and relations also appeared to him at night, as did familiar places, including Rome and Paris. Michael Duff, Lady Colefax and Harold Nicolson all pop up, the latter in a garden of fruit trees, beyond which is a fat woman swimming, 'Very naked – an enormous breast exposed and is wearing a black picture hat . . . also a very fat man bathing.' In brilliant sunshine on the Riviera, he is reminded 'of the Casati and think of what she was and what she is now'. In another dream his chauffeur, William, is indistinguishable from Robert when he is trying to pack a suitcase. The dream makes clear the intimacy he felt with William Crack and his reliance on Robert for practicalities. Gerald always addressed his loyal driver as 'William', unlike the other servants whom he called by their surnames, and he was doubtless sad to have seen him go soon after the move to Oxford.[290] In reality, William and Robert could hardly have been more different and the chauffeur's gentle manners often clashed with the Mad Boy's fiery chaos.

Places in his dreams are very precisely described – another indication of how settings and scenery were almost as significant as people to him: 'Diana Mosley and I go to Germany. We are walking through a field with long grass and a fringe of trees lining a road behind us. We ask to see Hitler. We are standing at the top of a flight of steps in front of a glass door. Hitler comes out and shakes hands with us. Very politely but there is no attempt at conversation. He then goes back.'

Some of Gerald's dreams are mildly erotic. He runs up the slopes of a sunny hill that resembles White Horse Hill 'with a sensation of great ease – (sexual). Two women lying on the grass – slightly lesbian in appearance. I want them to admire the way I run.' At another time, a rather pretty adolescent face on a scrap screen 'suddenly materialises into a real adolescent standing next to me. I lay my face against his and find that it is smooth and cool. We go out of the room together.'

In his fiction, Gerald made a joke out of his dealings with a 'trick cyclist', as psychiatrists were known in army parlance. Lord FitzCricket describes psychoanalysis as having 'the same sort of charm as going to a fortune-teller . . . You lie on a sofa and talk about yourself for hours and hours. That in itself is exhilarating for the Ego. All sorts of curious things were found in my Unconscious; a stuffed bird, a pair of gloves, a black rubber mackintosh, in fact the whole contents of a jumble sale. No wonder I felt queer.' Having got the hang of the jargon, Gerald does it to death for effect: 'Another thing the analyst found out was that my death-instincts were getting the better of my pleasure principle, and that it was something to do with my Oedipus-complex. It just shows how mistaken one can be about oneself. When I used to feel like that before I always thought it was my liver.'[291]

URING THE DARKEST PERIOD of Gerald's life, Robert was off on his most adventurous undertaking. Saudi Arabia was just as extraordinary as de Gaury had said, and they were treated as honoured guests of Ibn Sa'ud. Robert was kitted out in appropriate clothes – a dark camel-hair cloak, a silken Arab robe and a loose white turban. In his writings, de Gaury explained that men were also heavily scented (often with rose-water) and their 'eyelids were blued with "kohl"'. There is a powerful homoerotic tinge to his descriptions of the handsome young men, whether galloping across the sands or emerging from a tent into the cold dawn. Even more alluring are the scenes at the oasis:

By the reed-bordered pool a young man who had been bathing squatted
to comb out his uncut curls. I watched him part them, three long plaits
falling on either side down to his breast. As he finished he bent forward
from his haunches to use the pool as a watery glass. Then he drew
himself up erect in one movement, to stand straight and taut, his well-
muscled body gleaming in the setting sun.[292]

De Gaury took numerous photographs of Robert, posing in
native attire by just such a desert pool, a small beard adding gravitas,
cigarette in his gracefully slim hand. It was not long before the young
man disrobed and waded into the warm water naked – something
de Gaury didn't fail to snap. Later, Robert told friends that he 'was
given code books to look after and had lots of gold for King Saud', and
that 'it was very hot and the code books were very heavy'. As it was a
secret expedition, linked to Britain's national interests in the region,
extremely little is available on record. Robert was a notoriously bad
letter-writer and almost nothing remains of anything he wrote, so there
is frustratingly little of his own assessments and emotions. This lacuna
makes his letter to Gerald that November all the more interesting and
worth quoting in full, notwithstanding the poor grammar:

Darling G.

I have just arrived here from Jedda on the Red Sea, it took six days the
King had us sent up with a huge cavalcade, we started with 4 saloon
cars and six lorries, tents, kitchens and such like. We had about thirty
servants, and a guard of thirty soldiers, the answer to it all was we were
frightfully uncomfortable and everything broke down, no road just
a track for 300 miles, terrible going we were shaken to bits, after 300
miles we were decanted on to the desert, and put on camels it was very
impressive and awfully funny if we hadn't ached so much the second
day on camels was hell, if I didn't know that I should just die in the
desert I should have dropped off, we covered 100 miles in two days on
camels you tell that to Penelope [Betjeman] and I had never ridden one
before. The last day cars met us from Riaydh [sic] and took us to the

ROBERT POSING FOR GERALD DE GAURY BY AN OASIS IN ARABIA

Palace where we are staying with the King, you have never stayed in a Palace with a King, even though the Palace is built of mud?

I go for my audience with the King this evening and wear my Arab clothes which I look rather impressive in. I have got a lot of photographs but they can't develop them here so they will have to go to Cairo and come back, so it will be a very long time before you get them. Do you realize how grand it is to be here, only Twelve Europeans have ever been here I am the Twelfth. There is an American doctor here, so there is just De Gaury, Doctor and myself. I told you in my last letter that one is not allowed to wear European clothes, smoke or drink Alcohol. The people are very wild and long to kill all foreigners, so we have to be very inconspicuous and can only go out with a guard.

I have had no letters from you that are dated latter [sic] than 15th Oct. I hope I shall get one soon, as I miss them very much. There is a caravan leaving for Basra on the Persian Gulf tomorrow so I am giving it to them to take to the Br[itish] Council there, who I have asked to put it on Imperial Airways which stop there from India so I hope you will get this fairly quickly. I'm afraid that most letters to and fro will take a hell of a time. I do hope you are well and are happier now. I have not had much time to be unhappy, but when I ever am still I could cry. I hate this bloody abroad and being away from you and Faringdon, but still I'm very lucky so far.

Will you tell Morris [the head gardener] to cover up the *burners* if has not already done so.

De Gaury sends his best wishes. Please write often and cheer me up. I don't think the £60 the Government gave me for my horse has ever been paid into my bank, would you let me know. I am going to write a book, while I'm here, so you had better all look out!

The King is a great character, very good looking and has been very kind to us, and so have all his ministers, in fact it is a beautiful country.

Best love Robert

The Mad Boy doesn't sound very mad, even if he is not an elegant writer. He is homesick for Faringdon and Gerald, occasionally sounding more like a lost boy, veering between youthful pride at his derring-do and lonely tears. This burning Arabian desert was another world, the green fields of Berkshire or Shropshire as far away as Dorothy's Kansas from the Land of Oz. Predictably, Robert's threat to write a book never materialised, but it hints at the inadequacy he felt next to Gerald's intellectual accomplishments, and those of so many of their friends. A single page remains of another letter, probably from an earlier date, in which all the housekeeping points are typed up and numbered, perhaps as an ironic joke but also because Robert was keen that Gerald take up some practical matters at Faringdon. He is full of suggestions and evidently worried about Gerald and what he is going to do in a war that has still not seriously got going:

13. Why did you not thank me for the wire I sent you for your birthday [18 September]?
14. Is your house in Rome still let?

15. Had you thought of going there as an honorary diplomat?
16. Have you divided the best pictures all over the house and not stacked them all together?
17. Please see that none of the petrol tins that I stored leak.
18. Will you please forward enclosed letters. You can open them if you wish, but they won't interest you.
19. Tell Simpson to set the water hen trap again. They make excellent soup (they must be skinned first and also it will leave more food for the ducks).
20. Give me news of the ducks.
21. I am sure the Stevens brothers would give you a couple of Mandarin hens to put on the lake and they might breed there.
22. My address is: –

    <u>By Courtesy of Foreign Office</u>
    Robert Heber-Percy
    c/o Captain De Gaury,
    Foreign Office

At night, Robert and de Gaury would sit by the camel-thorn fire, wrapped in their cloaks and drinking bitter coffee after a meal of mutton or chicken with unleavened bread and dates. The old expert entertained his young companion by translating the ballads sung by the guards and Bedouin guides, and telling him Arab tales and explaining local ways. De Gaury enjoyed how easily one forgot 'the daily customs of smoking, of drinking, newspaper-reading, and speaking on a telephone'. He knew all about the Arab preoccupation with *sharaf* – generally translated as 'honour', but covering generosity, good breeding and manliness, and also including learning, courage and good manners.[293] Later, Robert would explain why he had been sent to Saudi Arabia by saying, 'The Arabs like good manners and I have them.' This was certainly not always the case, but he shared something else with them. De Gaury noted the Arab's volatility, marked by patience under physical hardship contrasted with 'sudden rages and excesses'. He may show 'a desire for quick friendliness' and then 'turn on his heel after weeks of companionship, to leave you for ever, with no more than a curt farewell . . .'[294] This could as easily have been written about Robert as the cloaked desert-dwellers.

De Gaury had sensed that something in Robert's nature would fit with the harsh, beautiful place he knew so well. Certainly, a close friend of Robert's in later life believed that his Arabian journey had been a catalytic experience. 'The intense atmosphere of Riyadh was almost a religious experience and confirmed Robert's attitude into one best described as pantheism.'[295] This was the first time that the Mad Boy had been removed from a familiar environment; his previous travels with Gerald had been well within the comfort zone of European culture and often surrounded by friends. This trip, on the other hand, entailed almost the subsuming of self to the wildness and differences of an unfamiliar civilisation. It has been suggested that Robert also carried out some intelligence work in the Balkans, but it is unclear when this would have been and with whom. It is possible that the success of the de Gaury trip led to something else, but sadly, no record remains.

HILE THE BEGINNING OF THE WAR appeared to mark the end of a worthwhile life for Gerald, Jennifer, like Robert, was swept up into new and formative experiences. Jennifer's parents were deeply disturbed by the war, each reacting in different ways: Geoffrey had a nervous breakdown, while Alathea became a Catholic. She was received into the Church by Father D'Arcy, a well-known Jesuit priest and Oxford-based philosopher linked to several famous conversions to Rome, including Evelyn Waugh's.

Jennifer left Oare to stay with Violet Wyndham at Parliament Piece as a paying guest. She took the bus into Swindon each day to learn shorthand and typing at a secretarial college and the teenage Francis would test her with passages from Proust. In 1940, Jennifer moved to Oxford, ending up in an airy two-bedroom flat at 6 Beaumont Street, a few minutes from where Gerald was lodging. Aged twenty-three, she got her first 'proper job' as a secretary, though there is no record of exactly where. One friend suggested it was at Blenheim, where MI5 was evacuated,[296] though later she said that she worked as a typist in a hospital. She learned to cook and keep house and decorated her flat with flair and subtle good taste. Alathea made sure that, whenever possible, something was sent from the farm at Oare – a cheese or some eggs to supplement meagre rations.

While Gerald felt that everything light and alluring would disappear during the war, Jennifer managed to maintain her style. As with Gerald and many of his friends, frivolity was an element in her rebellion – what some now saw as superficial, insignificant details like scent and clothes remained important to her. Even during the dullest years of clothes rationing and 'Make Do and Mend' slogans, Jennifer remained a glamorous figure. A fortuitous friendship with the dressmaker Pauline Hansford ensured that she was wonderfully dressed, and she used perfumes like Gardenia by Mary Chess, whose 'little luxuries' ('Roman' bath oils and 'friction lotions' as well as perfumes made from natural ingredients) had been popular throughout the 1930s and which were now all the more desirable.

Although Jennifer was determined to look good, life was not easy as the war took hold. Petrol was now rationed, and windows had to be blacked out at night, which became as depressing as it was inconvenient – even chinks of light could get you in trouble with the wardens. More worryingly, large numbers of male friends were disappearing off into the terrifying and opaque machinery of warfare. There were trips up to London for a party or to meet people at the Café de Paris – famous for the best cabarets, including the black band-leader Ken 'Snake Hips' Johnson – but the supposedly safe underground restaurant received a direct hit in 1941 and Snake Hips was killed along with many of the clientele. London was becoming increasingly dangerous and damaged, even if some did believe in the 'love-charm of bombs', and their contribution to seduction.[297] There were comical and surreal episodes – when the zoo was bombed, an escaped zebra reached

Marylebone before it was recaptured – but many, including Harold Nicolson, were fearful of 'being buried under huge piles of masonry and hearing the water drip slowly, smelling the gas creeping towards me . . .'[298]

With large numbers of Londoners escaping to Oxford and elsewhere, it was often tempting to stay put. At her flat, Jennifer read a huge amount, particularly contemporary British writers like Elizabeth Bowen, Henry Green and Evelyn Waugh, and she took refuge in music. She had a large collection of gramophone records: lots of Mozart, but also ballet music and popular recordings – American jazz singers like Billie Holiday and Ella Fitzgerald and the latest Broadway hits. She particularly liked anything by the 'young waif' of Paris, Agnès Capri, whom she had seen performing in the South of France. A rival to Edith Piaf, Capri sang in nightclubs and had a good line in ironic love songs, including 'Mes soeurs, n'aimez pas les marins' ('Sisters, never love a sailor') with lyrics by Jean Cocteau – 'As soon as they've come they go'. For dancing and parties, the most popular thing was the West Indian calypso, with its witty, clever lyrics and irrepressible rhythms. 'Edward the VIII' by the Trinidadian Lord Caresser had come out a couple of years earlier, but was still going strong: 'It's love, love alone / That caused King Edward to leave the throne.'

Oxford had changed enormously since the beginning of the war and by 1941 was 'in a state of mutilation; an extension of the Ministry of Food and Agriculture, the place swarming with civil servants carrying gas-masks'.[299] Most of the students and young dons had been called up, so there was a very different university population, with many younger and female undergraduates arriving and with students often studying only for a short time. Age-old enmities, like those between 'hearties' and aesthetes, now seemed irrelevant. 'Life in college was austere. Its pre-war pattern had been dispersed, in some instances permanently. Everyone paid the same fees . . . and ate the same meals.'[300] There were also numerous bureaucrats, medics and students who had been transferred from London, not to mention the European refugees. 'Czechs, Austrians and Germans crowded the pavements', and 'Women from Whitechapel treated their perambulators as tanks and mowed down everything before them.'[301]

Before long, planes were buzzing over Oxford day and night, and Australian and Canadian soldiers arrived 'who roared about all day long in cars with camouflage fishnets in which branches and bright green paper fuzzy stuff were stitched'.[302] New red-brick air-raid shelters appeared all over the city, and the charmed, indulgent days remembered by Oxford alumni now appeared extinct. Evelyn Waugh believed it part of a vanishing world that, along with large country houses and privileged aristocratic families, was worthy of memorialising in *Brideshead Revisited*. Ministry of Food regulations ensured a dull and restricted diet; Sebastian's plovers' eggs were long gone. Now it was tins of powdered hens' eggs if you were lucky.

One of Jennifer's closest friends was a pivotal figure in Oxford. Wilhelmine 'Billa' Harrod was four years older than her, fiercely opinionated, religiously devout, and already becoming a pillar of the architectural conservation world. But she also knew how to have fun – through the 1930s she had been just as enthusiastic a party girl as Jennifer. John Betjeman had fallen for Billa during his engagement to Penelope and remained a close friend, calling her 'my Turkish Delight' for her curvy figure and dark hair. And nobody could forget Billa's striptease, when she swung from a huge chandelier at a house party of Joan Eyres Monsell,* the clever, beautiful daughter of the First Lord of the Admiralty.[303]

In 1938, Billa had married Roy Harrod, a somewhat older historian and economist, and fellow of Christ Church. They quickly established themselves as a sparkling and gregarious couple at their house opposite the college. Socially confident and with the ability to dominate her friends, Billa was seen by some as having a tendency to bossiness: 'Billa was running Oxford,' quipped one friend.[304] The Harrods' circle included not only erudite and amusing dons such as Maurice Bowra and Isaiah Berlin, but also students and

* Later Rayner, then Leigh Fermor.

figures from the literary and social world like Nancy Mitford and Cyril Connolly.

Billa and Roy were already close to Gerald; indeed, he had hoped to go and stay with them in Oxford after he left Bowra's lodgings. Roy's letter from May 1940 makes it clear why that couldn't happen:

Dear Gerald,

Billa has been telling me that you might come and take up your quarters with us at 91 S. Aldates. It is a delightful idea and there is no one whom we should like so well to have.

But at the moment there is an obstacle. Billa is expecting a baby some time in September. That means the house being upside down with a monthly nurse in residence, presumably in the room which would otherwise be yours, and Billa unable for a considerable period to do housekeeping.

Some claim that Billa was an inspiration for Nancy Mitford's Fanny, the narrator in *The Pursuit of Love*. In 1941, Nancy reported on Oxford to her sister Diana after staying with the Harrods: 'Oxford society is very pleasant I think, everybody so amiable & nice, most unlike what one would imagine such a small highly cultivated world to be. Gerald has taken up his residence there. Apparently he has a mania for tea-shop life & Billa says it is a kind of task, undertaken in turns, to face Gerald across rather grubby check tablecloths at mealtimes.'[305]

Clearly this 'task' was something of a chore for Gerald's friends; the combination of his miserable spirits and the sparse offerings of the tea shops was far less appealing than teas in the drawing room at Faringdon. There was a whole set of particular and unexpected problems for those civilians left 'holding the fort'.

By 1941, many of Gerald's younger friends had joined the forces, though a few had not. John Betjeman volunteered for the RAF, but was allegedly turned down after telling the psychologist he was terrified of spiders. Following a year at the Ministry of Information, he was sent to Ireland as press attaché at the British Embassy and he and Penelope left for Dublin.[306] Cyril Connolly had started what was to become the hugely influential literary magazine *Horizon* in 1940, funded by Peter Watson, whose flamboyant millionaire's life was suspended in the name of art. As Cyril later wrote, 'he stepped, gay and delightful, out of a charmed existence like a Mayfair Buddha suddenly sobered by the tragedy of his time to become the most intelligent and generous and discreet of patrons, the most creative of connoisseurs, the possessor of a formative flair which sought out everything that was contemporary, international and alive in painting and music'.[307]

Cyril regarded *Horizon* as vital war work, and had direct access to a broad web of talented friends and acquaintances, including Stephen Spender as associate editor. Within ten weeks, the first issue of the small magazine that was to become 'a major contribution to the cultural life of the nation' was out. Printed on rationed paper (help came from Harold Nicolson at the Ministry of Information), it included pieces by W. H. Auden, George Orwell and Dylan Thomas. There would be art by many of the leading artists and photographers of the day: Barbara Hepworth, Graham Sutherland, John Craxton, Lucian Freud, Cecil Beaton, Bill Brandt, Paul Nash and many more.[308] Gerald later contributed a literary critical piece and two poems to the magazine, including his 'Surrealist Landscape', dedicated to Dalí, and the poignantly witty 'The Performing Mushroom', dedicated 'To Professor Jebb, author of *Inedible Fungi, the Toadstool and all about it*, etc., etc.'

Cyril was keen to promote young writers in the magazine and included the then unknown Denton Welch, who wrote about meeting the elderly painter Walter Sickert just before his death. When Welch, in bad health and fated to die young, tried to attract patronage from Gerald as he had from Cyril, he was disappointed. He had painted a bizarre and touching portrait of Gerald as a boy, dressed up as Robinson Crusoe, in shaggy goatskin with a macaw on his shoulder, basing it on a photograph in *First Childhood*. Inviting Gerald to his room at the Randolph Hotel in Oxford, he hoped the eccentric peer would buy the work, but Gerald, uncomfortably shy, took snuff 'furiously' from a gold box and made no offer for the painting, which then failed to sell at an exhibition.[309] Nonetheless, Gerald later encouraged the young man with his writing and Welch managed to get something out of the awkward and disappointing meeting, writing it up for *Time and Tide* as 'A Morning with the Versatile Peer Lord Berners in the Ancient Seat of Learning'.

OBERT RETURNED FROM HIS Arabian expedition in early 1940 to find himself confronted with the prospect of having to enlist. Moving rapidly from the sublime to the mundane, he entered the Army as a private in May 1940. This was an unusual choice for someone of his background, but less surprising given his lack of enthusiasm for discipline; the fiasco of his officer-training days in 1931 probably returned to haunt him. Travelling to Brighton, he joined the Royal Sussex Regiment, where he was duly weighed, measured, inspected ('Scar 3½ inches long oval upper patella, scar left groin'), questioned ('Religious Denomination: C of E . . . Occupations: Independent'), and given a number ('Private 6404613').

Gerald was terribly worried when Robert enlisted. Even without the horrendous slaughter of trench warfare, casualties were inevitable and news of death and injury was already a dreadful part of daily life. In the event, the Mad Boy never left England and few in his regiment saw active service, but such an unchallenging war was far from guaranteed at this stage in the hostilities.

Just when Gerald might have taken another turn for the worse, he met a new young friend with whom he was so taken that some thought she might even replace the Mad Boy. Clarissa Churchill was poised, slim and feline, with sharp, almond eyes, and known to be very intelligent. And she was only nineteen. Winston Churchill's niece, she had moved to Oxford at around the same time as Gerald. Billa thought her 'terribly attractive, and gay, and young, and pretty. And I remember Gerald really rather liked her and we almost thought in a sort of dotty moment that he might marry her . . .'[310] The new arrival was keen to do some studying and in the informal climate of the time, Roy Harrod quickly fixed Clarissa up with Freddie Ayer as a philosophy tutor. She could not have been less like the young female undergraduates Philip Larkin depicted in his novel *Jill*, 'carrying bulky handbags and enormous tattered bundles of notes; they smelt inimitably of face powder and (vaguely) Irish stew'. Clarissa was sophisticated and worldly beyond her years and she soon found herself at the heart of Oxford society. She was a frequent visitor at the home of Lord David Cecil, an old friend of her mother's, a fellow of New College and the younger son of the Marquess of Salisbury. Tall, lanky, clever and kind, he had a voice 'like a crate of hens carried across a field'.[311] David and his wife, Rachel, regularly gathered a stimulating group of people for dinners: Isaiah Berlin, Maurice Bowra, the Harrods, and on their visits to Oxford, Cyril Connolly and Stephen Spender. In spite of rationing, they somehow managed to feed their guests; pudding was usually sorbet made from Ribena, available without coupons from the chemist.[312] Although there is no evidence, it is highly likely that as a close friend of Billa's, Jennifer found herself at some of these evenings, even if she was sometimes intimidated by high-powered intellectuals, who reminded her of her father's disapproving attitudes.

In a corner of the Cecils' drawing room, Clarissa noticed 'there was often a small bald-headed man who rarely spoke and sat with bowed head. I eventually asked David who this character was and he said, "He's called Lord Berners. He's having a nervous breakdown."'[313] An unlikely pair, Gerald and Clarissa were soon intimates. She was attractive and opinionated; he was forlorn but full of surprises. 'He never opened up,' recalled Clarissa, 'but I didn't need that in a relationship. He was basically shy and his jokes were a defence against intimacy.'[314] It wasn't long before he had taken her by taxi to Faringdon and Clarissa was amazed at seeing the 'ravishing' eighteenth-century house. On another occasion, presumably when Robert was on leave, she noticed 'a figure in private's uniform' walking about outside, 'but never approaching us'. Asking Gerald who it was, he replied, 'Oh, that's my agent.'

'Who's that girl?' asked Penelope Betjeman of Clarissa Churchill, here posing under Gerald's instruction as a statue in a niche

Later, opening a drawer in the library, Clarissa came upon a pile of photographs, including famous characters such as Diaghilev, Stravinsky, Gertrude Stein, the Sitwells and William Walton. She would also have spotted 'the agent' in rather different circumstances. 'I was completely astonished,' she confessed. 'I had no idea about Gerald's past life.'[315] It is strange that Gerald should have kept Robert from Clarissa, though it appears that Robert was suspicious and even jealous of Gerald's relationship with the Prime Minister's niece, so perhaps there was avoidance on his part, and Gerald was merely being discreet. (In a magazine interview, Gerald later listed his 'favourite virtue' as 'tact'.)[316] 'Gerald never demonstrated affection,' Clarissa recalled. 'He was old-fashioned.'[317] She believed that some of Gerald's other friends were puzzled by the new addition to their ranks. On spotting her in the drawing room on another visit to Faringdon, Penelope Betjeman turned to Gerald and asked truculently, 'Who's that girl?'

Gerald was still gloomy about the war, but from late 1940, he gradually emerged out of his depression and started having weekends back at Faringdon. He bought antiques from Mr John's shop by All Souls in Oxford – Dresden vases with parrots and flowers, silver-gilt owls, cockerels and fish, that eventually decorated his home.[318] David Cecil recalled them reading aloud to each other what they'd been writing and how Gerald was very much part of the 'odd little enclave of society' that had grown up in Oxford since the start of the war. Although Gerald was not a talker in the expansive intellectual tradition, he was appreciated by many of those who were, including the brilliant Isaiah Berlin.[319]

Clarissa returned to London in the spring of 1941 to work in the Foreign Office, but she remained Gerald's favourite guest and there are numerous letters from the ageing man to the young woman, begging her to take the train from London to Faringdon again as soon as possible. 'My dear Clarissa . . . It is heartbreaking to think of you in the catacombs of the Foreign Office with your debutantes and your lentils, blown along the corridors by the blast, together with Lady Colefax like people in Dante's Inferno, instead of being here with us in the City of the Dreaming Dons.'

Gerald began coming back to life. In seventeenth-century Oxford, Robert Burton had recommended music as a treatment in his *Anatomy of Melancholy* and it was this beloved medium that accompanied Gerald's return from the vortex of 'black bile' that had nearly drowned him. There was a piano in his rooms in St Giles' and Gerald played for himself and the occasional visitor. His old friend Winnie, Princesse de Polignac (one of the many refugees from occupied Paris), passed through Oxford and together they went to Christ Church to hear Thomas Armstrong play the organ. Afterwards, Gerald persuaded Armstrong (later Sir Thomas, principal of the Royal Academy of Music) to give him music-theory lessons, in particular to learn the principles of the Renaissance composer Palestrina. Armstrong was impressed: 'His was the most alert and far-seeing brain I've ever had to do with in music.'[320]

Despite his finesse in composition, it has been suggested that Gerald's piano playing was not outstanding, if full of determination and spirit; 'a cross between Mr Toad on a clear highway and Wanda Landowska [a famous harpsichordist] crashing a water-jump,' suggested one critic.[321] Gerald's next composition was a two-piano polka for a 1941 Christmas pantomime (*Cinderella, or There's Many a Slipper*, performed by the Tynchewycke Society to raise money for the Radcliffe Hospital), for which he also composed one of his best-loved comical songs, 'Red Roses and Red Noses'.

In addition to composing, Gerald also found the energy to write no fewer than four novels, albeit slim ones. *Count Omega* is the fantastical story of a young composer (supposedly based partly on William Walton) who becomes obsessed with a youthful giantess, 'whose virtuosity on a trombone seems to offer the perfect climax to a symphony he is composing'. *Mr Pidger* tells a darkly comic tale concerning inheritance and the bad behaviour of a spoilt lapdog. *The Romance of a Nose* is an extraordinary creation about Cleopatra having the world's first nose job to correct her enormous protuberance. Like all his books, it combines a parodic lightness of touch with dark, sinister elements. Gerald's research, even for a slight novel like this, was prodigious. His notebooks are filled with musings and precise historical references to ancient Egypt and Greece ('Thebes, sweet-smelling, medicinal desert plants . . . geese caught by nets or shot with a bow') and details about Hippocrates, Cicero, Asclepiades and Caesar. The title of his book was not immediately obvious and he tried out a list: '*A Royal Nose, The Story of a Nose, The Queen's Nose, A Nose is a Nose* [presumably a playful nudge to his friend Gertrude Stein], *The End of a Nose, Roman Nose.*' There are little sketches, quotes from Dante, thoughts on music and some botanical notes. Sometimes, there is a page given over to the first line of a story that didn't get written: 'Prawling was an old dog who lived in the country . . .'

His next book, *Far From the Madding War*, is dedicated to David and Rachel Cecil, who had cherished Gerald in his darkest times. The novel is based in Oxford during the war and has a good deal of autobiographical content, featuring Lord FitzCricket, Gerald's alter ego. The heroine, Miss Emmeline Pocock, is widely believed to be based on Clarissa, though the ironic descriptions of her absurd choice of 'war work' are pure fantasy. The academic's daughter decides to pick apart an immense and valuable German embroidery, with ample breaks for tea, lunch, rests and perusal of *The Times*. Various other friends make appearances throughout the pages: Harold Nicolson is teased (yet again), appearing as 'Lollypop' Jenkins, a politician who makes mock-heroic speeches and tries to maintain his reputation as an *enfant terrible*. There are also characters apparently based on Penelope Betjeman, Maurice Bowra and Isaiah Berlin.

At last, Gerald was able to put his sadness and frustration into words. Expressing his loathing of war in a poem, 'The Romantic Charter', he describes his yearning for the sensuous and aesthetic pleasures that seem to have vanished. Some aspects of the poem might seem elitist, even snobbish, today; housemaids were now working in arms factories or driving ambulances and would never return to domestic service, and dinners 'all in evening dress' would dwindle along with Britain's colonies. Some of Gerald's rhymes edge towards doggerel, but he meant them. These were the things he loved and desperately missed, and the verses have a freshness and anger that are unlike the light ironies of some of his prose.

> I am not fighting for the Poles or Czechs,
> And only indirectly for the Rex.
> I do not greatly love the Slav or Greek,
> I cannot bear the way colonials speak.
> I loathe efficiency and Nissen huts,
> And as for 'bonhomie' I hate its guts.
> I am not fighting Germans just to get
> My democratic share of 'blood and sweat'.
> Dear Sir,
>   I feel that you may get the gist
> Of all MY War Aims from the following list . . .
> . . . Georgian houses, red repliquas of heaven,
> Split pediments, breakfast at eleven,

Large white peonies in big glass bowls,
Asparagus au beurre, whitebait in shoals,
Close cropped grass, huge trees and cawing rooks,
A sunny breakfast room, a library with books,
Clean white housemaids in new print frocks,
Coachmen turned chauffeur, footmen on the box.
Dinner parties, all in evening dress,
Glamorous women drenched in Mary Chess
Charades and paper games, hot-houses with the heat on,
Superficiality and Cecil Beaton.
Shrimps from Morecambe Bay, port that is tawny,
Claret and Beaujolais, soles that are Mornay,
Hot scones for tea, thick cream, the smell of logs,
Long country walks, thick shoes and spaniel dogs,
Ducks in the evening, swishing swans in flight,
Fires in bedrooms, flickering at night –
And of those *autres fois*, all those *mœurs*
Which are epitomized in '*Valse des fleurs*' –
Fresh shiny chintzes, an herbaceous border –
Death and destruction to this damned new order.

It was around this time that Gerald took to wearing little knitted skullcaps that some compared to tea cosies, while others noted 'a somewhat rabbinical design'. The knitter was Marie Beazley, wife of the noted archaeologist and expert on Greek vases, J. D. 'Jack' Beazley. Mrs Beazley was a mysterious woman with 'iridescent blue hair . . . very black oblique eyes, a long Oriental nose and the curved lips of an Archaic goddess'.[322] She was Jewish, wore overwhelming eastern perfumes, cooked unfamiliar Levantine dishes with rose petals and pistachios, and played Chopin on the piano with great feeling. Though Harold Acton adored her, Mrs Beazley was to some rather a figure of fun; such exoticism was a step too far for tweedy Oxford. There was talk of her *décolleté*, her formidable nose and even a little moustache, not to mention the tame goose that followed her around (and later died after eating the *Daily Mail*). Gerald appears to have enjoyed the Beazleys' company enough to visit them regularly – he surely appreciated the Epicurean and musical elements, and Jack had a lingering nostalgia for the ideals of Grecian youth that had characterised his wilder young days.[323] Certainly, Gerald was happy to wear the caps that warmed his bald pate and gave him an unusual aspect indoors. 'It gives me an air of Ali Baba and startled my landlady the first time she saw me in it,' he wrote with pleasure. The first one, in light green wool, was sent over when Gerald had 'a sharp attack of flu', but others followed in red and various colours and became quite a trademark over subsequent years.

It was through Marie Beazley that Gerald met Gregorio Prieto, a painter, sculptor and poet from Don Quixote's region of La Mancha in south-central Spain. A friend of García Lorca, the forty-four-year-old artist moved to London just before the war, and was introduced to a series of eminent sitters through the Beazleys. In 1941, he made two portraits of Gerald, both striking and capturing the subject's enigma in an interesting style that combines realism with fantasy. The first is a painting in which Gerald sits solemnly, almost miserably, before the sea. He is wearing outsize gloves with red stars, holds a big, gold fish and is topped with one of Mrs Beazley's red tea cosies. The second, more uplifting picture is a pencil drawing of a debonair Gerald in gleaming monocle and bow tie. He clutches a lobster, hinting at the surrealism and jokes he was known for, and pincered in the lobster's claw and clasped in Gerald's hand are butterflies, symbols, surely, of his lightness of touch, but also perhaps his vulnerable psychological state. Gerald once described himself as having a 'lepidopterous' character even if he was fundamentally an introvert.[324] Prieto also drew Clarissa Churchill, cool and girlish, with a book in her hands; Marie Beazley, with blossoms, doves and holding a volume of Dante; and Winston Churchill, staring implacably. Clementine Churchill disliked the portrait of her husband, but bowed to pressure from Clarissa and Gerald and allowed it to appear in a book which came out later, complete with various charming, Cocteau-esque drawings of half-naked youths in shorts.[325]

Meanwhile, the Mad Boy's military service was as patchy as might be expected. His older brother Cyril described a visit to his barracks, when the mention of Robert's name brought a hush to the guards, followed by a summons for the duty-officer. It turned out that Robert was in the guardroom under arrest for stealing a car. 'But he has one of his own,' replied Cyril. 'Is it a large Buick?' 'Yes.'

It emerged that Robert had been stopped by the military police and when asked whose car it was, 'just out of cussedness', replied, 'Whose do you think?' It seemed unlikely that a private would have such a fine model and they locked him up. Later Robert said, 'You know, it was interesting to see what it was like.'[326] According to Cyril, Robert's section 'consisted mostly of cockneys', and given their knowledge of how to work the system and Robert's car, they all had a grand time; 'The NCO in charge was kept well in hand.'

In July 1941, after 1 year and 61 days in uniform, Robert left the Army, discharged under Paragraph 390 (XIV) – 'ceasing to fulfil Army physical requirements. Permanently unfit for any form of military service'. According to Billa, he might have 'got a wound or something' (presumably during training) and was in a military hospital set up in St Hugh's College, Oxford, which specialised in head wounds. It is possible, she added, that 'it was just a sort of nervous thing'. Others have suggested a chronic problem with migraines; Gerald wrote to Penelope Betjeman that Robert had been 'granted unlimited leave' on account of his 'continuous headaches and the peculiar conformation of his brain'. Could he have taken a tip or two from John Betjeman and mentioned a few neuroses as well, encouraged by Gerald's psychoanalytic knowledge? In another letter, Gerald wrote, 'Robert has been removed from the army for being loopy.' Whatever the case, the Mad Boy was soon back at Faringdon. Gerald too headed over from Oxford when he could, usually staying Saturday to Tuesday. It was almost as if everything were back to normal, although, of course, it wasn't.

CHAPTER ELEVEN

Gosh I Think She's Swell

HEN ROBERT RETURNED to live at Faringdon in the summer of 1941, the place had changed. The house and estate had been requisitioned by the Army, and about a dozen Nissen huts had been erected in the trees to the side of the lawn. Men from the Royal Engineers and Royal Army Service Corps were stationed there, fixing army vehicles and preparing their food in a special cookhouse. The Folly was now the observation post for the local Home Guard (those on duty saw the glow from the Coventry bombing), and there were pill-boxes and holes in the roads all over the town ready for road blocks. At night, the whole area was darker than anyone had ever known. What with blackout blinds and cars with shrouded headlights, it was easy, walking through the marketplace in the evening, to bump into people. Accidents were legion.

Robert was in his element and set to work organising the estate again and trying to protect it from the soldiers. Gerald reported to Clarissa that 'Robert made a terrific fuss because a soldier broke a branch off a lilac tree but if one gets away with no further damage than that one may account oneself lucky.' Coming over for weekends from Oxford, usually by train, Gerald reported that the military were hardly noticeable. 'Except for distant motor-bikes they are as quiet as mice.' Robert worked hard on the farm, driving the tractor and joining Fred Shury, his lanky former groom, to plant wheat in the fields by Grove Wood. They managed to harvest and thresh it with help from Italian prisoners-of-war, who were brought in from a nearby camp to work in the fields.

As part of the 'Dig for Victory' campaign, ornamental grounds were to be planted with vegetables – London parks were now sporting carrots and onions rather than flowers, and St James's Square had rows of cabbages around the central statue of William III. There was an attempt to dig up the lawns at Faringdon, but the foundations of the old Elizabethan house broke the plough and the task was abandoned. Instead, six sheep were put there to graze, and if they were unable to provide the velvety green stripes of the glory days, at least they prevented the grass from getting too high. Vegetables and fruit were plentiful; Mr Morris, the head gardener, was too old to fight and though the urns were no longer filled with geraniums and areas were overgrown with weeds, there was plenty of garden produce. In the summer, plump, scented peaches and purple grapes still emerged from the greenhouses.

Fred Shury was now performing many jobs to cover for the staff who had left. It was he who drove into Oxford most weeks with a trailer of vegetables and surplus fruit. The bulk was donated to the Radcliffe Hospital, thereby gaining an extra petrol allowance for the maroon-coloured Austin 8, but a box of supplies was also dropped off with Miss Alden at 22 St Giles' for Gerald. Everyone, even the royal family, had been issued with a buff-coloured ration book to ensure that the entire population would be fed fairly, but Faringdon provided myriad opportunities for augmenting the careful measurements and dull, repetitive diet. *Soufflé de Berners*, with its brandy, eggs, cream and crystallised fruits, was not on the menu, but when friends like Clarissa, Cecil Beaton, Daphne Fielding or Peter Watson were invited for the weekend, there were meals that still met exacting standards. Cooking was done by Mrs Law, and while the food was 'not sumptuous', recalled Clarissa, 'lunch parties for fifteen people were normal'. Still, Gerald lamented the good old days and yearned for the delights of French cooking: 'For one who is greedy, the striking figure of Brillat-Savarin [author of *The Physiology of Taste*] is nostalgically present to the palate in these days of rationing and make-shift cookery.'

Mr Morris kept the vegetables coming from the garden and long-standing friendships with local farmers ensured a supply of dairy produce. Perhaps there were more carrots than usual – the carrot and Marmite soup sounds a dubious invention – but they were also cooked up with butter and sugar into a mouth-watering caramel. There was certainly no such thing as 'mock cream', 'mock duck' or other horrors of the wartime kitchen. Robert went off in the early mornings with a gun, returning with soft, bloodied rabbits or a couple of pigeons in his leather bag. In the early summer, he picked morels in the woods and in autumn field mushrooms in the rough grass above the lake. While Gerald was pleased to be back with his birds at Faringdon, he did not object to Robert setting traps for the moorhens and coots on the lake – both provided a dark, rich meat for the table. The exotic birds had been sent off to the zoo because their food was now unavailable, and nobody knows what became of the ornamental ducks that lived in a cage by the fountain on the back lawn. The urge to consume them may well have overcome scruples about their beauty.

Clarissa remained Gerald's preferred guest at Faringdon after her move to London, but she was not Robert's. The Oxford rumours that Gerald might even marry her would surely have reached the Mad Boy and Clarissa remembered, 'He was a bit prickly at the beginning. It must have been irritating. "What was I at?"'[327] Robert would have understood Clarissa's attraction, though she was surely not his type. His prickliness is unlikely to have been sexual jealousy; aged fifty-eight, Gerald gave the impression of being no longer interested in sex, and indeed admitted his relief at this development to A. L. Rowse.[328] It was more likely to have been a fear of being replaced as youthful confidant and companion by someone who possibly had more qualifications than him, particularly in intellectual terms. Gerald would discuss his writing with Clarissa, whereas Robert's role as 'manager' had given his position a practical and thus potentially slightly demeaning function. 'I had a rapport with Gerald,' admitted Clarissa. But she insisted that Gerald 'was madly in love with Robert . . . though perhaps there was a masochistic side to Gerald . . . But by that time they were an old couple. They were used to each other.'[329]

After her mother died in 1941, Clarissa became very ill and was hospitalised with a kidney complaint. The final part of her convalescence was spent at Faringdon, in the womb-like cosiness of the Red Room, with its wine-coloured wallpaper, damask curtains and four-poster drapes. Sleeping long hours in the red bed, she found it hard to wake in the mornings. 'Once, Robert came and banged on the door and told me it was one-thirty. There were lunch guests. "We're all waiting for you,"' he shouted, with more vehemence than was necessary. 'I was mortified,' Clarissa remembered sixty years later. Perhaps it was then that Robert accepted Clarissa – an exhausted, orphaned girl who slept the days away and was not about to take his place. 'He realised I wasn't after anything,' she said. Robert, too, suffered his own bereavement that Christmas, when he received the news that his father had died. He travelled to Shropshire for the funeral, where his thirty-seven-year-old brother Algy was now Lord of the Manor. This confirmed Robert's distance from the old family seat; Faringdon was now his home and his future.

During 1942, when Clarissa was back at her Foreign Office job, she continued to go down to Faringdon by train as often as possible. She was usually collected from the station by Mr Webb, the local taxi driver who regularly drove Gerald after William Crack joined up. Sometimes, though, Robert would take the wheel and, if Clarissa could run rings around him with cultured dinner-party conversation, he evidently managed to get back at her with his unreformed technique on the roads.

Dearest Gerald,

Just to thank you for a lovely weekend. We left you telephoning hard. Robert nearly killed a dog on the way to the station – the train was gone. Our journey to Didcot hell-for-leather in Mr Webb's Rover was a sort of 'Destry Rides again' – the car made a noise like the first aeroplane, only chance remarks were possible – I remember screaming 'Not another dog!' as we nearly killed a second one – we caught that train by a fraction of a second. Mr Webb was sweating and shaking.

Gerald sent letters to Clarissa reporting on his latest work. 'Publishers are delighted with Cleo [*The Romance of a Nose*] and want to get it out before Xmas. But I doubt if they do as printing etc is getting more difficult.' He thanked her for gifts with his usual humour: 'Dearest C, Thank you <u>so</u> much for the lovely chocs. Robert and I fell upon them as cannibals might fall upon a missionary.' He also sent picture postcards upon which he had drawn or added inappropriate comments. On Fra Angelico's *The Annunciation*, with the Angel Gabriel and the Virgin holding their hands crossed over their abdomens, Gerald wrote around the edge: 'HOW ODD THAT WE SHOULD BOTH HAVE TUMMY-ACHES. IT MUST HAVE BEEN THAT MELON.'

Gerald's wicked humour was clearly back on form by the time Dottie Wellesley published a slim book of poems with the Hogarth Press in 1942. Separated from Gerry Wellesley for twenty years (though they never divorced) and known since diplomatic days in Rome, Dottie took her writing very seriously and had been encouraged by her hero, W. B. Yeats. *Lost Planet and Other Poems* is grandly ambitious – the verses of an educated woman who does not shy from speaking of planets, eclipses, myths, ancient stones or from using anachronisms – 'thou hast' features quite regularly. This earnestness was too much for Gerald, who went through the book pencilling in cheeky comments and cartoons on every other page. The poem 'Mars' has '-Bar' added to the title. When Socrates, in an 'Elysian land . . . beyond the Pleiades', is called a 'wilful old tease', Gerald adds:

<u>Variants</u>
That pessimist sour
Old Schopenhauer.
That awful creature
Friedrich Nietzsche.
Better the bottle
Than Aristotle.

Throughout the volume, the numerous references to bones and stones are underlined or given asterisks, particularly the allusions to 'a phallic stone'. Dottie's 'Epitaph for Everyman' was too much. To the verse 'No bud of flesh, nor of spring, / No cross, no thought in stone, / Shall give Man anything / More beautiful than his bone', Gerald adds his own little creation beneath:

> <u>Bone Sweet Bone </u>see pp 16, 17, 24
> I sit alone
> On the Phallic Stone
> And moan
> And gnaw
> My Bone –
> My beautiful Bone.

Gerald was greatly amused to hear in the spring of 1943 that Dottie had behaved disgracefully at a grand poetry reading in Bond Street in the presence of the Queen. Given in aid of the Free French, it featured illustrious poets such as T. S. Eliot, Walter de la Mare, Vita Sackville-West and the Sitwells, all performing in alphabetical order. Dottie had allegedly got so drunk that she was not given her turn (which as 'Wellesley' was last). There were tears, insults, and Dottie hit Harold Nicolson with an umbrella while Vita (who had already done her reading) tried to soothe her and ultimately succeeded in taking her away in a taxi. Gerald later wrote to Edith Sitwell, joking that 'Dorothy Wellesley is suing Harold [Nicolson] for saying she was drunk – whereas it was merely a Dionysiac Frenzy. I am mad at having missed it all.'

F CLARISSA WAS Gerald's new best friend, he also remained loyal to his old ones – a defining characteristic throughout his life. Another clever beautiful young blonde woman he was close to was now in prison – Diana Mosley. In May 1940, Oswald Mosley had been imprisoned under Defence Regulation 18B – as a threat to national security – and Diana was interned in June. Gerald and Robert were among the few people who wrote in support on her first day in Holloway. 'What can I send you?' asked Gerald. 'Would you like a little file concealed in a peach?' What Diana and her friends did not know was that her sister Nancy had been summoned to the Foreign Office to give her opinion on whether Diana's friendship with Hitler and various other Nazis made her a threat to the country. Nancy announced that she considered Diana 'an extremely dangerous person', something that probably sealed her sister's fate, but Diana only discovered this decades after Nancy's death, with the declassification of MI5 documents in 2002.

Despite Gerald's depression and the warnings of Oxford friends that he was putting his own reputation in danger, he also went to visit her. Conditions of indefinite internment at F Block in Holloway were not pleasant, and Diana had been forced to leave behind her eleven-week-old son, whom she was breast-feeding. Gerald brought her Floris bath essence, which must have offered new olfactory delights wafting along the bleach-scrubbed prison corridors. He also sent her a copy of *Far From the Madding War*. Even after a year of incarceration, her tough *joie de vivre* remained intact. In a tight, girlish script that filled the page, she thanked 'dearest Gerald . . . for the 'wonderful book which made me simply scream with laughter so that the walls of my cell echoed with my laughing . . .' Her politics may have been abhorrent, but it is hard to deny the witty courage of Prisoner D. Mosley 5433E1/12, who sends her 'fondest love' to Robert, Penelope Betjeman, Roy Harrod 'or anyone who might like to have it'.

> I do a lot of cooking and my cell stinks of delicious garlic. My next experiment is going to be a (very inferior) imitation of your Tito's beautiful cake [in Rome] which was choc outside and sour cream inside – mine will have a sort of cheese that I make from milk. I am feeling very well because of the hot weather we are having – I will draw a veil over the winter here which lasted from September until the middle of June and which was an intensely painful experience.
> I promise when I get out if I ever do I will not be a prison bore or ever refer to it, but in case you want to know what it is like, it is an endless

journey 3rd class abroad in a rather crowded train with a very bad restaurant car.

Diana claimed that the happiest day of her life was when she was reunited with her husband and they were put in married quarters in the prison grounds. (When Diana's mother came by bus to visit, the conductor called out before the stop, 'Holloway Gaol! Lady Mosley's suite! All change here!'[330]) The Mosleys had a small garden where they grew vegetables and even *fraises des bois*, and the dark, ivy-covered walls reminded Diana of happier days at Gerald's house in Rome.

Other Faringdon friends had also gone down in the world. The Marchesa Casati, deeply in debt, had fled Paris for London, where she now lived in very reduced circumstances, swathed in ripped black velvet and grubby ostrich feathers, her eyes like dark coal-holes staring from a dead-white powdered face. Gone were the startling pets and masquerades of her Roman days and the pythons in glass tanks that she had taken to Faringdon. It appears from later evidence that Gerald helped Luisa Casati financially, something that may well have begun at this vulnerable stage in her life. Although her old friends sometimes found her a pitiful sight, La Casati attracted a new, younger set of admirers, and survived the war into the late 1950s.

Winnie de Polignac had set herself up in a modest flat at 55 Park Lane, where, exiled from the glamour and influence of her musical salon in Paris, she bought an upright piano and comforted herself playing Bach. The atmosphere in London was hellish: thousands of citizens were dying in air raids, and many buildings – including the House of Commons, Waterloo Station and the British Museum – had been devastated. Despite her terror at the air raids, the Princesse de Polignac made her way through bombed-out, glass-strewn streets to concerts and literary events and took the train for weekends at Faringdon. The old exiled Princess was a regular visitor until her death of a heart attack in 1943, and would sit out on the porch in the sunshine, gazing into the distance, perhaps remembering her happier days with Violet Trefusis (the two were not invited together). The grand old lady had come a

long way from mid-nineteenth-
century New York and Singer
sewing machines, via French
aristocracy and *belle époque*
Paris Lesbos, to being a major
influence on European music.
Now, a younger generation
of British writers became
acquainted with the powerful
woman whom Violet Trefusis
called 'Oak', amazed that she

WINNIE, PRINCESSE
DE POLIGNAC READING
THE PAPER ON THE
PORCH AT FARINGDON
NOT LONG BEFORE
HER DEATH IN 1943

represented a direct link to Proust. James Lees-Milne described her
sitting on a sofa, 'immobile, with a hat on, like a large Buddha'. There
was something 'very godlike' about her.[331]

Numerous Faringdon friends were among the well-heeled
Londoners who moved into the Dorchester – 'one of the SAFEST
buildings in London' as the hotel's advertisement claimed, pointing out
the eight floors of heavily reinforced concrete and virtually bomb-proof
ground floor. A 'glittering fortress during the Blitz', the bar continued
to serve champagne, the restaurant offered oysters and lobster, and
dance tunes were played by the orchestra until late at night. Some
said that spies and criminals mingled with the off-duty airmen, society
ladies and politicians. Certainly American officials favoured the place,
including General Eisenhower, who met Churchill there to discuss
D-Day. At night, a cockroach-killer was employed to crawl about on
knee-pads, making sure the vermin would not offend the illustrious
guests.[332]

Among the permanent occupants of 'the Dorch' were the two great
hostesses Lady Cunard and Lady Colefax, who abandoned their fine
London houses and established themselves on different floors. The
rival *salonnières* continued to gather what they could of the great and
the glamorous, war or no war. Naturally, some old friends were now
on active service, others evacuated and others too busy to be doing
with Emerald Cunard's teas or Sibyl Colefax's 'ordinaries' – lunches at

the Dorchester, after which guests would be presented with a bill for 10s 6d. But many of the old faithful did turn up, including those who continued to visit Faringdon, such as Harold Nicolson, Edith Sitwell and Cyril Connolly. Rumour had it that when the sirens announced a raid, Lady Cunard would crouch beneath the dining table amidst the gilt and ormolu in her seventh-floor suite and read Proust or Shakespeare to calm her guests.

Clarissa took up quarters on the Dorchester's (understandably unpopular) top floor along with her old school friend Pamela Digby, now Churchill, having recently married Churchill's son, Randolph, and famous for her astonishing success with rich and famous men. 'At one time or another, there were friends and acquaintances on every floor,' wrote Clarissa, who nonchalantly eschewed the bomb shelter for the foyer when the sirens went off. Cecil Beaton became a very close, lifelong friend, sending over boxes of flowers from Ashcombe and writing letters when abroad.[333] He had turned away from the fripperies of fashion and royal portraits (claiming 'I was sick to death of posing people round apple blossom'[334]), to snap bomb-wrecked streets, wounded babies and brave airmen setting off on missions. The Ministry of Information sent him all over the world on photographic assignments and he became the official photographer for the RAF.

In 1942, Doris Castlerosse, Cecil's unlikely girlfriend of the 1930s, came back to London from the US and also moved into the Dorchester. Lady Castlerosse had left behind her American lover, Eleonor Flick Hoffman (of the Venetian palazzo), and was rumoured to have become bitter and 'an acid misanthrope'.[335] During a trip to Washington, Winston Churchill had invited her to dinner and strongly encouraged her return to England. It appears he was worried that his portraits of this notorious, if titled, courtesan might fall into the hands of an American magazine and affect his gravitas as Britain's leader. Not long after seeing Churchill, Doris managed to obtain a highly elusive priority air ticket to London. Despite their bitter divorce dealings, Lord Castlerosse met his ex-wife at Waterloo Station and they dined together at the Dorchester before he left her there and returned home. (He would die the following year from a heart attack, allegedly after one of his habitually indulgent dinners.)

Doris then had a dreadful few days, sitting in her rooms, terrified at the bombs falling all around and the blasts from the huge anti-aircraft guns in Hyde Park, the three Churchill portraits still wrapped in brown paper. She sent a telegram to New York to try to discover whether she could obtain the money for some jewellery she had pawned there, only to find that the telegram was intercepted by British censors. Detectives turned up to question her about what appeared to be irregular financial dealings. She called friends and found them in an entirely different mood to previous times, critical that she had left Britain. Lonely and miserable, the 'enchantress of the Thirties' with a 'jester's cap of pure gold hair' felt she had lost her magical charms. A few days later she encountered the Duke of Marlborough in one of the Dorchester's carpeted corridors and he made a contemptuous remark about people who desert their country during war. Later she was found unconscious in her bed. Doris died some days later in hospital, aged forty-one. The coroner's verdict was open, but described a death from self-administered barbiturate acid poisoning.[336]

OR MANY OF Gerald and Robert's war-weary friends, weekends at Faringdon became an escape to another, forgotten era. It seemed almost inconceivable to find themselves back at this beautiful house, tucked up under satin eiderdowns in four-poster beds and fed with marvellous food. The war was provoking vast changes in society. The class system appeared to be crumbling and few imagined that large country houses filled with servants would be reinstated once the war was over. As James Lees-Milne travelled around England inspecting many of these increasingly dilapidated piles for the National Trust, he was aware that he was a witness to an entire way of life in its death throes. Evelyn Waugh agreed, believing that 'the ancestral seats which were our chief national aristocratic achievement were doomed to decay and spoliation like the monasteries of the sixteenth century'.[337]

Nancy Mitford, meanwhile, had been a night fire-watcher, had worked in a canteen for French soldiers evacuated from Dunkirk, and then with Jewish refugees. At last she settled in a job with her friends Heywood and Anne Hill at their unusual Mayfair bookshop that was more like a private house filled with first editions, pictures and toys as well as the latest publications, and a much-loved meeting point for a large network of friends that included Jennifer, as well as Gerald, Evelyn Waugh and the Sitwells. Nancy adored her visits to Faringdon, where Gerald not only provided a refuge of comfort and glamour, but encouraged her to write, telling her she could not leave her room until she had written the required amount for the day. It was also the place where she received the devastating news that her brother Tom had been killed in action in Burma. Gerald went to tell her in her room, and said she mustn't think of coming down for dinner, but Nancy insisted on acting as though nothing had happened.[338] Despite this, Nancy later recalled her times at Faringdon like trips to Paradise.

> I can remember, during the tedious or frightening but always sleepless nights of fire-watching in wartime London, that the place I longed to be in most intensely was the red bedroom at Faringdon, with its crackling fire, its Bessarabian carpet with bunchy flowers and above all its four-post bed, whence from beneath a huge fat fluffy old-fashioned quilt one can gaze out at the view, head still on pillow . . . Perhaps the greatest, most amazing conjuring tricks are reserved for the dining room. In this pleasant sunny white room, scattered with large silver-gilt birds and wonderful Sevres and Dresden china, a standard of culinary perfection has been maintained through the darkest days of war. Cook or no cook, raw materials or no raw materials, a succession of utterly delicious courses would somehow waft themselves to the sideboard, and the poor Londoner, starved, or sated with Spam, would see sights and tastes he had long ago forgotten to believe in.[339]

If old friends were astounded by Faringdon, the same was probably true of the American servicemen who were stationed there from 1942. The Nissen huts were vacated by the Royal Engineers and filled with 'Yanks', many of them black, as the US Army was segregated. The townspeople of Faringdon had become accustomed to unusual occurrences during the war, but the sight of so many assembled African-Americans impressed and sometimes startled them. Needless to say, the senior officers were white, and it was they who were billeted in the attic and basement rooms of Faringdon House. Gerald and Robert were able to keep the two main floors, but inevitably the atmosphere of the house altered. However careful they were, the soldiers could be heard as they trooped up the back staircase to their rooms, or as they drove their trucks to unload in the stable yard. There had always been an unpretentious, almost scruffy feel to the place and now, with little domestic help, pictures put away and blackout blinds to fix each day at dusk, the glamour was toned down. Gerald took over a ground-floor room, to the right of the hall, which had a dressing room and bathroom off it. He had his desk with piles of books and papers there, and he slept in an ornate painted Venetian-style day-bed, reminiscent of a boat, with gilded lions at its base.

The officers had their mess on the lower ground floor, but they were occasionally asked to dine with their hosts. Doubtless they had read the *Instructions for American Servicemen in Britain 1942* that warned about British reserve: 'On a small crowded island where forty-five million people live, each man learns to guard his privacy carefully.' It discouraged bragging about American wages, criticising the food or making fun of British accents – 'You sound just as funny to them.' The weather was equally daunting: 'At first you will probably not like the almost continual rains and mists and the absence of snow and crisp cold.' And of course, 'NEVER criticize the King or Queen.' An introductory section entitled 'Britain at War' gives a useful picture of the general situation in 1942:

> Every light in England is blacked out every night and all night. Every highway signpost has come down and barrage balloons have gone up.

Grazing land is now ploughed for wheat and flower beds turned into vegetable gardens. Britain's peacetime army of a couple of hundred thousand has been expanded to over two million men . . . Old-time social distinctions are being forgotten as the sons of factory workers rise to be officers in the forces and the daughters of noblemen get jobs in munitions factories.

But more important than this is the effect of the war itself. The British have been bombed, night after night and month after month. Thousands of them have lost their houses, their possessions, their families. Gasoline, clothes, and railroad travel are hard to come by and incomes are cut by taxes to an extent we Americans have not even approached. One of the things the English always had enough of in the past was soap. Now it is so scarce that girls working in the factories often cannot get the grease off their hands or out of their hair. And food is more strictly rationed than anything else.

Given the warnings not to misinterpret the dowdy clothes and un-soaped bodies, it must have been a surprise for these US servicemen to find their hosts not only stylishly arrayed, scented individuals who entertained beautifully, but able to place a fine spread on the table. Gerald described one such evening to Clarissa. 'Two of the officers dined the other night. One (from Carolina) agreeable and prepossessing, the other a New Yorker lamentably dull and slow of speech. Others I have met ditto. I am told that it is regarded in America as <u>politeness</u> not to spare one a <u>single</u> detail. But it makes <u>one</u> feel like a motor car going up hill with the brake on.' Despite the cultural gap, Clarissa remembered that the Americans 'were a source of resigned amusement to Gerald'. He wrote to her again when they were snowed up, with only enough food for a couple of days: 'If it continues we shall have to kill and eat a soldier. It might be interesting to try the major, who is thoroughly impregnated with whisky and might make an excellent haggis.'

The town of Faringdon changed with the presence of the 100th and 101st Ordnance Battalions. The roads were lined with vast piles of ammunition under camouflage tarpaulins – the stock-piling of shells and detonators ahead of D-Day. Young boys would approach the Americans guarding them, asking, 'Got any gum, chum?' The retort, often as not, was 'Got an older sister?' Some of them did, and there was a marked increase in the social life of Faringdon, with dances and parties livening up the gloomy evenings. The GIs offered not only chewing gum, but silk stockings and unusual items from their fantastic rations. Daphne Fielding (whose home at Longleat was now a US military hospital) particularly recommended American cough mixture, which 'tasted rather like Cointreau but acted like bath-tub gin'.[340] Gerald also reported her as saying she 'was "keeping up the morale of others by letting down her own morals" which seems to me a very amiable form of war-work . . .'[341]

The Americans were famously good as dance partners and more. 'Overfed, overpaid, oversexed and over here', complained disgruntled or anxious local males. British soldiers were 'underfed, underpaid, undersexed and under Eisenhower', retorted the in-comers.[342] The well-fed young Americans were not only appreciated by women, but also some men. Quentin Crisp eulogised their bodies bulging 'through every straining khaki fibre towards our feverish hands', and their voices 'like warm milk'. 'Never in the history of sex was so much offered to so many by so few.'[343]

When the winter got terribly cold the men living in Nissen huts had a tough time. Their quarters were heated by pot-bellied stoves, with only a bucket of coke per day as fuel, and they approached Robert to see if he could help. He told them they could take the stump of a large tree that had fallen by the lake, combining a charitable act to the soldiers with help in clearing the awkward obstruction. The Americans roped in one of their explosives experts to help speed things up and the ensuing blast was so strong that, while it blew the tree stump to conveniently sized pieces, it also shattered some of the house's windows.

IKE MANY PEOPLE, Jennifer was getting tired after three years of war, with its fears, bereavement and tedious discomfort. On her twenty-sixth birthday, she wrote to her mother, thanking her for what would have been an unlikely present during peacetime. There was probably also a cheque – despite her maladies, Alathea was always generous and good at sending money. Jennifer tries to be interesting but sounds drained: there's not enough to eat, it's hard to stay healthy and friends are dying – Eric Ravilious, the painter and family friend, would soon disappear on a reconnaissance flight.

6 Beaumont St

29.3.42

My darling Mummy,

Thank you a million times for your sweet letter and the <u>huge</u> cheese, darling, which you really shouldn't have sent me. I've never felt so rich in my life, and it will really help tremendously. Thank you so very much, my darling.

I was very upset about poor Peter, and <u>haunted</u> by the times we were together – all that first summer of the war. He was so sweet and gay, I can't believe he's dead. It all seems so real again, and I can't think of anything else. He had <u>such</u> a sweet character, and was always such an angel to me and I'm afraid I made him rather unhappy at one time. I can only pray that he's a prisoner – I think there may be a chance of that.

I have had flu again and feel rather run down and wretched but the weather seems nicer and that makes me feel better. If only I could get away for a bit, I think it's just tiredness that makes me get all these coughs and so on.

Have you read Evelyn's new book [*Put Out More Flags*]? Bits are very funny, I must say. You will laugh at the evacuees, – monsters – called the Connollys!!

I am so glad daddy seems better and is having quite a gay time. I'm <u>sure</u> that's the important thing for him, to see lots of people and go out a lot.

Oh darling I feel depressed and sad and wish I wasn't getting so old. I know it isn't old <u>really</u>, but one feels a hundred sometimes. I am reading Proust again and had forgotten how very funny he is sometimes – about Francoise and Tante Leonie. I do love it.

Bless you darling. Write when you can. I long for news of you and you seem so far away.

All love,

From Jennifer

While Jennifer gives her mother the impression of a quiet, maybe lonely existence in Oxford, her life was actually much more complex. She gave at least one cocktail party at her flat, which was judged a great success by her Oxford friends, and she remained as daring and open to new encounters and love affairs as she had been before the war. She often went up to London, where parties and nightclubs were going strong, despite, or even because of, the difficult circumstances. The Gargoyle Club, in Meard Street, Soho, was already a favourite place for the sort of smart bohemia in which Jennifer felt at home. Opened by David Tennant in the 1920s, it began as a place for eating, drinking and, especially, dancing. At the suggestion of Matisse, the walls were covered in small squares of old French mirrors, cut up to produce a general sparkle, and there was lots of red plush and gold. During the 1930s, it was chic but not flashy; the Prince of Wales and Wallis Simpson preferred grander places like the Embassy Club. The clientele at the Gargoyle included artists, musicians and writers and the club had a reputation for beautiful people, tolerance and intrigue; it seemed that half the clients were running off with one another's lovers at any one time. Its atmosphere was described by one fervent admirer as 'Mystery suffused with a tender eroticism'.[344]

During the worst of the Blitz, in the winter of 1940–41, the Gargoyle closed for a period, but it soon reopened and became a haven for many people in Jennifer's (and the Faringdon) circle. 'It was very difficult to stay away, and seemed like a never-ending party night after night and with constant changes of partners,' wrote Patrick Leigh Fermor, a regular, like many of his fighting friends, when they were in town. 'Hangovers were drowned like kittens next morning in a drink called a Dog's Nose or a Monkey's Tail: a pint of beer, that is, with either a large gin or vodka slipped into it. It worked wonders.'[345] Across the glittering room (some of the small mirrors now blown off by bombs), one might spot Dylan Thomas, Constant Lambert or Lucian Freud, not to mention a few secret-service chaps like Guy Burgess and a sprinkling of Europeans who had sought refuge in England, such as Arthur Koestler and George Weidenfeld. And, as usual, Brian Howard (lately moved on from MI5) would be calling out cattily from the bar.

Jennifer often saw Cyril Connolly at the Gargoyle, where he revelled in the intrigue at night and appreciated the cheap lunches in the day. Both of them moved easily between more alternative or artistic people and the smart, upper-class set and it was the ideal place for meeting contributors to (and readers of) *Horizon*, which was increasing in influence and success. Cyril had found new strength and courage in fighting his own war to keep European civilisation alive. The writer Peter Quennell described being caught in an air raid with his friend in a London street, bombs going off all around. 'And Cyril simply stood inside a doorway calmly waiting for the raid to end. I was visibly frightened, thinking any minute a bomb might hit us, but when Cyril saw the expression on my face he just looked at me and said, "Be calm. Really, you know, we've all had interesting lives."'[346]

Cyril and Jennifer also shared something new in common. Cyril had fallen in love with a much younger woman, Lys Lubbock, a former model, who soon became indispensable in the *Horizon* offices (her speedy typing was legendary) and in running a home for them both. Despite rationing, numerous guests were invited to parties and meals at their flat in Sussex Place near Regent's Park. Evelyn Waugh admired Lys's wartime skills in acquiring such rare luxuries as lobster and truffles and in cooking exquisite meals. When the war ended, the Anglo-Irish novelist Elizabeth Bowen wrote to thank Cyril for all he had done. She had worked as an air-raid warden and had had her London home bombed, but she deeply appreciated how he had kept a valuable 'evidence of continuity' through publishing *Horizon* and how his parties had 'real spirit'.[347] Privately, she had also noted that with '3 little girls in slacks' scurrying about doing all the work, Cyril looked 'rather like a Sultan in a harem'.[348]

When they met, Cyril was thirty-seven and Lys twenty-two. She was also married, though she soon left her husband, and when Cyril was slow-footed in obtaining his own divorce and marrying her, she deftly changed her surname to Connolly. Lys's ex-husband was a handsome, dark-haired, struggling actor, Ian Lubbock. He was also Jennifer's boyfriend.

Most accounts of Jennifer's life suggest that she threw herself freely into the wild fray of the civilian's war, where love was grasped more readily in the face of death, and drinking, dancing and casual kisses could become a kind of private battle or at least a refusal to surrender. 'It came to be rumoured . . . that everybody in London was in love,' wrote Elizabeth Bowen in *The Heat of the Day*. 'Life stories were shed as so much superfluous weight.' Malcolm Muggeridge referred to the Blitz as 'a kind of protracted debauch, with the shape of orderly living shattered, all restraints removed, barriers non-existent'.[349] In some ways, Jennifer had already been fighting her own battles as a part of a campaign to escape the cold, critical environment of her parents; it was not just the war that encouraged them. Despite her various love affairs during the early 1940s, Ian Lubbock appears to have been involved with her for up to a year, in 1941–42; her friends knew him as her regular boyfriend. It is tempting to imagine that Jennifer and Cyril laughed about their taking up with opposite elements of a couple – there was an implicit intimacy to it that would have appealed. They surely giggled over drinks in the early hours at the Gargoyle, comparing notes. Neither relationship was to last very long and Evelyn Waugh commented in his diary with perception: 'I read Connolly's *Unquiet Grave*, half commonplace book of French maxims, half a lament for his life. Poor Lys; he sees her as the embodiment of the blackout and air raids and rationing and compulsory service and Jean [his ex-wife] as the golden past of beaches and peaches and lemurs . . .'[350]

Ian's presence in Jennifer's life was strengthened when, like many London actors, he left the capital and joined the Oxford Repertory Players. The troupe performed at the recently opened Oxford Playhouse, just down the road from Jennifer's flat in Beaumont Street. A year younger than Jennifer, Ian had the sort of mixed background that appealed to her. His manner reflected his schooling at Eton; his father was a teacher there and came from an illustrious old Norfolk Quaker family. Ian's mother, on the other hand, was the classical pianist Irene Scharrer, who often played with the more famous pianist Myra Hess and who had Jewish origins. Ian was charming, though he was already known to drink too much, and his pursuit of an acting career was not going as well as he hoped. It must have seemed like a break when Ian was given a supporting role in a play by Lord Berners, to be given its 'world premiere' (as the *Oxford Magazine* put it) at the Playhouse in June 1942.

The Furies was a lightweight farce based on the story of Alfred Eversly, a writer, who tries to escape the pressures of an oppressive Mayfair social life by moving to Cornwall, and when that fails, takes off to Haiti. The furies are three ageing, aristocratic hostesses, based apparently on Gerald's old friends Lady Colefax and Lady Cunard. They pursue the writer, who has taken up with and then marries Vera de Pomeroy, a 'tart' who shares a liking for jewellery and sugar daddies with Doris (*née* Delavigne) Castlerosse. 'Marry him? Good God!' comments Miss de Pomeroy about a former admirer; 'That stingy little rat! He's as rich as hell and all he ever gave me was a diamond bracelet I had to look at through a magnifying glass. He doesn't know how to handle the girls.' Ian Lubbock took the minor role of Simon Montague, the writer's assistant – 'a good looking young man of somewhat ingenuous appearance' – who accompanies Alfred on his escapes and hopes to marry his daughter, Monica.

Many of Jennifer and Gerald's Oxford friends were in the audience and lots of them had lent a hand in the production in one way or another; A. L. Rowse typed up the manuscript, Robert brought over furniture for the stage from Faringdon and Daisy Fellowes was said to have produced the curtains.[351] 'A distinguished audience hugely enjoyed themselves,'[352] and the *Oxford Times* admired Lord Berners's 'gossamer-like wit, fast-moving comedy and admirably-observed characters', even if it did find the play far-fetched. Moving among some of Oxford's finest minds cannot be said to have prompted Gerald to write a subtle play. The women are all either money-grubbing young things or monstrous regiments of cackling 'old trouts', and the language is absolutely of its age: 'Papa darling, she's absolutely divine. Gosh I think she's swell,' opines Monica, before she is corrupted by the pornography-reading 'tart'. Possibly Gerald was working out his own internal battles between enjoying the superficial joys of society and dedicating himself to his art – 'Sometimes I feel like Orestes pursued by the Furies,' complains the hero – but the prevalence in the play of gin fizzes, Rolls-Royces and weekend trips to Paris places the victory firmly with the former.

OBODY HAS EVER come up with a very convincing explanation of how it happened that, only a month or so after *The Furies* was performed in Oxford, during the heatwave of early July 1942, Jennifer and Robert got married. Ann Jennifer Evelyn Elizabeth Fry, aged twenty-six, 'Spinster', listed her profession as 'Typist (Hospital)' on the marriage certificate. Robert Vernon Heber-Percy, aged twenty-nine, put his as 'Land Agent'. The ceremony took place at the Chelsea Register Office on the King's Road, and the only known wedding photographs are the three in the *Tatler and Bystander*. A small piece records the fact that Mr Robert Heber-Percy and Miss Jennifer Fry were married 'quietly' in London, with a reception afterwards at Claridge's. The picture of the nuptial pair is unfortunate; both look frozen with fear. Jennifer is pretty in a light summer frock, though the unusual plumed white fascinator only emphasises her anxious dark eyes. Robert is immaculate in a double-breasted suit, but his arms are clamped to his sides, his hands clenched. Perhaps the photograph was taken at a bad moment and they were

BRIDE AND GROOM
LOOKING TENSE AT
THE RECEPTION AT
CLARIDGE'S

smiling and laughing the rest of the time.

The bride's parents were there – Lady Fry in a marvellous hat, sitting on a sofa with a distracted look. No doubt she knew that Robert was Gerald's 'young man'; she certainly knew about being married to someone who liked young men. Sir Geoffrey, one of the witnesses, had a vaguely grumpy air. Gladys (Robert's mother) was the other witness – a widow of seven months. Some of the younger guests look happier, including Lady Elizabeth Clyde (daughter of Gerry and Dottie Wellesley). There was a lot of champagne and, despite the war, Claridge's still retained its art-deco glamour. Afterwards they all went off nightclubbing. There is no record of where the couple spent their first night, but it was probably back at the hotel.

Presumably Gerald was present, though the magazine article doesn't mention him. Understandably, he was not happy. This time, the Mad Boy had taken things too far. Sexual freedom was all very well, but neither of the two bachelors were 'the marrying sort', as the old euphemism went. The discussions must have been fraught. Did Robert go over to Oxford to sit in Gerald's dour parlour in St Giles', trying to make sure Miss Alden didn't overhear? Or were there heated arguments at Faringdon, away from American soldiers, gardeners and guests? Gerald definitely knew Jennifer – he had inscribed a copy of *The Romance of a Nose* to her a few months earlier and he had surely met her on her visits to Faringdon. But this development was unbelievable. And why the rush? Later, Robert would tell a friend that it had been Gerald who said, 'You should marry Jennifer,'[353] but this seems unlikely. Gerald's view of marriage was a jaundiced one, and he satirised and mocked it in his novels. Years earlier, he had been asked the ingredients for a happy marriage and replied: 'A long purse, infinite credulity, and no sense of humour, a combative nature and a stipulation that the man should be a man and the woman a woman – or vice versa!'[354]

Jack Fox was then a seventeen-year-old, helping out at Faringdon before he went off to join the Navy in 1943. Small-built with foxy-red hair, he would later become the estate's gamekeeper as well as a builder and stonemason. According to him, nobody among the staff knew about the wedding in advance. Jack always went rabbiting on a Saturday morning with Fred Shury and had gone over to help him pick vegetables before setting off with their guns. He found Robert's loyal groom (and now general factotum) in a state of bewilderment. Robert had gone up to London the day before and had just rung up and announced, 'I'm getting married this morning.' Naturally, nobody would have suggested that marriage was out of the question for the Mad Boy – he might have been Gerald's heir, but they were not viewed as lovers by the staff. Still, the secrecy was strange. Gerald and Robert's friends were, understandably, astounded.

Could it be that Robert and Jennifer had just decided to do something crazy? Was it a decision taken after too much champagne at the Gargoyle? Both were risk-takers in love and neither was having a 'glorious war'. During these years, many couples had rushed to marry; men were leaving to fight and you never knew where the next bomb would land. But why such haste in this case? Jennifer appeared to have a boyfriend (what did Ian Lubbock have to say?) and Robert had a well-established partnership. Naturally, some pointed to the age-old trigger for shotgun weddings and it is possible that Jennifer knew she was in the very early stages of pregnancy. It is unknown whether or not she used contraception, but the Marie Stopes clinic did a roaring trade in Dutch caps, and there were also 'things called Volpar Gels'.[355]

More significantly, abortions were available, particularly for those with money and contacts.

When, a while after the wedding, Fred Shury noticed that Jennifer was pregnant, he commented, 'I knew there must've been something.' In the meantime, everyone was puzzled.

CHAPTER TWELVE

The Pram in the Hall

I T WAS NOT INEVITABLE that the newly-weds would live at Faringdon; Gerald's tolerance had limits. He announced that they wouldn't fit into Faringdon, what with the Americans, and that he had found them 'a very nice nest' nearby. If the farmer wanted a wife, then he could do the right thing and set himself up appropriately for all this burgeoning domesticity. But in the meantime, until all the arrangements were made, the couple moved into the main house.

Jennifer must have been thankful to leave her flat in Beaumont Street; the heatwave had brought an infestation of mosquitoes to Oxford, so Faringdon, with its cool breezes gusting up from the Thames Valley, was particularly appealing. The bride was given a room on the southerly, more domestic side of the house, catching the morning sun and overlooking the lawns, where the sheep chewed the grass to a ragged thatch. Jennifer could look down on cars arriving at the front door, and across to the stone church, from whose carillon tower snippets of Bishop Heber's hymns chimed through the day.

There are no reports of what occurred during the first evening when Gerald, Robert and Jennifer had dinner at Faringdon together. And at breakfast? Gerald would have always been painfully polite. Or was there still breakfast in bed for ladies, in spite of wartime constraints? At this time of year there were magnolia flowers, large as creamy doves, ready to pluck from the curved walls flanking the house. Maybe Mrs Law continued the pre-war tradition and

239

placed one of the headily-scented offerings on the tray before taking it upstairs.

This was not the first time that Robert became sexually involved with a woman during his decade at Faringdon: there had been Maimie Lygon and Doris Castlerosse, to mention only two. But why get married? The dead hand of the law made it all so different. It is not known when Gerald was told about the pregnancy. He could never have imagined that he would test out Cyril Connolly's adage 'There is no more sombre enemy of good art than the pram in the hall.' Yet here he was, in his sixtieth year, confronting the prospect of Faringdon's airy entrance hall ringing out with the unfamiliar call of an infant, with its pram parked somewhere by the Victorian music boxes. But Gerald's anger and fears rapidly dissipated. After all the misery and depression he had suffered at the start of the war, maybe this didn't seem so tragic in comparison.

The situation was probably helped by Jennifer, who was easy on the eye and amusing – two highly significant qualifications for success with Gerald. She was neither dominating nor demanding, but happy to fit in, almost as though she were a guest rather than a spouse. It had always suited Gerald to be surrounded by bad behaviour and he enjoyed a peripheral atmosphere of naughtiness and unconventionality, while sticking to his own serious routines. He continued to get up early, work at whatever was his current project and invite friends for meals and weekends. During the week he went back to Miss Alden's lodgings in Oxford and left the Mad Boy and his bride to sort things out for themselves.

Among the wedding presents was an appealingly child-sized seventeenth-century book, *The Dictionary of Love, In Which Is Contained the Explanation of Most of the Terms Used in that Language*, by John Wilmot, Earl of Rochester. It was given to the bride and groom by Jennifer's old friend Glur and her husband, Peter Quennell. Their inscription now appears to be tempting fate: 'To Darling Jennifer / Robert / Who need no instruction in this important and perplexing subject.'

Sadly, it appeared that they did. No sooner had he married Jennifer than Robert changed. It was not that he didn't care about her, but the realisation of what he had done threw him into a panic and he rejected his bride. Jennifer was utterly bewildered. She was aware of Robert's complex sexuality, but had been confident that they would be able to make a success of their marriage. She assumed they would be lovers. His sudden angry coldness was shocking. She never forgot one night during what should have been their honeymoon, when she walked along the dark, blacked-out corridor from her room to his. The door was locked. She knocked, but he wouldn't open it. Desperate and lonely, she wept and begged for him to let her in, banging the wooden panels, rattling the brass handle. His rejection seemed inexplicable. What had happened to the crazy Mad Boy, who had been so entertaining, fun-loving and sexy? The humiliation of returning alone to her room was bitterly painful.

Jennifer's suffering made Robert withdraw even more – over-emotional women were not his territory. He didn't have it in him to be a good husband, he later admitted. In fact he didn't seem to have it in him to be any kind of husband. The prospect of a baby on the way only exacerbated his alarm. Until now, so much in Robert's life had been a game, a quick dare or passed in the irresponsible haze of too many drinks. At school he didn't give a damn, he had never committed to a regular job, army life had been undemanding and eventually shrugged off, and Gerald had let him get away with outrageously bad behaviour. Now a mad scheme had entrapped him in a situation that was only going to get much worse and was supposed to last until death.

All three members of the household were damaged in one way or another, with wounds that went back to their childhoods, but Robert was by far the least self-reflective of the trio. Gerald had already written about the miseries of his early years and had spent time on the analyst's couch discussing them. Jennifer was well aware of the disaster of her parents' marriage and the effect on her of her father's rejection. She had the language to discuss these matters and would later write

CECIL BEATON'S PHOTOGRAPH OF JENNIFER, GERALD AND ROBERT IN GERALD'S WARTIME STUDY-BEDROOM. NOBODY LOOKS HAPPY, BUT AT LEAST GERALD IS BUSY WITH HIS BOOKS

about them when she had psychoanalysis. Robert, on the other hand, expressed himself physically rather than through words, by losing control, making love or risking his life in daredevil stunts. As soon as people came too close, he removed himself. And though he had settled with Gerald, their unlikely relationship only lasted because of the large degree of independence they allowed each other and their fine balance of domesticity with a lack of intimacy.

The staff at Faringdon welcomed Jennifer to her new home. It was bizarre that there was now a lady of the house, but if she was not quite Lady of the Manor, she brought a new feminine element to a place that had been created and dominated by men. Naturally, there had always been numerous female visitors, but this was something different – the start of a recognisable family. A young, beautiful couple, cocooned from the violence and horrors of the war, like Adam and Eve in a version of Eden. Jack Fox recalled first seeing Jennifer: 'I never saw a woman with such a pretty face and a pretty figure. She was perfectly proportioned, like an hourglass. That summer, she'd lie out on a bed, sunbathing. She was brown as a berry.'[356]

Friends were agog to witness the highly unorthodox *ménage à trois*. There is no record of public arguments between the newly-weds, but it is hard to imagine that Robert hid his mood successfully. Jennifer probably managed better. Some people were close to all the members of what had become rather an un-erotic triangle. Billa Harrod, for one, was delighted at having her three friends brought together in this way. She was very close to Jennifer (a mutual friend suggested that her adoration bordered on her being in love), but she also got on extremely well with Robert and Gerald.[357] Billa had not approved of Ian Lubbock, and was notoriously forthright about these things. How marvellous, then, to be able to have them all under one roof at one of the loveliest houses she knew, and where she playfully signed herself into the visitors' book as 'Turkish' (in reference to John Betjeman's affectionate nickname, 'my Turkish Delight'). Now the mother of two young sons – Henry and Dominick – Billa encouraged Jennifer in her pregnancy; the baby would have two ready playmates. Other friends also came from Oxford, including Maurice Bowra. The growling-voiced, sharp-witted don didn't often appreciate feminine charms and he certainly didn't suffer fools, but he liked the Mad Boy's bride and was kind to her.

Another local friend who was charmed by Jennifer was the roguish queen of fashion and elegant indulgence, Daisy Fellowes. She often drove over, inevitably drawn by the intrigue at Faringdon, as well as by her affection for Gerald. She was also able to catch up with Winnie de Polignac, the beloved aunt who had brought her up. But for Daisy, it was not only her aunt who beckoned, but the American soldiers. 'Never have I seen her in such glamorous looks,' wrote Diana Cooper to her husband, Duff, after meeting Daisy at the Dorchester. 'The women were startled, the men looked avidly. She adores Compton Beauchamp – Oxford and Gerald within reach and an amorous American group to strengthen her morale.'[358]

Clarissa continued as a regular guest at Faringdon but didn't have much time for Jennifer or Robert. She was younger than both, but they seemed immature social butterflies compared to her and her overworked colleagues at the Foreign Office. 'I couldn't hang around having a lovely time during the war,' she said.[359] Jennifer felt this resentment coming from Gerald's special friend. 'Clarissa probably thought Jennifer silly; Clarissa was so busy *not* being silly,' remembered a mutual friend. Jennifer and Clarissa did have certain things in common, however. They both had a penchant for homosexual men – something that continued throughout their lives. However, Jennifer's voluptuous femininity was in obvious contrast to Clarissa's almost austere seriousness. While Jennifer dressed in beautifully made frocks and heels, Clarissa's favourite outfit was a manly trouser suit.

By the end of the year, Robert was ill and Jennifer's figure was swelling by the day. The prospective mother wrote to Alathea, who had closed up Oare House and moved with Geoffrey to Portmeirion, the Welsh resort designed by Clough Williams-Ellis. Alathea had sent another generous cheque to her daughter, who gives a good impression of the situation at Faringdon, without letting on that she and Robert are miserable.

Faringdon, Dec 30th [1942]

My darling Mummy,

How sweet of you to give me such a tremendous New Year's present.

You are an angel though I really don't think you ought to – but thank you, my darling, a million times –

How are you feeling and are you sleeping better? Don't worry about my clothes as I gave up that belt months ago, and now anyway would never be able to get into it! And I have a nice little red coat which looks quite pretty and keeps me warm – not that I need it here as the house is beautifully central heated except today, the coldest day of the winter on which the Americans have chosen to run out of coal. Very tiresome but we have electric fires so it's quite warm.

Poor Robert is in bed with jaundice and as yellow as a tea rose, as you used to say to me when I had it! He isn't nearly as bad as I was, I'm glad to say, but is a wicked patient and won't do as he's told and will send for Bovril when I'm not looking – his mother is staying here so she helps to keep him in order.

I'm sorry you'd read The Narrow Street. Wouldn't you like to change it? Nancy Rodd [Mitford], who works at H.[eywood] Hill would change it any time.

Will you really be in London in January? It will be lovely to see you again. I do miss you darling, and hope this time you will be better and we will be able to go to plays together.

Take care of yourself, darling, and don't get cold in this wretched weather. And all wishes for a Happy New Year from Robert and me.

Best love
From Jennifer
Best love to Daddy

As Jennifer waited out the last period of her pregnancy, numerous friends came to stay at Faringdon. There were old stalwarts like Coote Lygon (now a flight officer in the WAAFs, specialising in photographic interpretation) and Violet Trefusis, who put her nationality in the visitors' book as 'Bogus Aryan'. The most incongruous guest at the dining table was Pixie, Jennifer's beloved old governess and lifelong ally. She surely brought warmth and encouragement at a time when the baby's imminent arrival was making Jennifer very anxious. It was one thing to be a beautiful, suntanned bride in the summer, and quite another to be heavy with child during the dull, icy days of winter. It is tempting to speculate on the topics of conversation at mealtimes between Gerald and Pixie; two more different characters could scarcely be imagined. Robert laughed, scornful at needing one's nanny at such an advanced age, and would later enjoy recounting inaccurate or scurrilous stories about the pious, ageing spinster.

Pixie was not the only special guest that February. Prim, Jennifer's childhood friend from Oare, had had her first child three months earlier and came to stay with her husband, who happened to be one of England's most glamorous actors, David Niven, and the only British star in Hollywood to return to join up. Having given up romantic leads in films, he lived out a real one instead. Spotting Prim dressed in the powder-blue uniform of a WAAF at the Café de Paris, he fell for her and the couple married within two weeks – nuptials arranged as rapidly as the Heber-Percys'. Prim's fair 'flower-like beauty' could well have suited a screen role as the patient girl-next-door who gets her man in the end; Jennifer's darker, more provocative looks would surely have her cast as the girl who gets in trouble. David Niven loved Primmie's great kindness ('She was incapable of saying an unkind word'[360]), but he craved thrills. Leaving the Rifle Brigade for more action with the Commandos, he joined the Army Film Unit, where in 1942 he starred as an RAF squadron leader in *The First of the Few*, and later, in 1944, appeared in *The Way Ahead*. Prim had meanwhile left the RAF and taken up war work building Hurricane fighters in Slough, but she gave that up and moved to London when she became pregnant with her first child. When David Jr was born, the infant was visited by stars such as Laurence Olivier, John Mills and Noël Coward, who as godfather gave him a silver cocktail shaker inscribed 'Because, my Godson dear, I rather / Think you'll turn out like your father.'

If Jennifer and Prim went back a long way, to lessons with Pixie in the attic at Oare and walks on the chalky Downs, David and Robert also shared youthful memories. Both had attended Stowe in the mid-1920s, when the school had just been founded and there were relatively few pupils. So they remembered each other as adolescents, though they had not been close. It is easy to imagine the two handsome Old Stoics drinking cocktails by the fire and recreating their headmaster, J. F. Roxburgh's, rich, honeyed tone of voice that had fascinated them as pupils. Niven remembered him with great affection, particularly for the attitude he showed to Nessie, the exquisite seventeen-year-old London prostitute (a self-proclaimed "ore with an 'eart of fuckin' gold') whom the young Niven had loved from the virginal age of fourteen, and whom he had invited to visit him for picnics in the school grounds. On one such occasion, Nessie insisted on meeting the famous J.F. ('Look, dear, 'e'll never know I'm an 'ore. 'E'll think I'm yer bleedin' aunt or somefing . . .') The suave headmaster showed no dismay at the unusual school visitor, and finished their discussion by saying, 'David is very lucky to have such a charming visitor.'[361]

Perhaps Robert showed David a letter he had received from J.F. which congratulated him on his marriage. The Mad Boy had replied jokily,

Dear J.F.

It was fun hearing from you again and reading it aloud to myself in that mellifluous voice of yours which I remember so well.

Jennifer and I long to come and see you, and receive your blessing. You might read The Bride of Corinth to us.

Yours ever,

Robert H. P.

Doubtless Gerald was intrigued to meet Niven, an ideal man of the times – matinée idol with bright blue eyes and pencil moustache, as well as courageous soldier. Like Robert, Niven was sexually voracious and had ignominiously left the Army following an early attempt to start a career there after school. Unlike Robert, Niven was famously debonair and witty; he knew exactly how to sing for his supper at Faringdon, tempering society gossip (Noël Coward was far from being the only mutual friend) with a cultured and informed appraisal of the war. He would see enough action – including the D-Day landings – to remove any illusions about the romance of war, and claimed that he was scarred for life by his experiences. Jennifer and Prim would have secluded themselves for 'women's talk', probably sitting in Jennifer's bedroom. Though Prim was two years younger, she was one step ahead with motherhood and Jennifer was very apprehensive about the birth. Prim must have been nonplussed by Jennifer's choice of husband – she was more conventional and didn't share Jennifer's wild streak – but she was kind and encouraging. Her answers would have been soothing: 'Don't worry, darling. It doesn't really hurt. The birth will soon be over. Think what fun we will have together with our babies.'

Jennifer went up to London for the delivery and was admitted to the London Clinic in Harley Street. Her labour was difficult and long, and in the end she was completely anaesthetised and forceps were used. When she woke up, there was a perfect baby girl. 'All the nurses and doctors keep saying how pretty she is,' she wrote to her father a few days later, 'and I must say I think so! She has a mass of brown hair and huge eyes and very long eyelashes!' No jokes then about whether the grandfather would like to drown this baby in a bucket of water for not being male. Robert rose to the occasion and arrived at the clinic by taxi from Covent Garden, having bought up what looked like half the flower market's supply. He filled Jennifer's room to overflowing with hothouse blooms and scented spring flowers. There is no record of the Mad Boy's reaction to his daughter, but the general consensus was that he was a proud father. And nobody could deny that the baby was beautiful. They decided to call her Victoria – the name of Jennifer's Aunt Vera, but also a tip of the cap to the old monarch whose presence was felt in so many offbeat ways at Faringdon, and whose name suggested the old-fashioned dignity and security that was lacking in the turbulent days of war.

'I am feeling wonderfully well and am delighted with my daughter who really is very sweet,' continued Jennifer to Sir Geoffrey, although it wasn't actually so easy. The new mother tried to breastfeed but the baby didn't appear to be drinking well. The nurses weighed her before and after each feed and announced she was not putting on the required ounces. The challenge was enough to make anyone feel tense if not impotent and Jennifer was accustomed to being seen as inadequate since childhood. After three days, she gave up trying and little Victoria was given a bottle. Sugar was added to soothe the baby and cod liver oil for good measure. Jennifer later confessed that she had cried for three days at her failure.[362]

When mother and child returned to Faringdon after a couple of weeks, Jennifer's former bedroom had been turned into the nursery and she moved into the Red Room across the landing, which had its own bathroom. A green baize door was put up to close off this section of the first floor and to muffle the sounds of the infant's cries. Jennifer wrote to thank her mother for another 'wonderful present' (i.e. money) and to say she hoped her relationship with Victoria would be as special as hers with Alathea.

> I've so much to tell you I don't know where to begin. First of all the Nanny is an angel, though I hardly dare say it so soon. She's obviously completely reliable and very intelligent too, about feeding etc – as she discovered poor little Victoria's tummy was very upset, and her bottom was terribly sore as a result, so she has taken her off the sugar and cod liver oil and she is better already. They really should have told me all this in the Clinic and not sent her home in that state. I am thankful to have Nanny, as she is so sensible and is marvellous with the servants – Mrs Law, the cook, is mad about her, and can't do enough to help her! I hardly dare say all this so soon, but my fingers are crossed.
>
> The Nursery is the prettiest room I've ever seen. I can't wait for you to see it, and Victoria looks so sweet in her cot. She has been lying out in the sun in her huge pram, and looks very well and beautiful
>
> . . . It's looking too beautiful here. The garden full of primulas of every colour, and grape hyacinths everywhere.
>
> The head gardener [Mr Morris] has just died and now we have no gardeners at all except an old man, who's really the woodman, and there's such a lot to do at the moment – it's very worrying, and we can't

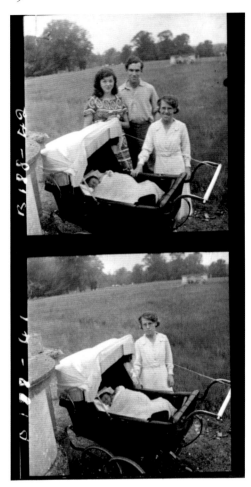

CECIL BEATON'S PHOTOGRAPH OF THE NEW
FAMILY WITH THEIR NANNY

get a land girl as there's nowhere to billet her. How I wish we could get someone like Ackland [the gardener at Oare], but I suppose that's too much to hope for.

In the event, the nanny didn't turn out to be such an angel and there were several others over the first year or so. Baby manuals explained the 'proper' way to care for babies, which was a strict feeding regime on a four-hourly cycle, plenty of lying outside in a pram to get fresh air, and a strict avoidance of 'spoiling' their character by too much indulgence. This approach was not a natural one for Jennifer's lenient character, but the nannies tended to make sure that both mother and baby accepted that 'Nanny knows best'. Having been accustomed to this mantra since her own childhood, it was easy for Jennifer to surrender to Nanny's command. Each time the nannies were sent away, Pixie was sent for to help out until a replacement was found.

If Robert had rejected Jennifer in the early months of their marriage, they appear to have established a modus vivendi after their daughter's birth. Robert was busy on the farm and now that Mr Morris had died, he had to solve the problem of the gardens too. Jennifer was inevitably wrapped up with Victoria, even if she had help, and there were various visitors who came to stay and to admire the baby. It was Gerald's reaction, however, that was the most surprising. During all his years at Faringdon there had been exotic bird calls, avant-garde music and, recently, the Yankee twang of American soldiers trooping up the back staircase, but none produced as unfamiliar, even disconcerting a sound in the house as a tiny baby's cry. Gerald loved animals, but a mewling newborn was far beyond his remit. Some of his friends

had children, but they were not of
particular interest to him. (He would
surely have chuckled in agreement
with Nancy Mitford's *bon mot*, 'I love
children – especially when they cry,
for then someone takes them away.')
The green baize door had seemed
like the erection of a barrier between
him and the baby, but then something
unforeseen happened: he liked the little
girl. It helped that she looked so lovely,
but it was surely heartening to see this
new life, tucked under lacy blankets in
her impressively sprung Rolls-Royce of
a perambulator and pushed along the
drive for walks. Gerald felt old, there
was a war that seemed to be destroying
everything he loved, but here was a small sign of hope.

GERALD WITH VICTORIA. 'GERALD WAS UNEXPECTEDLY NICE TO BABIES', SAID BILLA

'Gerald was unexpectedly nice to babies,' remembered Billa. 'When
Victoria was a child he was frightfully good and nice. I remember him
discovering how to get the pram up the front steps. Can you imagine
it? I remember him saying, "I've discovered how to do it by turning it
around." It was so unexpected of Gerald.'[363] Friends were flabbergasted.
Lord Berners pushing a pram! Whatever next?

Gerald asked Cecil Beaton to come and take pictures. Back from
one of his many trips as a war photographer, Cecil swallowed his
dislike of the 'Horrid Mad Boy' and obliged, setting up tableaux to
capture the essence of this implausible new family. The props were
familiar objects – a gilt cockerel, the portrait of Henry VIII that was
'after Hans Holbein', exquisite flowers that always flooded the house in
the good old days and still managed to put in an appearance. In some
of the pictures, the baby is held by her father or mother, who are both
handsome but tense.

In some pictures Gerald takes on a grandfatherly mien. Sporting one of Mrs Beazley's knitted skullcaps, he cradles the frothy-dressed little girl in his arms. This is the nearest he could ever come to having his own child or grandchild and he was enjoying it. The *Sketch* published some of the photographs under the title 'Faringdon House-Party: Lord Berners and the Heber-Percys'. Robert and Jennifer (in giant sun-hat) are shown with the pram, his hand over hers on the handlebar. Cecil was probably revelling in directing them for his camera, forcing the Mad Boy to act like a responsible father, yet revealing the strain between the parents. Jennifer and Robert are looking in different directions, appearing almost stranded in a sunny tangle of overgrown garden by the orangery that Mr Morris's demise had left like a romantic, eighteenth-century wilderness.

In September there was a christening at All Saints'; the arched wooden door in the wall was opened and family and guests trooped through into the churchyard. The seven-month-old baby was dressed in

October 6, 1943   *The Sketch*   175

FARINGDON HOUSE-PARTY: LORD BERNERS AND THE HEBER-PERCYS.

Conversation-piece at Faringdon. Lord Berners is holding baby VICTORIA GALA, while her parents, MR. and MRS. ROBERT HEBER-PERCY, sit on either side of the fireplace.

In the garden.

CECIL BEATON'S PHOTOGRAPHS OF LORD BERNERS AND THE HEBER-PERCYS PUBLISHED IN THE *SKETCH*. JENNIFER AND ROBERT PUSH VICTORIA'S PRAM THROUGH THE OVERGROWN GARDEN

an elaborate, lacy christening gown at least a yard long and was given the middle name Gala, presumably after Dalí's indomitable wife. Gerald composed some music in honour of the occasion and played it on the church organ. Photographs show the parents with the godparents and Gerald as the symbolic *pater familias*, bursting with pride. Even Robert is beaming in some of the pictures. Jennifer looks delighted – dressed in a clinging raw-silk suit with a perky hat. Clarissa was there, as she often was during those times, still very close to Gerald, but uninterested in the rest of the household. In the photographs she looks unamused.

The godparents were chosen from both sides of the family: Prim Niven, as Jennifer's oldest friend, who came in a sensible wartime coat, and Aunt Nora (Geoffrey Fry's older half-sister), who couldn't make it to the ceremony. Robert chose Michael Duff, the man who

Victoria's christening at All Saints', Faringdon. From left: Robert, Jennifer holding Victoria Gala, Primula Niven, Michael Duff, Gerald and Clarissa Churchill

had introduced him to Gerald twelve years earlier. Michael had been an RAF intelligence officer for the Eagles – a group of American volunteers who fought with the British before the US joined the war – though according to some, he was mostly 'arranging their parties'.[364] After contracting jaundice in Tangier on a reconnaissance expedition, he was invalided out and was now managing Vaynol, which had become a hospital. He signed himself into the visitors' book as 'Tired airman'. The final godparent was also in the RAF, first as a rear-gunner and then as a physicist: Derek Jackson (married to Pamela Mitford) was too busy working on British air defence and improving bombers (for which he was much decorated) to attend the baptism. Both godfathers were, like Robert, men who normally favoured men but who got involved with and married women – Jackson managed six times.

Friends of the Faringdon triangle continued to be amazed by the almost surreal turn of events; it was the perfect subject for entertaining, if partially inaccurate, gossip. Frances Partridge wrote to Heywood Hill, 'Babies are in the air all right – Isobel [Strachey] has been describing Jennifer Fry's, which is a Bright Young Person already – exquisitely beautiful with huge dark eyes and hundreds of young titled godparents.'[365]

The guest lists at Faringdon and Jennifer's sporadic letters to her mother give the impression of a life as pleasant as any could be given the continuation of the war.

> My darling Mummy,
>
> . . . We have been to Oxford this week to see Noël Coward's new plays which were very enjoyable, especially one called 'Present Laughter' – just as good as anything he's ever written – and one called 'This Happy Breed' – ten years of family life on Clapham Common and obviously sincere and straight from his heart but somehow didn't quite come off. Though there were some excellent characters – a wonderful Christian Scientist sister-in-law – Joyce Carey.
>
> You must try to see them when you're in London. We went to see him afterwards and he is just as attractive as I've always thought – tremendous charm.

It was lovely seeing Prim and David [Niven] last weekend. They seemed so happy.

In November, Coward came to stay at Faringdon and afterwards wrote to tell Gerald how much he had enjoyed it. He had evidently liked the new feminine elements in the household, as he joked: 'Give my love to Jennifer and Victoria. I am trying to find the latter the second movement of "Sacre du Printemps" for Christmas because she is an old-fashioned girl.' Jennifer managed to make trips up to London, leaving Victoria with the nanny and catching up with her old friends. She often made an appearance at Cyril Connolly's parties, held with Lys at his flat in Sussex Place. They were filled with members of the artistic and literary set, whether in uniform or not, and among the scruffier, arty girls, Jennifer struck a glamorous note with her perfect outfits and elegant hair and make-up. On one visit to London, Jennifer met her disreputable former flame, Hamish St Clair Erskine, who had just arrived back from war. Bizarrely, given his reputation for being a dandified ne'er-do-well, he had been awarded the MC for bravery. Having gained a commission with the Coldstream Guards, Hamish managed to blow up a German tank and survived serious wounds. He ended up in an Italian prisoner-of-war camp, from which he escaped by doing what he had always enjoyed – dressing up as a woman. He hid from Nazis in ditches – probably dressed as 'the *Marchesa della Piccola Mia*', suggested Nancy Mitford when she heard the tale.[366] James Lees-Milne went for drinks with Hamish and found Jennifer there, and she entertained them with stories. Apparently, wrote Lees-Milne, 'She once laughed so uncontrollably in the High Street, St Albans, that she did herself a mischief, as my Aunt Dorothy expresses it. People noticed, yet she could not help herself. It happened outside an inn. When she looked up she saw the name of the inn was The Waterspout. She was so convulsed that she started all over again.'[367]

Extensive travel by car was impossible, given petrol rationing, but Mr Webb's taxi was regularly used for both the inhabitants of and visitors to Faringdon – within the prescribed twelve-mile radius.

When they had to go further, say to Oxford, they would be met by another hired car at Kingston Bagpuize to take them the rest of the way – something like changing horses in pre-motoring days. Mr and Mrs Webb had a daughter the same age as Victoria, and when Phyllis Webb drove Jennifer to Faringdon station or out to the shops, the two women compared notes on their babies. The Webbs' black-and-silver Armstrong Siddeley was later replaced by several impressively large, albeit left-hand-drive, American cars, brought over by the US servicemen stationed in Faringdon; they struck a jaunty note in the quiet country lanes.

In addition to his farming activities, Robert joined the local Auxiliary Fire Service, an organisation through which part-time volunteers went on night duty every few days, supplementing the full-time professionals in the National Fire Service. There was look-out duty up on the Folly and an enormous water tank in the middle of the Market Place ready for emergencies. The Mad Boy was kitted out in a dark blue uniform with brass buttons and a cap with a badge, and, according to local sources, made the whole thing great fun, taking beer down to the headquarters and creating a party atmosphere whenever it was his night on duty.

Gerald, meanwhile, continued writing music. He was commissioned to produce the soundtrack for *The Halfway House*, an Ealing Studios film, and later wrote an orchestral version of the polka (that had first been played for the hospital Christmas pantomime in Oxford), as well as one of his most mischievous and popular songs for Alberto Cavalcanti's 1944 film, *Champagne Charlie*. 'Come On Algernon' is a music-hall parody, full of double entendres, that tells of insatiable, youthful and above all female sexuality. It features Daisy, always sighing, begging and crying to Algernon:

> Come on Algernon,
> That's not enough for me
> Give me some more
> The same as before . . .

N NOVEMBER 1943, after three years in prison, Oswald Mosley was released due to ill-health and he and Diana left Holloway amidst much popular protest. They were placed under house arrest and stayed at first with Diana's sister Pamela and her husband, Derek Jackson. 'For the first time for three and a half years, we slept in soft, fine linen in soft, warm beds', albeit with journalists lurking outside who would write up the Jacksons' yapping dachshunds as 'baying hounds'.[368] When the authorities realised that the notorious traitors were staying with a man who was doing secret scientific work for the Air Ministry, they were quickly instructed to leave, and moved with their two sons to an inn called the Shaven Crown in the Cotswold village of Shipton-under-Wychwood. Gerald went to visit them there and Diana managed to get permission to go house-hunting, accompanied by two policemen. It should not be surprising, given her immense charm and beauty, that she persuaded the officers to let her stop off for luncheon at Faringdon House. She described herself as 'in the seventh heaven, to visit the charming house once more and eat Gerald's delicious food and listen to his jokes was like being transported back in time to happy days before the war'.[369]

Diana was curious to meet the newest member of Faringdon's *ménage*, but Jennifer was horrified by the prospect of seeing the well-known Fascist. She had long detested the racism and anti-Semitism of the Mosleys and their British followers, and was a lifelong advocate of liberal tolerance. As a small, personal protest, Jennifer locked herself in her bathroom and refused to come out, something of which Lady Mosley was presumably not aware. After lunch, Diana requested a glimpse of the infant, and Gerald took her upstairs to meet Victoria. The nanny showed off the perfect baby, whom Diana described – with icy Mitfordian irony – as being 'like an expensive doll with huge eyes'. Tearing herself away, Diana continued on her house-hunting excursion; 'when [Gerald] saw me off with my two uniformed policemen in front, he said frivolously: "You're the only person now with a chauffeur and a footman on the box."[370]

In London, the war had turned life drab. So many houses were bomb-damaged that most streets seemed to sport gaping gashes. Cyril Connolly wrote of London's 'shabbiness and expense, its dirt and vulgarity'.[371] And with no end in sight, it was all made worse by getting older – Cyril had hit forty the same month that Gerald reached sixty. Gerald wrote to Clarissa, 'And dear old Cyril. He was rather sad I thought and less effervescent than usual – like Eno's [liver salts] that has been left to stand.' And yet at Faringdon, in spite of the American soldiers' presence, it was almost possible to forget the traumas taking place outside the walls. The spring bulbs made a wonderful display along the side of the drive, with tall red tulips poking up among the hyacinths and narcissi. There were beautiful young people and even a charming baby sprawled in the sunshine.

The diaries of James Lees-Milne mention two visits to Faringdon. On one, he drove there from Oxford with Billa.

> A day of unexcelled loveliness, the apex of springtide, warm sun and no wind. At Faringdon House Jennifer Heber-Percy was sitting in the sun, on a swing seat, against the curved retaining wall. There were small chickens running around. This frightened Billa for she hates birds. We talked until 1.45 when we lunched off chicken (she doesn't mind eating them) and rice. Lord Berners, wearing a green knitted skull cap and yellow bow tie, was positively cordial. He is a considerate host. Robert came in to lunch from driving a tractor on the farm. He was wearing a pair of battle-dress trousers and a yellow aertex shirt open at the neck. Very bronzed by the sun, youthful and handsome. He is the enfant terrible, all right. What a curious family they were, sitting round this large round table. But they know how to live. I thought how enviable their ménage.[372]

Later in the day, Billa went for a walk with Jennifer and Gerald showed Lees-Milne around the house, discussing architectural details with him and doubtless catching up on the news of their mutual London friends like the Ladies Cunard and Colefax, Harold Nicolson or Maimie Lygon. The diary continues:

The house is attractively untidy in an Irish way, with beds, but beautiful ones, scattered in the downstairs rooms. Much confusion and comfort combined. Jennifer's baby Victoria playing on the floor like a kitten. Lord B. said that this afternoon one of the Negro soldiers – and the place is stiff with them – accosted him in the garden with the request, 'Massa, may I pick just a little bunch of flowers for our colonel?'[373]

CHAPTER THIRTEEN

Put in a Van

HE 'CURIOUS' FAMILY may have looked enviable to some onlookers, but its fundamental flaw remained. Though the set-up was agreeable to the oldest and youngest members of the household, it was far from ideal for Jennifer and Robert. They were not lovers and keeping up the pretence of marriage was a strain on two people for whom freedom – and particularly erotic freedom – was fundamental. During the summer of 1944, as the huge offensive for the D-Day landings was finally set into motion, they separated. Jennifer decided to return to her parents' home at Oare with Victoria, and Robert located a van to transport mother, baby and their belongings to Wiltshire. It must have been with sadness that Gerald bade them goodbye; he had enjoyed the pram in the hall, and the feminine presence in the house had brought a sweetness and domestic tenderness that he had never known before. When he published his second volume of memoirs, A *Distant Prospect*, the following year, he dedicated it to Jennifer Heber-Percy.

It was a troubled summer for many people, even by the harsh standards of the past five years. It was double summertime, so evenings remained light until well after ten, but the weather was cold and rainy. Thousands of British and US troops were slaughtered on the Normandy beaches, and to make matters worse, the Germans' fearful new V-1 flying bombs started landing on London and southern England. Everyone quickly learned about the terrifying nature of these pilotless bombs; there was no warning and when the engine cut out, you knew that seconds later there would be dreadful damage and numerous deaths wherever it landed. You could only hope it would be somewhere else. Both Faringdon and Oare were safely out of reach of Hitler's 'secret' weapon, but it was a miserable time for both households.

Many years later, when she was attending a Jungian psychoanalyst, Jennifer wrote a stream-of-consciousness account of this period of her life in a notebook. It now reads like a list of clues as to what happened, with some more obvious and others that remain opaque.

> Anna Karenina – The Race – the Fall – Robert. The pain. The Bed and the far away wing – the tears. The speechlessness – the Famous, Renowned and old. The kindness of Freddy, Maurice, with slight but loving malice. And back to the four poster and letters and tears. The three in bed. The herbs over the door. The Toy, and the [illegible] – the best food and the van I was put in with my baby and half my luggage. All my underclothes and love letters left in a drawer and read and laughed at by Cecil and Clarissa.

The first mystery is Anna Karenina. Why is Jennifer recalling the famous horse-race scene, where Vronsky falls and his beloved dark mare is injured and has to be shot? Could Jennifer have seen Robert ride and fall at the Grand National in 1937? Might they have had some sort of relationship then? It is hard to associate Jennifer and Robert with such an intense love story as Tolstoy's, but perhaps there was a time of high passion. 'The pain' is surely Robert's rejection after the wedding, and 'the speechlessness' with the 'Famous, Renowned and old' sounds like a Faringdon re-run of what Jennifer had suffered at her father's dining table in her youth. It must have been a strain making conversation at dinner with the Princesse de Polignac or various Sitwell siblings, when Robert was sulking across the table and she would have preferred a quiet evening to talk to her reluctant husband, or at least an escape to a party with cocktails and dancing.

Half a lifetime after the events, Jennifer appreciated the small kindnesses of Frederick Ashton and Maurice Bowra (albeit with 'slight but loving malice'). The 'three in bed' sounds as though it might be with Robert and someone else, but is anyone's guess, and the herbs and 'the Toy' remain unexplained. The van became a symbol of Jennifer's ignominious departure – a sign that she was packed off with her baby, flung out into a world of war and uncertainties without ceremony. This story became a tragicomic one, repeated over the years by Jennifer and then Victoria, the bathos marking the finale to their Faringdon era. The most painful sentence is the part referring to Jennifer's intimate belongings that she forgot to pack. How did she find out about Cecil Beaton and Clarissa Churchill reading the letters and laughing? Jennifer was well aware that Clarissa did not appreciate her presence at Faringdon, but after all she had suffered, the image of the two friends cackling as they leafed through her silken knickers to fish out her most private, hidden correspondence must have been a devastating humiliation. Perhaps it was not like that at all, but the shameful, burning soreness it left is clear.

Jennifer had sent a telegram to her parents, and although Oare was closed up, they made a part of it available to her. She and Victoria were not to be alone; Billa and her two young sons, Henry and Dominick (aged five and four), were to join them there, leaving Roy behind in Oxford. He would be able to go over for some weekends and the arrangement would not only provide Jennifer and Victoria with company but give the young boys some space and country air. Billa's letters to her husband indicate that they were installed at Oare by mid-July and the leitmotif is 'poor Jennifer!' with just a touch of irony.

> Poor Jennifer has got Victoria on her hands now, <u>&</u> the daily who cooks the breakfast has been called up. However I think we shall get someone else. The village are very shocked because we have 3 dailies. It is quite absurd as they only come for a few hours each. Anyhow I don't care if they <u>die</u> of shock, so long as I don't have to work! Yesterday we made some lovely strawberry jam . . . Poor Jennifer is <u>very</u> exhausted having had to look after Victoria for a fortnight which makes me laugh! Luckily her nanny comes on Saturday.[374]

The house may have been mostly closed, but the two mothers

and their three children made
themselves at home for the
best part of the next year. Each
time the nannies left, Jennifer
sent urgent telegrams to Pixie
begging her to come and
help – which she did. Despite
being out in the middle of the
Wiltshire countryside, they
were not isolated. American
soldiers came over in Jeeps
to take Jennifer and Billa to parties and there were expeditions to
Stonehenge and Avebury. Prim and David Niven visited when David
was on leave, bringing their son with them, and Violet Wyndham was
close by and remained a treasured and broad-minded friend in whom
Jennifer could confide. At Oare, they kept donkeys, made quince jelly
and went for walks along the lanes that Jennifer had loved as a child.
When their old friends Peter and Glur Quennell visited, they cooked
jugged hare, using the blood, according to the traditional recipe. When
the bottom fell out of the casserole, they merely scraped up the dark
stew and served it as though nothing had happened. The two women
were thrown into a panic when 'Sir Geoff' came to stay in his own
home, and he cannot have been thrilled by the idea of three noisy
children, though he always liked his only granddaughter. Indeed,
according to some, Victoria was the only person in the family who was
not afraid of him.

Robert sometimes came over to visit, acting as though everything
was perfectly normal. He felt guilty as well as relieved at his failure to
make a good husband and father. Jennifer was less resilient, and Billa
was known to snap: 'Do stop bursting into tears.'[375] Billa confessed to
Roy that she herself was not always happy at Oare. 'I get terrible moods
of horror about myself and see myself as ugly, useless, unpopular etc
which is all just absurd and unreasonable as I have got endless devoted
friends.' She also had to cancel one of Roy's visits in late September

VICTORIA WITH
JENNIFER AT OARE

because Jennifer was miserable: 'I don't see much hope of the weekend as though I have hinted dozens of times Jennifer is in a very depressed state and says she doesn't want anyone for the weekend. It seems such a shame as the weather is lovely and it really is heavenly here.'

It was not long, however, before Jennifer acquired a lover; she might even have met him before she left Faringdon – the timing is unknown. Michael ('Mickey') Luke was a handsome boy of nineteen. The son of a diplomat, he had left Eton the previous year and was commissioned into the Rifle Brigade where he learned to drive tanks and work big guns. According to the story, a duty officer spotted him reading Proust and quickly transferred him to military intelligence instead. His black wartime witticism 'It's awfully chic to be killed' was used by Anthony Powell in *A Dance to the Music of Time*, but some found him 'too charming for his own good'.[376] He and Jennifer were soon embroiled in a passionate affair.

Billa's letters to Roy describe the early trysts. 'Our little soldier came to dinner last night, he writes poetry and draws, both very badly but is so sweet, just like an undergraduate. We cooked some salmon for dinner which Jenny had bought in London.' On a later occasion, 'Mickey stayed nearly a week; how he gets so much leave no one knows. He is a <u>dear</u> boy, so sweet and sensitive and angelic with the children.'

When the situation with nannies allowed, Jennifer would dash up to London for crazy nights with Mickey at the Gargoyle Club. All the usual suspects would be there, watched over by Brian Howard, 'forked tongue and cloven hoof, swivelling on a bar-stool waiting to release his unexpended venom on suitable prey'.[377] On one occasion, Jennifer and Mickey arrived, with Mickey in the Rifle Brigade's dress uniform, to be greeted by Howard: 'How wonderful to see you, Jennifer. And you've brought your chauffeur!'[378] He might have been young, but Mickey had fallen deeply in love. Although Jennifer loved him too, it was never an easy relationship. He became increasingly obsessed, threatening suicide if he couldn't see her and throwing jealous scenes because she would not commit herself more fully. If Robert had been stand-offish and cold, Mickey took things to the other extreme.

Billa quickly became disenchanted with Jennifer's 'young man'; the couple's heavy drinking and what she called 'misbehaviour' became tiresome. It was clear that Mickey wanted Jennifer all to himself, to the extent that he was sometimes even jealous of Victoria. Billa also found the explicitly erotic nature of the relationship hard to cope with – Mickey had transformed their cosy matriarchal household into something unstable and combustible. Once, Francis Wyndham was visiting Jennifer at Oare when she was getting dressed up to go to London to meet Mickey. Francis and Billa admired Jennifer's clothes and she laughed: 'Of course, it will all be torn off when I get there.' Billa looked revolted and said to Francis, 'Isn't sex disgusting!' 'Billa was very possessive about Jennifer', recalled Francis. 'She was bossy but adoring – it was a very unequal relationship . . . Jennifer was very liberated and enlightened on sex . . . and Billa was jealous of Mickey.'[379]

While Jennifer was starting to enjoy life again with her young soldier, Robert was doing very much the same thing himself. At around the time that Billa's first letter was sent from Oare in July 1944, a dark-haired, twenty-six-year-old officer called Hugh Cruddas began signing himself into the Faringdon visitors' book. Robert had met Captain Cruddas in London, possibly at some sort of military reunion, and was taken with the sweet-natured young man. Hughie, as he was known, was the son of a lieutenant colonel in the Indian Medical Service. He had been wounded in the leg, then captured in North Africa in 1941, then imprisoned in an Italian POW camp near Parma. When Italy surrendered in 1943, he and many others escaped into the nearby hills before the Nazis arrived to escort the prisoners to Germany. Along with two companions, Hughie walked the 500 miles down through German-occupied Italy to reach the Allies in Bari. Back in England, he had got engaged to Juliet Heygate, a twenty-four-year-old RADA-trained actress who had been a driver and then a subaltern in the Army. But in early June 1944 a notice was placed in *The Times*: 'The marriage arranged between Captain H. Cruddas and Miss Juliet Heygate will not now take place.' It seems possible that the Mad Boy played some part in this cancellation.

'Gerald couldn't have minded Hugh Cruddas because he was so sweet, nice and pleasant,' remembered Clarissa. 'He wouldn't have impinged.' If Clarissa had not been impressed by Jennifer, she was no more so by Hugh, though he was easier to stomach: 'He was a sort of non-character as far as I was concerned.'[380] Hugh's gentle ways and good nature quickly made him a regular visitor and then a part of the household. 'The Captain' (as he was known by estate staff) had many practical attributes, including an interest in arranging flowers, and he was famous for mixing marvellous Bloody Marys. It wasn't long before he was taken on as 'Farm Manager', with his name printed on the Berners Estates Company paper, but he would never achieve anything like an equal partnership with Robert. The Mad Boy was soon treating Hughie badly, as he seemed to with almost anyone he was close to, yet he didn't quite break up the relationship.

Maurice Bowra, in a characteristically mischievous yet intriguing analysis, commented on this new Faringdon set-up with a Shakespearean parallel. He suggested that if Gerald could be viewed as King Lear, Robert and Hughie were Goneril and Regan, the two ruthlessly grasping, older daughters, while Clarissa was Cordelia, the virtuous, loyal youngest. John Betjeman would be cast as the Fool.[381] Although it was an acidic joke, there must have been those who thought that Robert was abusing Gerald's love for him by bringing first a wife and then a boyfriend to Faringdon. There is no sign, however, that Gerald was upset by this domestic development; indeed some have suggested that he took rather a liking to the fresh-faced captain, even to the extent of annoying Robert. When Hughie went to Tripoli in Lebanon, Gerald wrote him a letter which shows no sign of jealousy or tension: 'Is it very Oriental or just sordid and suburban? Beverley Nichols was here last weekend. He taught Robert Backgammon which is maddening as Robert is trying to teach me and I think it is the most boring game in the world and anyway I can't count. Robert misses you very much and whines as poor Shine [a dog] did when Robert was out of the room.'

Later, there is evidence that Hughie provided a useful element in Faringdon's second, but longer-lasting, *ménage à trois* – as the butt of jokes. Both Robert and Gerald were inveterate, sometimes cruel, teasers and it was irresistible to pick on the genial Hughie. In 1948, Gerald wrote to Diana Mosley, mentioning her older sister: 'Nancy has I'm afraid been rather naughty making mischief with Hugh. She told him a lot of things that Robert and I were supposed to have said about him which, even if we <u>had</u> said them ought not to have been repeated. But, as David Herbert said, all one's friends <u>do</u> make mischief. With Nancy I think it is "anything for a shriek!"'

HEN PEACE WAS DECLARED in May 1945, Gerald and Robert were at Faringdon with guests for lunch. Elizabeth Bowen described the scene as the fountain on the back lawn was turned on for the first time since 1939:

After lunch we all went out and stood on the terrace; Robert did something to the fountain; there was a breathless pause, then a jet of water, at first a little rusty, hesitated up into the air, wobbled then separated into four curved feathers of water. It was so beautiful and so sublimely symbolic – with the long view, the miles of England, stretching away behind it, that I found myself weeping. I think a fountain is much nicer than a bonfire; if less democratic.[382]

The end of war gave hope for some sort of fresh start in a country that had changed so drastically over six exhausting, tragic years. And yet, despite the relief, joy and dancing in the streets, much of the bleak, frugal atmosphere continued. There was a sense of disorientation for many who had been used to living on the edge, ready for death or disaster. Now, there was a vacuum. Cyril Connolly was deeply gloomy about post-war England: 'Most of us are not men or women but members of a vast seedy, over-worked neuter class, with our drab clothes, our ration books and murder stories, our envious, stricken, old-world apathies and resentments – a careworn people.'[383] With Attlee's Labour government voted in, some believed that the era of the grand country

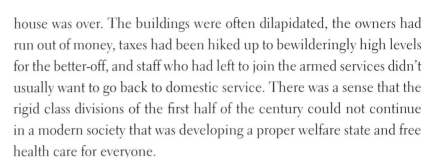

house was over. The buildings were often dilapidated, the owners had run out of money, taxes had been hiked up to bewilderingly high levels for the better-off, and staff who had left to join the armed services didn't usually want to go back to domestic service. There was a sense that the rigid class divisions of the first half of the century could not continue in a modern society that was developing a proper welfare state and free health care for everyone.

At Faringdon it was possible to cut back without doing anything too radical. The house in London was sold and via Foro Romano was let. Faringdon itself was a *mignon* country estate and had always had an unkempt edge. 'Any room of Gerald's would be in the same muddle,' remarked Robert.[384] 'There was luxury but it was rather uncomfortable,' remembered Rachel Cecil, who often came over with her husband from Oxford. 'It wasn't very grand or highly organised. Things were quite in a mess . . . A very pretty room but it wasn't quite like a bedroom. You'd have nowhere to hang your clothes.'[385] The house didn't need large numbers of servants to function perfectly well and in any case there were evidently enough local men who returned from the armed forces and needed employment.

With Robert and Hughie running the practical side of the farm and gardens, Gerald was able to continue much as he always had; given the trials and miseries he had been through during the war, he was impressively active. In 1946, he wrote the music for Alberto Cavalcanti's *Nicholas Nickleby*, an Ealing Studios film that came out the next year. More significant was another collaboration he undertook for the first new ballet for Sadler's Wells after it moved to Covent Garden's Royal Opera House. *Les Sirènes* was a re-gathering of old friends who worked together at Faringdon in preparation for the production: Freddie Ashton did the choreography, Cecil Beaton (back from an unlikely romance with Greta Garbo) designed the costumes and Margot Fonteyn danced the part of the Spanish Beauty who is pursued by a poor young man and a rich old king. It was a light comedy featuring a car, a balloon and mechanical waves on a beach, and although some found it 'divinely pretty and funny',[386] and even Lord Berners's 'most brilliant work',[387] the production was generally considered to have been a flop. In the sober climate that followed the war, people apparently didn't care for a frothy pastiche that epitomised the giddy excesses of the 1930s. It was just the sort of criticism that had been levelled at *Cupid and Psyche* when it was performed in the worrying days of 1939 as war was looming. Billa looked back on this episode as an attempt by Gerald to retrieve a golden era. 'All the nice things had gone, and I suppose he tried to bring it back by writing a ballet like that, and then they didn't come back at all. Then there was all that terrible time of austerity . . . really horrible. Endless shortages. Still evacuees . . .'[388]

At Faringdon, there were well-tested ways of getting around the rationing, and visitors still flocked there. Among the many loyal friends who adored Gerald and Robert and who saw him regularly were the Betjemans, the Harrods, the Mitfords and the Lygons. Nancy's *The Pursuit of Love* was published in 1945 with great success, and the depiction of Gerald as the glamorously *sui generis* Lord Merlin was a tip of her cap to the man who had provided such a refuge and such friendship to her and her sisters. In the book, the heroine, Linda, often rides over to chat with Lord Merlin for hours on all sorts of subjects. 'He knew that she had an intensely romantic character, he foresaw much trouble ahead, and he continually urged upon her the necessity for an intellectual background.' This was clearly a trait of Gerald's, many of whose friends were far from being intellectuals, yet who had himself been saved over a lifetime by pursuing his interests with seriousness.

Of course, sometimes the interests failed to catch Gerald and he plummeted into depression. He was also increasingly plagued by physical ailments for which he visited various fashionable and certain experimental doctors. By 1947, his already failing eyesight was badly affected, possibly due to his doctor's prescriptions, and he wrote in a large, childish hand to Nancy Mitford, lamenting how he could hardly see:

> That arch beast Pierre Lausel! He gave me an overdose of an unknown
> and apparently dangerous drug, Vitamine E, believing it to be of the

order of dear old Vitamine B. I just lapped it up unsuspectingly, with the most appalling results – the worst being this misfortune to my eyes. Lausel ought really to be warned off, defrocked or whatever is done to delinquent doctors who treat their patients as guinea pigs.

Gerald had long been attracted to the idea of a wonder cure for body and psyche. Back in the early 1930s, he had dined with a Swiss millionaire who owned a pharmaceutical business and learned about a drug (supposedly sold from a particular pharmacy in Paris) '*qui rend la vie merveilleuse*'. For a time, Gerald fantasised that this miraculous medicine would permanently remove his *accidie* and render his life 'marvellous'. Until, of course, he took it and it didn't.[389] Later in 1947, Gerald went to a clinic in Richmond, outside London, where Dr Gottfried gave him two weeks' 'electric treatment' for his heart condition. Gerald found the enthusiasm to write a little description of Richmond as a place he had come to appreciate during his 'enforced sojourn' there. 'Were Richmond in the Salzkammergut or in some foreign part of the world it would have been patronised by the wealthy and fashionable, for it holds all the delights of a foreign watering-place without the bother of the waters.' He sent a letter to Nancy Mitford, declaring, 'Did you know that one's status in the nursing home depends entirely on one's flowers? Robert brings me enormous chrysanthemums looking like poodles from les serres [greenhouses] de Faringdon and I stand very high.'[390] However, he was not so positive about the therapy itself. He wrote to Edward James that it 'has made me <u>look</u> better but <u>feel</u> worse. I suspect him of being a beauty doctor.' Cecil Beaton was devoted to Gottfried – and apparently based Professor Higgins's house in *My Fair Lady* on his Wimpole Street rooms[391] – but Gerald was far from impressed. Indeed, other friends, including Harold Acton, believed that Dr Gottfried was a quack who had actually made them much worse.[392]

The various complaints continued. Gerald told Osbert Lancaster, 'I am permanently depressed,' and confessed to Siegfried Sassoon that he had such problems with heart trouble and high blood pressure that he could barely walk, 'let alone write, paint or compose music . . . Between 7 and 8 in the morning when formerly I felt delight in life and the prospect of another day, is now the time when I chiefly long for death. I have had these periods of gloom before and have got over them, but this time (as one likes to associate oneself with greatness) I fear it is the last, as with Cowper and Ruskin.'

Some of Gerald's friends tried to pull him towards religion – it was rumoured that Penelope Betjeman had been assigned Lord Berners as a 'conversion target' by the Roman Catholic Church (while Evelyn Waugh had been given the 'impossible assignment' of Cyril Connolly).[393] But far from keeping an open mind, as he had claimed to some at the start of the war, Gerald became fed up with his friends recommending God. 'Why should I listen to them? It is all such *bosh!*' he railed.[394] When Diana Mosley reported that Waugh was praying for him, Gerald got quite cross and said, 'God doesn't pay any attention to Evelyn.'[395] It is hard to know whether or not Gerald's description of Robert being ill after the end of the war is true to life or exaggerated, but it appears that even the Mad Boy (encouraged by Penelope Betjeman?) didn't rule out God as an appropriate companion for one's final hours.

> Robert is getting awfully dotty. He had a slight temperature yesterday and went to bed in the drawing-room and said that he had got consumption and that the red damask from [illegible] would make a very pretty death-bed scene and asked the gardener to send in some lilies. He also wanted a Roman Catholic priest as he thought a death bed conversion would be very effective. However, he seems better today and is going out hunting.[396]

There were periods of recuperation when Gerald's spirits lifted. He read a great deal, taking particular pleasure in the classics. Writing to Cyril when he was ill, he said, 'I've put in a good deal of reading: Balzac, Proust, and "Middlemarch", Old Horse-Face's masterpiece – which I had not read before.'[397] He also enjoyed contemporary writers, including Angus Wilson, Jocelyn Brooke and André Gide. In 1947, after Gide was awarded the Nobel Prize for Literature, he was given an honorary degree at Oxford. The organisers were nervous about the French writer's notoriously unconventional character and his homosexuality, and they came up with Lord Berners as a solution for the social side of the visit. Gide was taken to Faringdon for lunch the day after the ceremony. The house party included David and Rachel Cecil and Cyril and Lys Connolly; notwithstanding clinics, ill-health, depression and post-war austerity, Gerald and Faringdon seemed once more to be at the centre of European culture. Gerald was thrilled and claimed he considered Gide 'the best writer in Europe and the most delightful of men'. He surely agreed with Gide's aphorism 'Believe those who are seeking the truth. Doubt those who find it.'

During another period of optimism, Gerald hoped to create a scent of his own and even consulted his old friend Elsa Schiaparelli, whose 1937 launch of Shocking had been wildly successful. He abandoned the plan, however, when he learned that 'the base of all scents is something quite obnoxious, like some secretion from the civet cat, which in itself, smells terrible, but which acts as an agent to blend all the other elements'. He feared that if he dropped some of this on the carpet there would be no way to get rid of the smell other than abandoning the house – something he was not prepared to do.[398]

HEN THE WAR ENDED, Jennifer had considered staying in the countryside and even bought a house near Oare, but the city beckoned. She took Victoria and made their new home in South Terrace, South Kensington, but her life remained unsettled for several years. She continued to seek out the best nightclubs, enjoying 'low life' as well as classier places. Lucian Freud recalled visiting a club where a drag queen took Jennifer's fur coat as a prop for his act and stroked his face with it. She was an alluring, glamorous figure for him, a regular at the seedy dives he also loved.[399] Mickey's continuing obsessive love proved wearing if not impossible. 'He was glowering and furious,' recalled Francis Wyndham. 'Always threatening suicide, always desperate. And Jennifer was much older, as was often pointed out by Billa.' There were terrible rows at South Terrace, with Mickey smashing piles of records on the floor in fury and throwing things out of the window. Victoria also liked to fling things from her third-floor bedroom window, emptying glasses of water and sugared almonds on the heads of passers-by, so locals may have learned to avoid the pavement outside No. 21 in the post-war years. According to Jennifer, Mickey had a 'violent horror of his own violence', and at least he was never sexually violent. As she wrote in a notebook, he 'knew so much about psychology, poetry, music, everything'.

At the end of 1945, Prim Niven gave birth to a second son, Jamie, and not long after, she and David gave a large farewell party at

DAVID AND PRIM NIVEN WITH NEW BABY ON A VISIT TO SEE JENNIFER

Claridge's, announcing that they would soon be leaving for America. David and Prim decided that the guests would all have a common characteristic: 'at some time in our lives they had been specially nice to us. It was a funny mixture – duchesses, policemen, actors, generals, hospital nurses . . .' with David taking pleasure in weeding out any gatecrashers.[400]

David crossed the Atlantic first and Prim made the trip with her young boys the following spring. It was in May that Jennifer received the terrible news from Hollywood: Prim was dead. There had been a freak accident. Prim and David had been invited to a party – a barbecue by the pool at Tyrone Power's house, followed by games. They decided to play 'Sardines' and Prim opened a door thinking it was a cupboard, when it was actually stairs leading to the cellar. The hospital initially thought she merely had concussion, but she died the next day. It was of course a tragedy for David Niven and their two young children, but it was also a dreadful blow for Jennifer. She and Prim had grown up together and were true friends; they had seen each other through teenage parties, wartime marriage and childbirth. Prim was Victoria's godmother. She was only twenty-five.

Jennifer could barely mention Prim afterwards, and this surely added to what was already almost a phobia; she even avoided funerals of her close friends and found it impossible to discuss death. A few years after this loss, Cyril Connolly wrote out some pages for Jennifer, in which he numbered a long list of what *must* happen to us after death if you confront the subject rationally – something he knew both he and Jennifer found hard:

> C.C.'s cure for the fear of death.
> To be taken LOGICALLY
> I. Either there is survival after death or there isn't (extinction).
> II. If there is survival it cannot be bodily survival for we know the body decays. Therefore it must be spiritual survival.
> III. Spiritual survival may be impersonal or personal. If impersonal we have nothing to fear, for the experience of spirit without personality cannot be painful, if personal (and it is difficult to imagine personal spirit) it cannot be very different from our own most spiritual moments in this life and they without exception are blissful, timeless and exalting.
> Etc.[401]

n 1947, Robert and Jennifer were divorced. The next year Jennifer decided to give a joint party with Hamish Erskine, bringing together many of their old friends as well as more recent ones. After his heroic deeds during the war, Hamish was also finding it hard to re-make a life. Like others who began as the butterflies of the brittle and sybaritic existentialism that followed the First World War, the prospect of 'settling down' was neither appealing nor feasible. Hamish eventually became the *homme d'affaires* for Daisy Fellowes, Gerald's old friend and country neighbour. Debonair and worldly, he spoke French and Italian, which was useful for Daisy's international, yacht-set society, but middle age and post-war puritanism made the endless indulgence in revelry less appropriate. Many felt that the old ways they had embraced did not exist any more; perhaps the party was an attempt to see if they did. The only record that remains is an excoriating description by James Lees-Milne, who hated it in spite of the number of people present he counted as friends.

> I believe my generation to be, for the most part, 'unreal'; cliquey, dated, prejudiced, out of touch with the new world and preposterously exclusive – arrogant, arrogant, with few redeeming qualities of any kind. They have nothing original to impart . . . I don't truly care if I never see these people again. They are only tolerable singly or in very small groups. In a mass they are detestable and contemptible. Am I one of them?[402]

Lees-Milne might have seen this cliquey circle as 'unreal' but it included people who were among the most interesting, creative individuals of the time. Jennifer remained close to Cyril, who brought her to the heart of literary and artistic London, and her next love affair was with another writer – Henry Yorke. He was older (forty-three to her thirty-two) and, under the nom de plume Henry Green, the author of numerous successful if experimental novels whose titles mostly end in '-ing' (*Living, Loving, Concluding*, and later, *Doting*). He produced writing that was strange, sparse and sometimes bewildering, with a penchant for working-class argot ('It makes me 'eart drop when I remember the way 'e be-'aves, 'is own flesh and blood too.').[403] But nobody doubted it was spectacularly good, even if some said he was 'a writer's writer'. Tall, with dark, slicked-back hair and a pale, handsome face, Henry had been at Oxford in the 1920s with Cyril and that well-known group of aesthetes and writers that included Harold Acton and Brian Howard. Maurice Bowra had teased him about his heterosexuality.[404] During the war, Henry had served in the Auxiliary Fire Service in London, a terrifying and exciting experience he wrote about in *Caught* (1943), though he did not puff up the characters with false heroism. In reality, one of the great advantages of the AFS was the opportunity for meeting women who liked the idea of a brave fireman. 'Who are you going out with tonight, darling?' girls would ask. 'Is it someone you'd like to die with?'[405]

Henry was also married. 'Dig' (*née* the Hon. Adelaide Biddulph), his wife since 1929, was universally recognised as 'sweet' and 'nice' and 'almost as inscrutable as Henry'.[406] When they were first married, they were known as 'the Bright Young Yorkes', and Dig's friends included the Duchess of York (later Queen Elizabeth), who stood as godmother to their son, Sebastian. Dig was so nice that she seems not only to have turned a benevolently blind eye to her husband's many girlfriends (who included Rosamund Lehmann and Mary Keene), but to have kept them close as friends. Later, when Jennifer remarried, Henry and Dig saw her regularly.

Evelyn Waugh mockingly called his old friend (and literary rival) 'Mr H. Yorke the lavatory king' on account of his parallel career with Pontifex, his family's factory in the Midlands, which made, among other things, plumbing parts. Henry always tried to keep his writing life as Green quite separate from his business and personal life as Yorke. His *Who's Who* entry listed his favourite pastime as 'romancing over the bottle, to a good band' – an interest he shared with Jennifer. In 1948, Waugh wrote to Nancy Mitford about Henry's liaison with Jennifer, and she replied, 'I should think Miss Fry and Henry very well suited both so sexy.'[407] When asked about the inspiration for *Loving*, Henry replied with provocative English dryness mixed with eroticism. He had got the idea, he said, from 'a manservant in the Fire Service during the war. He was serving with me in the ranks, and he told me he had once asked the elderly butler who was over him what the old boy most liked in the world. The reply was: "Lying in bed on a summer morning, with the window open, listening to the church bells, eating buttered toast with cunty fingers." I saw the book in a flash.'[408]

Henry was already drinking too much and starting to neglect his appearance; by 1952 he had written his last novel and was becoming a somewhat pitifully lugubrious figure. Nevertheless, in the late 1940s, he was attractive enough to appeal to Jennifer, not to mention other young women – his subsequent relationship was with Kitty Freud, whose marriage to Lucian Freud was breaking up. Above all, Henry was interesting and intelligent and, after the childish antics of Mickey, it was refreshing for Jennifer to be with somebody older and probably wiser.

Henry's 1950 novel, *Nothing*, features John Pomfret, a middle-aged widower whose younger lover is supposedly based at least partially on Jennifer, though there are also elements of her in other characters. The opening scene depicts an event which actually occurred at Jennifer's house. John visits his former mistress, Jane, and enacts a mock marriage ceremony with her young daughter, Penelope. The game is taken one step too far and the young child ends up crying in her mother's arms. Victoria had in fact dressed up as a bride when aged about five, to play this somewhat inappropriate game with Henry, though she has no memory of the tears.

Jennifer adored her daughter, but despite her struggles at Oare with only sporadic help she had little idea of the physical reality of motherhood; women in her milieu did not generally spend much time with their children and it was assumed that you hired people for the practicalities. Once, Jennifer took the four-year-old Victoria shopping at Harrods and then went home, totally forgetting her. Racing back, she found the child quite unperturbed in the fabrics department, entertaining herself by removing and replacing price tags on bolts of material.

It was a painful irony that Jennifer should have made some of the same mistakes as Alathea had in her time. Most crucially, she employed a nanny for Victoria who was bad-tempered and aggressive. Wrapped up in her own struggle to establish a new life after the Faringdon debacle, Jennifer relied on Mardie, a forceful, middle-aged, chain-smoking Scot, to take on much of the day-to-day childcare. Jennifer knew that Mardie shouted and railed, but she failed to grasp the extent to which the nanny was bullying her daughter. Victoria travelled up to Scotland with Mardie for long holidays over the summer where she would not see her mother at all (when Jennifer asked whether she might join them for a visit, she was told it would be better if she didn't). Just as her own nannies had conspired to make Alathea an almost obsolete figure who could be idealised from a distance, so Jennifer allowed Mardie to keep the nursery a world apart.

Although Jennifer did not return to Faringdon for many years, she and Robert collaborated so that their daughter could spend time with her father. Victoria would be sent over with a nanny for a few days at a time and later for longer periods during the school holidays. There are photographs of Victoria, aged about three, sitting on Gerald's lap, and he continued to feel huge affection for the child, and showed her kindness despite his worsening health. Robert arranged pony rides and visits from other children and generally tried to do what was expected of a father. He still cared enough about Jennifer to show signs of jealousy and on one visit tried to teach the young Victoria a rhyme involving a parrot and the line 'Mickey's gone to visit Pixie's sister', evidently hoping that she would recite it back home. A surviving letter from Robert to Sir Geoffrey indicates that Victoria was sometimes sent across from Faringdon to Oare; bizarrely, these two bisexual, self-centred men found themselves discussing the practicalities of childcare in the post-war years when bread, butter, sugar and meat were still rationed. Written on Berners Estates Company paper ('Directors: RT. HON. LORD BERNERS, R. V. HEBER-PERCY, Farm Manager – Capt. H. H. Cruddas

M.C'), it probably dates from about 1948, when Victoria was five, and when Jennifer was in London making secret dates with Henry Yorke.

> Dear Geoffrey
>
> I hope Victoria arrived safely.
>
> Jennifer has got her ration book. I don't know if you will be any more successful than I was at getting it.
>
> We find that eggs or cream have a disastrous effect on both stomach and temper, otherwise she has been very sweet and good.
>
> Yours,
>
> Robert

Only a year later, the affair with Henry was over, and Jennifer was getting married for the second time. Alan Ross was exceptionally attractive – dark-eyed, black-haired, slim and athletic – a poet and a keen cricketer, and combined a sophisticated love of glamour with sensitivity and a tendency to depression. Six years younger than Jennifer, he had been born in Calcutta and had undergone the conventional miseries of children sent to boarding school in England, where he desperately missed the Indian servants and his ayah, who had spoken to him in Hindustani and given him the security he now lacked. He had gone up to Oxford in 1940, studying modern languages at St John's and becoming a cricket and squash

VICTORIA SITTING ON GERALD'S LAP DURING ONE OF HER VISITS

Blue, so he might have passed Jennifer unknowingly in the streets or at the Playhouse bar. His contemporaries included Philip Larkin and Kingsley Amis. After five terms he joined the Navy, participating in the Arctic convoys and suffering the terror of being bombed and torpedoed by the Germans. As his flame-filled destroyer had flooded with icy water and he struggled to fight the fires, he found himself treading on the bodies of his comrades and friends floating in the darkness. These were experiences that would haunt him and his poems for life.

> Beneath the ice-floes sleeping,
> Embalmed in salt
> The sewn-up bodies slipping
> Into silent vaults.[409]

After a spell in Germany in 1945, Alan was finally demobbed, but rather than return to Oxford to complete his degree, he wrote, travelled and became a keen frequenter of Soho's artistic watering holes. When he married the thirty-three-year-old Jennifer, he was twenty-seven, but he had already entered London's literary life. John Lehmann published his first poems and he became friends with Cyril Connolly, who was keen to act as master of ceremonies, if not matchmaker, for the relationship with Jennifer. The couple combined the perfect mix for Cyril – intelligence with beauty, worldliness with feeling – and he was happy to keep them close. According to their friend Francis Wyndham, Cyril repeated this pattern of encouraging and 'masterminding' couples where he was somewhat in love with the woman and 'a tiny bit of the man'; another was Caroline Blackwood and Lucian Freud. Mickey described Cyril as 'Old Miss Matchmaker, that rival to Swan Vestas'.[410] But Cyril also had his vulnerable side, and his own love life was often a mess; he warned a friend who said he would like to edit his letters, 'You'd find letters to two women threatening suicide, written within half an hour of each other, and then one to a third, written quarter of an hour later, asking her to lunch at the Ritz.'[411] Cyril's vulnerability was something Gerald recognised; once, when the ever-pugnacious Evelyn Waugh had been making spiteful comments (as he frequently did about Cyril, whom he enjoyed tormenting), Gerald memorably remarked, 'To attack Cyril Connolly is like shooting a sitting robin.'[412]

The photographs from the October wedding show Alan boyishly anxious yet happy in a dark suit, and Jennifer smiling confidently, dressed in a pale autumnal dress, cinched in at the waist. Wedding guests included the two painters who had shared a house with Alan, Keith Vaughan and John Minton, and the as-yet-undiscovered Soviet spy Donald MacLean. A letter congratulating Jennifer on her unexpected wedding was sent by a friend who had evidently followed Jennifer's complex romantic life, though the second page and signature is missing: 'Poor Robert will feel it I think and I wonder how Cyril feels. And Henry! To say nothing of Micky [sic]!'

The six-year-old Victoria adored her new stepfather and he enjoyed this role. The following year, they all travelled to the Italian Riviera and stayed at La Mortola, a beautiful villa near Ventimiglia, built on steep, verdant slopes above the sea – an enchanted high point in Victoria's childhood. At last Jennifer appeared to have found love and stability with someone who was also handsome, intelligent and sexy. Alan added to the family's new-found happiness when he announced that he could not stand to have Mardie living in

JENNIFER AND ALAN ROSS ON THEIR WEDDING DAY, 1949
ALAN ROWING

the house with them and the dreaded nanny was sent away. Jennifer wrote to her mother in 1950, thanking her for sending butter from Oare – 'such a treat . . . after National Butter!' – then adding, apparently ingenuously, that Victoria looks very well and seems very happy. 'You won't believe it but she is <u>quite different</u> since Mardie left. She is full of ideas for games and so on which she never was before as she was never given time to think or turn round with Mardie barking at her day and night.' There is no mention of why Jennifer had allowed a nanny to 'bark' and terrorise her daughter for so long.

Y 1949, GERALD's health was rapidly deteriorating. He had heart problems, high blood pressure and it appears he had suffered some sort of thrombosis, though he still had the spirit to write letters to friends: 'Do you find that <u>everything</u> disappears. "Panta rei" (I can't write Greek letters any more) as Heraclitus says. The moment I put a paper down on a table it disappears into space. It is also largely Robert I suspect.'[413]

Those close to Gerald were increasingly worried but nobody seemed to be clear quite what he was suffering from. Some suggested a brain tumour, others that it might have all been somewhat psychosomatic. Nancy Mitford wrote to her sister Diana after visiting him: 'He is quite well I think but furious if one says so!' When Diana went to see him, she found him lying 'like a log with two nurses and all the paraphernalia of terrific illness and I believe he dreads getting better for fear of his depression coming back (he is not awfully depressed now). We talk of his coming to Crowood [the Mosleys' home] and he says he <u>longs</u> to, but you know he won't even open his eyes!'[414] Diana continued to visit and sometimes managed to drive him in his dressing gown to the farm, where he enjoyed seeing the cats in the cowshed.[415] Writing later to Robert, Diana noted 'how gentle and thoughtful' he was with Gerald during this difficult time.

Gerald's decline can only have been worsened by the news coming in of old friends dying: Gertrude Stein in 1946, Emerald Cunard in 1948. When writing to Cecil Beaton, he thanked him for news about Salvador Dalí and requested that his love be sent to him and Gala. 'All my old life seems to be vanishing,' he wrote; 'I feel like a ghost. Perhaps I am really dead and just earth-bound. It is a curious and not wholly pleasant sensation, anyhow I can't write more than a few lines to living friends and must end now. Also it's lunch time.'

In spite of his vulnerability, many people Gerald cared about continued to arrive for weekends. Elizabeth Bowen described 'sitting on the terrace tangled with loops of honeysuckle, drinking champagne, with this enormous smoke-blue Berkshire distance reaching away below . . . Robert Heber-Percy's exquisite 5-year-old child Victoria is here; all the Betjemans' children arrived over, and we spent a very nice demented midgy afternoon boating on the lake.'[416] Clarissa was still a regular visitor, but there were also people from the theatre like Freddie Ashton and Constant Lambert, and others, like Edward James, from the heyday of the 1930s, and Gerald de Gaury, who had snapped up the Mad Boy for their *Boy's Own* Arabian adventure. Cyril Connolly's signature crops up many times in the visitors' book, revealing his own domestic changes as Lys's name disappears and Barbara Skelton (soon to be Connolly) appears. Robert kept the whole place running, even when Gerald wasn't up to much; inevitably he was now less like the young Mad Boy running riot in Gerald's shadow. And it was a reflection of this that Cyril wrote him a jokey thank-you letter on *Horizon* notepaper.

Dearest Robert,

I don't suppose you get many bread and butter letters so I am sending you one. You looked after me as well as I am accustomed to, even at Faringdon. One or two small points – you should serve champagne in the bath on a salver, with a small hand-towel. And one CAN'T be expected to use the same bath-salts two baths running. But one must not carp . . .

Was up all night twice last week, most enjoyable, the rising sun over
the lake in Regent's Park was everything you . . . used to crack it up to be.

Lots of love from Cyril

Cecil Beaton pronounced that Gerald was fading fast, reporting a
conversation in his diary (later published in *The Happy Years*): 'Gerald
comes blinking into my room. "It's really quite serious: it's the sort of
thing that people die of. Oh well, it's not worth getting upset about . . .
but I might as well take a month off, for after all, health is everything,
isn't it. And it's never quiet at Faringdon with Robert about.' Cecil
visited Gerald on one of his sojourns at the Richmond nursing home,
where the patient was sad to be missing Faringdon at a lovely time of
year: 'The bore is I'm missing the spring there. Now, let me see – when
I come out of the home it will be 1 June. The syringa will be coming out
and the greenhouse peaches will be ripe.'[417] Cecil included accusations
in the same book that Robert had not cared well for Gerald during
his illness, adding to his suffering and loneliness rather than assuaging
it. When these diaries were published, many years later, friends who
knew the situation at Faringdon rallied in defence of the Mad Boy.
Billa said she was quite certain that Robert did not neglect Gerald,
and Daphne Fielding pronounced that both Robert and Hughie were
'Pure Gold' as far as tending to Gerald was concerned. Diana Mosley
was angered that Cecil spread what she saw as unfair and untrue details
about Gerald that would give entirely the wrong impression of the
situation at Faringdon.[418]

In early spring 1949, Gerald wrote a letter addressed to Robert, the
envelope announcing: 'To be opened and attended to immediately
upon my death', and expressing the not-uncommon concern that
pronouncement of death and even burial might take place before the
person was fully deceased.

March 19 1949

I wish Mr Robert Heber-Percy to superintend all matters and formalities
involved by my death.

GERALD LOOKING
UNWELL AND
MISERABLE ON THE
DAY-BED IN HIS STUDY,
WHICH HE NOW USED
AS A BEDROOM

I wish to be cremated.

If however there is any difficulty about this and I have to be buried in
the ordinary way I wish it to be made certain – by any doctor – that I am
truly dead by the severance of the jugular vein or by any other means.

By early 1950, Gerald was clearly in the final stages of his illness.
Robert rang Clarissa in London suggesting that she come. The two had
never got along, but he knew how much she and Gerald meant to each
other. The patient was lying on the Venetian day-bed in his downstairs
bedroom and 'was clearly going'. 'He was completely unlike himself,'
Clarissa remembered. 'He didn't want to be seen . . . he was past being
interested.'[419] She stayed for five or ten minutes and then left; she never
saw him again.

Gerald knew he was dying. According to Robert, he never complained. During his last days, Sir Thomas Beecham wrote an article saying that Lord Berners was 'the greatest English composer' and that he would make new recordings of his compositions. Despite Gerald's withdrawal from the world, this made him very happy.[420] On 19 April, 'Two hours before he died a new doctor came from London and Gerald said: "Thank you for coming, but I'm afraid I've rather wasted your time." Those were the last words he spoke as he slipped peacefully into unconsciousness.'[421]

Gerald's body was placed in a plain white coffin covered with purple velvet, which remained on trestles in the hall at Faringdon for several days. The funeral was arranged according to his wishes; he eschewed the churchyard at the end of the lawns in favour of the more modern method of cremation that was gaining popularity in post-war England. The coffin was carried out of the house to the hearse by estate workers Freddie Law and young Jack Fox. William Crack, Gerald's beloved chauffeur from before the war, joined them, looking pale and upset. Cars were provided by Mr Webb and Robert travelled with Diana Mosley and the estate's accountant. The few other people attending included Hughie, John Betjeman and some Oxford friends.

The service took place at Oxford's crematorium at Headington, a plain brick 1930s building. Quantities of white flowers were sent by Gerald's cousin Vera, who also put in an appearance with her mother. The forty-eight-year-old Mrs Williams was now 15th Baroness Berners, but she evidently was not acquainted with Gerald's friends, producing what Diana Mosley called 'a note of pure comedy Gerald would have enjoyed'. When the two women asked someone whether they should go to Faringdon after the funeral, the answer was 'Better ask Mr Percy', to which they replied, 'Who is Mr Percy?'[422] Later, there were rumours that the Berners relations were surprised and disappointed to learn that Gerald's will left his house and all his possessions to Robert.

Robert was thirty-nine when Gerald died. Although he was still known as the Mad Boy, he was now a man, and looking back over what were almost two decades of life together, he realised that Gerald had been family, mentor and protector. Gerald had educated him, indulged him, loved him and – importantly – let him be. He had given him stability and freedom, and now in death had given him almost everything he owned (bar some legacies to servants). For the youngest Heber-Percy son, who had had to leave his childhood paradise in Shropshire, it was an extraordinary gift and one that gave his life the shape, substance and purpose it would not otherwise have had. Robert had known that Gerald was dying and must have prepared himself, but after his death he felt bereft. In reply to a condolence letter from Osbert Sitwell, he wrote:

> I do miss him dreadfully as you say 'All the particular things of which only he would see the point have become pointless', and also what you would realise but that most people never understood was his fund of wisdom. I never made any decision without either mentally or actually considering his reaction, and though I fell into many pits he always rescued me with such effective ease, that it left me grateful but bewildered and now I feel quite lost and haven't an idea what to do with the rest of my life.

CHAPTER FOURTEEN

'From Catamite to Catamite'

ATER, PEOPLE WOULD COMMENT that after Gerald's death, Robert's life was founded on preserving and cherishing Faringdon House. It was as though the Mad Boy transformed himself into a dutiful caretaker, a guardian of the flame of Lord Berners's memory. Their shared home would become almost like a shrine. There may be some truth in this, but the process was not a straightforward one. In the beginning, Gerald's friends commiserated with Robert and with each other over their loss. John Betjeman wrote to Diana Mosley, 'I had so taken him for granted that I forgot how good a friend he was, and how scornful of all pretension and how loyal in trouble, effortlessly loyal it seemed. It's hell without him, isn't it?'[423] He then penned an obituary for the *Listener* that tried to put into words the magical atmosphere Gerald had created around himself: 'Envious dry blankets who did not know him, and those who read of his luxury and the world of beauty with which he could afford to protect himself, may regard him as a relic of a civilized age. They can think what they like, the dreary form-fillers . . . They cannot be expected to understand the pleasure and thankfulness those people feel who had the privilege of his friendship.'[424]

Evelyn Waugh wrote more cattily to Diana, 'The Mad Boy has installed a Mad Boy of his own. Has there ever been a property in history that has devolved from catamite to catamite for any length of time?'[425] In fact, Hughie (now thirty-two) does not appear to have been anyone's idea of a mad boy or a catamite; nor did he provide a solution

Charges to pay
___ s. ___ d.
RECEIVED

POST OFFICE
TELEGRAM
Prefix. Time handed in. Office of Origin and Service Instructions. Words.
91

At ___ m
From ___
By ___ XWB 2079 12.14 WEST LONDON T 27

At ___ m
By ___

HEBER PERCY FARINGDON HOUSE FARINGDON-BERKS =

GREATFUL YOUR MAGNIFICIENT GESTURE WAS DEEPLY
MOVED BY NEWS AT THE BANK OF CONTINUATION OF
GERALDS GENEROSITY THANK YOU ALWAYS = LUISA CASATI

+ + LUISA CASATI + XW

GRAMS ENQUIRY" or call, with this form
'd by this form, and, if possible, the envelope.

DESPITE THE TURMOIL AFTER GERALD'S DEATH, ROBERT MANAGED BY THE NEXT MONTH TO ARRANGE THE CONTINUED PAYMENT OF AN ALLOWANCE TO THE AGEING MARCHESA CASATI. BOTH MEN WERE DISCREET ABOUT THEIR GENEROSITY TO FRIENDS

for Robert who was thrown into turmoil by Gerald's death. The crisis was serious enough for him to debate whether he should stay at Faringdon. He once told Jennifer that there had been a point when he climbed to the top of a hill and pondered on his future, coming to the decision to stay with Gerald and make Faringdon his life. It would involve giving up some independence, and the possibility of another sort of life (as a married farmer?), but it was a conscious choice. Faringdon was surely Robert's dream, the place he had known for the last fifteen years was destined to be his. Suddenly, however, with Gerald gone, it didn't make sense. As he had confessed to Osbert Sitwell, he felt 'quite lost' and didn't know what to do with his life.

Not long after his bereavement, Robert vacated the main part of the house and moved downstairs onto the lower ground floor, into a panelled room that Gerald had used for many years as his library. It looked out from beneath the terrace, towards the fountain on the back lawn and the parkland beyond. In order to bring more daylight into the room, Gerald had designed a system of holes cut in the terrace, with glass prisms refracting the light inwards. It was fine as a workroom, but after the airy brightness of the house it must have felt gloomy and subterranean. In November 1950, seven months after Gerald's death, Robert gave an interview to the *Daily Express*. Described as a 'neighbour of Berners', Robert was said to have inherited most of the £214,000 that Lord Berners had left in his will, but changes were evidently afoot. The heir was described as living 'in the basement'. The drawing room would stay open for Christmas, Robert said, but 'then it is to go under dust sheets for good'.[426] The article claimed that the upper rooms of Faringdon House – 'the meeting place of famous people' including George Bernard Shaw, Constant Lambert and Margot Fonteyn – had now been turned into three flats, though this was somewhat misleading as they were actually on the attic floor that had been occupied by servants in the 1930s and US Army officers during the war.

Some insight into Robert's emotional state comes across in his words to the journalist: 'Lord Berners and I were friends for 20 years. I am his literary and musical executor. But we did not share a single interest. I am a farmer and I like horses.' It seems as though Robert had not only suddenly realised how different he was to Gerald, but that he might be unable to keep the show running. Partly, this was financial – there were daunting death duties to be paid – but it was also psychological. Over those two decades, Robert had got to know great men and women of letters, music, the theatre and politics. He had learned about culture, manners and food by merely being there and was excused any shortcomings on account of being Gerald's 'Mad Boy', who provided youth, beauty and a picturesque degree of crazy behaviour. Now, in his fortieth year, Robert seems to have had a loss of faith: 'We did not share a single interest.' Had he ever really been a part of all this? And how could he continue without the force of Gerald's personality?

Although some of the old friends continued to visit Faringdon in the ensuing months, among them Coote Lygon and Billa Harrod with her family, the visitors' book stops abruptly in September and is not continued again for four years. During this time, Robert changed his plans and made the place his own. Jack Fox (now returned from the Navy) was among various estate employees who renovated bedrooms, put up partitions and added bathrooms. Jack remembers constructing a tiny bathroom for the Crystal Room, suspended over the back staircase – you could tap the bottom of the pink enamel bath when you went downstairs. It was painted throughout with a fantastical landscape of jungle and desert by the artist Roy Hobdell, who had produced

ROY HOBDELL'S MURAL IN THE BATHROOM BUILT BY JACK FOX

murals for Robert and Gerald's old friend Lord Faringdon at Buscot Park. Other decorations were added by Hobdell: a *trompe l'œil* of Lord Berners's books and a portrait of a scantily clad young man (the Mad Boy?) went on some cupboard doors in the drawing room; the wooden canopy of Victoria's four-poster received a wreath of pink roses encircling the gilded words 'Victoria, Her Bed'; and at a later date, a blocked-up window at the lodge house that Jack Fox moved into was painted with a fox reading the *Faringdon Standard* between lace curtains.

By the time Michael Duff was signing himself back into the visitors' book as 'Michael of Vaynol', he had married the beautiful,

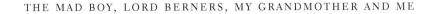

ONE OF ROY
HOBDELL'S *TROMPE
L'ŒIL* WORKS
COMMISSIONED BY
ROBERT. THE BOOKS
ARE ALL MUSICAL
AND LITERARY WORKS
BY GERALD, THE
HANDSOME YOUTH
SURELY INSPIRED BY
THE MAD BOY

bisexual Lady Caroline Paget, previously lover and inspiration to Rex Whistler. Michael's chaotic family life rivalled or even exceeded Robert's. When Caroline became pregnant, it was generally assumed that Michael had little to do with it. Some speculated that the father was her uncle-by-marriage, Duff Cooper, while others believed it was Anthony Eden, the future Prime Minister (who at fifty-five would soon marry the thirty-two-year-old Clarissa Churchill). When Caroline lost the child, she and Michael adopted a baby boy they named Charley, whom Michael largely rejected, to the extent of disinheriting him.

According to the grown-up Charley Duff, Robert had 'the indoor boyfriend and the outdoor boyfriend' at Faringdon during the 1950s. Rumour had it that the latter was not allowed in and the former was not allowed out. If Hughie was the person who kept indoor life on a more even keel than it might have been, then 'Garth' (as he was known, after an action-adventure cartoon character) was the man on the outside. In fact, as Hughie was farm manager, he did go out; and although Garth was estate foreman, he did go in. One friend recalled that Garth came up to the house during the day, but not in the evening or for meals. Nevertheless, the newly married Barbara Connolly recorded in her diary a visit with Cyril, for Christmas 1950. 'Met by Garth at the house who acted as hostess and said, "Pleased to meet you again." He poured us out a delicious iced gin cocktail sugared round the edge. The house was very centrally heated, a strong smell of incense that Garth said was smouldering rosemary they'd put on the fire.'[427] Clarissa was also there for this first Christmas after Gerald died – mysteriously, given her lack of rapport with the Mad Boy. They saw the Mosleys and the Betjemans among others; Robert was evidently staying close to the old friends. Barbara continued: 'Clarissa Churchill had not changed, as I had been made to, for she had no evening dress with her. There were two other queens. A very pretty American who didn't say much but seemed intelligent and kept pursing up his mouth; a blue-eyed airman called Ken, snobbish and self-assured who never stopped talking, anxious to be a social success. The whole weekend I found a strain. Lengthy meal sessions, messy food with little wine and a row of watchful eyes with everyone making guarded statements or listening to Pungle [Cyril] holding forth.'[428]

Garth's real name was Clarence, though most people called him Bob. Ten years younger than Robert, he was born into a family of Yorkshire miners, but swore he would never go underground. He worked on the Duke of Devonshire's estate before serving in the Medical Corps during the war, when he was injured and captured as a prisoner-of-war. In around 1947, Robert made him foreman at Faringdon – a job some thought he was not qualified for. Heavily built with thinning fair hair and blue eyes, he was a handsome rogue in the mould of Charlton Heston, a cigarette always hanging from his lips. Others noted his bad skin and uncouth ways. 'Captain Cruddas never had a bad word for anyone, but he did for Garth,' recalled Jack Fox. 'Those two were at daggers drawn.' 'He was not a very nice man,' said another acquaintance. To complicate the picture, Garth had married a local woman in 1947, and when their daughter Susan was born in

1949, Robert was made godfather. After Garth had a spell in prison for drink-driving, he and his family lived in a flat on the top floor of Faringdon House. Susan learned to count using Robert's roulette chips and her parents would watch out of their attic window as guests arrived at the front door below, with Garth telling his wife their names.[429] Some believed that the foreman had a strange hold over Robert, others couldn't understand why he needed to travel abroad with him 'to carry the money' after the house in Rome was sold. And Garth and his wife were regularly seen driving Robert's sports car when they went out for the evening. Michael Duff spread a story that he had asked Garth, 'What do you do?' and that the reply was 'I digs.'[430]

Whatever the attraction, the liaison with Garth was formalised with proper terms of employment. For Robert, as for both Gerald and Jennifer, the affection for employees was sometimes among the most lasting and significant sort. Gerald's fondness for William, his driver, or Jennifer's love for Pixie, her governess, were other examples of the intimacy that could occur in these unequal relationships. Though Robert was kind to Garth and his family in many ways, he still paid his lover a pitiful agricultural wage.[431] While it was probably their fiery characters that frequently led the two men to have noisy and sometimes violent quarrels, the unequal power balance must surely have played a part.

Notwithstanding the periodic separations and the complications with Garth, Hughie adopted an increasingly 'wifely' role at Faringdon, taking great pride in the place, its beauty and history. Unlike Robert, Hughie added a more effeminate atmosphere to the household. His favourite party trick was impersonating the Queen Mother, and having stuffed a cushion down his front and a toque on his head, was said 'to actually become her' as he waved his hand in the royal manner. Hughie's flower-arranging was also noted, becoming increasingly extravagant, so that 'huge, voluptuous cornucopias with every sort of flower' were placed around the house.[432] Gin was distributed liberally, even to underage visitors, and guests were made to feel at ease. When Candida Betjeman came over to play with Victoria, and later to stay on her own and ride, it was Hughie who became her confidant and, 'like a slightly illegal uncle', gave her advice about boys. 'He was a lady-in-waiting' to Robert, suggested one friend.[433] 'He was a kind of buffer,' said another.[434] When Robert lost his temper, was rude to people or drank too much and got out of control, it was Hughie who smoothed things over. With Hughie by his side, Robert was able to continue as a Mad Boy, even if he was now Lord of the Manor, running an estate and watching a daughter grow up.

ENNIFER AND ALAN'S SON Jonathan was born four years after their wedding, in 1953. Aged ten when her half-brother was born, Victoria was overjoyed: 'It was the best thing in my childhood.' Jonathan completed the family with her mother and beloved stepfather. The family divided their time between South Terrace and, from 1955, Clayton Manor, a Georgian house beneath the Sussex Downs. Alan was writing poetry and became the *Observer*'s cricket correspondent; Jennifer and Victoria joined him in Australia where he covered the Ashes series in 1954–5. He also contributed to John Lehmann's *London Magazine*, a monthly literary publication that he was eventually to take over as editor. His stewardship was largely subsidised by Jennifer, who supported his interest in young, undiscovered talent, and helped turn the publication into a far more daring international one than it had been. Many writers and poets remain grateful to Alan for giving them an opportunity when they were still unknown; he spotted and published a young Caribbean poet, Derek Walcott. Jennifer often read manuscripts for Alan and had a strong sense for when something worked or not. 'She had perfect pitch about writing,' said Francis Wyndham. 'I am often credited with having discovered Jean Rhys, but it was Jennifer who found out about her and recommended her to me.'[435]

The Rosses' *ménage* looked marvellous from the outside. Jennifer and Alan were good-looking, intelligent and sociable. They continued their London life during the week but took pleasure in creating a more substantial country home. Clayton Manor was charming and comfortable, with many books, and furniture picked up in antique shops in Brighton. There were paintings by contemporary artists, including Alan's old friends John Minton and Keith Vaughan, and Jennifer's friend Adrian Daintrey (a regular at Faringdon), plus pictures by Augustus John and Eric Ravilious that had come from Oare. The lovely gardens contained an ancient ginkgo tree (whose leaf was used as the *London Magazine*'s logo), a swimming pool and a tree house, and there was enough room for a few friends, often writers and artists, to stay. An Italian couple lived in and guests were provided with delicious food, including many Italian recipes, which were still unusual in those post-war days of dull English fare. Cecil Beaton described visiting 'the Alan Rosses' in Sussex in the 1960s, when, among others, Violet Wyndham was there (she was still an important confidante of Jennifer's, and Jonathan's godmother). Cecil described a 'most friendly, highly civilised evening of quiet talk, discussing the quality of charm and why it is not enjoyed by the younger generation'. But all was not well between Jennifer and Alan, and even Cecil noticed on another occasion that Alan was 'tense and rather hard on nice clever Jennifer'.[436]

Jennifer and Alan's marriage had begun to unravel from early on. Alan started having affairs and then Jennifer began seeing Mickey again. After Jonathan's birth, the couple stopped sharing a room. At Clayton, Alan took over a small, austere bedroom with a single bed, while Jennifer's was a large, bay-windowed feminine place, where she was brought breakfast in bed (grapefruit, Ryvita and honey, tea with lemon). Shades of Geoffrey and Alathea were haunting the marriage. Alan had a masculine, book-lined study, where he took interesting male guests for cigars and literary conversations, or to watch the racing on television – he owned racehorses and chose for his colours Schiaparelli shocking pink and chocolate brown. He kept a sporty convertible in the garage and organised cricket matches, bringing in people to play against the village team.

When Jennifer wrote notes, years afterwards, about the failure of her second marriage, she used the third person: 'Sexual failure early on – as he marries her for wrong reasons and suffers from what is called Don Juan Syndrome – seducing all her friends – voyeurism, prostitutes etc. She meets her lover again. Affair starts again.' It wasn't long before she yearned for the days in London and hated the endless train journeys and the 'deathly weekends in the country'. Eventually, Mickey married and had children, and as Alan's star rose, Jennifer's declined. Coming from a family where health was a favourite preoccupation, she became increasingly concerned with what Virginia Woolf called the 'daily drama of the body'. Her liver reacted badly to cream, the east wind brought headaches, and tranquillisers and drink offered blurred relief from anxiety and sadness. However, her anguish was tempered by her forgiving nature and years afterwards she wrote some loving lines for Alan.

> I lie awake at night and think of you.
> Cradled at Clayton
> The beeches guarding you like an army, the Gingko [sic] a sentinel.
> Creating the childhood house you never had.
> No dog, no scrapbook.
> No person.
> Now you have a stream, a pond with birds.
> All your own doing.

Cranking up the pain, Alan had a fling with Cyril's ex-wife Barbara, who was now unhappily married to George Weidenfeld. Not entirely justifiably, Cyril was outraged. Worse, he tried to involve Jennifer in preventing it, accusing Alan of 'plotting alibis with her [Barbara], all the James Bond stuff'. The two men fell out, not for the last time, over a woman ('The moral of all this is Fuck Women!' wrote Alan in reply).[437] Another of Alan's dalliances was with Deirdre Craven, a beautiful, blonde, married, much younger woman, who would go on to marry Cyril in 1959 and bear him two children, Cressida and Matthew. The cross-cutting stresses might have prevented friendship for others, but Cyril and Deirdre lived in Sussex and were among the most regular visitors to Clayton, the legacies of the past forgotten or swallowed along with stiff drinks before Sunday lunch. Jennifer was asked to be godmother to Matthew (along with John Betjeman and Diana Cooper), and became lifelong friends with Cressida, who exhibited her father's intelligent wit and charm from a precocious age. But the shifting sands of her marriage had an effect on Jennifer. Indeed it was Deirdre who noted a transformation, particularly after Jennifer dyed her hair in the early 1960s, when she went from an energetic, dark-haired person to a blonde who sat, Alathea-like, on the sofa in the drawing room she had filled with pretty Victorian knick-knacks.[438]

The merry-go-round of love had not been stopped by the war and the intricate patterns of marriage, betrayal, compromise, reconciliation and separation continued within a remarkably tight-knit social group. Many of Jennifer's friends, like Cyril or Cecil, also knew Robert and had known Gerald. And if it had seemed that Alan was from a different milieu to Faringdon society, life with him was equally complex. Later, Jennifer tried to analyse the similarities between herself and her second husband in terms of their sexuality: 'Alan said he was a hustler once. So was I – he did it for money probably. I did it for fun and revenge. His father and grandfather were Evangelist preachers. Mine were Quakers. And we both had to break away. Differently – but the same.'[439] It appeared that part of what brought them together also drove them apart. Jennifer would describe Mickey as 'the love of my life', and while their relationship was always fitted into the interstices, she found solace with him when Alan's rejections became too painful.

Although Alan had more worldly success than Jennifer, he had had several severe bouts of depression that he linked directly to his horrifying experiences during the war. Jennifer thought their source, at least in part, might be the guilt he felt about how he had been so blatant with his extra-marital relationships. Alan was hospitalised and received electric-shock treatment, while Jennifer remained loyally by his side – an experience she again made notes on, writing in the third person: 'Winter of snow and loneliness and journeys to nursing home through snow. Utterly alone, pitied by friends. Husband recovers and leads active work travel life – including more flaunting affairs. Never tells but friends do. Unable to make much of her life. Living in two places with man she has no mutual life with is nearly killing her.'

Some observers believed that Alan used Jennifer's wealth and that he would have left her long before he eventually did if it hadn't been for that factor. She never mentioned this aspect of their relationship, but later, she did write a passage that was probably never given to Alan, but shows she was far from naive about the issues:

> Tonight when you talked about being anti Arts Council Grants, you didn't seem to realise that I am now <u>your</u> Grant, enabling you to live in comfort in two houses, with no responsibilities, telling me perpetually that I do nothing, when I could give you a very long list of what I do to make <u>your</u> life comfortable, whereas you do next to nothing for me.
>
> You don't understand my emotional needs – for affection, talk of subjects that <u>I</u> am interested in. Of course I know your flawed childhood, your war life – but who in a way hasn't suffered? I think you are selfish, inconsiderate and would have gone some years ago if it hadn't been for many things better not put in writing. I also have great admiration for you – and affection as well as the opposite.

Quoting Maria Callas (whom she loved), Jennifer finishes the unsent letter: 'Communication is the most important thing in life – it is what makes the human predicament bearable.'

 N 1950, WHEN VICTORIA was five, Jennifer sent her to Lady Eden's School for Girls, an exclusive institution in South Kensington which prioritised dance and the arts and mixed old-fashioned formality with a cosy homeliness. It was run by the sister-in-law of the Prime Minister Sir Anthony Eden, and pupils were dressed in checked pinafores with frills and tweed coats with velvet collars, and curtsied to their teachers. Victoria loved ballet, acting and poetry and

was generally good at lessons; she skipped a year to be in an older class. However, she often had minor illnesses and Jennifer indulged her daughter by allowing her to miss school if she claimed to feel unwell.

During the school holidays Victoria always visited Faringdon. At a young age she was accompanied by Mardie, but later, when she was a bit older, she went alone or with her best friend, and was cared for by Mrs Shury, the affable wife of Robert's groom. 'Robert tried terribly hard,' remembered Victoria, regretting that his efforts didn't help make a connection between them. 'He organised parties and invited friends.' But none of this made them close. She came to agree with a doctor friend of Robert's who, many years later, told her that her father was 'emotionally autistic'. Both Garth and Hughie were very friendly with their lover's daughter. Garth built a three-storey wooden house for her hamster, Jenny, and Hughie was the most approachable person at Faringdon. He chatted to Victoria and sat with her at Gerald's piano, teaching her the beginning of Beethoven's *Moonlight Sonata*.

Gladys, Robert's mother, came to live near Faringdon to be close to her adored youngest son and occasionally saw Victoria. 'Granny Heber-Percy' had very high cheekbones and a somewhat severe mien. She had remained a formidable rider, insisting on galloping side-saddle, and claimed to have broken every bone in her body; not much had changed since she laughed when she heard her young sons had tumbled from their pony's panniers while out with their nurse. Gladys bought her granddaughter a young Arab pony that Victoria named Pegasus and which thrilled its young rider. But although Victoria liked horses, she was not a daredevil rider like her father and grandmother. 'I used to think that Candida Betjeman would have been the ideal daughter for Robert instead of me, because she loved him, she was a very good rider and she was confident and worldly.'

Victoria passed her Common Entrance exam a year early, aged eleven, and went to Cranborne Chase in 1956, only ten years after the small boarding school for girls had been founded in Crichel House in Dorset. Robert came every term to take her out, but despite his attempts to do the right thing and to establish a bond with his growing daughter, she felt that he didn't actually like her. 'I couldn't think of what to say to him, and later he said that as a child, nothing had been quite right for me. We were the wrong kind of animal for each other – we didn't "get" one another.' When Victoria was about thirteen, a friend told her that Robert was 'queer' and this only increased her sense of distance and difference from her father. While she felt rejected by him, she also played a part in the lack of rapport. Once, when Robert visited his daughter at school, he had given her £5 and she refused to take the money, handing it back to him. He had been hurt, he later confessed. For her part, Victoria later said, 'I think that without thinking it out, I rejected Faringdon before it rejected me.' Victoria also enjoyed shocking people when she was young by saying, 'My father has never given me a Christmas present and has never written me a letter.'

VICTORIA, AGED FIFTEEN, WITH HER ADORED HALF-BROTHER, JONATHAN, AGED FIVE

Although father and daughter were not close and Victoria felt that Alan played a more significant role in her life than Robert, there were times when she appreciated Robert's generosity and style. In 1959, when Victoria had her sixteenth birthday at Cranborne Chase, she rang her father to tell him she wanted to throw a party and Robert sent Hughie over with a van filled with marvellous food. 'There were maybe twenty roast *poussins*,' she remembered, and although it was February, the weather was warm and the whole class had a picnic. 'It was a typically grand gesture.'

Soon after this birthday party, Victoria left school, saying she felt homesick, and joined her mother and stepfather in London, where she took a few independent lessons and planned her future. It was at this point that Cecil Beaton asked to take a photograph of the beautiful teenager. He got her to stand by a gauzy-curtained window and then, without asking her permission, published it in *Harper's Bazaar* with the caption 'Victoria Heber-Percy: the reluctant debutante' – though she was not a deb and never would be. Victoria was already attracted to a different approach to life from that of her parents. Her belief in simplicity and the idea of being 'natural' became an instinctive principle and one that increasingly marked her apart from her glamorous, well-dressed mother and particularly from her father, with his obsession with his grand house and his lack of emotional involvement.

In September 1959, Victoria went to St Clare's, a crammer in Oxford, to do A-levels. Early the next year, just before her seventeenth birthday, her recently ex-boyfriend Michael Brett took her to a party. It was there that she met Peter Zinovieff, a twenty-six-year-old geologist who was known in Oxford as a 'mad Russian'. His parents had left St Petersburg as child-refugees of the 1917 revolution, and he was known for wild behaviour and the sort of alcohol-fuelled pranks that recalled the heyday of *Brideshead* Oxford – running round the quadrangle in a woman's corset, stripping naked, setting fire to his hair or making bets as to who could be the first to drive to London and return with a policeman's helmet.[440] In order to call off his engagement to a second-generation Russian in Paris, Peter had concocted a crazy scheme that involved accompanying his fiancée to the opera, where he pretended to have a fit and jumped out of the box into the stalls below. After working in Cyprus, he was now at Oxford doing post-doctoral research.

Peter's first encounter with Victoria was not by chance. He had come across Cecil Beaton's photograph of the teenager and, enchanted by her looks, had cut it out of the magazine and carried it around in his wallet. When he serendipitously discovered that Michael Brett knew this beautiful girl, Peter insisted that he engineer a meeting.

They were ostensibly an unlikely pair. Victoria was depressed following her break-up with Michael, and was particularly immature for her age (she had only reached puberty the previous year). Peter, despite his reputation for wildness, was still a virgin and his family background equalled Victoria's for complications. His parents had separated when he was a child and his remarried father had been killed in a train crash when Peter was eighteen. His mother had been born Princess Dolgoruky, but created havoc in the exiled White Russian community not only for becoming a dedicated Communist but for her many love affairs. She worked with the French Resistance during her internment in a Nazi camp in France and was now being monitored by MI5. This 'Red Princess' worked for the Communist travel agent Progressive Tours, taking groups of socialist tourists to visit the Eastern Bloc; she delighted in showing off her parents' palaces in St Petersburg, adding what a good thing it was that they were now state-owned.[441]

VICTORIA AGED SIXTEEN, PHOTOGRAPHED BY CECIL BEATON. IT WAS PUBLISHED IN *HARPER'S BAZAAR* AND INSPIRED PETER TO SEEK HER OUT

By the summer, Victoria and Peter were enough of a couple for the forty-four-year-old Jennifer to take them on a holiday to Greece. They rented a house on Aegina, where Peter and Jennifer drank lots of wine and got on so well that she was delighted when her schoolgirl daughter announced that she and Peter were getting married. Peter fainted from over-excitement most nights at dinner, to the extent that they took to positioning a mattress behind him as a precaution. The only person to suggest that seventeen seemed rather young for matrimony was Alan, who came out to Greece with Jonathan towards the end of the holiday. But the event went ahead anyway.

In November 1960, Victoria and Peter were married at the Russian Orthodox Church in Exile in Emperor's Gate, Kensington. Robert, now almost fifty and starting to go grey, was dashing in a morning suit. He had been scheduled to give the young bride away, but there was a muddle and in the end it was Alan who did – symbolic of how Victoria had adopted him as more of a father-figure. Jennifer wore a fur hat with a fitted silk suit and winkle-pickers and seven-year-old Jonathan carried the icon, as is the way in Russian church weddings. It probably looked quite exotic to the English crowd; there were crown-bearers and large candles and the front section of the bride's voluminous veil burst into flames and had to be torn off and beaten out. This all added drama to an event Victoria recalled as 'like having the main part in the school play'. The headmistress of Cranborne Chase attended, in addition to many of Victoria's old school-mates, one of whom was the maid of honour. Hundreds of guests went on to a reception at the Ritz, where formal photographs were taken – the Russian émigrés on one side of the couple and Robert, Jennifer and Alan on the other. After the party, the bride and groom took the night train to Scotland for the first part of a honeymoon. The second part was in Iceland.

Early the next year, the couple took a driving holiday to Italy in a newly invented and highly fashionable Mini. Victoria was struck with a mystery illness in Rome, where she felt very sick and, worried it might be appendicitis, Peter raced her back to London. When the British GP asked whether there was a chance Victoria could be pregnant, they both had to admit that the thought hadn't occurred to them.

Before the baby was born, Victoria took Peter to stay at Faringdon for the first time. There was a splendid dinner the night they arrived and the following morning Peter let himself into the darkened, shuttered drawing room. Inspired by the stories of Lord Berners, Stravinsky, Constant Lambert and others, he sat down at the Bechstein and began to play. An accomplished amateur pianist, he improvised something he thought might fit the place and its extraordinary history, but before

VICTORIA AND PETER'S WEDDING RECEPTION AT THE RITZ, 1960. *L to R*: PETER'S UNCLE, KYRIL ZINOVIEFF; HIS MOTHER, SOFKA SKIPWITH; THE BRIDE AND GROOM; JONATHAN ROSS; ROBERT HEBER-PERCY; JENNIFER ROSS; ALAN ROSS

he got very far, Robert rushed into the room. 'What the hell are you doing, buggering around in here?' he shouted. 'Get out!' Peter stopped, mortified. 'I'd only been trying to do something positive,' he recalled. 'I was so shocked that I cried!' The couple stayed on miserably for the rest of the day, and left early the next morning. Why Robert was so furious remains unexplained. Although Gerald's piano was precious, it was not

an untouchable relic – Hughie often tinkled on it after dinner – and it is hard to imagine that this was the reason. Perhaps the ageing Mad Boy was unable to stomach the young mad Russian. Peter knew just as much about breaking conventions and behaving badly as Robert; was there too much reckless male energy in one house? Maybe Peter was not playing by Robert's rules, about which he was increasingly particular. Whatever the cause of Robert's outburst, Peter never went again during his father-in-law's lifetime and it was years before Victoria did.

In 1961, Alathea offered Victoria and her new husband the opportunity to take over Oare. Geoffrey had died just before the wedding and his widow didn't want to keep the place on. But neither of the newly-weds wanted to establish a life with the constraints that a large country house would bring and it was eventually sold.

N November of that year, I was born at the Royal Northern Hospital in Holloway. Peter fainted and the obstetrician had a heart attack, but the teenage mother (already an early advocate of natural birth) did very well. They named me Sofka after my paternal grandmother and I lived with my parents and two grey whippets in Ebury Street, Belgravia. This was a road whose previous inhabitants included Mozart and Tennyson, and from where Vita Sackville-West set off from her marital home dressed as a man for evenings out with Violet Keppel. I was christened in the Russian Orthodox Church, though I barely returned there during my childhood. Peter was becoming interested in computers and experimental music, leaving behind the geology and a job at the Air Ministry that had formed his career until then. Victoria was now receiving an income from a trust fund set up by her maternal grandfather, Geoffrey Fry, to provide for Jennifer and her descendants. The new parents gave dinner parties where the guests wore evening dress, and they often went to Clayton for weekends and

L to R: JENNIFER (AGED FORTY-FIVE), VICTORIA (NINETEEN), HOLDING THE AUTHOR AS A BABY, AND ALATHEA (SIXTY-NINE) AT OARE, 1962

took trips abroad. Their house was decorated by designers sent in by Jennifer, with beautifully made curtains and silk cushions.

Fifteen months after me, my brother Leo was born, and by the time my mother was twenty-three she had a third child, Nicolas, later known by the Russian diminutive 'Kolinka'. But the marriage was not going well. Peter had started having affairs within weeks of the wedding and Victoria had soon followed suit. She felt dominated by Peter's large personality and was periodically depressed. Husband and wife were following in the tradition of their parents in terms of their chaotic infidelity, and Robert took the opportunity when he could to come between the young couple. On one occasion he invited Victoria to a party at the Clermont Club – a grand gambling outfit in Berkeley Square – to which only one half of every couple was allowed. Peter sat at home, believing he had been cut out of a party thrown especially for his wife, and became so angry and miserable that he started smashing the windows at 4.30 in the morning. Victoria returned home to the sound of breaking glass.

A few years later, Victoria and Peter transformed their milieu, embracing the fashionably bohemian ethos of the time and moving from Belgravia to Putney. Gone were my mother's fitted dresses and shiny shoes from the early period of her marriage; now she wore long Indian skirts, went to pottery classes and smoked the odd joint while listening to Leonard Cohen. Trips to St Tropez had been replaced by holidays in the Hebrides, in a remote croft house they renovated. My father built a computer-music studio in our Putney garden, which ran almost underneath a railway bridge and down to the Thames. The place was filled with a mass of winking lights and electronic wires and innards – 'probably the most advanced studio in the world', Peter told a reporter for the *Evening Standard*.[442] In 1968 there was a concert at the Queen Elizabeth Hall with his *Partita for Unattended Computer* and it was not long before experimental composers and musicians of all sorts were flocking to Putney. Meanwhile, the children went about barefoot, didn't have many haircuts and weren't taught manners on principle.

The same year, Victoria decided to leave Peter and it was Robert who suggested she join him and a friend, Lady Primrose Cadogan, on a cruise to South Africa. That Robert was keen to facilitate a distance between his daughter and her husband is comprehensible. It is more unexpected, given the lack of warmth she felt for her father, that Victoria agreed. At least it provided an escape from a situation that was increasingly unhappy. It was both brave and reckless when the twenty-five-year-old Victoria gathered up her offspring, aged six, four and nearly two, flew to Venice and boarded an Italian ship bound for Cape Town. Perhaps she was encouraged by the example of Alathea, who had taken up travelling the world on cruises since Sir Geoffrey's death. Rumour had it that Alathea perked up no end as a widow, taking quite a shine to the sailors, though she was to die on one of these voyages, aged seventy-four, this same year. She was buried at sea.

I remember nothing of Robert from that journey down the west coast of Africa and he was apparently not impressed by his three unruly grandchildren, preferring the bar and the gaming tables. If he was trying to facilitate a divorce between my parents, it didn't work. After the cruise, my mother, gripped by the depression that continued to dog her, returned to my father and they struggled on with their marriage for another five years.

THE AUTHOR, AGED ABOUT TWELVE, AT HOME IN PUTNEY

CHAPTER FIFTEEN

The Nazi

ROSA PROLL WENT TO WORK at Faringdon in the late 1950s and it was she, more than Robert's indoor boyfriend or the outdoor one, who was to mark his tenure. Fiercely industrious and loyal, Rosa got rid of the other house staff, only tolerating old Mrs Shury till her retirement and allowing a daily cleaner to come in from the town for some years until she too was banned.

It was not long before Rosa controlled every aspect of the domestic environment. Already a phenomenal cook, she took on the weighty mantle of producing food that matched the standards Robert had learned at Gerald's side. Eventually, Rosa also cleaned the house, polished the silver and the brass, washed the walls, mended the linen and, in her spare time, embroidered tapestry chair covers for the dining room. It was she who barred the shutters after everyone had gone to bed and who opened them in the morning before laying the fires. She had the trays ready for the ladies' breakfast in bed, observed a military strategy for preparing a three-course lunch and kept a close eye on what was going on in the gardens. 'She was a bloody terror,' remembered Des Ball, the gardener at the time. 'You couldn't move without her coming to check.' Trespassers on the estate became a thing of the past as Rosa patrolled the grounds with a large dog; even children who played by the stream in the woodland a good mile away from the house were chased off with shouts and threats.

Robert had spotted Rosa's culinary talents when visiting the house of his friend Peggy, Countess of Munster, and was so impressed by the

Austrian's cooking that he went into the kitchen and 'stole' her. He would have known that this was extremely bad form, if not immoral. Many years before, Gerald had written to Nancy Mitford congratulating her on *The Pursuit of Love* and his alter ego, Lord Merlin, but adding, 'I must take you to task for Lord Merlin's only lapse . . . I should never dream of attempting to snaffle anyone else's cook – that is a form of wickedness in which I should never indulge.'

In her early thirties when she arrived at Faringdon, Rosa had high, flushed cheekbones, brown hair scraped into an unforgiving bun and exuded a nervous energy that sometimes verged on the wild-eyed. She had grown up in a small village near Linz, where she was probably recruited to the League of German Girls. When she worked on a farm during the war, she obeyed the command to avert her eyes if passing the nearby Mauthausen concentration camp – notorious as 'the bone-grinder' for 'Incorrigible Political Enemies of the Reich'.[443] Certainly, Rosa was believed to be sympathetic to the late Führer, and her own servility and self-abasement before Robert, whom she worshipped, hinted at an affinity with totalitarianism. 'Rosa was a Tartar, no doubt about it,' said Des Ball. 'That's why she and Robert got on so well.' Des learned to harvest the vegetables when they were only just visible, and therefore of the correct dainty dimensions and sweet taste to be worthy of the dining room. Rosa declared that 'Mr Heber-Percy will only have the best . . . isn't it?' as she often rhetorically concluded her sentences. Robert was certainly the principal force in Rosa's existence and she filled her life with Faringdon House. Many thought that she was in love with him. 'She had an idea she was Mrs Heber-Percy,' said Des.[444] There was a sister back in Austria, and she made occasional visits there, but there was scant sign of any other family or friends.

It wasn't long before Rosa's food was as legendary as that in Gerald's time. People who had known the place before the war would now go to the kitchen to praise Rosa after a meal that contained dishes they knew and loved – the fillets of sole in cream and horseradish, or lobster Thermidor. But Rosa also developed her own favourites, like rack of lamb, and concocted spectacular puddings and cakes, simultaneously rich and delicate. The world was changing, many country houses were unable to keep going, but at Faringdon, with Rosa's perfectionism, friends felt as pampered as they had ever been. Frederick Ashton was a great favourite with Rosa and particularly generous with the tips; it must have seemed miraculous to return to the place that retained so many elements of Gerald's generosity, if not the enchantment of the man himself.

Rosa did not appreciate Hughie; her devotion to Robert seemed to produce equivalent negative emotions towards his lover. She avoided serving the Captain at meals, neglected his bedroom – leaving his waste-paper basket to overflow and hiding his clothes – and humiliated him when she could. If Robert was ever away and Hughie returned to the house alone, Rosa would lock him out. Robert did not reproach her, colluding with her tendency to torment the Captain. Although Hughie and Robert were involved for decades, the former was never given any 'rights' in the house, and while he was unanimously considered 'nice', many criticised him as 'spineless'. He 'panted about behind Robert like a dog', remembered one local friend, and as he thickened around the middle, it was suggested by the less charitable that Robert was 'kind' to keep Hughie on when he was so boring.[445] There was quite possibly an element of masochism on the younger man's part – something that had been noted in Gerald too. In annoyance, Robert was known to pour a bottle of red wine over his lover at dinner and Rosa once poured cold water over Captain Cruddas's head from the first-floor landing. Many witnessed Robert sending Hughie out to buy him cigarettes from the pub in the middle of a formal lunch. Hughie 'would scuttle off looking whipped'.[446] Rosa, bringing the food to the dining room, would gloat with triumph at the humiliation, while Hughie called Rosa 'the Nazi' behind her back.

On the surface, Rosa could scarcely have been more different from Robert. With his silk shirts, irresponsible episodes at the casino, trips abroad and decadent entertaining, the Mad Boy was still overtly sexual and extravagant. Rosa, on the other hand, exaggerated her humility, emphasised her frugality and was almost asexual in her appearance.

She adored the aristocracy, believing they were 'a race apart'. 'I'm just a servant,' she would say emphatically.[447] If she served only the best for her master, she announced herself content to eat cold porridge or stale bread. She dressed in thick, home-knitted pullovers and sturdy shoes and presented herself as someone with only two concerns – to do her job better than anyone else and to guard her master. If Hughie was a loyal Labrador, Rosa was a fierce-eyed Rottweiler.

Some years later, when Richard Burton arrived at Faringdon to film some scenes from *Laughter in the Dark*, accompanied by his wife, there was understandable excitement about welcoming the most celebrated and sexiest couple in show business. While Burton acted, Elizabeth Taylor hung around drinking gin. Jack Fox was dispatched to collect a case for Miss Taylor from Ferguson's, the wine merchant, 'and she nearly drank it all in three days'.[448] Taylor was wearing the colossal diamond ring her husband had recently given her – a 33-carat, octagonal stone famous for being one of the largest flawless stones in the world. At one point, the dazzling, violet-eyed actress took it off to show Rosa and suggested she try it on. Rosa took the outsize gem in her large, work-reddened hands. They may have done dainty work with a knife or a needle, but her fingers were thick as sausages and the ring wouldn't fit over them.

Despite their differences, Robert and Rosa shared certain characteristics. Both were stubborn and had fiery tempers. They were united in their desire to put Faringdon first, even if they sometimes had diverse opinions as to the method. If Rosa retained a fondness for Teutonic discipline, Robert never lost the disdain for authority that had created such problems at school and in the Army. He fought the town council so that Irish travellers could make an encampment outside the estate's walls and always gave camping space in the grounds to the elderly Fred Abel, who travelled the country in his caravan pulled by two donkeys. Abel's menagerie included his famous flea circus in a glass box, nineteen rats and three dogs. Rosa was instructed to make him welcome and give him some milk every day. One year, Robert was away in Africa when the showman arrived and was annoyed on his return to learn that old Fred had not been given his milk. Ignoring Rosa's protests that there wasn't any to give Mr Abel, Robert opened the fridge, took out a bottle of milk and poured it over her head as she sat at the table peeling potatoes. 'She didn't say a word,' recalled Martin Webb (son of Gerald's old taxi driver, Reginald), who had driven Robert from the airport. 'She didn't react. She just didn't want to take Fred Abel his milk.'

There seem to have been other incidents with milk. Jack Fox witnessed Robert and Rosa having 'a hell of a row' when he was walking past the kitchen, and saw Robert pick up a bottle of milk and pour it over the housekeeper's head. She stopped her shouting and 'let out one manic scream, ran off to her room and slammed the door. Captain Cruddas came running and said, "Ring up the Bell and book lunch and dinner as we're not going to get any food today."' Those who were close to Robert knew that he had a cruel and aggressive side. To some, his unpredictable temper, occasionally violent behaviour and his unapologetic selfishness were off-putting. To others, they were parts of a multifarious character that refused to stay within anyone's boundaries. For every person who admired or loved him there was another who thought him dreadful. He was generous and stingy, welcoming and rejecting, a person who insisted on good manners and who was appallingly rude.

Robert was godfather to Jack Fox's son, who was named after him, but Jack didn't trust Robert not to trick him when it came to business. 'I need it in writing 'cause I don't bloody trust you,' he said after Robert offered him a job in his latest commercial activity – a building and undertaking company. While Robert was busy converting parts of the house into flats, he decided to organise the work himself rather than pay what was demanded by Baker's, the local firm he used. Luring away from Baker's a carpenter called Russell Spinage, Robert set him up as director of a building business that he named after him. The team carried out various jobs inside the house (ignoring regulations for Grade I listed buildings), turning dank service areas into garages and workshops and creating a new room for Rosa's kitchen, close to the dining room, so food was no longer carried up and down a flight of stairs.

It was traditional for country joiners to make coffins and Jack joined Russell Spinage as both a stonemason and an undertaker. 'I'm not afraid of dead bodies. It's not horrible when you get used to it,' he said. Later, when Baker's closed down, Robert took over their undertaking business too. Friends couldn't contain their hilarity at the idea of the Mad Boy as an undertaker. They'd enquire, 'How are the coffins?' But he took it surprisingly seriously, even claiming that he had been to the annual undertakers' conference in Blackpool. Robert made sure that he returned from his almost yearly winter trips to Africa 'in time for the burial season'. He said this came 'early in spring when all the old folk who had been hibernating, poked their noses out, thinking the weather was getting warmer, caught flu and died'.[449]

In the early 1960s, Robert decided to build an office for Mr Rich, his accountant, who initially came down from London, but ultimately moved to Faringdon. Robert converted the old chapel that extended from the main body of the house on the lower ground floor by the stables, and Jack was involved in the renovation. On the windowsill of the chapel sat a small oak box. Inside it were Gerald's ashes that had been there since the cremation in 1950. 'What shall I do with them?' asked Jack. 'Bury them,' replied Robert. 'Where?' 'Over there,' said Robert, pointing towards the front lawn. Jack took the box and walked over to the two large flowerbeds filled with delphiniums near the gateway to the churchyard. Gerald had loved the mad firework flash of blue that these tall flowers created for a few weeks each year and Robert had continued the tradition despite the work involved in staking the fragile, ephemeral spires. Jack dug down into the earth between the delphinium beds until he reached the stone foundations of the old Elizabethan house, placed the box there and filled in the hole. Robert had adored Gerald and there were those that felt he dedicated his life to commemorating Gerald's, but there was no ceremony, no marker for these dusty remains. On the nearby path, by the churchyard wall, there was a row of dogs' graves that had been given much greater

ROBERT IN THE 1960S
WITH MANLEY, THE
GREAT DANE

consideration. There was Manley, the Great Dane that died of rickets, and a lovely stone for Towser, a Jack Russell that belonged to Rosa. Everyone on the estate dreaded Towser as a 'silent biter', but even he was honoured with a small pyramid, engraved 'Towser: A short life but a gay one'.

If Robert seemed slapdash in some ways, in others he was

meticulous. He would lose huge amounts of money at Mayfair gaming tables and return home with unsuitable young men, whom Rosa avoided at all costs. But on a Monday morning, he'd be up at 7.30, directing the gardeners and groundsmen about their day's work. He took enormous care to improve the house and grounds, re-rendering the building, buying statues, reclaiming areas that were grown over and insisting that standards were not lowered when it came to raking the gravel or planting up the urns with colourful geraniums and lobelia. He created a 'gloom garden' down by the lake, in the shade of dark yew trees, with hellebores and bleeding hearts, and he planted a monkey-puzzle walk, where flowering cherries were interspersed with the spiky trees most associated with suburban gardens. A peacock and peahen were brought in, producing offspring, but the male became 'over-sexed and over-fed', alienating its owner by attacking what it believed was an enemy bird in the Jaguar's shiny hub caps. Robert asked Jack Fox to 'shoot the bloody thing' but it ended up along the road in Lord Faringdon's wood at Buscot.[450]

By middle age, the Mad Boy had the confidence to insist on his own taste. Like Gerald, he appreciated the kitsch and unconventional as well as the traditionally attractive. He bought a chest of drawers that leaned to the side as though someone had pushed it or Dalí had designed it, and he was unafraid to add plastic tulips to the grand spread of spring bulbs cultivated along the drive, or fake lilies to the vases of real ones in the house. Among the Victorian needlework and beaded cushions on the day-bed was a soft doll of a 'dirty old man', complete with grey woollen hair and a beige raincoat that opened to reveal the daintily sewn genitals. And if someone was shocked, so much the better.

'He avoided conventions and categories,' remembered Candida Lycett Green, whose parents, John and Penelope Betjeman, remained among Robert's greatest friends. 'And he was fantastically astute about people. Faringdon was a bit like a royal court, with people always wanting to be in it. He understood if people were being sycophantic.'[451] Though Robert had considered shutting up the whole place after Gerald's death, he actually became a generous and active host; the visitors' books testify both to the many who continued to visit over generations and the new friends who became regulars. In 1960, just before Victoria's wedding, Robert welcomed the most famous and fashionable newly-weds in the country – Princess Margaret and her photographer husband, Tony Armstrong-Jones, now Earl of Snowdon. He was close to Jeremy Fry, an inventor and entrepreneur who, with his wife Camilla, was a lifelong friend of Robert's. They were part of the 'fast set' that the royal pair were drawn to, with wild parties, casual flings and a liking for drink and drugs. Jeremy was also a cousin of Jennifer's, and like her was dogged by the epithet 'member of the Fry chocolate dynasty'. He was also dogged by a conviction for a homosexuality offence, something that led courtiers to make him stand down as Armstrong-Jones's best man on account of 'jaundice'. Like Robert, both Jeremy and Armstrong-Jones appreciated women while also being attracted to men. None of them were obviously gay or had camp manners, but they were all at home in the company of other men who were. And it was not until 1967 that England decriminalised homosexual acts in private between two men aged over twenty-one.

Jeremy eventually separated from Camilla (after they had had four children) and started living openly 'out of the closet' with a man. But Camilla too had a complicated love life. Robert was possibly romantically involved with her and certainly adored her; he told Victoria that he had loved Camilla more than anyone else in his life (though he told someone else his great love had been Garth).[452] To add further intricacy to the tangle of threads, one of Camilla and Jeremy's children turned out to have been fathered by Armstrong-Jones shortly before his wedding. The Snowdons and the Frys remained friends and acted as godparents to one another's children, but it was only in his late seventies that Lord Snowdon agreed to take a DNA test to confirm what many had long suspected.

Robert had no problem progressing with these new younger sets from the excesses of the 1930s to those of the Swinging Sixties. If parties were now fuelled by amyl nitrate rather than cocktails from silver shakers, and the music was the Rolling Stones rather than Cole

Porter, the fundamentals had not changed so much. Nancy Mitford considered that the young people of the 1960s were 'sobriety itself' in comparison to the wilder hedonism of her own youth.[453] The Mad Boy was naturally attracted to the younger generation and in several cases, the children of his or Gerald's friends continued the tradition by returning to Faringdon and establishing their own friendships with Robert. One of these was Constant Lambert's son, Kit, who described Robert as his godfather, though there are doubts as to whether there had actually been a ceremony. By the time Kit went to Oxford in the mid-1950s, he had inherited his father's traits of intelligence, charm and a propensity to drink. Both shared a self-destructive tendency that would end their lives prematurely; Constant had died only a few years earlier, when sustained alcohol abuse combined with undiagnosed diabetes killed him two days before his forty-sixth birthday. Unlike his father, Kit was homosexual, though he was not always open about it, despite what many recognised as gay manners and decadent ways. After a stay at Faringdon in 1957, he signed himself into the visitors' book as 'Kit Lambert, Life Member of the Society for the Extermination (painful) of American Debutantes'.

Following university, Kit led the life of an often perilously impecunious, diminutively sized playboy. But everything changed when he decided to make a film about English rock and roll. He came across a band ('ugly in the extreme') called the High Numbers and became their manager. Taking a loan from Robert and another from his paternal grandmother, he shaped them into a ground-breaking rock band and changed their name to the Who. Kit quickly made lots of money, which enabled him to party to an even more outrageous extent; he took as many drugs, if not more, than the band. He still dressed in dark suits and cut his hair short, and managed, despite the riotous behaviour, to have a huge impact on the music and style of the group. Predictably, he failed to take care of the accounts properly, something that would later catch up with him, but not before he encouraged and nurtured Pete Townshend through creating the innovative and later legendary rock-opera *Tommy*.[454]

According to Robert, Kit never paid back his original investment in the Who, but offered him holidays at the exquisitely lovely Palazzo Dario, a Renaissance palace on Venice's Grand Canal that he bought in 1971. The partying continued at a dizzying pace and the use of drugs increased. In 1973, Kit's entry in the Faringdon visitors' book looks like that of an addict: 'I have lost <u>all</u> my skin, you are lucky to have not lost your – skin. Me, me, me.' Like his namesake, the painter Christopher Wood, Kit had a fatal tendency to fly too high. Robert himself drank excessively and knew about losing control, but even he realised that Kit was in trouble, taking heroin as well as other drugs and alcohol, and eventually sacked by the Who for massive financial incompetence.[455] Robert tried to help, though there was little that could be done by this stage; Kit's physical deterioration and self-abuse followed a similar path to that of his father's, and he died thirty years after Constant, in 1981.

UGHIE'S PERIODIC BANISHMENT by Robert eventually became permanent exile; in the late 1960s, he moved into Waterfall Cottage, a small, thatched house near Uffington. Friends described him as heartbroken, his days devoid of meaning, the war wound in his leg keeping him awake at night.[456] Typically for Robert, once his partner had left he proved generous, providing him with wood and driving over to the cottage with supplies of wine. But deprived of Robert and his beloved Faringdon, Hugh died some years later of a heart attack, lonely and rejected.

As Robert got older, he surrounded himself with increasing numbers of women friends of different ages. Though he was still active sexually with men, the relationships grew more perfunctory and impersonal; he was unafraid of 'real rough trade', commented one friend. However, for company and travel, he far preferred vivacious, worldly women. Some of these were from a younger generation, like Camilla Fry and Joy Skinner, whose husband, James, said that he and Camilla's second husband John Fairbairn 'trailed along', tolerated by Robert so he could maintain his friendships with their wives. Others had known the Mad Boy since his arrival at Faringdon as a boy of twenty, with windswept hair and pink cheeks, like Gerald's fictional Millie. Daphne Fielding and Diana Mosley both continued to visit, and to write about their memories of Faringdon and Gerald in various publications. Diana was utterly unrepentant about her past, and astonished people by continuing to insist on how nice Hitler had been and how Mosley had got it right all along. As a child, Candida Betjeman was so appalled by her 'still banging on about Hitler', that she threatened to her parents, 'I'm going to pick my nose at Lady Mosley!' The Mad Boy, however, loved Diana's kind of unconventionality and cherished her, not only for her friendship, beauty and intelligence, but her willingness to go against the tide and not care what the world said.

Another loyal companion was Coote Lygon, who had known Faringdon since the early 1930s. Coote had been very fond of Gerald, but she idolised Robert; some say she had always been in love with him. In the intervening years, she had farmed in Gloucestershire, worked as a governess in Istanbul and lived in Athens, becoming Social Secretary at the British Embassy.[457] Later, she worked as an archivist for Christie's and lived in a houseboat on the Thames. She had never married, and she remained as pudding-faced and plump as she had been when young. While her beautiful sister Maimie always managed to look stylish, even if she'd had too much to drink, Coote appeared awkward, her clothes unflattering and her thick spectacles unfortunate. Back in the pre-war days, Coote had gone to a fancy-dress ball where both she and Diana Cooper were dressed as nuns. Robert had remarked then that 'Diana looked like an actress playing a nun, Coote looked like a nun.'[458] But age sometimes works in favour of the less attractive, whose other qualities can shine brighter than those who have lost their looks. Coote had always been astute, considerate and an intrepid traveller and she was a successful addition to Robert's house parties and travels. A keen horsewoman who hunted side-saddle, she often accompanied Robert out on the horses. Above all, she was a steadfast friend in whose normally discerning eyes Robert could do no wrong.

During the 1960s, Lady Primrose Cadogan was another close friend to Robert, putting him up in London, visiting Faringdon and accompanying him on many trips abroad. She had a penchant for Dom Pérignon, which she called 'bottled sunshine', and her nickname for Robert was 'Shoe' (or was it 'Chou', as in *mon petit*?). They went gambling together, betting in opposite ways in roulette, so if he won she lost and vice-versa, and if they weren't exactly lovers, evidence suggests that they ended up in bed together at least once. Robert's liking for Africa was increasing and the pair travelled to several destinations on the Dark Continent together. For many years, he also went almost annually, though alone, to Tanzania to stay with a doctor friend, Andrew Crowden, in his small flat in Dar-es-Salaam. Robert's wild claims about what he got up to with young, handsome African men probably had at least an element of truth to them. 'It was very easy there if you had money,' commented one friend. Once at a dinner someone said something racist to Robert about Africans to which Robert replied, 'You're so wrong. They may be a bit boring sometimes at breakfast, but they're wonderful.'[459] His defence against racism was not exactly politically correct.

As Robert got older, he became more confident about honouring Gerald's legacy. For a long time, he had tended to ignore enquiries about Lord Berners by people interested in his music, writing or painting. Letters went unanswered: 'I didn't reply because I knew I'd give a wrong reply. That's slightly worse than giving none.'[460] In 1972, however, there was a concert of Berners's music at the Purcell Room, organised by the composers Peter Dickinson and Philip Lane. John Betjeman gave readings from his old friend's work and Robert collaborated, sending a van with pictures and furniture from Faringdon to lend atmosphere. It was the first sign that a revival might take place of a composer who had been sidelined in the twenty-two years since his death.

When Primrose Cadogan became ill with cancer, Robert took

care of her loyally; on holiday in Jamaica, he had given her a huge diamond ring, which she insisted on returning to him when she knew she was dying. Afterwards, he 'wore it in his button-hole instead of a carnation at parties', said Laura, Duchess of Marlborough, the person who largely replaced Primrose as Robert's bosom friend. Laura Marlborough had been briefly married to the 10th Duke, though she had already been Viscountess Long, Countess of Dudley and Mrs Canfield during previous marriages. As she grew older, she was much happier dashing around the world on bibulous trips with Robert and playing backgammon (to a competitive level) with him. Both she and her sister Anne (who was married to Ian Fleming) were among his closest friends. When Laura tried to commit suicide with whisky and sleeping pills, it was Robert who made her turn the corner, arriving with so many beautiful lilies that they extinguished the smell of the elderly and incontinent which normally pervaded the nursing home. He went further:

> Then he apparently told a number of people he wanted to marry me. He declared this at a dinner party, which caused Diana Cooper to telephone me saying what lovely news it was, to which I replied, 'What news?' She said, 'I hear you are to marry the "mad boy". I said I knew of no such news, but nevertheless it gave me the boost I needed; for once I didn't care if the William Hickey column picked up this daydream, which of course they did.[461]

A few years younger than Robert, both Laura Marlborough and Anne Fleming had been photographed by Cecil Beaton as young society beauties of the 1930s. Although Robert and Cecil had never got along, their mutual loathing was to reach new heights at a late stage in their lives when Cecil published another volume of his diaries in 1972 that covered the period of Gerald's last illness: 'Pathetic Gerald! When he returned to Faringdon life was made no easier for him. He was not even allowed his breakfast in bed. It was not long before, in desperation, he turned his face to the wall.'[462] Robert was outraged and deeply unhappy about the accusation that he had not cared for

THE OLD MAD BOY, HORNED AND READY FOR A PARTY

Gerald in his final illness, and the implication that his inheritance had disappointed the Berners family. The Mad Boy considered and then decided against suing Cecil; friends from the old days knew it wasn't true, but to be portrayed as opportunistic and cruel violated Robert's sense of honour and wounded him deeply. Two years later, the chance for revenge arrived.

In March 1974, both Robert and Cecil were invited to a birthday party at the Cheyne Row house of their old friend Peter Quennell. There were lots of familiar faces, including Laura Marlborough, Cyril Connolly and John Betjeman (now quite openly involved with Lady Elizabeth Cavendish, though not divorced from Penelope). Robert came face-to-face with Cecil as the latter was leaving and followed him to the front door wearing what Cecil called 'his asinine grin'. Without warning, Robert punched the eminent seventy-year-old photographer on the chin. According to shocked witnesses, Cecil stumbled down the three front doorsteps and fell, hitting his head against a car. Cecil's subsequent diary entry makes claims that observers (and Beaton's biographer) believe are untrue, but that indicate how violated he felt.[463] He recorded that Robert tried to kick him in the balls, and continued beating him with a 'maniacal fury' while taunting, 'Now run! Now run!'[464] In fact, it was Robert who ran off into the wet London night; Cecil was helped back into Peter Quennell's house, dizzy, sore-faced, but with nothing broken.

Martin Webb had driven Robert up to the party and, once he

had discovered what had happened, 'drove round and round London trying to find him. It was pouring with rain and there were police cars everywhere because it was the night someone had tried to shoot Princess Anne. I couldn't find him anywhere and decided to go home, but then I spotted him outside Harrods. He was quite drunk (he always had a few drinks when he went to a party), but said he felt much better having hit Cecil Beaton on the nose.'[465] Cecil, on the other hand, felt worse the next day. He was cold, shivery and shocked, and undecided as to whether he should sue his 'lifelong enemy'. The incident was the talk of London and Cecil's phone rang all day with sympathy callers and others wanting to hear the titillating tale first hand.[466] It was only a few months after the horrifying murder by stabbing of James Pope-Hennessy, Cecil's old friend, and it seemed as though London's ageing, artistic high society was under serious attack.

On his lawyer's advice, Cecil didn't start legal proceedings, but he was no doubt pleased when George Weidenfeld quipped, 'The TV and newspapers are full of violence, thuggery, and people who behave like Robert Heber Percy.'[467] Cecil's friends thought his stroke, one month later, was a direct consequence of the attack.[468] Robert was unrepentant, laughing and declaring that Cecil deserved it. Cecil lived nearly another six years, but miserable, weak and without the use of his right hand, so unable to take photographs, draw or write. Despite visits from loyal friends like Clarissa (now Lady Avon), and one from Greta Garbo, he became increasingly disillusioned and isolated. When Cecil died aged seventy-four, there were many who believed that the Mad Boy had killed him.

CHAPTER SIXTEEN

Robert's Folly

OT LONG AFTER MY FIRST VISIT to Faringdon in 1979, Robert invited me back. I asked if I could bring the same boyfriend, Jeremy Newick, a designer and a keen sailor and boat-builder. Now eighteen, I had already left home by default as my father and stepmother had moved to the remote Scottish island where we had always holidayed. They had no telephone and the only means of contacting them was by letter. During term time, I was lodging in Oxford and attending my final year of school, but at weekends and holidays I stayed with Jeremy in his decrepit but elegant Georgian terraced house at the top of a hill in Bristol. I learned how to sand floors and paint banisters, I wrote my essays and played the piano with fingerless gloves against the cold, and I hardly noticed some of Jeremy's friends' quizzical looks at this rangy thirty-one-year-old taking up with a schoolgirl.

My mother, with whom I had not lived since the age of eleven, was now a follower of Bhagwan Shree Rajneesh, an Indian mystic who had dozens of Rolls-Royces and was called the 'Sex Guru' by the tabloids. Her latest boyfriend was a *sannyasin*, and she had joined the many thousands who dressed in orange or shades of red and pink, wore a mandala with a picture of Bhagwan around their necks, and were given new names by their leader. She spent weeks or months away visiting ashrams in California and Oregon. Her comrades-in-orange all called her Gala, her middle name, which had appealed to Bhagwan when he bestowed her new identity. I sometimes went to stay with my mother in London, where both my brothers lived in a house that was often

326

filled with 'orange people'. There was lots of dancing, hugging and meditating, and rumours filtered back about the incredible orgies in Oregon, though Bhagwan ordered the use of rubber gloves in addition to condoms, predicting that AIDS was going to decimate the world. Victoria still claims she has never been happier than at this time.

Throughout the early 1980s, Robert kept inviting me to stay, and once or twice a year Jeremy and I went to Faringdon for a weekend. But there was no closeness in the relationship with my grandfather, no sense of complicity in the fact that we were related. I suspect he liked adding me into a weekend house party as a wild card: a surprise element that might entertain the other guests. There were regularly people who reacted with astonishment at meeting me. Some didn't even know that Robert had a child, let alone a grandchild. Others assumed he was exclusively gay. I enjoyed playing along with his game. The place and the people I met were so different from the rest of my life and it was exhilarating to feel as though I was someone else for a couple of days.

The house was always perfectly set up on a Friday to receive guests. Gravel was raked, flowerbeds weeded and Des, the gardener, brought in whatever was agreed in the way of vegetables, cut flowers and hothouse plants. A collection of pots was placed beneath the double staircase so that the heady scent from stephanotis blossoms or the bell-like blooms of daturas wafted about as you passed through, just as they had in Gerald's day. Rosa arranged flowers in tall vases for the drawing room and dining room and smaller ones for the bedrooms, and every piece of silver and brass glistened, newly cleaned.

Guests were usually instructed to arrive in time for pre-lunch drinks on Saturday, or sometimes for Friday evening. It was like walking into a production where you had to play a part, with nice clothes and funny stories ready. Often there were a few people invited just for drinks who were expected to know to leave before the music boxes in the hall chimed their tunes and the rest of the guests were summoned to the dining room by Rosa. Robert would have worked out a *placement* in advance, calculating who the most senior woman was and inviting her to sit on his right. He always occupied the same chair at the large round table, within reach of an electric bell underneath; it took me some time to work out how Rosa knew exactly when to reappear after one course and clear away the plates and bring in another. There were white linen napkins and tablecloths, supple from years of washing, and crystal glasses, quickly filled with a golden, nectar-like Mosel that was Robert's habitual wine (neither he nor Gerald had ever been wine buffs who made a fuss about domains and vintages). The dining room contained furniture, pictures and ornaments that must have been from the old days – an articulated silver-gilt fish the size of a salmon and painted blackamoors on columns – but there were also some more modern touches like a flashing-light sculpture by the Greek artist Takis.

Once everyone was seated, Robert would direct the ladies to serve themselves from a range of dishes on the sideboard, starting with the most important guest and then letting the men get going. There might be a light salmon coulibiac, already sliced, with a frothy hollandaise sauce; the system was perfect if, like me, you wanted to discreetly avoid the pheasant or rack of lamb. It was like a highly orchestrated ceremony, with Robert as the master who was allowed to break all his own rules and Rosa as his handmaiden.

Returning to Faringdon, I got to know some of the regulars. Coote was among Robert's closest friends, having moved first into a cottage in a nearby village and then into a somewhat dour modern house in Faringdon. I didn't know that both had been bought by Robert, nor that Coote was paying a mortgage to him. Coote seemed almost part of the furniture at Faringdon – a calm, modest foil to Robert's mercurial ways. Sometimes her sister Maimie was there too. You could tell that Maimie had been a beauty, though age and drink had extracted their toll since the 1930s when she and Robert had rolled almost naked on the sand at Ostia. She still had the air of a coquette and carried about a badly behaved, incontinent Pekingese that recalled the one-eyed predecessor that Evelyn Waugh had described half a century before: 'the malignant Cyclopean-eye of Grainger winking across the Ritz lounge'.[469] Neither sister had been back to their beloved Madresfield for decades as they detested their older brother's wife, Else.

Other neighbours who frequently appeared were Susanna and Nicholas Johnston. Nicky had been the architect for what was probably Robert's greatest addition to the gardens – the 'stairs to nowhere' by the orangery, and the pool at the top of them. The great flight of stone steps surrounded by yew hedges was the first idea, built up a bank opposite the orangery and ending mid-air. This surreal tease was such a success that Robert decided to go one further and build a swimming pool up there. Nicky devised a way of incorporating a tank, and – after being rung in the middle of the night by Robert shouting, 'I want to go High Gothic' – then designed a castellated pepper-pot changing room with a floor of old pennies. Robert located a pair of very expensive seventeenth-century stone wyverns (winged, serpent-like dragons), which he bought with money won through gambling, and they were incorporated into the structure. The result was a triumph – Robert's own Folly, created forty years after Gerald made his tower.

After we had helped ourselves to the raspberry Pavlova or redcurrants frosted in icing sugar and served with buttery, bean-shaped shortbread, we would move back to the drawing room and drink coffee from gilt cups sculpted with scenes and figures like something Benvenuto Cellini might have made, encasing a tiny porcelain interior. Then we would often meander over to the pool. The size precluded laps but made it ideal for wallowing; like the interior of the house, it was heated to an indulgent degree. Robert would sit on an antique marble throne by the edge, but some of us would dive off the ledge by the wyverns or float in a dreamy haze.

Occasionally, I would play the piano at the green end of the drawing room. I would leaf through the piles of music I assumed had belonged to Lord Berners and find some Bach or Chopin that I knew. I hadn't heard the story about my father's disgrace and I never suspected that Robert might be eyeing me suspiciously as the progeny of the dreadful mad Russian; quite the reverse, as I could tell he liked me and I was pleased. When Jeremy and I made a jokey present for Robert, assembling a collection of false moustaches and framing them like a butterfly display, he hung it in the drawing room alongside formidable works of art by Corot and Gerald. It felt like an outrageous honour. I didn't know then that long before, Robert and Gerald had decorated Berners ancestral portraits with moustaches, or that there is a Lord Berners piece called 'L'Uomo dai baffi' ('The Man with the Moustache'). But moustaches were evidently in the ether. There were still plenty of other jokes: Gerald's mechanical toys remained arrayed on a grand marble-topped table, added to over the years; fake pink pearls spilled from delicate porcelain shells; and small, snooty busts of a jowly Queen Victoria were reflected in sumptuous rococo mirrors.

Getting to know Robert was unlike any other family relationship or friendship I had encountered. We rarely had a personal conversation, and both circumstances and his character discouraged intimacy. He told stories that made his guests laugh, often recycling episodes from long ago with characters interchanged at will. Was it Sachie Sitwell, or Emerald Cunard, or perhaps the arrogant Lady Stanley (who wondered whether, when she arrived at the pearly gates, she would be addressed as 'Portia' or 'Lady Stanley') who arrived at Faringdon all in a fluster? 'The policeman stopped us in the car and was preventing us from leaving, so I had to tell him who we were.' (Or sometimes it was: 'The head waiter at the restaurant did not know who we were.') To which Gerald's reply was always: 'And who *were* you?' This stinging retort had appealed to Gerald and Robert, as they shared a hatred of pomposity and a delight in deflating anyone too puffed up. Like Gerald, Robert wanted to be amused and to amuse others, and scorned anything too earnest. For my seventy-year-old grandfather, life was still for living dangerously, in the moment and with indulgence. And yet I had also seen his tender, hands-on care of the gardens, his planting of trees he would never see mature, the detailed curating of sculptures, ornaments and vistas around the estate. Whenever I came to some conclusion about the man, another angle came into view that contradicted it.

I never had the kind of discussion with my grandfather that gave me much insight into his life or his deeper emotions; everything had to be deduced or guessed. And later, when I came to write this book, Robert was the hardest character to get close to. The absence of written documents left a void that was not filled by the fond recollections of friends and admirers or the scathing remarks of enemies and critics. Sometimes he appeared to be a vulnerable figure, taking refuge in bad behaviour, but he could also seem to be selfish, rude and vain, without a thought for other people's feelings. There were points where his mischievous rebelliousness was appealing and others where it was tiresome.

During one stay at Faringdon, Robert gave me a present – a compact, square bottle of scent with a gold label. He explained that Joy was his favourite: 'We used to sprinkle it in our gumboots.' The smell was intoxicating, like tuberose and jasmine mixed with the mysterious fragrance of the opulent magnolia grandiflora that Rosa would place on the breakfast tray she brought me in bed, nestling next to a set of the prettiest mottled green china I had ever seen. I didn't know it, but Joy had been created in France in 1930, just before Robert met Gerald; it was famous for being 'the world's most expensive perfume'. When I wore it, I felt transported into the world of Faringdon's heyday. I didn't know much about it then and felt I had little in common with this unusual grandfather, but I could sense the seductive indulgence and mischief. I realise now that it was largely through the senses that I got closer to Robert – by putting on Joy, by sleeping in his house, walking in his gardens and eating his food. And now this seems appropriate, as he was a man for whom the physical aspects of life often took priority.

Sometimes, Robert's love of controversy and tendency to shock became obvious. Several drinks in, a precariously unflicked inch of ash on the cigarette in his hand, he would make remarks that left the table speechless. The anti-Semitism that had been de rigueur in the Shropshire homes of his childhood and the London parties of his youth was like regurgitated bile. He chose to ignore that this had become an appalling faux pas in the post-Holocaust, increasingly politically correct era of the 1980s. There was never a theory or policy, just an in-built prejudice that was difficult to know how to tackle. 'It wasn't any more than many of his time and class,' remarked several friends of his whom I questioned. But it wasn't something I had encountered before.

By this time, I had left school and was studying social anthropology at Cambridge; it was unbearable to be in a situation where someone joked that a lampshade had been made from Jews' skin. I was close to my Russian grandmother, who had brought me up on Holocaust literature, and who was later posthumously awarded a medal and recognised as Righteous Among the Nations by Israel for her bravery in helping Jews during the war. I only witnessed Robert expressing anti-Semitic sentiments once and I tried to confront him. It became immediately clear, however, that there wasn't a discussion; he wasn't making these remarks to open a dialogue; it wasn't a democracy at Faringdon. It could have been a point to break off relations. For someone of my generation, this sort of racism was unacceptable. To walk away might have been morally braver, though I knew it wouldn't make any difference to him. I had the impression, though, that maybe it was all a trick or a test and that he didn't mean it at all. To challenge him was like aiming at a moving target that kept changing shape. After all, Robert sometimes had Jewish friends to stay and he didn't seem to have a problem with them. Other liberal-minded people kept coming. I let the matter hang uneasily – a canker in the bloom.

In the afternoons there was tea, and then everyone retired to bathe and change, emerging like new creatures of the evening – the women in long dresses or at least something smarter, the men in suits, their hair brushed. It was at this time that the elements in the house's own scent were at their most potent: steamy bath essence and the spritz of newly applied perfumes dominated upstairs, while the tempting hint of a buttery sauce floated out from the kitchen, and the smell of beeswax furniture polish gave a low note to the ambient aroma. Added to this was the heartening tang of woodsmoke, as fires were lit, even in the summer. In cooler seasons there was no dread of the chill so familiar to English country houses; as in Nancy Mitford's day, 'Faringdonheit' was kept heated to a luxurious degree, with radiators blasting and electric fires in the bedrooms. Lighting, on the other hand, was always kept low, with small lamps glowing like candle-light. Combined with the speckled old mirrors, one's reflection became more romantic, unblemished by the strong lighting of a modern era. The steady flow of alcohol added a further dose of mystery. Evening drinks were served, possibly with a new set of people chosen from local or Oxford friends as temporary entertainment, and then there was dinner.

On Sunday, the whole thing started over again with the addition of Sunday papers, sometimes read sitting in the morning sun on the porch. Not long after, there'd be a giant jug of Bloody Mary with celery and lots of Worcestershire sauce, maybe taken out onto the terrace where one would find a place on the low, honeysuckle-covered wall. Someone might get out the croquet set and we'd thwack the coloured balls around on the turf. Or a child would wind up the music boxes in the hall, or pull the lead on the Victorian model pug, which would open its lower jaw to reveal a small-toothed pink mouth and let out a rasping bark. There might be an expedition to climb the Folly, take the punt out on the lake or have drinks somewhere else. Once, Robert took us to Oare and we slipped into the gardens through a side gate. I'd never seen the house where my grandmother had grown up and it had been sold when I was a young child. We wandered along to the swimming pool – a perfect turquoise rectangle surrounded by green – and looked around before leaving, unobserved, the way we had come. It came just as naturally to me as it did to Robert to sneak in the back way, to add a touch of the forbidden. Perhaps we bonded over that without needing to talk about it.

Once, Robert asked me to come to Faringdon alone, without Jeremy, though he knew that we were living together in Cambridge. We had bought a tiny two-up two-down with no bathroom and Jeremy was now extending it into the garden to where the privy had been. For a long time, there was a tarpaulin instead of a roof and lots of dust. Robert had been given an invitation to a ball held by the new Lord Faringdon, the nephew of Gerald and Robert's old friend who had inherited the title and Buscot House in 1977. The party was intended as a celebration for his son's twenty-first birthday and as I was about the same age, I was invited. My grandfather wanted me to go alone. I knew nothing of Robert's attempted manipulation of my mother's relationship with

THE AUTHOR WITH ROBERT, MID-1980S

my father, but I sensed that he wanted some control over me – strange, perhaps, because he seemed to like Jeremy. I was sent a cheque for £100 to buy a frock and I found something in a second-hand shop that was very old and made of black silk chiffon. It looked like it was from the 1930s – bias-cut and delicate as spider's web – and cost £25. I kept the change without telling Robert, slightly guilty but pleased to subsidise student costs.

When the night arrived, my grandfather drove me to the ball and, after a drink with the 'grown-ups', left me there. People were kind – some girls took me to an upstairs bedroom where they were fixing their hair – and there was a glittering marquee, dinner and then dancing to pop hits of the day. I felt terribly out of place and, predictably, my nearly disintegrating dress was unlike any of the brightly coloured, stiffly ballooning confections that were fashionable in the early 1980s. I also knew I had to wait until a respectably late hour before I asked for my arranged ride back to Faringdon. When I did, there was a tray in the hall with milk and biscuits, laid out as I imagined had always been done after countless hunt balls, where young people had drunk too much and, in the pre-dawn hours, were starving from all the dancing and flirting. It was like something out of *Brideshead Revisited*, which I was watching each week on television. All that was missing was a darling old nanny up in an attic bedroom whom I could visit the next morning for advice after a night of excess or an amorous disaster.

When I left at the end of a weekend, I'd sign myself into the visitors' book, laid out on one of the wooden chests in the hall near the Dalí ink drawing of a horse and rider and the wartime Prieto portrait of Gerald holding a lobster and butterflies. Once, when I wrote my name under two of the regular guests I'd met as Deirdre and Johnny Grantley, I didn't understand why she had written her full name and he had only put his surname; it was the first time I learned that lords make a habit of that.

I once made the mistake of asking to stay over on Sunday night as it fitted my plans better for travelling on somewhere the following day. I heard a mild reluctance in Robert's acceptance, but only understood afterwards why that had been. On Monday morning, the place was completely different; the show over. The drawing room was shuttered up, the cleaning equipment was out and by the time I got up, Robert was dressed in a darned sweater, clutching a mug of Nescafé laced with brandy and back from consulting with the gardeners. It was like going back-stage after a play, where the actors were taking off their make-up and the scenery was being put away by technicians. After decades of observing how it was done and with Rosa's extraordinary capabilities, Robert was now the creative director of what was often a weekly production. But the audience needed to play by the rules. By Monday, it was back to rehearsals and repairs.

DIDN'T KNOW IT THEN, but Jennifer went to visit Robert after one of my early trips to Faringdon. In their mid-to-late sixties by then, they had more in common than they might have admitted. Both used alcohol as a crutch and dreaded the degradations of old age. Both also retained the optimism required for sexual escapades despite the fragility of a body that betrayed. 'Isn't it horrible being old?' Robert said to Jennifer around this time. Neither had a permanent partner; Hughie was long gone and the predictable if painful divorce from Alan had finally gone through. Clayton had been sold and Jennifer was now back in London. 'I am waiting for the telephone to ring. I have a whisky, light a cigarette, put it out. Pour another drink. The room seems stifling. I open the window and look at the trees, trying to relax.'[470] It was a sad time to be single, and Alan was now involved with a woman of Victoria's age.

When Cressida Connolly, Cyril's daughter, was finding her feet in London after leaving school, she lived with Jennifer for a while. Cyril had died when she was only thirteen and Jennifer had become something of an honorary godmother. 'She was very brave in many ways,' remembered Cressida. 'She didn't confide her problems, even though she sometimes complained a lot. And she was witty about her moaning. One autumn evening, at dusk, when she was shutting the curtains as usual, she said, "Darling, I can't stand this time of day . . . or year . . . or life."' Or when Cressida asked what they would cook that evening for dinner, Jennifer would announce deadpan, in her tinkling, pre-war voice, '*Petti di* fucking *pollo*'.[471]

Younger people often loved Jennifer for her humorous sparkle and for being unshockable; she never judged anyone's behaviour. Jonathan's friends flocked to her for advice over a drink or two. She was still attractive enough to have what she called 'the odd adventure', often with a much younger man, but this was done discreetly. Even at this point, she was still Pixie's darling; she continued to shelter her beloved governess from anything that might shock her, and she had the saintly old lady (now heading for a hundred) to live in her house before she moved into a care home. At one point, Jennifer decided to do some voluntary work and, taking a lead from her ancestor Elizabeth Fry, visited prisoners' wives. Though Jennifer didn't have the practical or financial problems of the women she tried to help, she identified with their unhappiness; she was lonely herself. It was often the small things that made her miserable, as though the underlying problems were too great to confront. One friend remembered going on holiday with her to Italy and on the first morning she appeared at breakfast 'totally shattered'. When asked what the matter was, she said, 'The leaves.' It seemed that the geraniums outside her window had been 'clattering together all night'.[472]

Jennifer never spoke to me about the visit to Faringdon one hot summer weekend, or about her feelings towards Robert, but she left a description.

> I woke early, apprehensive but soon felt better and at 11 a handsome man with a Range Rover arrived to fetch me. I didn't know him but he turned out to be the son of Gerald's chauffeur – Webb. Strange is hardly the way to describe my arrival as I was talking to him and didn't notice we were in Faringdon until we were at the Door. The pigeons were a brighter colour but otherwise at first glance all was the same as ever – including Robert. I was glad to have a drink – 12.30 by then, and I was shaken, and to find I was in the same room no – the same bed, as the rooms have been changed round.
>
> . . . My heart was so full of memories and my own thoughts and gossip and old times – so different to the times of now. I must try and remember more. I cried now and then but no one knew.
>
> Robert said that's your bag. I said 'where?' and saw it on a chair. He said no, it was a straw fish-shaped bag with a cane handle, under a picture of me. How long had it been there? My voice must have trembled a little.[473]

Among the guests staying that weekend was the publisher Jonathan Burnham, then an undergraduate at Oxford. He had recently become

such a favoured friend of Robert's that Rosa detested him. Jonathan
recalled that Robert had been in a state of anxiety to get everything
perfect in preparation for his ex-wife's stay. Jennifer, on the other
hand, evidently felt very emotional and her large, dark eyes frequently
brimmed with tears. After lunch, when others went home or disappeared
for siestas, Jennifer suggested a walk and the student and the slightly
tipsy woman in her mid-sixties strolled down to the lake in the
afternoon heat. They sat on a bench by the summer house and talked:
Jennifer confessed how much she had loved Robert. Then she asked
the young man whether he would like to join her for a swim. When
Jonathan protested that he had no trunks, Jennifer retorted, 'Don't be
so silly, darling,' stripped naked, lowered herself into the green-tinged
water and swam off with a ladylike breaststroke. Jonathan followed suit
and later commented that although nothing else happened between
them, Jennifer's behaviour appeared to be 'a kind of seduction', as well
as an expression of freedom from stuffy conventions.[474] Like Robert,
Jennifer refused to let her age get in the way of the sort of flirtation or
unexpected behaviour that had always been a part of her character.
Other friends who came for Sunday lunch that weekend recalled
that Robert and Jennifer got on well, making something of a comic
double act out of their shared memories. Afterwards, when his ex-wife
was leaving, Robert said, 'Do come back soon, darling,' and Jennifer
quipped, 'Perhaps I will. This time for good.'[475]

Y THE TIME ROBERT WAS seventy-four his health
was failing. He had had a stroke followed by some
smaller ones and had nearly drowned on holiday
in Majorca. Frail, unable to walk far without
a stick and later, humiliatingly, a Zimmer frame,
he took to driving almost everywhere, even within
the estate. There was a Range Rover and a Mini
and although he had always tended to crash, there were now brushes
with death on a regular basis. It was customary to see new cement work

patching up the front steps of the house after yet another collision. There had been several stays in hospital in Oxford, from where there were also escapes. Being shut up and restrained was unbearable for him. Once Robert persuaded Don Pargeter, the groundsman at Faringdon, to come and get him from the John Radcliffe. When he got home, it emerged that he had ripped out the tubes and discharged himself; the drip was still inserted in his hand.

Robert was desperate to be at Faringdon, but even there life was no longer easy. He had bouts of increasing gloom, while being cheered up by visits to and from friends. His relationship with Rosa became progressively more fractious. Once, he peed in his trousers in front of her, stepping out of them and leaving her to clear up the mess as if he was a naughty toddler challenging his mother. His fingernails grew long and yellow and sometimes he refused to wash. Rosa threatened to hand in her notice several times, but their lives were so entwined that such a prospect probably seemed impossible to them both.

Friends were worried about Robert, but they were flabbergasted when, in 1985, they heard that he was engaged. The shock was not just that he planned a second wedding, but that the bride was to be Coote. For a man who was known to be fundamentally gay and who had always prioritised beauty, Lady Dorothy Lygon was among the most unlikely choices. True, the pair had been friends all their adult life. Coote's stalwart devotion to Gerald and Robert had been limitless, and it had long been rumoured that Coote was always secretly in love with the Mad Boy. But marriage was surely beyond her most outrageous dreams. The *Daily Express* wrote, 'A Darby and Joan engagement just announced in *The Times* has led to much chuckling on the grouse moors this week . . . Both are in their early 70s and were not expected by friends to marry.'

Some thought it one of Robert's cruel jokes – a nod to the sort of thing he and Gerald had concocted when they placed advertisements for elephants or when the papers announced that Lord Berners was marrying the sapphically inclined Violet Trefusis. However, all doubt about the seriousness of the case was dispelled when anyone spoke to Coote. Known for her sharp mind and placid manner, she now appeared like a giddy girl, confessing, 'I know I'm seventy-four, but I'm starry-eyed.'[476] Robert's fiancée went to a health farm to lose weight, bought a smart handbag and showed off an impressive sapphire engagement ring. Evelyn Waugh had been dead almost twenty years, but she would surely have loved to tell him that his humiliating tease of 'marrying off Coote' – with the implication of its unlikeliness – was now obsolete. Notwithstanding the general consternation, Coote viewed her first marriage with genuine delight and to mark the day she had a cushion embroidered:

> To celebrate the marriage between
> Lady Dorothy Lygon
> And Mr Robert Heber-Percy
>
> on
>
> 10th September 1985

Astonishment led to perplexity. Why? Couldn't they just go on being close friends and neighbours? After all, Coote was so often at Robert's social events that she was seen as 'a cross between an ADC and co-host'.[477] Was it something to do with inheritance or tax? Maybe Robert wanted to 'look after' his old friend, who was far from well off. Or was it that the old Mad Boy still enjoyed shocking people and being unpredictable? Some recalled an equally unlikely marriage over thirty years earlier between Tom Driberg and his middle-aged Labour Party friend, Ena Binfield. Driberg was well known for his rampant appetite for casual sex with young working-class men, and his friends (including many of the Faringdon set) were astonished and, in some cases, appalled at what appeared to be either a big joke or a horrible mistake.

People noticed an expression of annoyance cross Robert's face when confronted with Coote's romantic interpretation of his proposal; whatever his motives, he hadn't expected to see her as his blushing bride. Rosa was beside herself, fulminating as if she were a jilted wife. The plans went ahead anyway. Dozens of loyal friends turned up for the party at Faringdon which preceded the civil ceremony. I was unable to go, having just driven out to Greece to start two years of research for an anthropology PhD, but I heard a number of reports. Most guests were staggered that Rosa, whom they considered among the finest cooks in the country, provided a very disappointing meal. 'She was in a proper bolsh,' said Algy, Robert's nephew, who drove over from Hodnet Hall. 'We'd expected a splendid lunch for an important family event, but it was very modest with two or three plates of ham sandwiches. So the coronation chicken and the lovely salads were nowhere to be seen.' 'It was so, so sad,' said Susanna Johnston. 'Rosa was in a filthy temper and made a filthy meal, slamming down plates of sandwiches.'

Twenty-five years after being turned down by Buckingham Palace as Tony Snowdon's best man, Jeremy Fry was appointed as Robert's. Who better to comprehend the complexities of being gay, married, divorced? The nuptial pair made their way to the car with the help of sticks, and Martin Webb drove them to Wantage Register Office. On the way, Jeremy Fry asked Coote who would represent her and she said, 'Martin.' So Lady Dorothy Lygon was 'given away' by the son of the man who had driven her from Faringdon station up to Faringdon House over half a century before. Martin then chauffeured Robert and Coote to Heathrow, from where they set off to Venice with Andrew Crowden, the doctor Robert had often stayed with in Dar-es-Salaam. Robert had failed to book early enough and the only hotel they could find was something very unsatisfactory in the industrial town of Mestre, on the edge of the lagoon. By all accounts, the two-week honeymoon was not a success.

Fuelled by ferocious jealousy, Rosa refused to stay even one day in the same house as the woman she accused of marrying Robert for his money. By the time Robert and Coote returned, Rosa had finally implemented her threat to leave. She was helped by Alan Heber-Percy, Robert's nephew, who provided her with accommodation and work in Gloucestershire. However, Rosa wanted to witness the full impact of her vengeful departure and concocted a plan. She booked Martin Webb to drive her away immediately after he had brought the returning honeymooners back from Heathrow. Robert was so angry when he discovered what was going on that he tried to block the driveway with his car to prevent them leaving; poor Martin was caught between two people who were masters of creating a drama. Eventually, Rosa won and she was driven off, leaving Robert and Coote alone in a house full of unwashed plates and debris from the wedding party. Lady Dorothy Heber-Percy's first night in her marital home consisted of scraping mouldy food from platters and washing champagne glasses, with Robert in a rage.

Robert's uxoriousness had not increased during the intervening forty-two years and his second marriage was even less successful than his first. From the day they began cohabiting, he was unkind and spiteful to Coote. 'I've gone from being his best friend to being his worst enemy,' Coote confessed, her expectations of sharing a room quickly dashed. 'He treated me like an unwanted guest as soon as we were married.'[478] Just as Robert had adored Jennifer and was then unable to have anything to do with her after the wedding, now he was foul-tempered with the woman who considered herself his closest companion. Worse, he expected Coote to take over Rosa's duties and cook, clean and shop – there was no persuading Rosa to return, however much anyone begged or bribed. For an elderly woman who had always lived alone during a peripatetic life and had never focused on domestic skills, these were almost impossible challenges. To compound the problems, Robert didn't provide any money for household expenses and Coote was forced to use her meagre savings to provide for them both. The newly-weds were utterly incapable of looking after themselves, and though sporadic help came from Garth's widow and estate workers, the situation quickly became unbearable. 'Poor Coote didn't stand a chance,' said one friend.[479] 'But she behaved like a gentleman,' recalled another; 'she left so that Rosa could come back.'[480] And sure enough, no sooner was Coote back in Lime Tree Cottage than Rosa returned.

URING THE TWO YEARS that I carried out the research for my PhD in the Peloponnese, I made the odd trip back to England, but I had become so attached to my adopted country that even after I finished my research and was writing up my thesis, I spent at least half the year in my apartment above a grocer's shop in Nafplio. I had changed during the time it took to learn Greek and make myself at home. Jeremy and I separated in Greece and it seemed to me as though I'd left my English life behind. Living out of a couple of suitcases, with furniture picked up from the street, made me feel light and happy – there was a sense of relief at abandoning my past. I liked the Greeks' lack of class obsession that I realised was so prevalent in my home country, where someone's accent, their school or their parents all counted for so much. It was also good to be away from the chaos of my parents' lives; my father's drinking had taken a deep plunge for the worse, he had left his second wife and their three young daughters and, shortly after the divorce, had married an eighteen-year-old within a week of meeting her. I was pleased I had no telephone (it took years or significant clout to acquire a line in the Greece of the 1980s), and although my landlord allowed important incoming calls to his neighbouring apartment, I usually queued up for the crackly connections of the telephone exchange in the centre of town. Slow letters still formed the most normal method of communication to England.

In 1987, on one of my visits home from Greece, Robert got in touch and asked if I would go to see him. I drove to Faringdon from London on a cold grey day. It was early springtime and there was a jazzy carpet of crocuses and aconites along the drive as I approached the house. Robert seemed frail but lucid. We had drinks and then ate lunch prepared by Rosa, who was back in charge as though nothing had ever happened. Ben, the boxer dog, wandered around between master and mistress. Afterwards, we sat by the fire in the drawing room. Robert said, 'Would you go into the study and look in the top drawer of the desk.

There should be a will there. Bring it here.' I did as he requested and returned with the legal document. 'Does it say that I leave everything to you?' he asked. I flicked through the pages and, apart from a few small legacies, what caught my eye was the name Alan Heber-Percy, repeated over and over in different clauses. I had never met Alan, but I knew that he was the son of Robert's brother Cyril. I had also heard that he was (at least until the marriage to Coote) Robert's intended heir. Alan was a businessman in his early fifties and married for the second time to someone with a large house in Gloucestershire. He was already caught up with Faringdon as a shareholder, he managed the farm and he owned a company in the town.

'I think it says you leave everything to Alan,' I said. 'Well, I want to leave it to you,' replied Robert. I can't remember how I reacted, but I suppose it was an expression of shock. I was so stunned I felt almost sick. It was an extraordinary gift and yet it seemed inappropriate to my character, age and situation. I was deeply flattered but also afraid. I realised that Robert was eccentric and wilful, but this was extreme. 'Do you know a solicitor?' asked Robert before I left. 'Yes,' I replied. 'Can you bring him here?'

I drove back to London in bewilderment. I couldn't imagine myself living like Robert. And how else might one live at Faringdon? Perhaps it would be different when I was older. My mother was astonished and far from happy when she heard the news. She had systematically tried to get as far away as possible from the way of life represented by Faringdon, and had made it clear to anyone who asked that she was not interested in inheriting her father's house. Nevertheless, Robert never consulted her about this 'and it would have been nice to be asked'. Victoria told me that her consternation was not that she felt disinherited – far from it – but she feared what would happen to me. For her, Faringdon represented a snobbish, mannered, loveless environment. Now, her daughter was being pulled right back into the epicentre. She worried that I would change into a different sort of person – that I would become like them.

I soon went back to Greece, carrying the bizarre piece of news like heavy extra baggage. I hoped that Robert would live a long time and provide me with many years in which to process this bizarre, almost terrifying development.

CHAPTER SEVENTEEN

Purple Dye

BOUT SIX MONTHS after Robert made me his heir, he died. It was a sunny October day and I was in my apartment in Nafplio typing up notes. Mr Mimis, my landlord, called me downstairs to his shop; there was a call for me. I could speak on the telephone by the cash register. My mother sounded shocked. I should arrange to come back as soon as I could. 'Don't be sad,' comforted Mr Mimis when he saw my tears and I explained that my grandfather was dead. 'He was an old man.' I didn't explain why the situation was more complicated.

Leo, my younger brother, collected me from Heathrow the next day and drove me to Faringdon. The sky was colourless and the air was cold. As we parked in front of the house, several people came out onto the porch: my mother, Rosa and a man who introduced himself as Alan Heber-Percy. We went into the study, where a fire was lit. Rosa, red-eyed and hand-wringing, brought tea. Alan sat on the leather fender-seat, welcoming and apparently in control. Urbane and handsomely silvering, he gave no sign that I had ruined his prospects, and was full of affable, practical advice. I went up to Robert's room to see his body. He looked slight and unfamiliar, laid out on a narrow four-poster. The room was very cold – the windows open – and I stood, chilled and fearful, in front of the man who, by dying, had made such a huge impact on my life.

My mother and I stayed at Faringdon for a few days. I slept in the room next to Robert's, where I was haunted by the image of him lying

346

on the other side of the wall. During the day, we went for walks in the cold mist, sometimes accompanied by Ben, the boxer, who lolloped about cheerily. The house was still and quiet, dominated by the corpse that was soon transferred into a coffin on trestles. I don't remember that I organised much for the funeral or did anything practical, though my mother had been to Russell Spinage and chosen the plainest coffin available before I arrived. I now suppose that it must have been Alan and Coote who organised the service. It was Jack Fox who laid out the body of the man he'd known since the 1930s, and about whom he said, 'One minute he was as good as gold, and he'd give you anything. And then he'd bury you in the earth.' Now it was Jack's turn to bury him in the earth, or as good as.

Rosa cooked for us and continued to care for the house, outwardly confident that I was Robert's chosen replacement and that I would learn to step into his shoes. She made sure that I sat in his place at the table and that I learned how to use the electric bell to summon her. There was a system and Rosa was not about to change it. There was no question of our making ourselves something to eat in the kitchen – that was Rosa's domain. Even a cup of tea was brought on a tray, with the large white teacups and saucers edged with a gilt key pattern. During those first days, I got to know the three men who worked outside, taking a special liking to Des Ball, the gardener, and Don Pargeter, the groundsman, who I later learned had been asked to 'look after' me by Robert. One of Don's jobs was to dye the fantail doves and it was his suggestion that we colour them purple as a sign of mourning for their master.

The day of the funeral was Robert's birthday – 5 November. He would have been seventy-six. The mauve doves picked flies from the wheels of the cars that drew up before the house, belying their role as sombre symbols of grief. Seeing Rosa crying, Alan said, 'Oh my God, can't she be given a tranquilliser?' Also gathered at the house was Cyril, Robert's brother (and Alan's father) – a charming, white-haired old man carrying a shooting stick, who picked up coloured pigeon feathers from the gravel to stick in his bowler hat. As the coffin was carried out of the

ROBERT'S COFFIN IS CARRIED FROM THE HOUSE TOWARDS THE CHURCH. HIS WIDOW, COOTE, HEADS THE LINE
OF MOURNERS WITH HIS NEPHEW ALAN, FOLLOWED BY MY MOTHER, MY BROTHERS AND ME, THEN JEREMY FRY,
ANDREW CROWDEN, GARTH'S WIDOW BETTY AND DAUGHTER SUSAN, AND ROSA

front door, Coote was first in line, dressed in widow's black and fur
hat, supported by Alan, who wore a morning coat and striped trousers.
Behind them was my mother on Leo's arm, then my younger brother,
Kolinka, with me. Following us were the two 'best men' from Robert's
second wedding – Jeremy Fry and Andrew Crowden. Garth's widow
Betty and their daughter Susan were there, and last out of the house
was Rosa, who locked the front door and caught up with the slowly
moving line as we crossed the damp expanse of lawn. The private
wooden doorway into the churchyard was open and we filed through it
and entered the church.

   The pews were filled with a wide variety of people: elegant women
of a certain age whose appearance hinted at a past of wild parties and
trips to the Riviera; young friends who had appreciated Robert's mad
excesses; gay men who had found refuge at Faringdon at a time when
their relationships could have landed them in prison; local Faringdon
people who had liked the eccentricity of the old squire; and estate tenants
and employees. I was disorientated, aware of the curiosity many must

have been feeling about me in my unlikely new role. Andrew Crowden gave the address, in which he described Robert's wartime Arabian trip as fundamental in forming his priorities in life. Emphasising Robert's love of Faringdon, and particularly the grounds, he said that his life 'was given to Marvell's "green thought in a green shade"', something I didn't understand until I looked up the seventeenth-century poet.

> The mind, that ocean where each kind
> Does straight its own resemblance find;
> Yet it creates, transcending these,
> Far other worlds, and other seas;
> Annihilating all that's made
> To a green thought in a green shade.

Robert was cremated in Oxford's crematorium where Gerald had ended up thirty-seven years earlier. We were a small group of mourners watching the traction belt pull the coffin into the furnace.

After the funeral, I was in shock. On the surface, this surprising set of circumstances looked rather romantic. Sometimes, as I walked down through the field to the lake, I felt as though I was viewing myself from the outside – like watching a film, or like those visions that dying people supposedly see, along with the tunnel leading to a bright light. I could appreciate the spectacular beauty of the place and the intriguing drama that had brought me there, but it was hard to make sense of how I would incorporate this twist of fate into my life. It was deeply confusing to find myself in what seemed to be almost a feudal set-up, where I was 'Miss Sofka', apparently Lord of the Manor, despite my gender. I was shown the special pew in the church that was allocated to me and told that I owned the rights to Market Place. It was so unfamiliar, it was anyone's guess whether there'd be some arcane *droit de seigneur* and local virgins would turn up for inspection.

I was Lord of the Manor but Rosa was the master of ceremonies. 'You are not just Sofka any more,' she crowed, wagging her forefinger at me in a threatening manner. 'You are quite someone. You are lady of this house. People will respect you and you must show them who you

are – isn't it?' In a letter to a friend I recorded that, after these episodes, 'I would flinch or feel like bursting into tears, but I have also managed to laugh a lot.' Once I tried to explain to the manic housekeeper that it was still important for me to carry on with my studies in Cambridge and Greece, adding that I wasn't about to take up flower-arranging or looking for a suitable husband. 'There could be worse things to do,' she replied knowingly.

In the days that I stayed at Faringdon before returning to Greece, Rosa took me to meet the tenants who lived in the various flats in and around the house. The seven or eight occupants were mostly single women, known by all as 'Miss Crack' (the daughter of Gerald's old chauffeur), 'Miss Stone' and so on. Rosa, however, was always Rosa, never Miss Proll. There was one young man. Rosa was very excited one morning before breakfast to pass on the gossip that he had been arrested as a peeping tom – something that only added to the slightly creepy, Gothic element in this hidden community.

We reached their homes by descending into the long basement corridor – the world of 'downstairs' that I had previously only known from films. Many of the old service rooms (game larders, sculleries and early incarnations of kitchens) had disappeared, but the atmosphere remained one of servants and practicalities. Gone were the creamy cornices and parquet floors of upstairs. Here, the walls were coloured institutional greens and greys, the floor was concrete, and a stream of people, from gardeners and gamekeepers to postmen and plumbers, entered the area freely from the stableyard, with no impression being made on the main part of the house. There were more tenants living up the back staircase on the attic floor, in the stable block and in some scattered cottages. None of them were allowed to walk in front of the house or make themselves evident to its occupants. At one end of the corridor was the small office where the elderly Mr Rich kept the accounts and managed business matters for the estate. Sometimes there would be a line of men queuing outside the office, wanting their annual permission to fish in the lake. (Robert's original permit cards had the unappealing warning: NO DOGS OR WOMEN ALLOWED.) Mr Rich looked like a benevolent tortoise and explained he had been begging Robert to let him retire for decades; his firm had been involved since Gerald's day. He was off like a shot when I agreed and a local chartered surveyor working on the probate values was brought in to replace him.

Back in Greece I was bewildered by the burden of guilt that descended along with this gargantuan bequest. It was like adding lead weights to the lightness I had discovered living in Nafplio with few belongings, when I believed (pitifully, it now seemed) that I had shed my past and the petty annoyances of the British class system. I did not share my mother's fear that I would change, but I wondered how the world would react to me. How would I know if people were interested in me or my house? Would others take against me on account of my bizarrely bestowed privilege? Robert's lasting influence from beyond the grave was becoming apparent; I recalled my undergraduate reading list on the complex implications of giving and receiving: Mauss's *The Gift* describing the American Indians' potlatch festival, where prestige was gained by giving away the largest amount of belongings, and Malinowski's Trobriand Islanders negotiating the finer points of social status according to what one person could bestow on another. Even in

Greece, I had noted how it is the host lavishing the guest with food, drink or presents who has the upper hand. You only have to witness the arguments over who will pay a restaurant bill to realise that it is giving and not receiving that incurs honour and influence. Everyone knows there is no such thing as a free lunch and it seemed the same was true in relation to a house.

All the same, it was a relief to step back from the situation. In Greece, Faringdon became irrelevant. I was back to being a graduate student who stood out only because female English anthropologists were a rare sight in provincial Peloponnesian towns. As I tried to come up with a plan, I pondered different solutions. Could I turn Faringdon into something useful? An orphanage for musical children? An anthropological research centre? The financial situation at that stage seemed too fluid and precarious for grand schemes: not only would Coote need to be given a widow's legacy (something Robert had overlooked), but Alan had to be bought out from the farm and his quarter-share of the whole estate. There would also be taxes to pay and there was talk of selling the entire contents of the house to pay death duties.

When I returned to England, I went to Cambridge for seminars and library work and stayed at Faringdon when I could. Rosa continued her scheme to turn me into a suitable replacement for her master, transferring her single-minded loyalty from him to me, but disapproving of the other 'young people' she encountered in my wake. She insisted that I should take over Robert's bedroom, and she got her way, though I made a point of decorating it and having a different bed. Rosa's techniques were not subtle, but it was far from easy to resist. She was simultaneously domineering and submissive – a tyrant and a slave. When I asked to make my own bed she ignored me, and the prospect that I might cook something for myself was beyond her imagination. Her traditions were implicitly those established in the pre-war days, shored up by time and by the objects she venerated – the fine linen hand-towels with the Berners crest, the washed-thin sheets she kept alive by sewing them sides-to-middle, and the silver cutlery we used at table. When a sharp-toothed pike was caught in the lake, Rosa cooked dainty *quenelles de brochet* in a cream sauce. I could imagine Gerald discussing that in his day. It was impossible not to be pulled into this self-contained world.

My friends couldn't help being amazed when they came to stay for weekends. Some liked the gauzy, Hollywood glamour of the Crystal Room, while others preferred the courtesan's-boudoir intensity of the Red Room. Some felt the presence of benign ghosts, others liked going through the books and photographs and playing the piano. They all enjoyed sitting on the porch steps in the morning sun, drinking coffee and reading the Sunday papers. I became aware of how we were part of a physical continuity: I had sat on the front steps with Robert when he was an old man, but there was also the picture of him and Gerald posing there in the 1930s with Gertrude Stein, Alice Toklas and others. Then there were the faded photographs from the early twentieth century, with Gerald's mother and stepfather, who sat there in wicker chairs and allowed their parrot out for a breath of air. I supposed the habit had stretched back to the 1780s, when Pye the Poet Laureate first surveyed the gardens and church from his newly built villa.

Opening drawers, we found more old photographs of famous visitors from the 1930s and '40s and were conscious that we were treading in their footsteps and sleeping in their beds. My mother told me that the painted day-bed in the drawing room had been Gerald's bed, and when we lounged on it among the Victorian needlework and beaded cushions it was hard not to think of his short, stout figure in the same place. Did the pictures give any clues? High on the green walls above the piano was a collection of some of the ugliest, most unappealing portraits in oval frames. They seemed to be a joke, all either 'simpering or morose', and we competed to find the most grotesque, debating whether they were Berners ancestors and why they had been hung near the beautiful paintings of Victorian agricultural animals, Henry VIII, and the elegant young man in a doublet.[481] Occasionally, stays at Faringdon felt almost like time travel or trespass. We would fish about in wardrobes and dress up in brocaded robes that Gerald had donned for photographs, or crimson 'pink' hunting jackets cut to fit Robert's torso. I adopted my grandfather's tailored black wool and cashmere coat – long and slightly baggy on me, its blue velvet collar dainty as a vole.

I wondered about the scandals, love stories and rows that had taken place within the walls that now contained me and my friends, who were mostly in their twenties. But the past often seemed distant and elusive, as it can to the young. Coote regularly came over for meals, braving Rosa's venomous expression and giving away nothing of her own terrible experiences with Robert. Following her estranged husband's death, the decades of friendship with him and Gerald became the over-riding narrative; the rest was not mentioned. Robert had left her the rights to Gerald's literary and musical output and she quickly set up the Berners Trust to promote his legacy. I was made a trustee and there were meetings in the drawing room followed by lunches along the lines of what many of the trustees had known in earlier days.

I often tried to get Coote to tell me some stories about what it had *really* been like, to reveal a few of the secrets and lies, but her nature was founded on the value of tact. We did, however, spend hours going through the photograph album, although Coote stuck strictly to names and the occasional mysterious detail. She identified Doris Castlerosse as 'a courtesan', which I couldn't understand at all, especially as the woman in question looked rather prim in a buttoned-up coat on the porch at Faringdon. Did this mean prostitute? Evidently not, but Coote would not elaborate. She would never have gossiped, and though I knew a little about Madresfield and her closeness with Evelyn Waugh, she would only say what a good friend he had been. Coote pointed out her sister, Maimie, déshabillée, frolicking with Robert on the beach at Ostia, but there was no talk of their relationship or why the word 'SHIT' was written on his back. And in the black-and-white pictures of Coote herself as a young woman – on a horse with Robert and Gerald, or at a party in the house – she looked remarkably the same as she did in her seventies. It was only much later that I came across a letter she had written Robert just after he told her about Gerald's death and it helped me to understand more of her tight-lipped approach:

THE FARINGDON PHOTOGRAPH ALBUM SHOWING ROBERT, MAIMIE AND OTHERS ON THE BEACH AT OSTIA, NEAR ROME. CENTRE LEFT: A RARE PICTURE OF GERALD IN A BATHING COSTUME, STANDING IN WHAT APPEARS TO BE A FOUNTAIN. COOTE NEVER REVEALED THE STORIES BEHIND THE PICTURES

Darling Robert,

Just a line to say I was so very sorry to hear about Gerald when you rang up just now. I am sure you must be missing him so much . . .

He reached a standard of true civilisation, which we will never be able to explain to the young, but we were very lucky to have known it.

Although the weekends I offered to friends and family were not the polished productions of Robert's era, let alone Gerald's, it felt as though there was a default setting for how a weekend would unfold. Rosa would discuss the menu plans and who would be 'dining'. Even when it was my oldest friend, Sarah Horrocks, with whom I'd got into trouble for printing an 'unsuitable magazine' during Putney High School days, there was something of the Faringdon traditions that directed our behaviour. Sarah would make her way from a Bermondsey council flat where she lived with her toddler, Samuel, to scented baths in the early evening (even if our evening dress was probably jeans); drinks by the fire in the drawing room; meals in the dining room cooked by Rosa. Samuel liked the music boxes in the hall and played with the mechanical barking pug, though his favourite object was the doll-sized cushion of the mackintoshed flasher.

Since Robert's death, Rosa seemed to be increasingly unbalanced and Ben, the temperamental boxer, was following her example. When Ben began to eye Samuel as though he were a rabbit, I felt worried, and it was only thanks to one guest's lightning response that the roaring lunge was intercepted before it turned into a nasty bite. Rosa was unable to appreciate that this was serious; the implication was that Samuel was too young rather than that Ben was a dangerous dog.

When we shrieked and giggled at dinner and lay down under the dining table, it felt subversive, as though we were being mischievous children. We made jokes about Rosa being a Fascist, recalling a sketch from *Dr Strangelove* where Peter Sellers has to hold down his right arm to prevent himself automatically making a Nazi salute. Could she really celebrate Hitler's birthday? we gasped. Sarah found a copy of Hitler's *Mein Kampf* in the bookshelves, with what I believed was a fake inscription in German from the Führer himself: 'To my dear Gerald.' I suspected it was part of the provocative joke begun by Gerald after his trip to Germany in 1935 – something similar to the pornography contained inside the cover of a Bible or the defaced photographs of society ladies. But predictably the infamous book produced mayhem among my friends whenever it was dug out from the shelves. I ended up hiding it, ashamed of the dark seam of history that ran through what was now my house. Although I tried to make things less formal and more appropriate for a student and her friends, it was all so inappropriate anyway that it was a hopeless task.

ust as ROBERT switched from expansive host at weekends to running the estate during the week, so I was expected to take over this role when I was there. One day, Des and Don, the two ageing gardeners, asked me to come and 'throw plates' along the drive. It sounded like some peculiar medieval custom, until they explained that they were planting bulbs for the spring display. Robert's technique for achieving a completely random, 'natural' pattern was to throw paper plates into position and the comic ritual was enacted each year. I duly took a pile and started making as haphazard a planting scheme as possible. Des also took the opportunity to make a few changes in the gardens and, with my agreement, the work-intensive, expensive and vulnerable delphinium beds were cancelled for the following year and something more practical put in their place. Don initiated me into the secrets of the dove-dyeing, letting me watch him as he washed the birds, gently bathed them in a bowl of brightly coloured pigment, and then placed them in boxes in the warm boiler room to dry off. Later, they'd be released into the sunshine and they'd strut about as if proud of their outrageous plumage.

If choosing plants and trees and learning about the thrice-yearly dyeing routines were newly-discovered pleasures that pulled me closer to Faringdon, there were other aspects of my inheritance that were less appealing. I found myself attending frequent meetings with Alan, the accountant and the solicitors and having to act as though I understood much more than I really did about taxes, milk quotas and company law. Alan was a director and shareholder in the Berners Estates Company and was well informed about management issues. When we met in the study at Faringdon, he sat on the fender-seat, confident and apparently sanguine about his abrupt disinheritance. He was friendly – though when he greeted me, kissing both cheeks, he clenched my shoulders with such intensity I wondered whether there wasn't a subconscious desire to raise the vice-like grip upwards towards my neck; how could he not detest me? But he seemed magnanimous. 'You can buy yourself a car,' he assured me. 'There's money available.' Nevertheless, money was flowing out at an alarming rate, to prop up the estate, make long-neglected repairs to tenants' cottages and pay off endowments. Alan agreed with the accountants that finances were dodgy enough for the youngest gardener, Martin, to be 'let go'. One of the more harrowing moments in my early times was asking Martin into the study so I could fire him. There'd been no training for that in Cambridge's anthropology department.

During that first winter, my mother came to stay at Faringdon several times, attempting to convert her reservations and distaste into something more positive, banishing the ghosts of rejection and trying to embrace the new era. She was not envious of my inheritance, but it stung that Robert had not even thought to leave something personal – a painting, say – to his only child. It was also painful to her that he had not thought of my two younger brothers, and in a reversal of the common pattern of English inheritance, where the oldest male takes it all, in this case, it was a female. My brothers were extraordinarily understanding and generous-spirited about it, but there was no getting away from the fact that it was unfair.

My mother always slept in the room that had been hers since babyhood. The green baize doors on the corridor were long gone, but there was still the painting on the wooden canopy, 'Victoria, Her Bed'. She usually came with her partner, Simon Craven, and, in the early days, I tried to persuade them that they should try living or staying at Faringdon for a while. I would have loved to visit the place as a guest, delaying any attempt to make it mine. By the sort of erotic twist that characterised so much of Faringdon's history, Simon was Cyril Connolly's stepson (his mother was Deirdre, Cyril's last wife). He and my mother had been together, on and off, for over ten years. Their alliance had started in 1976, when, aged fourteen, I gave a summer party at Clayton, Jennifer's Sussex house. I brought a whole train carriage of teenagers from London, all of whom had signed an agreement for some worried parents that they would not take drugs. We walked across fields from the station, danced to music from speakers suspended in the beech trees, swam naked in the pool, and after a mostly sleepless night, boiled eggs in tea urns for breakfast. Jennifer had suggested that I invite Cyril's fifteen-year-old daughter, Cressida (her father had died two years earlier), and it was her older half-brother who brought her along from Eastbourne. Simon had long golden hair, a tan and was extremely handsome. He was twenty-two, which placed him out of the young teen orbit and into that of the only other non-teen in evidence that evening, thirty-three-year-old Victoria. Shortly afterwards, he moved in with her in London and they began a relationship that, despite various partings, would last decades.

On one of my mother's visits to Faringdon during the winter after Robert's death, we scattered his ashes. Alan and Coote came too. Robert had specified in his will that he wanted his ashes thrown by the sculpture 'in the style of Barbara Hepworth' that sat at a particularly gloomy point along the shady monkey-puzzle walk. This was odd. I had always been told that this quasi-Christian stone structure had been put there by Robert as a tactic to stop the local council compulsorily purchasing the land for the neighbouring school. His claim that this was where Lord Berners's ashes were buried and that it was consecrated land had been entirely successful in preventing any slice being removed from this part of the estate.

It was a dull, freezing day when Alan drove us along the carriage drive from the house, down through the park, over the ornamental bridge by the lake and up the other side, along the avenue of lime trees. We parked by Jack Fox's lodge, where the *trompe l'œil* fox looked out from a window and dead birds were strung up in the vegetable garden to warn off their poaching comrades. Patchy snow lay on the ground and our faces were pinched from cold and tension. Alan carried the small wooden box provided by the crematorium and we made our way to the angular-cut stone with its cross on one side. Having decided that we would each throw some of the ashes, we then discovered that the lid was screwed down on the box and wouldn't come off. Alan walked back to his car and returned with a screwdriver. Taking turns, we angled the plastic bag within the box and poured little dribs of what remained of the Mad Boy around the stone. We stood around awkwardly, with no priest or ritual to give structure. Neither praying nor saying much, we eventually turned back towards the car and the warmth of the house. Later, on walks, I noticed the ashes stubbornly fixed in a damp, grey circle around the base of the monument, not absorbed by the earth or blown away by the wind. Once, Ben cocked his leg and peed on his master's remains.

Although Victoria and Simon eventually decided against moving into Faringdon, my brother Leo and his fiancée Annabelle Eccles took up the challenge instead. They organised their spring wedding there, and in a mirror-image of the funeral that had taken place five months earlier, entered the gardens through the wooden gateway in the churchyard wall accompanied by young velvet-clad bridesmaids and pageboys. Hundreds of guests gathered in a marquee erected over the fountain and there was dancing and flowers and delicious food. Jennifer came, swathed in chiffon scarves, drinking too much and misleading us all by hinting that this was the first time she had returned to Faringdon in many decades.

After their honeymoon, Leo and Annabelle settled into the house and I sometimes came to visit. Leo spent time with Don, learning about tree-felling and planting and incorporating Faringdon timber into his furniture-making work. Annabelle helped Des in the gardens, weeding and picking vegetables for the twice-weekly sales, when locals made their way to the potting shed for fresh produce. It had long been Robert's way of making a little money on the side and off-setting taxes for the company, and while the first pickings went to the house, the soft fruit and bunches of frothy-leaved carrots were snapped up by townspeople.

Rosa had always been strange, but now she began to seem unhinged, admitting that she found it hard with 'all these young people'. 'The first time she saw me after our marriage, she called me Mrs Leo,' remembered Annabelle, who was only twenty-four and daunted by the dominating custodian of a lost way of life. 'Then she ignored us completely. If I passed her and said hello she would have to

My brother Leo's wedding to Annabelle Eccles, mirroring the journey of Robert's coffin in the other direction only five months earlier

acknowledge me, but she basically pretended we weren't there. She was subtly destructive, sulking in the back room . . . a menacing presence.' Friends who had known the place for a long time commented that Rosa's undermining, even threatening behaviour was reminiscent of her approach to Hugh Cruddas in the old days, or to Coote in more recent times. Just as this tyrannical servant had always been loyal to Robert, she was never critical of me, favouring his chosen successor. But she was like a fearsome guard dog who growled at anyone else, irrespective of what I wanted. Rosa had stopped cooking for the young couple, and although she cleaned the house, she maintained a steady stream of minor acts of sabotage. When the situation became too tense, I asked Rosa whether she might not be more comfortable in a larger flat below the main part of the house. Her new quarters were off the corridor that runs the length of the house at semi-basement level and leads to the stableyard at one end. This passageway quickly became her domain; she received visitors there and among them Alan would be spotted bringing in his muddy riding boots and hunting gear so she could clean and polish them. Well known as an astounding cook, she also began to do some part-time jobs cooking for other people.

That summer, when Annabelle was several months pregnant, she and Leo went to London for a few days. When they returned, they found the kitchen and dining room in a chaotic state, with sugar and salt thrown about on the floor and tablecloths and various objects apparently missing. 'We immediately knew something bad had happened, but we thought that Rosa must have done it,' remembered Annabelle. The pair went down to see Rosa, who said that the place had been like that for two days. 'I thought Sofka must have instructed for the silver to be taken to the bank,' she said in a sullen voice, looking at the floor. Although Robert would sometimes send valuable paintings to be stored in the vault at Barclay's, Faringdon, when he travelled, Rosa's suggestion seemed absurd, and, returning to the scene, Leo and Annabelle realised that all the silver was missing: candlesticks, cutlery, teapots, coffee pots and all the salt-cellars and sugar-shakers – hence the spillage on the floor. Gone too were the gilt basket and the wonderful large gilt fish from the dining table.

The police were called and Sergeant Brown began the interviewing process. After speaking with Rosa, he took a different, more aggressive approach with Leo and Annabelle. 'What did you have for breakfast that day? What time was it when you left for London?' A silver teaspoon was located in their car – Annabelle had taken it to eat a yogurt and remembered waving spoon and plastic pot at Rosa as they departed. Based on evidence given by Rosa, Leo was arrested and taken to a police cell in Witney, where his belt and shoelaces were confiscated. The pregnant Annabelle was driven up to London by a police officer to search their flat for stolen goods. I learned about the debacle in Cambridge, where I was packing before my return to Greece the following morning. Horrified at what had befallen my brother and his wife, I rang up the police station. 'You can't arrest my family,' I protested. 'It would be like arresting me.' 'Don't tell us how to do our job, Madam,' came the response. There were no other lines of enquiry being pursued.

By the end of the day, Leo was released from custody and Annabelle was back at Faringdon, both deeply shocked. Rumours were starting to circulate that maybe it had been Rosa who had set up 'the young people' and hidden the stash of silver herself. I later realised that I should have cancelled my trip and gone to Faringdon to support my maligned family, but I was so appalled by the whole episode that my instinct was to get as far away as possible. I didn't know then about Rosa leaving the washing-up from Robert and Coote's wedding to greet them on their return from honeymoon, but later these events came to look like a parallel way of revelling in destruction and wreaking unhappiness. The police started a fresh investigation and sent frogmen to drag the lake. Nothing was found.

The place had been filled with poison by Rosa. Friends joked about Mrs Danvers from Daphne du Maurier's *Rebecca*, but the prospect of Miss Proll burning down the house felt only too likely in the circumstances. In Greece, I wondered whether I would ever be able to face going back, outraged on behalf of Leo and Annabelle and full of distaste for what I had taken on. When I did return to Faringdon after a couple of months, it was with trepidation. I was clear that Rosa would have to go. She had stopped coming into the house anyway, and although no cache of stolen goods had been located, there were many who felt she had been, at the very least, negligent and spiteful. I knocked on the door of her flat, nauseous about the task ahead. It needed to happen, I told her. We would help her find somewhere in the town to live, we would pay her compensation, but she must go. 'I will never leave this place,' she screamed and sank to her knees on the floor. Threatening suicide, she grasped onto me, her strong, swollen fingers gripping my legs as she pulled herself closer. 'Don't make me go. The only way I will go from here is in a coffin.'

Traumatised, I fled the scene. I had forgotten that only a few years earlier Rosa had left Faringdon of her own accord out of vindictiveness, abandoning Robert when he had needed her most through jealousy of Coote. Instead, I only felt guilt at what I was doing, mixed with anger and sadness at the troubles Rosa had brought to our lives. Eventually, with Alan as a go-between, Rosa did leave, moving to a house in Faringdon and continuing to work for various people in neighbouring villages, producing the extraordinary food for which she was famed. Often, she was spotted close to dawn or dusk, silently picking her way through Faringdon's walled garden along with the diminutive Muntjac deer that favoured these quiet hours for feasting on buds and bulbs. She had previously kept a narrow, enclosed strip of vegetables and flowers and there was still rhubarb growing, along with the herbs she used so cleverly in her cooking.

Y VISITS TO FARINGDON gave rise to a range of emotions. I appreciated its extraordinary beauty and originality and it was strange and wonderful to invite friends to stay. Don continued to teach me about the history and ways of the place, from explaining how to choose the right day to dye the doves, to helping me decide which trees to plant by the lake. He often told stories about Robert and pointed out the quirks and history of the house and grounds. I gradually got to know the people whose lives were entwined with the estate, and each one had their own complications. According to Robert's will, Garth's widow Betty had been left a lifelong tenancy at an annual rate of 10p, and when her house needed fixing, I was the one who had to decide what we could do. Many tenants took the opportunity of a new regime to request repairs that Robert had refused to carry out.

After Leo, Annabelle and their young son moved out to a house they had renovated in a neighbouring village, I occasionally stayed at Faringdon alone, mooching around, flicking through first editions that had belonged to Gerald, or uncovering stashes of photographs that revealed something new about the place. Sometimes, I tried to get on with writing up my thesis there, but it was extremely difficult to retreat from what seemed like a steady flow of people who needed me to be 'captain of the ship', as one person put it. I found myself being offered a variety of roles and relationships that apparently came with the inheritance and that were bewildering to someone in her mid-twenties from a very different background. I was asked to become president of the local horticultural association and to ceremonially switch on the town's Christmas lights. People I didn't know invited me to dine at nearby large houses. Fearful of being sucked into a way of life I hadn't chosen, I refused. I worried that the line between real friends and the curious, the snobbish or the ambitious would become blurred. I was apprehensive about what effect this hugely beautiful yet weighty appendage would have on the way my life evolved.

I must have seemed stand-offish to some, but I also tried to do the right thing. All of Robert's local obituaries mentioned his kindness in the community: there was a tea party each year for the Silver Threads social club, scouts came camping and charity events were allowed. I had seen the old photographs of fetes and Gerald crowning the May Queen. I tried to continue some of these activities, and when the gardens were opened twice a year under a national scheme, I often sold tickets or helped with preparations, half proud of how lovely the place looked, half awkward at being thrust into the role of chatelaine. When the town's annual firework party was held in a field by the lake on Guy Fawkes Day – also Robert's birthday – I agreed to give a welcome speech. There were hundreds of people and I was taken to a caravan to speak into the booming PA system. A Greek friend staying gave me brandy to quell my nerves. 'My grandfather would have been very pleased . . .' I heard myself say, in a voice that sounded squeaky, shaky and like a pitiful imitation of minor royalty without the elocution lessons.

Various issues cropped up that forced me to take a position. Would I allow the local hunt to continue to ride over the estate? My initial reaction was: absolutely not. As someone who barely knew one end of a horse from the other and who believed that hunting was outdated, snobbish, brutal and unnecessary, I said I'd prefer to keep the place as a fox sanctuary. It was only after the thoughtful and charming Master of the Hounds and his deputy showed up for a drink and I heard about the alternatives – farmers shooting, trapping and wounding foxes, the problems created by what was classed as vermin – that I took in some of the complexities. Who was I to turn up and stop them having their fun? Wasn't I an anthropologist who tried to empathise with other cultures? We made a compromise: no blocking foxholes and sending the terriers in to kill the cubs and a 'fox reserve' to be respected around the house. From my bedroom window, I would often see a red glint slinking across the rough field above the lake, provocative on a frosty morning.

Harder to resolve was the situation when Alan was finally bought out. He had become a director and an investor in the Berners Estates Company after Robert had got into trouble with severe gambling debts and Alan had stepped up with the cash in return for shares. There was a selling spree to produce the money for him. Among other things, Gerald's beloved paintings by Corot were auctioned and many more would follow in subsequent years, including the portrait of Henry VIII given by the king himself to the Lord Berners of his day. There were too many long meetings with people I described at the time as 'be-suited, grey-faced, heavy-shoed, tax-scheming, middle-aged men'.

Along with the rumours that people passed on about my own inheritance, I was given several stories about why Robert ditched Alan at the last post: some said it was because his preferred nephew had separated from a first wife whom Robert adored, though that had been years before; others that Robert didn't like the second wife. (At least she owned a place in Gloucestershire that was much larger than Faringdon, so I had no additional guilt that Alan's lost expectations would affect his quality of life.) An estate worker claimed that Robert had said, 'Sofka is the only one with any bloody sense.' An old friend of Robert's suggested that he liked the serendipity of this unlikely choice. Just as *he* had been a surprise for more conventional types when he acquired everything in 1950, so he liked the idea of creating a rumpus. 'He said it had been so amazing for him when he inherited Faringdon from Gerald – like *Kind Hearts and Coronets*,'[482] a film where an oblique inheritance is the subject of much scheming and merriment, not to mention Ealing Comedy murder.

When we had finally fixed all the financial details, Alan announced that he refused to go without my signed agreement that sixty-two-year-old Jack Fox would be given the shooting rights for life on the estate. He would be able to take shoots (presumably with Alan or his friends, if required) all over the estate to gun down wild birds and the pheasants he raised in Grove Wood and Bennet's Pen, a copse near the lake. My initial reaction was indignation. I didn't like the idea of shooting anyway, and I was being forced to give away something against my will. Although Alan was always scrupulously polite with me and I admired his sang-froid in the face of what must have been a nasty disappointment, I realised I was an uncomfortable thorn in his side. His hand-in-glove relationship with Rosa, whom he continued to visit bearing his muddy riding boots, was awkward enough, but now he wanted to take away my control of something at Faringdon, probably for decades to come.

Adding to my unhappiness at Alan's arm-twisting was an unfortunate phobia. Like Gerald, who 'found a dead bird' inside him during his wartime psychoanalysis, I had been horrified by this symbol of death since earliest childhood. While I never minded another animal's corpse, the claws and feathers of a lifeless bird provoked a cold-sweat panic. I looked the other way or even avoided passing Jack Fox's garden so I wouldn't see the splayed wings of pigeons or, worst of all, greasy black crows hung up by their legs and waving in the breeze. One of the first things I had done after inheriting Faringdon was to get rid of the numerous stuffed birds from Gerald's collection. Alan had offered to remove from the dining room some glass domes sheltering long-tailed birds-of-paradise, loading them into his car after one of our early meetings. The most gruesome item of all was a sinister screen made up of two glass panels, between which were placed the boneless bodies of numerous coloured birds. One of Cecil Beaton's photographs of my mother as a baby shows her posed in Jennifer's arms in front of it, Robert's reflection in the glass only adding to the creepiness.

Alan was just as stubborn as I was and a far more experienced negotiator. I was trapped. In the end he won and, miserably, I capitulated.

There were other times when I learned how to get the upper hand over the grey men in suits. When my solicitor announced that the only way forward in Faringdon's management was through a trust, he offered himself and a colleague as trustees. 'Could one have someone else?' I asked, inspired on a whim. 'Does it have to be a lawyer, or could I have, for example, two friends?' Within a short space of time, I was back in the panelled conference room off the Strand with Sarah Horrocks and Tessa Charlton, my two oldest friends, who had supported me through the peculiarities of the early months at Faringdon. They had even less experience of these things than I did, and the atmosphere was one of suppressed hilarity and high tension as we tried to concentrate on unfamiliar terms like 'the statutory and equitable rules of apportionment' or 'deeds of Indemnity'. Tessa took drops of her Bach Flower Rescue Remedy to combat her terror of 'suits', and we all eyed one another conspiratorially across the heavy table. Unreasonably, it felt like a coup of the young and female over the old and male. Afterwards, the newly appointed Trustees of the Robert Heber-Percy Will Trust took me to a pub where we collapsed in fits of nervous laughter, downing vodka to put us back on track.

It was not all financial meetings and dealing with the burdens of tradition. The second summer after Robert's death, Mario Testino asked whether he could do a photographic shoot at Faringdon. He was a friend of my younger brother Kolinka, who had once taken Mario to see Robert. They had been fed smoked salmon and champagne – 'That's all he ate, no?' said Mario, who had been impressed by the place and the man. The previous year, Mario had taken atmospheric black and white wedding photographs for Leo and Annabelle. Ever since his arrival from Peru a decade earlier, he had noticed how many from his social and professional circle in England were fascinated by the era that Beaton had captured so memorably in his photographs. 'They were very deferential to that group of people – Cecil Beaton, Gertrude Stein, Elsa Schiaparelli,' he said. 'My editor at *Harpers & Queen*,

Hamish Bowles, was obsessed with Beaton. We were inspired by the importance of decor and environment and his pioneering use of androgyny.'[483] Mario's own interest in the influential photographer had increased. People would later compare the Peruvian photographer to Beaton – both for his ability to create a story and an unusual *mise en scène* for a picture, but also for his ground-breaking portraits of royalty.

Mario and Hamish showed up with an impressive collection of models, stylists and make-up artists, and created what was essentially a 1980s fantasy of the 1930s using the idea of an Agatha Christie-style murder story. The dining room was turned over to make-up and hairdressing, while the study was filled with racks of slinky evening dresses and piles of red satin slingbacks, co-respondent brogues

THE AUTHOR AND MARIO TESTINO (IN ONE OF GERALD'S ROBES) AT FARINGDON, DRESSED FOR EASTER DAY, 1988

and sparkly gold heels. Actors as well as models became aristocrats *manqués*, a butler, a poetess – inevitably called Sappho – and an exotic femme fatale. Most of them stayed in pubs in the town, while those who could be fitted stayed in the house; with only five bedrooms, the hosts at Faringdon had always needed to limit their guests. Hamish, as willowy and gimlet-eyed as Cecil Beaton, wafted down the stairs for dinner dressed in the sort of Edwardian evening gown that his muse had donned in more frivolous moods.

Mario had already visited Faringdon several times since Robert's death and believed 'You could really feel the energy, the madness

VICTORIA'S WHIPPET
NIFTY, DYED MAUVE

that inhabited the place . . . The lake, the folly . . . England has so much history, you can relive it. Everything you do is related to the past.' Once when he was staying, and as if to prove my links to the Mad Boy and Gerald who had fantasised about coloured sheep and cows, I dyed my mother's grey whippet mauve. She had left Nifty with me when she went on two weeks' holiday and I persuaded Don to help me colour him, applying the shade used on the doves for Robert's funeral. In the old days, Gerald and Robert had done the dyeing outside the house, in 'great basins of magenta, copper green, and ultramarine dye, and with the help of men-servants ceremoniously dipping, one after another, his white pigeons and once . . . some swans, a duck, and a white poodle'.[484] With echoes of the past becoming almost deafening, the multi-coloured doves fluttered obligingly for the beautiful visitors, and a purple streak was to be seen racing across the expanses of green lawn between the house and the churchyard wall.

My future at Faringdon continued to seem very unclear and I became increasingly convinced that I could not live there and be true to myself. I wrote at the time to an anthropologist friend that my relationship with Faringdon might be a bit like an arranged marriage. I don't have a passionate love for it, as I do for Greece, nor do I have the deep, family sort of love that I do for Raasay. Faringdon is like a very handsome, rich, eligible husband, but one who was chosen by someone else. In some arranged marriages the love and even passion develops, but in others I suppose this can never be. The best I can do, as the privileged bride, is to give it a chance and see what develops. And at least, using the metaphor of marriage, I am able to be polygamous!

CHAPTER EIGHTEEN

Blood Ties

ESS THAN FIVE YEARS after I inherited Faringdon, I returned from abroad to stay there in very different circumstances. Rosa's words that I could do worse than find a husband and take up flower-arranging returned to haunt me. Although I was not married, I arrived with a man and I was six months pregnant. As I walked about the gardens with my expanding abdomen, I picked flowers and placed them around the house in Gerald and Robert's old vases. The place felt utterly different – transformed by love.

I had met Vassilis two years earlier in Moscow. Having finished my PhD, in 1990 I had gone on a trip to what was still the USSR, partly on a quest for my Russian roots and partly to write a couple of articles as a freelance journalist. One of the pieces I was investigating was about the Greeks of the Soviet Union and I had arranged an interview with the Greek Consul in Moscow. The Consul stood me up, but Vassilis spotted me out of the Embassy window and took over. He was the press attaché, he said, so ideally placed to help. Some weeks after, Vassilis appeared in London, and not many months after that I returned to Moscow to live with him.

It took Vassilis over twenty years to admit that when I drove him to Faringdon from London for the first time and we spent the weekend alone there together, he was troubled. From my point of view he had seemed appealingly blasé, and I later appreciated that Vassilis was not weighed down by the historical burdens and class awareness of the

British. But in reality, he had been perplexed. What sort of person will she be, if this is her house? he had wondered. Vassilis had by now been transferred to the Greek Embassy in London and was leaving Faringdon in the dewy mornings to catch a train up to work and arriving back by early evening. We had quiet weekday suppers in the kitchen, spotting deer picking their way daintily across the lawn towards the walled garden, or watching in dismay as a hawk dive-bombed a coloured dove, leaving a pile of candy-coloured feathers on the grass as it carried its meal away.

We made plans for improving the house, pondering how it might pay for itself as increasingly worrying accounts appeared. A few old friends like Sarah and Tessa came down for weekends, and Leo and Annabelle would come over with their two young sons. Rosa's menacing presence as housekeeper had finally been expunged by a dark-haired young Scottish woman, Patricia Howie. An art-school graduate with a passion for cooking, she brought a new warmth and informality to the place, while rising happily to the challenge of creating imaginative feasts when we had people to stay. We also threw the occasional party. Friends gathered from Russia, Greece and around the country for the 'Green Party', at which everyone dressed in green. Even Coote showed up in a floor-length pastel chiffon number. Sarah wore a green wig and rode a monocycle along the terrace, and Tessa was overwhelmed by admirers from Moscow. (Later, developing her photographs, she discovered that someone had used her camera to take a close-up of his penis, something one imagines the Mad Boy might have done in his day.) The carpets were taken up for dancing, with music provided by DJ K, a Greek disc jockey called Kostas, who crossed Europe by bus for the gig. Some friends camped in the garden, others took rooms in local pubs, and in the morning we gathered at the orangery for breakfast, where two musicians played Indian music and people climbed the stairs to nowhere and took dips in the pool.

Faringdon was changing, emotionally and practically. All over the house were additions from Russia, where Vassilis had spent the last four years collecting art, furniture and curiosities; anyone paid in foreign currency was rich in Soviet terms, and he was a regular at the auctions and street markets. In the green part of the drawing room near Gerald's piano there was now an ornate old harp, a double bass and a *belle époque* wind-up gramophone, all of which looked as though they'd been there since the 1930s. In the study, where Gerald's red wax models of horses stood on a shelf, we placed a garland of trumpets, saxophones and trombones. As we began to reclaim the attic floor, in the hope of letting out the whole house for holiday rentals, we furnished some of the rooms with Russian wardrobes and desks and hung paintings Vassilis had bought in Moscow's Arbat. Teasing was a tradition we easily adopted; we put a giant plaster bust of Lenin in the corner of the attic room under the pediment, now gazing not towards a glorious revolutionary future, but at the coloured pigeons that perched, cooing, on the window ledge.

Our daughter Anna was born in Oxford's John Radcliffe hospital in August 1992 and we returned home the same day. After half a century, Faringdon once more had a pram in the hall. This time, though, there were no nurses, nannies or green baize doors. The house seemed airy and light, reinvented by a new life. We walked the baby around the walled garden to pick mulberries and wheeled her through the park and down to the lake, shooing away the curious heifers that gathered to inspect the unfamiliar contraption. We lay, the three of us, in a capacious string hammock, bought the previous year in Mexico and slung beneath the Scots pines at the top of the lawn. Rooks cawed from their nests above, the church carillon chimed out Bishop Heber's hymns through the warm afternoons, and somewhere in the distance, beyond the buzz of insects in the mock-orange flowers, was the rhythmic hum of Don mowing the grass at the back of the house.

My mother's half-brother Jonathan came to take some photographs of our new family. Only too aware of the history, he arranged us in the drawing room, as Robert and Jennifer had been by Cecil Beaton in 1943. My brother Leo filled the place of Gerald, nonchalantly reading a book on the day-bed. To imitate Robert, Vassilis donned his gumboots, holding Anna in the place where her grandmother had been before her.

IMITATING THE CECIL BEATON PHOTOGRAPH OF 1943, IN 1992 MY UNCLE JONATHAN PHOTOGRAPHED
MY BROTHER LEO (ON THE DAY-BED), VASSILIS HOLDING THE NEWBORN ANNA, AND ME TAKING UP MY
GRANDMOTHER'S POSITION

Three summers later, Lara was born, and it was around this time
that my mother learned something bizarre.

Jennifer had fallen down the stairs some years earlier and due to
brain injury or possibly a stroke, she had changed profoundly. She was
not always aware of what was going on and her speech was affected and
often unintelligible. Even stranger was her outspokenness on subjects
that she had been discreet about in the past. Alan had not been a good
husband – he was a 'bad man', she declared. She also exhibited an
occasional uncharacteristic prudishness: she disapproved of her young
Australian nurse having a boyfriend. One day, Victoria took her mother
for a walk in the nearby London park and Jennifer remarked, 'You don't
look at all like Robert.' 'Is he my father?' asked Victoria, who had heard
a few whispers that there might be some doubt, but nothing more

substantial. 'Oh no,' replied an ingenuous Jennifer, in a devastatingly casual, almost sing-song voice. 'Well, who is?' asked Victoria. 'I can't remember,' came the disturbing reply. Then, 'Ask Billa. She knows.'

Victoria didn't approach Billa directly but asked for help from another old friend of Jennifer's, the writer Jonathan Gathorne-Hardy, who lived near Billa in Norfolk. Almost a month later a postcard arrived from Jonny, who had invited Billa to dinner. He quoted her as saying, 'The person that springs to mind is Ned Fitzmaurice.' It was an unusual way to learn about a possible father.

Lord Edward Norman Petty-Fitzmaurice was the youngest son of the 6th Marquess of Lansdowne. He had been killed fighting in Normandy in August 1944 at the age of twenty-two. Billa sent a photograph of a sweet-faced boy, with fair colouring and a slightly snub nose. He was sitting with two friends and a dog, and when Victoria showed the picture to Jennifer she pointed to Ned and said he was the one. She added that she and Robert had slept together, but suggested that it had not been often.

Understandably, Victoria was thrown into turmoil. She was not helped by the fact that everyone she spoke to seemed to have their own opinion, never previously divulged to her. Some said they'd always known that Robert had rescued Jennifer when her lover was killed in the war. Others said it was Lord Berners's arrangement, or Billa's bossy scheme. When my mother approached Billa herself, the ageing Lady Harrod was furious. She now regretted saying anything, given the rumpus. Nothing was certain, anyway, she added. Equally incensed was Coote, whose famed kindness deserted her when Victoria consulted her. 'Coote snapped my head off,' remembered Victoria. 'She said, "It's really snobbish of you," as if I'd preferred Lord Lansdowne instead of Robert Heber-Percy Esq.'[485] Such apparent disloyalty to her oldest (if not necessarily most loyal) friend was anathema to Lady Dorothy Heber-Percy.

Victoria managed to arrange a meeting with the Duchess of Devonshire (*née* Mitford), the youngest sister of Gerald and Robert's old friends Diana and Nancy. Debo had been very close to Ned and his older brother, Charlie, the Marquess of Lansdowne from 1936. Charlie had been killed in Italy, blown up in his tank, only nine days after Ned went down in a blaze of machine-gun bullets while leading his platoon. According to a lance corporal in his regiment, Ned was 'the gamest little lad I have ever seen . . . No one could ever imagine him to possess the guts he had.'[486] Debo had often visited the brothers at Bowood House, their dazzling and gigantic Wiltshire home. The Bowood Ball was renowned as one of the most splendid events in the social calendar. Although large sections of the house were knocked down after the war, Ned's bedroom and dressing room were in a part of the house that is still known as Ned's Tower. When the Duchess met my mother for tea in Curzon Street (fresh from trying on hats for Ascot), she looked her up and down – 'as if she was examining a horse' – and said, 'You have the ankles of the Lansdownes!'[487]

The Lansdowne family had been devastated by the deaths of Ned and Charlie, and their two sisters, Elizabeth and Kitty, were still haunted by the double tragedy. The title and inheritance of Bowood House had gone to a cousin. Kitty (who had inherited the family's Scottish title, Baroness Nairne) was now in her early eighties. She was such a close friend of the Mitford sisters that her nickname was 'Wife'; Debo described her as quiet, discreet, intelligent and witty.[488] Kitty agreed to meet my mother and the two women immediately felt a bond and discovered much in common. Ned had been 'sensitive if not over-sensitive' and the whole family had suffered from depression, something that continued to plague my mother and that she now saw as a family trait; Kitty's eldest brother had 'fallen under a train' aged twenty. If Kitty felt she was meeting the child of her beloved brother who had died fifty years earlier, Victoria believed she was meeting the sister of a young man who was rapidly becoming her idealised father. 'I liked the idea of Ned,' she said. 'He was so much more sympathetic and cultured than Robert. I was keen on the idea of anybody other than Robert being my father. We just couldn't get on – we were like a cat and a dog. He admitted to me that when I was born he had felt no more interest than if there had been a newborn animal in the house.'[489]

It was a cataclysmic experience for my mother to have to revise her own life in the light of this possible new narrative. To discover that your unloved legal and social father might have had nothing to do with your biological make-up can be bewildering but also exhilarating. Victoria had undergone enough years of psychoanalysis to know about the 'inner father' and the large, framed, black-and-white photograph of a freckle-faced boy that now took pride of place in her bedroom became a 'guardian angel'. For me, the episode was a very different sort of experience. 'Maybe Faringdon doesn't really belong to you now, if Robert is not your "real" grandfather,' suggested some. This seemed an inversion of the reluctance some of the Lansdownes initially showed my mother, fearing she might be a bounty-seeker. While I didn't fear the legal or practical implications, there was no doubt that this changed the story. My conversations with people who knew the characters involved didn't lead me to any firm conclusions about who my 'real grandfather' was, and while I sympathised with my mother's anguish and hopes, I realised that when it comes to the biology of one's grandparents, it all seems more remote and less urgent. One sperm didn't seem to make a fundamental difference by the third generation.

It wasn't until I came to write this book that I tried to weigh up the evidence more systematically and to ponder on the implications of my own descent and inheritance. First, I tried to find out more about Ned. There was no evidence that he and Jennifer had been seriously involved; the most likely scenario was a brief fling, like the many adrenaline-fuelled passions that lasted a night or two during the war, when nobody knew whether they'd survive the next day. My mother had discovered a few things about Ned. He had been an undergraduate at Oxford before he joined the Army and he was artistic, drawing and painting for pleasure. Apparently, he had hoped to be a writer. Victoria had managed to look through Ned's old letters to his family, but the only reference she found about her mother was that he reported meeting up with Jennifer and Billa and finding them both 'middle class'. Hardly a reflection of intimacy or romantic intent. Worse, it seemed an indication of a snobbish superficiality that may have been prevalent then among the titled class, but now sounds bad. When I asked Ned's descendants whether I could take a look at the papers myself, they refused. Kitty died only four months after getting to know Victoria and had left strict instructions in her will that nobody should see the letters until after the death of her younger sister, Elizabeth. According to one of the relations, the dates of Ned's whereabouts made it virtually impossible that he was Victoria's father, but without access to the papers I was unable to verify this.[490]

Gerald's old friend Clarissa had been close to Ned's older brother, Charlie, but she was surprised to hear that Ned was a possible candidate. 'I didn't know he was old enough,' she said, recalling a 'little boy', though she then remembered that he had been 'charming and gentle with a little bit of malice – a kick at the back'. As Lady Avon dug back into her memories, she recalled that Ned had become a great friend of Gerald's when he had been an undergraduate at Oxford. 'Ned was amusing – he had a half-smile on his face as if he was about to say something. And Gerald liked being amused. I presume that Gerald picked him up in Oxford and Ned began going to Faringdon. I saw him there.' I scoured the visitors' book and, sure enough, found Edward Fitzmaurice staying for the weekend of 27 June 1942, a couple of weeks before Jennifer and Robert's wedding. Other guests included Winnie de Polignac, Constant Lambert and Margot Fonteyn. There is no sign of Jennifer's name.

At this point, I began to look at dates. My mother had been born on 28 February 1943, so when did Jennifer become pregnant? An online service calculated conception on or around 7 June 1942. Assuming that Jennifer's next period was due a couple of weeks later (say, 21 June), that she waited at least a week before getting a pregnancy test (29 June), and that the test took at least a week to produce results, she would not have confirmed the situation before at least 6 July, five days before she and Robert got married (11 July). Even given the propensity for last-minute weddings during the war, the pace of developments is uncannily rapid. It would have taken some doing to gather parents, relations and friends from around the country for the London nuptials, especially during a time of chaotic communications when there were plenty of more urgent problems. Was twenty-year-old Ned invited? He didn't die until August 1944, around the time when Victoria was eighteen months old and she and Jennifer had left Faringdon for Oare. A letter from Billa to Roy at that time reveals that Nancy Mitford 'wrote to Jennifer about a book and asked her to tell <u>me</u> how sorry she was for me about . . . Ned. I thought that so <u>very</u> sweet of her.' Was this Nancy's tactful way of sending condolences to Jennifer?

Then when I spoke to Francis Wyndham, Jennifer's old friend who had been at Oxford for part of the war, he threw a spanner in the works. According to him, Jennifer's regular boyfriend in 1941–2 had been Ian Lubbock, the dark-haired actor who had played in Gerald's *The Furies*. 'My mother [Violet] always thought that *he* was Victoria's father. Ian was struggling to make a career in rep, he was married (and separated) and he drank too much. Violet didn't think there was any future in the relationship. She assumed that when Jennifer found out she was pregnant, the last thing she'd want was for it to be Ian's.'[491]

Armed with a new bundle of suspicions, my mother set off to Norfolk to speak to some Lubbock relations – Ian had died in 1977. They hadn't felt right, she reported afterwards. It was a question of instinct, but also physical looks. Ian's mother had been Jewish and her children inherited her dark colouring, whereas Victoria was fair. Seeing as both Robert and Jennifer also had dark hair, this was setting her firmly back on course for Ned, whose light hair and freckled skin matched hers, as did his darker disposition.

It only made things worse when someone mentioned a Canadian airman as a candidate. Another friend from later days said, 'Well, I know Harry Cust was often mentioned. "The Sergeant." I think he was a US Air Force sergeant. He was also involved with Robert.'[492] Increasingly, my mother wondered whether Jennifer had simply not known who the father of her child was.

Almost everyone I spoke to on the subject said something different or contradicted the evidence. One theory was that the Mad Boy had stepped gallantly into the breach to help an old friend out of a tricky situation. In this scenario, Jennifer found herself alone and pregnant at a time when the only feasible alternative to an abortion was marriage. Given that neither a young student headed for the Army, nor a boozing, still-married actor were appealing prospects, she favoured Robert. But then, as someone who was fundamentally gay and had cohabited with another man for the last decade, the Mad Boy was hardly the ideal husband either. And if it was all a charade to avoid scandal, why was Jennifer so bitterly disappointed when Robert failed to take on the part of a real husband and locked her out of his bedroom?

'Robert might have been pleased to be married and give the impression of having a daughter,' said one old friend of Jennifer's who knew those involved at the time. 'It helped cover up bugger life. The bloody-mindedness of the police towards any kind of buggery, even during the war, was awful.'[493] At a time when homosexuality was illegal and the penalties were daunting, there is little doubt that a wife and child provided a useful alibi. But why would Robert have grasped at this opportunity all of a sudden in the middle of wartime, when nothing else in his life ever showed that he was fearful of having relationships with men and being seen to do so? Gerald had always given him the freedom to have flings with women and men; why would he introduce such a volatile element to their fundamentally stable set-up?

'Did Robert want a son and heir, perhaps?' asked Sarah Gibb, daughter of Peter and Glur Quennell and friend of Victoria's who had often stayed at Faringdon when they were growing up and knew the rumours. Robert had always seemed pleased to have a daughter and was very keen to have her at Faringdon, where she went during most school holidays. 'He did lots to entertain us, asking other young people over, organising picnics, boat trips on the lake, Christmas parties for teenagers. I don't remember him not being nice to Victoria, but maybe they didn't have one-on-one time – they were always surrounded by people.'[494] 'Robert had no doubts that you were his granddaughter,' said Richard Brain, a close friend and neighbour to the Mad Boy since the 1950s. 'He talked to me about whom he should leave the estate to and he never really considered Coote as someone who should inherit Faringdon.' Several people added to this theory by saying that if Robert believed that he was not Victoria's father it would have emerged at some point. He often drank too much and said outrageous things; surely if it was all a big secret, he would not have managed to keep it undisclosed over a lifetime of blurting things out. Logically, then, Robert must have thought that there was at least a possibility that Jennifer was pregnant by him. 'And anyway, you look like him,' remarked Charley Duff, who had just quoted his father's description of Robert as an 'attractive ape'.

My mother had initially agreed that it might be worth carrying out DNA tests and I began to investigate. I uncovered a website that offered clients 'peace of mind' and a 'quick, confidential and compassionate' service. The details proved trickier. If the putative father were no longer alive, samples could be taken from the remains – a bone fragment from the shaft of the femur or two teeth would do. Robert had been cremated, so that was out of the question. I wasn't sure what had happened to Ned or Ian's bodies, but I couldn't imagine we'd get to the stage of digging them up. It was suddenly becoming slightly creepy. Couldn't you take samples from relations?

Just when I was wondering how I could start the process, I received a warm email from Robert's nephew and current owner of Hodnet Hall, Algernon Heber-Percy. Although I had never met Algy or his family, I had asked whether I could visit to see the place where Robert had been brought up. Algy invited me to stay at Hodnet and I was welcomed as family. I was given the largest bedroom I've ever stayed in, which turned out to be the old sitting room and study of Gladys, my great-grandmother. Or was she? The windows gave on to the water gardens and beyond, a bucolic scene of cattle grazing on velvet swells of green field. As I made myself comfortable amidst drapes and swathes of rosy chintz and wallowed in a bluebell-scented bath, I idly wondered whether I'd be able to sneak some hairs from a Heber-Percy hairbrush. It didn't seem the right way of approaching the enigma.

When I asked Algy whether he knew of the rumours that Robert was not Victoria's father, he said he had always heard that Jennifer was pregnant by the son of an Irish peer and that when her lover was killed during the war, Robert offered himself as a solution. The story went that the lover's family was only too happy to find their problem solved. When I explained that Ned had been killed two years after the wedding, Algy pondered a while. 'Was Jennifer what they called a "popular girl"?' I agreed she had been. Algy suggested that it seemed likely that if his crazy, unreliable uncle Robert had known he was definitely not Victoria's father, it would have emerged over the years. 'He could get cross and nasty . . . which meant that either your mum meant an enormous amount to him – and he was very proud of her, after all, she was stunning and it would raise your stud fee to be her dad – or he didn't believe there was anything to think about. In that case, maybe he was the father.' Later, when I rejoined the family after some time in Gladys's room, Algy said, 'Well, *we* all think that you look like a Heber-Percy. You've got the fine hair.' Somewhere between my mother's Fitzmaurice ankles and my Heber-Percy hair lay the truth.

By the time I discussed the matter of DNA testing again with my mother, she had decided that she didn't want to go ahead. She preferred to stay with her image of lost innocence – Ned, the golden boy who could stand in as an idealised father-figure. It would be too disappointing to find out that it had been Robert all along. She didn't want him as her father, even if he was. As Francis Wyndham said, it was like a Henry James story with these three varied possibilities: Ian Lubbock, the actor-son of a Jewish pianist and a Quaker teacher who ended up an alcoholic; Ned Fitzmaurice, the scion of an old English house who was killed in the war; and Robert Heber-Percy, the Mad Boy who created havoc all over again at the end by choosing an unlikely heir to his estate. Even after all the investigation I had done, I didn't believe that a conclusion was clear from the evidence. Perhaps Jennifer herself didn't know. And while it was a twist in the tale of my relationship with Robert, it hadn't made a difference to how I thought of him and I wondered whether it would have changed anything for him either. Whatever the case, the scientific route would evidently not be taken and the solution would have to remain inconclusive – a mystery that each person could guess or solve as they preferred. As they say, 'It is a wise child who knows his own father.'

CHAPTER NINETEEN

Dust and Ashes

NE WEEKEND when Lara was not yet one, we had a robbery at Faringdon. It was a warm, still summer night and the baby had been unsettled. I had been up with her for what felt like hours at a time, and at 7 a.m. Vassilis finally gave up hope of more sleep and went downstairs to make coffee. He returned quickly, looking shocked. Something awful had happened. The drawing room looked completely different. Rushing down to look, I felt the chill morning air blowing in through the door to the terrace, which had evidently been forced open. The room had been half-emptied. After the initial feeling of being punched in the stomach, I had to admit that it had been a surgically precise job. No paintings or easily identifiable objects had been taken, nor large, unwieldy pieces of furniture, but anything that could be lifted quietly by a couple of thieves in rubber-soled shoes and taken out onto the terrace, down the steps and over to where a van had evidently been waiting. There were now gaps where there had been gilded mirrors, aged globes, painted blackamoors, portable chairs, tables and bookcases, and all the Victorian beaded needlework cushions from Gerald's day-bed. I couldn't believe we hadn't heard a thing. Worse, I knew we were partly to blame for not having closed the large wooden shutters on the drawing room windows. It had always been the rule – Rosa's task in the old days – but the five minutes spent unfolding and barring the three pairs of shutters on each of the five tall windows was always a bother last thing at night. Surely, I had reasoned, burglars would not be able to smash their way unnoticed into a house full of family and friends?

Since the silver heist in Rosa's day, we had suffered other burglaries, but not inside the house. Each time we opened the gardens to the public, there was a subsequent swoop on urns or statues in the grounds. One gang had even removed the bronze fountain of a lissom young Dionysus that I had commissioned as a memorial for Robert from the sculptor Nicholas Dimbleby. They had sawn him off at his shapely ankles, leaving his feet behind. He was later found by a policewoman at an antiques fair, wrapped in a blanket like a stowaway in the back of a van. He was duly repositioned in the circular pond at the back of the house. An unpleasant phase followed of putting up electric gates at the end of the drive, upgrading the burglar alarm and positioning security cameras. We stopped opening the gardens. It was a distressing process that went against all my instincts of leaving the doors open and welcoming people in. Yet there seemed little alternative other than asking Rosa to come back with a vicious dog.

Within days of the burglary, Vassilis was offered a tempting posting in the Greek Embassy in Rome and given twenty-four hours to decide. In the four years we had been together in England, Faringdon had become like home. Not only had we repaired, renewed and decorated, we had tried to get the finances back on track by renting it out for holiday lets. We had also, in spite of the burglaries, become relaxed there in a way that I hadn't managed in the first years. The presence of two young children had confirmed the metamorphosis so that while I could still marvel at the absurd serendipity of owning the place, I could also feel that I belonged there. Now all this could be thrown up in favour of the unknown. It was a daunting prospect to set off again, and although Vassilis had spent his student years in Venice and spoke Italian like a native, I knew that I would have to start from scratch once more with a new country and language. But perhaps I could return to the freelance journalism I had enjoyed during my time in Moscow, I thought. We wrote a list of pros and cons, as Darwin had before he married his cousin, and came up with a 'yes', in favour of embracing

the new. After all, we could always come back, we reasoned. And wasn't that how Gerald lived his life, with long stays in Rome?

Over the next years we returned to Faringdon periodically, but it was proving difficult to keep the place afloat financially. The short-term lets were erratic and the tenants themselves were unpredictable – some didn't respect the fragility of the house, whilst others were absurdly demanding. We decided to let Faringdon out for a longer period as a way of balancing the books. We were very fortunate in having a housekeeper, Patricia Hornbuckle, whose vast energy and capacity to cope under any conditions provided the foundation for trusting that we could leave the house. We stored away more of our personal belongings and prepared for a long wait before our next stay.

A variety of tenants ensued, some delightful and appreciative of the unusual spirit of the place, others less so. One tenant tried to commune with the ghost of Lord Berners while wandering the grounds at nightfall. Another had a wedding there at which the bride demanded that the doves be dyed 'gold'. Yellow was the best that could be managed by Andrew Smith, the man who replaced Don after his retirement and became just as dedicated a gardener, groundsman and dove-dyer, not to mention inspired restorer of the disintegrating lake house, orangery and Victorian greenhouse. A few who rented the house were dismayed

On the back lawn during a visit to Faringdon, Easter 2009: the author's daughters, Anna (playing guitar) and Lara (dancing), their cousins (Leo's sons) Alyosha, right, and Tom, dancing, and Lydia, a friend from Greece

by the scruffy side that often exists in English country homes, where power showers are unheard of, historic carpets are frayed and the wiring hasn't been replaced in a lifetime. However, many of our tenants were friendly and welcoming and Vassilis and I became accustomed to the initially unsettling experience of being invited as guests for drinks or meals in our own house.

After five years in Rome, we made the decision to move to Athens. Vassilis had been offered a job there and we were happy to move on and settle in a place we both loved but had never lived in together. Anna and Lara would grow up as bilingual, bicultural children, something we could only view as positive. We still managed the occasional stay at Faringdon, while using it to generate enough income to pay its bills.

Our friends and family also made use of the times between lets. When my old friend Sarah decided to celebrate her civil partnership with her girlfriend Julia, Faringdon, with its history of unconventional marriages and gay unions, was the ideal setting for her family party. Sarah's son Samuel, who had first visited Faringdon as a toddler and was now a grown man, gave a moving speech.

Over the years, several of the significant characters in the Faringdon story died. In 1998, Alan Heber-Percy had a fatal heart attack aged only sixty-three. Coote died three years later, just short of her ninetieth birthday. After decades of self-imposed exile from Madresfield due to family tensions, she had recently returned to visit after the estate passed out of the hands of a hated sister-in-law and into those of a beloved niece. Coote's funeral was held in the place that had meant so much to her, in spite of its association with great pain. In her thoughtful way, Coote had left her small house in Faringdon (which passed to her after Robert's death) back to the Faringdon estate. Despite the honourable intentions, there was gossip; apparently a loyal nephew had been expecting it. This was the second time that, quite without trying, I usurped a legator's nephew and presumably became very unpopular.

Jennifer's death came in 2003, when she was eighty-seven. I had never tried to speak with her about who my mother's real father was; it was often hard enough to have any kind of normal conversation, though the sweet nature and silvery laugh of her youth remained till the end.

Rosa's end was as dramatic as her life. She was killed by a lorry on Faringdon's ring road in 2010. Aged eighty-five, she was still working as a cook, and was walking the several miles to her job in the early morning when she was hit. After decades of frugal living, her savings turned out to be over half a million pounds, and apart from her house and a few small legacies, she left it all to a children's charity in London. I was over from Greece and helped spread her ashes around a tree by the lake at Faringdon. Despite the many years since we had last met, it was easy to picture her striding across the field, red-cheeked and eagle-eyed, her grey hair tightly pinned. She'd be gathering mushrooms or

ANDY SMITH DIGGING FOR GERALD'S ASHES, HELPED BY JACK FOX

chasing trespassers, a large dog at her side. I imagined she would have been rather pleased by the thought of this little autumnal gathering and the wind that gusted small clouds of grey crematorium dust into the air.

When I began researching for this book, one of the invaluable sources of information going back to the 1930s was Jack Fox. Although there had been a degree of tension after Alan's forced deal with the shooting rights, Jack and I found common ground and great enjoyment in the detective work that is involved in an investigation of this kind. I had no idea what had happened to Gerald's ashes until Jack told me the story of burying them at the top of the lawn when the estate office was built. We even had an archaeological dig to try to retrieve them. Jack turned up with a variety of probing tools from his undertaking days, Andy the gardener dug trenches into the grass he had recently mown and Des, the long-retired gardener, came along from his lodge on his mobility scooter. I had hoped we'd find the oak box and possibly rebury it somewhere with a monument for Gerald, but sadly, though we found the old foundations of the Elizabethan house, there was no sign of the ashes. Either the flowerbeds had changed position and we were digging in the wrong location, or Gerald's remains had become one with the place he had so lovingly fashioned after himself.

Jack was determined that we should try another excavation and the matter remains open. While discussing burial rites, Jack also mentioned that, unbeknownst to anyone else at Faringdon, Alan Heber-Percy's widow had returned to the grounds with her husband's ashes. She had taken them to the stone sculpture in the monkey-puzzle avenue, where we had scattered Robert's a decade or so earlier. 'The ashes just sat there, all white, for ages,' said Jack, 'so I went and dug them into the ground a bit.'

CHAPTER TWENTY

The Bell and the Blue Plaque

PRIL 2013, the coldest spring in England for half a century. I left Athens bathed in scented sunshine and landed at Heathrow to sleet sliding down the windows. Over the dozen years since I had settled in Greece with Vassilis, Anna and Lara, I had often travelled back to England and made my way to Faringdon. Occasionally, it was to stay in the house, but more often the house was occupied by tenants and I spent a couple of days with Leo and Annabelle in their nearby home, going over to Faringdon to make plans in the gardens with Andy and plough through the accounts and the latest problems in the estate office: a lead roof needing to be replaced, a historical group requesting a visit, the perimeter wall that has collapsed, the town sewage pipe which is gushing inexplicably, dangerously near the lake, just like it did in the 1930s . . . This time, though, Leo and his family were away in Scotland and I booked myself into a pub for a couple of days.

I'd had a few drinks over the years at the Bell Hotel in Faringdon's Market Place, but it never crossed my mind I might stay there. It smelled of beer and fried food and had the sombre hush of a winter afternoon before the first drinkers arrive. The landlady, Mel Gravestock, had a hennaed crew-cut and a nose stud and told me she and her husband had been managing the place for two years. 'It's tough work that never stops – on duty twenty-four hours a day.' The building is an old coaching inn, with sections apparently dating back to medieval times; there were narrow stairways and unevenly floored corridors to negotiate before we reached what had been described as the 'bridal suite'. A low-beamed attic room, it gave on to rooftops and the back courtyard and offered a large, windowless bathroom with a beaten-up circular bathtub. The temperature felt sub-zero. On enquiring, it emerged that the heating oil had run out and wouldn't be delivered for two days. Electric fires were brought, blankets piled on. It could have been the beginning of one of Gerald's stories. A camel might arrive at the front door, or a fur-wrapped *marchesa* pass by with her python in a glass travelling box, heading up towards Faringdon House. Perhaps a flock of vibrantly coloured birds would swoop down before returning to a magical place where a lord wears masks, plays music on a piano in his car and throws wild parties for the famous, rich and beautiful with a mad boy.

I had come to Faringdon this time to unveil a blue plaque. Recently, quite unexpectedly, an email had come from Eda Forbes, my ancient-history teacher from Oxford High School. I remembered her well – a clever classicist with hair wound high on her head. She had been surprised to find me in her class. I had arrived at the school aged sixteen, a rebel from Wheatley Park Comprehensive following a move with my father to an Oxfordshire village where he had gone in search of the good life. Accustomed to the precociously erudite daughters of Oxford dons, Miss Forbes had looked at me sadly after my first homework assignment and said, 'Sofka, you don't know how to write an essay, do you?' Now retired, she worked as secretary of the Oxfordshire Blue Plaques Board, which had agreed that Lord Berners should be honoured and that the ideal location was his tower on Folly Hill. She wondered if I could give a little speech.

The next morning, an icy wind was blustering around the hill as I walked up towards Gerald's Folly. I was glad I'd brought my old astrakhan coat, acquired decades before in a Soviet state outlet in Leningrad before it reverted to St Petersburg, as my Russian grandparents knew the place. A small crowd was gathering around the square brick base of the tower. Miss Forbes wore the additional decades very well and her hair was still arranged as I remembered. There were three mayors, including Oxford's, all of whom sported gleaming gold chains. A few journalists took notes and snapped photographs. Eddie Williams, the man who has galvanised an enthusiastic group of supporters into repairing, restoring and cherishing the Folly, was beaming with pleasure. There were all sorts of local people who have made this tower theirs, who walk their dogs, organise parties or take friends up on open days to look out across expanses of England.

Robert handed over the Folly to the town in the 1980s when it was at its crumbling nadir – unsafe to enter and scarred by vandalism and graffiti. There were various attempts to patch it up over the years. When I inherited Faringdon House, I automatically became a trustee of the tower, along with the mayor and the accountant. Inevitably, I was influenced by the way Robert always treated the place, recalling how he would bump us up the track in his car to the tower after lunch, fumble with some keys in the thick, bank-vault door (put in after the other was destroyed), and let us creep up cautiously to the top and push open the trap-door to the viewing platform. I, in my turn, also kept a key and would take friends there. Some of my daughters' birthdays were celebrated within the turreted top, with a cake and picnic carried up the creaking stairs. Now things are different. What began as one man's indulgence or as a gift to his wild young lover, is now a municipal amenity. There are information boards to explain the history, health and safety regulations, volunteers on a rota. Some of the romance might have been lost, but it is the exclusive romance associated with the old ways of privilege, inappropriate in this age.

Gerald and Robert were always amused by teasing their more conventional neighbours, and at the time there were many who were outraged at the prospect of this imposing construction. Now the last laugh is with the townspeople, who have adopted Lord Berners and his tower both as a local attraction and a trademark for Faringdon. A charitable group called the Pink Pigeons Trust is 'Bringing the spirit of Lord Berners back to life!' Local artists and voluntary groups are encouraged to produce work in a surrealist, humorous spirit that is then placed around the town and the Folly. Model pink pigeons are attached to windowsills, comical signs hung on walls and unusual sculptures placed in the trees on Folly Hill. In September 2013, on the anniversary of Gerald's birth, a Berners Night dinner was organised at a local restaurant: 'quirky quocktails, qurious qanapes . . . kinky koffee and folly fancies' were provided and among the entertainment was a 'Queer Quiz' with Gerald as its subject.

Lord Berners is becoming a brand. A retired magician and entertainer, Peter Wentworth, dresses up as Berners whenever the occasion warrants, with a pink plastic pigeon on his bowler hat, a Dalí-esque black moustache and an ornate silk waistcoat. A local hotel put in a request for Andy to provide dyeing lessons at Faringdon House so that they could colour their own flock of doves (though eventually it didn't happen). When Bob Canning, a Californian playwright, wrote *Faringdon Follies*, based on the lives of Gerald and Robert, it was given its highly successful premiere as a reading in the aisles of Budgens, the local supermarket. A full staging of the play might have proved more challenging in that setting: act I begins with the two heroes chasing each other naked around the drawing room.

Before the celebrations of Gerald's centenary in 1983, he was seen as an obscure footnote to musical history – an eccentric aristocrat who had been largely forgotten by all but his friends and a few specialists. Since then, however, his star has risen. To mark the centenary of Lord Berners's birth, there were recitals of his music and readings from his books in the Wigmore Hall and the Purcell Room, an exhibition at the Royal Festival Hall (all events enthusiastically supported by Robert) and widespread interest was shown by the media. Thanks largely to the work of Peter Dickinson and Philip Lane, who have championed and performed Lord Berners's music for many decades, there are now recordings of all his major compositions. Mark Amory's 1998 biography provoked new interest in Gerald's life, as did the subsequent collection of interviews and critical appraisals of Lord Berners's work by Peter Dickinson. The Berners Trust has also provided support and funding for all sorts of performances, recordings and publications and Gerald's fiction and non-fiction has been re-released and appreciated by a new generation of readers. The frolics of the elite 1930s in-crowd can seem

THE AUTHOR
UNVEILING THE BLUE
PLAQUE FOR LORD
BERNERS ON HIS
FOLLY, 2013

distasteful, but there is also a fascination with their extremes, their passions and their creativity.

At the unveiling in 2013, there were some introductions, then I gave my speech about Lord Berners and pulled back a blue velvet curtain to reveal the plaque. It quotes from the epitaph that Gerald composed for himself and which neatly encapsulates his attitude to life, with its oblique playfulness and its failure to mention his great love of music, his offbeat creativity or the Mad Boy:

> Here lies Lord Berners
> One of the learners.
> His great love of learning
> May earn him a burning
> But, Praise the Lord!
> He seldom was bored.

It was strange to be taking the part of unveiler – as if in some way I was Gerald's spiritual great-granddaughter, though of course that's rubbish. I wondered what he would think to see me doing the honours for him. I suspect he would be amused by the tangle of inconsistencies that landed me there. There are so many contradictions. Yes, I inherited the Mad Boy's house, but I don't live there – my home is in Greece. And although I think of Robert as the long-lost grandfather I came to know and care about, he might not even be my blood relation. The fact that I have a Russian name many find impossible to pronounce and that my Russian grandmother was a card-carrying British Communist to the end of her days merely adds further twists.

ARLIER THAT MORNING, when I had gone downstairs
for breakfast at the Bell, Mel advised me to go to
the bar, where her husband was blowing on a few
pieces of coal, trying to get a fire going. I sat at a
large table in the bay window, and while Mel
prepared scrambled eggs, doorsteps of toast and
coffee, I looked out at the Market Place. There
were people hurrying to work or out on errands, farmers passing in
Land Rovers, a pretty teenage girl dawdling, the flower shop putting
out its wares, a queue for the Oxford bus. It was a contemporary version
of the reproduction engraving in the pub of exactly the same view in
the nineteenth century: women with crinolines and parasols stroll by,
a shepherd drives his flock down the slope. From my chair, I could
see the gates to Faringdon House up by the church. This was a new
vantage point for me – the outsider looking in. It was strange to look
at a place that was both mine and not mine. I sensed the mystery of
the house that can't be seen from the town but that dominates it in
a certain way. This novel angle was enjoyable, though I also recalled
the awkwardness and shame I felt emerging from the gates, soon after
inheriting the estate, and being taken down to the market stalls on a
Tuesday so the new estate manager could introduce me. He collected
the rents: £5 from the egg stall, something else from the chap with
the baskets. That seemed a long time ago and I was pleased to sit
anonymously in this window, watching the world pass. 'Did you tell
the landlord at the Bell who you were?' a friend had asked the previous
evening. It made me think of Gerald's old retort: 'And who *were* you?'
Back in the early days, a conversation was overheard by my brother
Leo, while having a drink at the Bell: 'Do you know about the new
owner of Faringdon House? It's some Czech woman.' Another person
said they'd heard that the chatelaine was 'a very old lady'.

This vista from the pub brought the realisation that I had taken a
step back from the place I've now been involved with for half my life.
My new perspective was not just spatial but temporal. From my beer-
scented breakfast table, the history of all the people who have been

linked to Faringdon House appeared slightly different. After several years researching and writing about their lives, I had become deeply involved with the people who came before me, and could look with much more understanding right back to Gerald's birth in the depths of Victorian Shropshire, to Robert's arrival twenty-eight years later and Jennifer's in the middle of the First World War. I had become fascinated by all three characters and how their lives were moulded by their rejection of their gentrified backgrounds. All of them suffered from critical or absent fathers, and mothers who were fonder of horses or drugged bed-rest than being with their children. All had close relationships with people they employed and troubled ones with those who loved them. And all created their own revolutions, running from the stifling conflicts of their parents' homes and pursuing pleasure with impunity. They refused to live along the conventional lines that were mapped out.

From far off, Lord Berners and the crazy Heber-Percy couple had looked funny, even foolish, but the closer I got to them, the more I empathised with their complex natures and their individual suffering. In these more puritanical but certainly fairer times, it is easy to deprive them of their rights to an unbiased judgement. Their huge material advantages and luxury-loving natures make them easy, even automatic targets – 'like shooting a sitting robin', as Gerald put it, or perhaps a rose-hued dove. We eschew the older bigotries of racism, sexism, ageism and homophobia, but class discrimination remains, with a denigration of 'chavs' and an easy prejudice encouraged against the rich and privileged. But privilege is not immunity from pain. I was increasingly aware that, whatever their shortcomings, the Faringdon set deserved understanding. I had been pulled into their world by Robert's last big risk in leaving me his beloved house – a development almost as unexpected as when he took Jennifer there as his bride – but it was the process of writing about Faringdon that provided me with a new sort of intimacy.

By the time I finished my coffee in the Bell's bay window, the fire was burning nicely and the chill in the bar was easing. At this point,

I felt able to step back from my own place in the story. I hadn't told the landlord 'who I was'. Looking at the black wrought-iron gates to Faringdon House, I became aware of how Lord Berners, the Mad Boy, my grandmother, my mother and me are just a few elements in a long story of so many other people – those who lived and worked in the same spaces before us, and the others who were there before that, in the old Elizabethan house. Of course it doesn't stop there either. And for many centuries of that time, the Bell was here in some guise, providing ale for locals, breakfast for travellers and a view up to the intriguing gateway of Faringdon House.

Notes

CHAPTER ONE
A Fish-shaped Handbag
Appearing on page 5

1 Alan Hollinghurst, 'Pink Doves', short story, Festival Internazionale di Roma 2006

CHAPTER TWO
Behind the Rocking Horse
Appearing between pages 11 and 29

2 Quennell, p. 138
3 Charles Duff, interview
4 Dickinson, p. 78
5 Acton, *More Memoirs of an Aesthete*, p. 34
6 Hart-Davis, p. 120
7 Berners, *First Childhood*, in *Collected Tales*, p. 5
8 Ibid.
9 Berners, unpublished notebook
10 Berners, *Far From the Madding War*, in *Collected Tales*, p. 383
11 Carpenter, p. 102
12 Fielding, *The Face on the Sphinx*, p. 2
13 Sitwell, p. 180
14 Berners, *First Childhood*, in *Collected Tales*, p. 82
15 Rowse, p. 48
16 Amory, *Lord Berners*, p. 73
17 Mary Gifford, 'Aspects of a Biography', pp. 30–31
18 Letter to Clarissa Churchill, 1941
19 Dickinson, p. 7
20 Berners, *First Childhood*, in *Collected Tales*, p. 53
21 Berners, *A Distant Prospect*, p. 45

22 Berners, *First Childhood*, in *Collected Tales*, p. 65
23 Ibid., p.107
24 Berners, *A Distant Prospect*, p. 65
25 Berners, *First Childhood*, in *Collected Tales*, p. 194
26 Ibid.
27 Berners, *A Distant Prospect*, p. 61
28 Berners, *Dresden*, p. 84
29 Ibid., p. 91
30 Ibid., p. 84
31 Brinnin, p. 354
32 Desmond Guinness, 'At Home with a Musical Eccentric', *Irish Times*, 23 May 1975
33 Stravinsky, *Selected Correspondence*, p. 153
34 Berners, *First Childhood*, in *Collected Tales*, p. 46
35 Berners, *The Château de Résenlieu*, p. 1
36 Ibid., p. 18
37 Ibid., p. 41
38 Ibid., p. 62
39 Nancy Mitford, 'Faringdon House', *House & Garden*, Aug.–Sept. 1950

CHAPTER THREE

Russians, Radicals and Roman Catholics

Appearing between pages 32 and 49

40 Harold Nicolson, p. 132
41 Berners, *Far From the Madding War*, in *Collected Tales*, p. 392
42 Alan Wykes, 'Lord Berners', *Music and Musicians*, Sept. 1983
43 Berners, *Percy Wallingford*, in *Collected Tales*, p. 29
44 Gavin Bryars, interview with author
45 Lane, 'Lord Berners'
46 Stravinsky, *Selected Correspondence*, p. 140
47 Constant Lambert, 'The Musical Peer', introduction to Osbert Lancaster's 'Uncommon People', *Strand Magazine*, April 1947
48 Constant Lambert, 'Tribute to Lord Berners', BBC Radio 3, 16 February 1951
49 Stravinsky, *Memories and Commentaries*, p. 83
50 Dickinson, *Lord Berners*, p. 24
51 Grigoriev, p. 226
52 Gifford, 'Lord Berners and the Triumph of Neptune', p. 11
53 ibid., p. 13
54 *Gramophone*, December 1926
55 Fielding, *The Face on the Sphinx*, pp. 2–3
56 Mary Gifford, 'The Eccentric Lord Berners', lecture at Wantage Festival, 2013

57 Wellesley, *Far Have I Travelled*, p. 134
58 William Crack, interview with Gavin Bryars
59 Ibid.
60 Ibid.
61 Amory, *Lord Berners*, p. 113
62 Rose, p. 376
63 Kahan, p.240
64 Glendinning, *Vita*, p. 253
65 Kahan, p. 252
66 Brett, 'Musicality, Essentialism, and the Closet', in Brett, Wood and Thomas, pp. 16–17
67 Christopher Wood, letter to mother, in Ingleby, pp. 105 and 162
68 Rose, p. 129
69 Alan Hollinghurst, 'The Dandy in the Desert: Ronald Firbank After the War', Graham Storey Lecture, 2012
70 Berners, in Kyrle Fletcher, p. 145
71 Hobson, p. 146
72 Berners, in Kyrle Fletcher, pp. 149–50
73 Aberconway, pp. 124–5
74 Acton, *More Memoirs of an Aesthete*, p. 42
75 Sitwell, p. 181
76 Amory, *Lord Berners*, p. 66

CHAPTER FOUR

A Delightful Youth

Appearing between pages 51 and 71

77 Heber-Percy, pp. 21–22
78 Ibid., p. 32
79 Ibid., p. 18
80 Ibid., p. 20
81 Ibid., p. 30
82 Ibid., p. 18
83 Deirdre Curteis, interview
84 Mitford, Ross *et al* (eds), p. 22
85 Wheen, p. 27
86 Ibid.

87 Niven, p. 34
88 Heber-Percy, p. 118
89 Martin Green, p. 27
90 Heber-Percy, p. 117
91 Carpenter, p. 172
92 Fielding, *The Duchess of Jermyn Street*, p. 124
93 Luke, p. 27
94 Jonathan Burnham, interview
95 Houlbrook, p. 51
96 Tamagne, p. 46

97 Ackerley, p. 175
98 Meyrick, p. 22
99 Gardiner, p. 628
100 Luke, p. 31

101 Susanna Johnston, interview
102 Diana Mosley, *Loved Ones*, p. 104
103 Berners, *The Girls of Radcliff Hall*, p. 39

CHAPTER FIVE

Et in Arcadia Ego

Appearing between pages 74 and 98

104 Diana Mosley, *Loved Ones*, p. 104
105 Letter from Gerald Berners to Cecil Beaton, copy in Berners Archive, British Library
106 Diana Mosley, *A Life of Contrasts*, p. 105, and Edward James, interview with Gavin Bryars
107 Rose, p. 376
108 Dickinson, p. 78
109 Michael Duff, p. 94
110 Jonathan Burnham to Mark Amory, *Lord Berners*, p. 127 and note
111 Letter from Gerald Berners to Cecil Beaton, October 15 1933, in Berners Archive, British Library
112 A. L. Rowse to Mark Amory, *Friends and Contemporaries*, p. 214 and note
113 Henry James, p. 222
114 Dickinson, p. 74
115 Bridget Dickinson, interview
116 Wheen, p. 72
117 Ibid., p. 54
118 Edward James, interview with Gavin Bryars
119 Mark Girouard, 'Faringdon House, Berkshire: The Home of Mr Robert Heber-Percy', *Country Life*, 12 and 19 May 1966
120 Nancy Mitford, *The Pursuit of Love*, p. 41
121 Rose, p. 376
122 Nancy Mitford, 'Faringdon House', *House & Garden*, Aug.–Sept. 1950
123 Alan Wykes, 'Lord Berners', *Music and Musicians*, Sept. 1983
124 Owen, p. 70
125 Berners, *The Romance of a Nose*, in *Collected Tales*, p. 304
126 Rowse, p.62, and Dickinson, p. 96
127 Nancy Mitford, op. cit.
128 Berners, unpublished notebook
129 Stravinsky, *Memories and Commentaries*, p. 84
130 Rose, p. 376
131 Berners, *First Childhood*, in *Collected Tales*, p. 29
132 Berners, interview in *Lilliput*, vol. XXIV, no. 1, January 1949
133 Derek Jackson, interview with Gavin Bryars
134 Wilson, p. 109
135 Kavanagh, p. 211
136 Cyril Connolly, *Enemies of Promise*, p. 34
137 Interview with Diana Mosley, in Dickinson, p. 91
138 John Betjeman, 'Lord Berners: 1883–1950' (obituary), *Listener*, 11 May 1950
139 Harris, p. 291
140 Diana Mosley, *A Life of Contrasts*, p. 191
141 Dickinson, p. 105
142 Carpenter, p. 263
143 Wilson, p. 104
144 Berners, unpublished notebook
145 Gavin Bryars, 'The Versatile Peer', *Guardian*, 22 February 2003
146 Interview with Harold Acton, in Dickinson, p. 56
147 Charlotte Mosley, *The Mitfords*, p. 86
148 Dickinson, p. 75

CHAPTER SIX

Boys and Girls

Appearing between pages 100 and 115

149 Mulvagh, p. 47

150 Byrne, p. 131

151 Ibid.

152 Ibid., p. 147

153 Ibid., p. 176

154 Ibid., p. 185

155 Mulvagh, p. 41

156 Luke, p. 91

157 John Betjeman, 'Lord Berners: 1883–1950' (obituary), *Listener*, 11 May 1950

158 Glendinning, *Edith Sitwell*, p. 104

159 Vickers, *Cecil Beaton*, p. 74

160 Evelyn Waugh, 'Footlights and Chandeliers', *The Spectator*, 21 July 1961

161 Deirdre Curteis, interview

162 Vickers, *Cecil Beaton*, p. 183

163 Alan Pryce-Jones, *Adam International Review*, nos 385–90, 1 January 1974

164 Fielding, *The Duchess of Jermyn Street*, p. 170

165 Ibid., p. 174

166 Ibid.

167 Dickinson, p. 85

168 Fielding, *The Duchess of Jermyn Street*, p. 170

169 Vickers, *Cecil Beaton*, p. 161

170 Hugo Vickers, unpublished diary

171 Vickers, *Cecil Beaton*, p. 162

172 Hugo Vickers, interview

173 Ibid.

174 Vickers, op. cit.

175 Thomson, p. 75

176 Ibid.

177 Daphne Fielding, 'Spirit of Ecstasy', *Harpers & Queen*, 1989

178 Thomson, p. 159

179 Amory, *Lord Berners*, p. 148

180 John Byrne, introduction to Berners, *The Girls of Radcliff Hall*, p. vii

CHAPTER SEVEN

Fiends

Appearing between pages 116 and 131

181 Devonshire, p. 41

182 Ben Macintyre, 'Those Utterly Maddening Mitford Girls', *The Times*, 12 October 2007

183 Diana Mosley, *A Life of Contrasts*, p. 267

184 Ibid.

185 Gardiner, p. 433

186 Green, p. 322

187 Devonshire, p. 41

188 Deirdre Curteis, interview

189 Gardiner, p. 439

190 T. S. Eliot, 'Burbank with a Beedeker: Bleistein with a Cigar', 1920

191 Luke, p. 91

192 Interview with Robert Heber-Percy, in Dickinson, p. 79

193 Berners, unpublished notebook

194 Clarissa Eden, interview

195 Acton, *More Memoirs of an Aesthete*, p. 31

196 Lees-Milne, *Prophesying Peace*, p. 24

197 Sitwell, p. 181

198 Diana Mosley, *A Life of Contrasts*, p. 97

199 Harold Nicolson, 'Marginal Comment', *The Spectator*, vol. CLXXXV, 12 October 1950

200 Nichols, *The Sweet and Twenties*, p. 158

201 Woolf, 'Am I a Snob?', in *Moments of Being*, p. 195

202 Nichols, *The Sweet and Twenties*, p. 165

203 Ibid., p. 159

204 Richardson, p. 47

205 Amory, *Lord Berners*, p. 161

206 Dickinson, p. 95

207 Ibid., p. 94

208 Constant Lambert, introductory talk to concert of Lord Berners' music, BBC Third Programme, 16 February 1951

209 Berners, *First Childhood*, in *Collected Tales*, p. 66

210 Noel Annan, 'The Camel at the Door', *New York Review of Books*, 7 October 1999

CHAPTER EIGHT

Follies and Fur-lined Wombs

Appearing between pages 133 and 155

211 Glendinning, *Vita*, p. 223

212 Vickers, *Cecil Beaton*, p. 261

213 Berners, *Far From the Madding War*, in *Collected Tales*, p. 385

214 Gibson, p. 72

215 Richardson, p. 291

216 Interview with Robert Heber-Percy, in Dickinson, p. 107

217 Ibid.

218 Cohen, p. 138

219 Gibson, p. 191

220 Edward James, p. 2

221 Gibson, p. 241

222 Edward James, interview with Gavin Bryars

223 Amory, *Lord Berners*, p. 160

224 Richardson, p. 296

225 John Betjeman, 'Lord Berners: 1883–1950' (obituary), *Listener*, 11 May 1950

226 Rose, p. 56

227 Amory, *The Letters of Evelyn Waugh*, p. 234

228 Diana Mosley, *Loved Ones*, p. 127

229 Dickinson, p. 33

230 Stein, [ebook, no page numbers]

231 Nichols, *Are They the Same at Home?*, p. 50

232 Kavanagh, p. 211

233 Berners, unpublished notebook

234 Sitwell, p. 178

235 Glendinning, *Edith Sitwell*, pp. 26–8

236 Sitwell, p. 178

237 Motion, p. 187

238 Salter, p. 78

239 Buckle, p. 42

240 Rose, p. 358

241 Cyril Connolly, *Previous Convictions*, p. 282

242 Rose, p. 184

243 Malcolm, p. 159

244 Stein

245 Malcolm, p. 64

246 Jack Fox, interview

247 Toklas, pp. 285 and 283

CHAPTER NINE

The Orphan on the Top Floor

Appearing between pages 161 and 185

248 Sturgis, p. 601

249 Gathorne-Hardy, p. 80

250 Christopher Hussey, 'Oare House, Wiltshire, The Property of Mr Geoffrey Fry', *Country Life*, vol. LXIII, no. 1625, 10 March 1928

251 Byrne, p. 110

252 Taylor, p. 61

253 Davie, p. 300

254 Letter to Harold Acton, in Amory, *The Letters of Evelyn Waugh*, p. 38

255 ibid., p. 40

256 Janetta Parlade, interview

257 Cressida Connolly, interview

258 Francis Wyndham, interview

259 Amory, *The Letters of Evelyn Waugh*, p. 51

260 Francis Wyndam, interview

261 Martin Green, p. 241

262 Francis Wyndham, interview

263 Hastings, p. 73

264 Taylor, p. 203

265 Francis Wyndham, interview

266 Cressida Connolly, obituary of Jennifer Ross, *Independent*, 19 December 2003

267 Cressida Connolly, interview

268 Lewis, p. 200

269 Jack Fox, interview

CHAPTER TEN
In the City of the Dreaming Dons
Appearing between pages 186 and 214

270 Fielding, *The Duchess of Jermyn Street*, p. 178
271 Haste, p. 28
272 Amory, *Lord Berners*, p. 177
273 Kavanagh, p. 245
274 Lees-Milne, *Diaries, 1942–1954*, p. 10
275 De Gaury, p. 18
276 Ibid., p. 174
277 Isaiah Berlin in Lloyd-Jones, p. 18
278 Haste, p. 38
279 Lewis, p. 107
280 Luke, p. 35
281 Carpenter, p. 97
282 Berners, unpublished notebook
283 Diana Mosley, *A Life of Contrasts*, p. 155
284 Olson, p. 186
285 Haste, p. 54
286 Letter from Ann O'Neil (later Fleming) to Gerald Berners, in Berners Archive, British Library
287 Billa Harrod, interview with Gavin Bryars
288 Ibid.
289 Rowse, p. 51
290 Sylvia Crack, interview
291 Berners, *Far From the Madding War*, in *Collected Tales*, p. 417
292 De Gaury, p. 44
293 Ibid., p. 174
294 Ibid., p. 21
295 Andrew Crowden, eulogy for Robert Heber-Percy
296 Francis Wyndham, interview
297 Feigel, p. 4
298 Olson, p. 194
299 Ross, p. 142
300 Larkin, p. 11
301 Berners, *Far From the Madding War*, in *Collected Tales*, p. 406
302 Haste, p. 53
303 Kavanagh, p. 206
304 Francis Wyndham, interview
305 Charlotte Mosley, *The Mitfords*, p. 183
306 Wilson, p. 145
307 Skelton, p. 218
308 Sheldon, p. 80
309 De-la-Noy, p. 137
310 Billa Harrod, interview with Gavin Bryars
311 Haste, p. 33
312 Ibid., p. 34
313 Ibid., p. 42
314 Clarissa Eden, interview
315 Haste, p. 33
316 Lord Berners, 'Private Opinion Poll', *Lilliput*, vol. XXIV, no. 1, January 1949
317 Clarissa Eden, interview
318 Rowse, p. 61
319 David Cecil, interview with Gavin Bryars
320 Sir Thomas Armstrong, interviewed on Radio 3 on 11 December 1992
321 Michael Ratcliff, 'Lord Berners, that Most Versatile Peer', *The Times*, 3 September 1983
322 Acton, *Memoirs of an Aesthete*, p. 139
323 Rowse, p. 290
324 Amory, *Lord Berners*, p. 36
325 Prieto, *Paintings and Drawings*
326 Heber-Percy, p. 119

CHAPTER ELEVEN
Gosh I Think She's Swell
Appearing between pages 217 and 237

327 Clarissa Eden, interview
328 Rowse, p. 72
329 Clarissa Eden, interview
330 Diana Mosley, *A Life of Contrasts*, p. 173
331 Kahan, p. 364
332 Sweet, p. 115–16
333 Haste, p. 60
334 Vickers, *Cecil Beaton*, p. 248
335 Ibid., p. 217
336 Leonard Mosley, p. 183
337 Cannadine, p. 635
338 Hastings, p. 158
339 Nancy Mitford, 'Faringdon House', *House & Garden*, Aug.–Sept. 1950
340 Fielding, *Mercury Presides*, p. 210
341 Amory, *Lord Berners*, p. 194

342 Gardiner, p. 552
343 Crisp, p. 160
344 Obituary of Michael Luke, *Independent*, 19 April 2005
345 Luke, p. 174
346 Sheldon, p. 63
347 Lewis, p. 398
348 Letter from Elizabeth Bowen to Charles Ritchie, in Glendinning, *Love's Civil War*, p. 51
349 Muggeridge, p. 104
350 Davie, p. 608
351 Rowse, p. 72
352 *Oxford Magazine*, 4 June 1942
353 Joy Skinner, interview
354 Dickinson, p. 17
355 Joan Wyndham, p. 45

CHAPTER TWELVE
The Pram in the Hall
Appearing between pages 243 and 259

356 Jack Fox, interview
357 Francis Wyndham, interview
358 Cooper, *A Durable Fire*, p. 310
359 Clarissa Eden, interview
360 Niven, p. 230
361 Ibid., p. 44
362 Victoria Zinovieff, interview
363 Billa Harrod, interview with Gavin Bryars
364 Charles Duff, interview

365 Hill, p. 173
366 Hastings, p. 141
367 Lees-Milne, *Prophesying Peace*, p. 28
368 Diana Mosley, *A Life of Contrasts*, p. 178
369 Ibid., p. 181
370 Ibid.
371 Sheldon, p. 115
372 Lees-Milne, *Prophesying Peace*, p. 53
373 Ibid., p. 54

CHAPTER THIRTEEN
Put in a Van
Appearing between pages 262 and 286

374 Letter to Roy Harrod, undated, 1994, in Billa Harrod's private papers

375 Amory, *Lord Berners*, p. 218

376 Obituary of Michael Luke, *Daily Telegraph*, 11 April 2005

377 Luke, p. 172

378 Obituary of Michael Luke, op. cit.

379 Francis Wyndham, interview

380 Clarissa Eden, interview

381 Francis Wyndham, interview

382 Amory, *Lord Berners*, p. 220, refers to Glendinning, *Elizabeth Bowen: Portrait of a Writer*

383 Cyril Connolly, *Horizon*, vols xv–xvi, August 1947

384 Interview with Robert Heber-Percy, in Dickinson, p. 84

385 Rachel Cecil, interview with Gavin Bryars

386 Glendinning, *Love's Civil War*, p. 100

387 Constant Lambert, 'The Musical Peer', introduction to Osbert Lancaster's 'Uncommon People', *Strand*, April 1947, p. 62

388 Billa Harrod, interview with Gavin Bryars

389 Diana Mosley, *Loved Ones*, p. 102

390 Amory, *Lord Berners*, p. 232

391 Vickers, *Cecil Beaton*, p. 462

392 Billa Harrod, interview with Gavin Bryars

393 Lewis, p. 413

394 Quennell, p. 137

395 Diana Mosley, *A Life of Contrasts*, p. 200

396 Amory, *Lord Berners*, p. 224

397 Ibid.

398 Diana Mosley, interview with Gavin Bryars

399 Francis Wyndham, interview

400 Niven, p. 247

401 Cyril Connolly, *London Magazine*, Feb.–March 1975

402 Lees-Milne, *Diaries, 1942–1954*, p. 330

403 Henry Green, p. 58

404 Treglown, p. 53

405 Feigel, p. 44

406 Ibid., p. 92

407 Charlotte Mosley, *The Letters of Nancy Mitford*, p. 254

408 Terry Southern, 'Henry Green, The Art of Fiction No. 22', *Paris Review*, Summer 1958

409 Ross, p. 196

410 Obituary of Michael Luke, op. cit.

411 Lewis, p. 428

412 Diana Mosley, *Loved Ones*, p. 128

413 Berners, letter to William Plomer

414 Charlotte Mosley, *The Mitfords*, p. 260

415 Diana Mosley, letter to Lady Redesdale, quoted in Amory, *Lord Berners*, p. 235

416 Elizabeth Bowen, letter to Charles Ritchie, Glendinning, op. cit., p. 126

417 Beaton, *The Happy Years*, p. 130

418 Diana Mosley, *Loved Ones*, p. 130

419 Clarissa Eden, interview

420 Diana Mosley, letter to Lady Redesdale, quoted in Amory, op. cit, p. 235

421 Robert Heber-Percy, draft letter to unknown person, private papers

422 Diana Mosley, letter to Lady Redesdale, quoted in Amory, op. cit.

CHAPTER FOURTEEN

'From Catamite to Catamite'

Appearing between pages 288 and 309

423 Diana Mosley, *Loved Ones*, p. 131
424 John Betjeman, obituary of Lord Berners, *Listener*, 11 May 1950
425 Obituary of Lady Dorothy Heber-Percy, *Daily Telegraph*, 17 November 2001
426 *Daily Express*, 30 November 1950
427 Skelton, p. 97
428 Ibid., p. 98
429 Betty (Garth's widow), interview
430 Charles Duff, interview
431 Susan Hazel, interview
432 Candida Lycett Green, interview
433 Deirdre Curteis, interview

434 Richard Brain, interview
435 Francis Wyndham, interview
436 Vickers, *The Unexpurgated Beaton Diaries*, p. 371
437 Cyril Connolly papers, courtesy of Jeremy Lewis
438 Cressida Connolly, interview
439 Jennifer Ross, unpublished notebook
440 Thynn, p. 21
441 Zinovieff, pp. 304–305
442 Maureen Cleave, 'The Performer at the Bottom of Mr Zinovieff's Garden', *Evening Standard*, 11 January 1968

CHAPTER FIFTEEN

The Nazi

Appearing between pages 311 and 325

443 Barbara Gilmore, interview
444 Desmond Ball, interview
445 Susanna Johnston, interview
446 Ibid.
447 Judith Webb, interview
448 Jack Fox, interview
449 James Skinner, interview
450 Jack Fox, interview
451 Candida Lycett Green, interview
452 Jonathan Burnham, interview
453 Taylor, p. 110
454 Motion, p. 336
455 Ibid., p. 351
456 Candida Lycett Green, 'The Way Home', blog: www.candidalycettgreen.co.uk, April 2010

457 Obituary of Lady Dorothy Heber-Percy, op. cit.
458 Amory, *Lord Berners*, p. 141
459 Mark Amory, interview
460 Interview with Robert Heber-Percy, in Dickinson, p. 86
461 Marlborough, p. 235
462 Beaton, *The Happy Years*, p. 130
463 Hugo Vickers, interview
464 Vickers, *The Unexpurgated Beaton Diaries*, p. 361
465 Martin Webb, interview
466 Vickers, op. cit., p. 374
467 Ibid.
468 Hugo Vickers, interview

CHAPTER SIXTEEN
Robert's Folly
Appearing between pages 328 and 342

469 Byrne, p. 163
470 Jennifer Ross, unpublished notebook
471 Cressida Connolly, interview
472 Jonathan Gathorne-Hardy, interview
473 Jennifer Ross, unpublished notebook
474 Jonathan Burnham, interview
475 Susanna Johnston, interview
476 Ibid.
477 Joy Skinner, interview
478 Victoria Zinovieff, interview
479 Candida Lycett Green, interview
480 Deirdre Curteis, interview

CHAPTER SEVENTEEN
Purple Dye
Appearing between pages 353 and 370

481 Nancy Mitford, 'Faringdon House', *House & Garden*, Aug.–Sept. 1950
482 Joy Skinner, interview
483 Mario Testino, interview
484 Rose, p. 376

CHAPTER EIGHTEEN
Blood Ties
Appearing between pages 376 and 383

485 Victoria Zinovieff, interview
486 Devonshire, p. 132
487 Victoria Zinovieff, interview
488 Devonshire, p. 155
489 Victoria Zinovieff, interview
490 Lady Joanna Mersey, interview
491 Francis Wyndham, interview
492 Richard Brain, interview
493 Janetta Parlade, interview
494 Sarah Gibb, interview

Select Bibliography

Note: Unpublished documents come from a number of different sources. Most of Lord Berners' papers, including letters and notebooks, are gathered in the British Library – thanks to the Berners Trust for permission to quote from them. Letters from Billa Harrod to Roy Harrod are in the archives of the Norfolk Record Office (ACC2005/362 box 7). Other letters, diaries and notebooks are in private collections. Diana Mosely letters are reproduced by kind permission of Charlotte Mosely and the Mitford Archive.

Aberconway, Christabel, *A Wiser Woman: A Book of Memories*, Hutchinson, London, 1966

Ackerley, J. R., *My Father and Myself*, NYRB Classics, New York, 1999

Acocella, Joan, 'A Dog's Life', *New Yorker*, 7 February 2011

Acton, Harold, *Memoirs of an Aesthete*, Methuen, London, 1948

—— *More Memoirs of an Aesthete*, Methuen, London, 1970

Amory, Mark, *Lord Berners: The Last Eccentric*, Chatto & Windus, London, 1998

—— (ed.), *The Letters of Evelyn Waugh*, Weidenfeld & Nicolson, London, 1980

Beaton, Cecil, *Ashcombe: The Story of a Fifteen-Year Lease*, Batsford, London, 1949

—— *The Happy Years: Diaries 1944–48*, Weidenfeld & Nicolson, London, 1972

—— *The Strenuous Years: Diaries 1948–55*, Weidenfeld & Nicolson, London, 1973

Berlin, Isaiah, *Personal Impressions*, Pimlico, London, 1998

Berners, Gerald, *A Distant Prospect*, Constable, London, 1945

—— *The Château de Résenlieu*, Turtle Point Press and Helen Marx Books, New York, 2000

—— *Dresden*, Turtle Point Press and Helen Marx Books, New York, 2008

—— *Collected Tales and Fantasies of Lord Berners*, including *Percy Wallingford*, *The Camel*, *Mr Pidger*, *Count Omega*, *First Childhood*, *The Romance of a Nose*, *Far From the Madding War*, Turtle Point Press and Helen Marx Books, New York, 1999

—— *The Girls of Radcliff Hall*, Introduction by John Byrne, Montcalm Publishing, New York, and the Cygnet Press, London, 2000

Betjeman, John, and John Piper (eds), *Murray's Berkshire Architectural Guide*, John Murray, London, 1949

Bowen, Elizabeth, *The Heat of the Day*, Vintage, London, 2008

—— *Collected Impressions*, Longmans, Green and Co., London, 1950

Brett, Philip, Elizabeth Wood and Gary C. Thomas (eds), *Queering the Pitch: The New Gay and Lesbian Musicology*, Routledge, London, 1994

Brinnin, John Malcolm, *The Third Rose: Gertrude Stein and Her World*, Weidenfeld & Nicolson, London, 1960

Brown, Susanna, *Queen Elizabeth II: Portraits by Cecil Beaton*, V&A Publications, London, 2013

Buckle, Richard (ed.), *Self Portrait with Friends: The Selected Diaries of Cecil Beaton*, Pimlico, London, 1979

Byrne, Paula, *Mad World: Evelyn Waugh and the*

Secrets of Brideshead, Harper Press, London, 2009

Cannadine, David, *The Decline and Fall of the British Aristocracy*, Yale University Press, New Haven and London, 1990

Carpenter, Humphrey, *The Brideshead Generation: Evelyn Waugh and His Generation* (later editions *His Friends*), Faber & Faber, London, 1989

Cohen, Harriet, *A Bundle of Time: The Memoirs of Harriet Cohen*, Faber & Faber, London, 1969

Connolly, Cyril, *Enemies of Promise*, University of Chicago Press, Chicago, 2008

—— *Previous Convictions: Selected Writings*, Hamish Hamilton, London, 1963

Connolly, Matthew (ed.), *The Selected Works of Cyril Connolly* (vol. I), *The Modern Movement*, Picador, London, 2002

—— (vol. II), *The Two Natures*, Picador, London, 2002

Cooper, Artemis, *Patrick Leigh Fermor: An Adventure*, John Murray, London, 2012

—— (ed.), *A Durable Fire: The Letters of Duff and Diana Cooper*, 1913–1950, Collins, London, 1983

Cooper, Diana, *Autobiography: The Rainbow Comes and Goes; The Light of Common Day; Trumpets from the Steep*, Faber & Faber, London, 2008

Crisp, Quentin, *The Naked Civil Servant*, Jonathan Cape, London, 1968

Dalí, Salvador, *The Secret Life of Salvadore Dali*, trans. Haakon M. Chevalier, Dial Press, London, 1948

Davie, Michael (ed.), *The Diaries of Evelyn Waugh*, Weidenfeld & Nicolson, London, 1976

de Gaury, Gerald, *Arabian Journey and Other Desert Travels*, Harrap, London, 1950

de la Mare, Walter, *Early One Morning in the Spring: Chapters on Children and on Childhood as it is Revealed in Particular in Early Memories and in Early Writings*, The Macmillan Company, New York, 1935

De-la-Noy, Michael, *Denton Welch: The Making of a Writer*, Viking, Harmondsworth, 1984

Devonshire, Deborah, *Wait for Me! Memoirs of the Youngest Mitford Sister*, John Murray, London, 2010

Dickinson, Peter, *Lord Berners: Composer, Writer, Painter*, The Boydell Press, Woodbridge, 2008

Duff, Charles, 'Sex, Slate and Snowdon', unpublished memoir

Duff, Michael, *The Power of a Parasol*, Marlowe Galleries, London, undated

Feigel, Lara, *The Love-charm of Bombs: Restless Lives in the Second World War*, Bloomsbury, London, 2013

Fielding, Daphne, *The Duchess of Jermyn Street: The Life and Good Times of Rosa Lewis of the Cavendish Hotel*, Futura, London, 1974

—— *The Face on the Sphinx: A Portrait of Gladys Deacon, Duchess of Marlborough*, Hamish Hamilton, London, 1978

—— *Mercury Presides*, Eyre and Spottiswoode, London, 1954

Gardiner, Juliet, *The Thirties: An Intimate History*, Harper Press, London, 2010

—— *Wartime: Britain 1939–1945*, Review, London, 2005

Gathorne-Hardy, Jonathan, *The Rise and Fall of the British Nanny*, Hodder & Stoughton, London, 1972

Gibson, Ian, *The Shameful Life of Salvador Dalí*, Faber & Faber, London, 1997

Gifford, Mary, 'Lord Berners: Aspects of a Biography', unpublished PhD thesis, King's College London, 2007

—— 'Lord Berners and the Triumph of Neptune', unpublished MA project, Southampton, 1999

Glendinning, Victoria, *Edith Sitwell: A Unicorn Among Lions*, Weidenfeld & Nicolson, London, 1981

—— *Vita: The Life of Vita Sackville-West*, Penguin, Harmondsworth, 1984

—— (ed.) with Judith Robertson, *Love's Civil War: Elizabeth Bowen and Charles Ritchie, Letters and Diaries from the Love Affair of a Lifetime*, Simon & Schuster, London, 2008

Green, Henry, *Caught*, The Hogarth Press, London, 1943
Green, Martin, *Children of the Sun: A Narrative of 'Decadence' in England after 1918*, Constable, London, 1977
Grigoriev, S. L., *The Diaghilev Ballet 1909–1929*, trans. Vera Bowen, Constable, London, 1953

Harris, Alexandra, *Romantic Moderns: English Writers, Artists and the Imagination from Virginia Woolf to John Piper*, Thames & Hudson, London, 2010
Hart-Davis, Rupert (ed.), *Siegfried Sassoon Diaries 1920–1922*, Faber & Faber, London, 1981
Haste, Cate (ed.), *Clarissa Eden, A Memoir: From Churchill to Eden*, Weidenfeld & Nicolson, London, 2007
Hastings, Selina, *Nancy Mitford*, Vintage, London, 2002
Heber-Percy, Cyril, *Us Four*, Faber & Faber, London, 1963
Hill, Heywood, and Anne Hill, *A Bookseller's War*, ed. Jonathan Gathorne-Hardy, Michael Russell Publishing, London, 1997
Hobson, Anthony (ed.), *Ronald Firbank: Letters to His Mother 1920–1924*, Verona, Stampena Valdonega 2001
Houlbrook, Matt, *Queer London: Perils and Pleasures in the Sexual Metropolis, 1918–1957*, University of Chicago Press, Chicago and London, 2005

Ingleby, Richard, *Christopher Wood: An English Painter*, Allison & Busby, London, 1995

James, Edward, *Swans Reflecting Elephants: My Early Years*, ed. George Melly, Weidenfeld & Nicolson, London, 1982
James, Henry, *Collected Travel Writings: Great Britain and America*, Library of America, New York, 1993
Jones, Bryony, *The Music of Lord Berners (1883–1950): 'The Versatile Peer'*, Ashgate Publishing, Aldershot, 2003

Kahan, Sylvia, *Music's Modern Muse: A Life of Winnaretta Singer, Princesse de Polignac*, University of Rochester Press, Rochester, 2003
Kavanagh, Julie, *Secret Muses: The Life of Frederick Ashton*, Faber & Faber, London, 1996
Kyrle Fletcher, Ifan, *Ronald Firbank: A Memoir*, Duckworth, London, 1930

Lancaster, Marie-Jacqueline (ed.), *Brian Howard: Portrait of a Failure*, Timewell Press, London, 2005
Lane, Philip, 'Lord Berners', unpublished BMus. thesis, University of Birmingham, 1972
Larkin, Philip, *Jill*, Faber & Faber, London, 1985
Lees-Milne, James, *Diaries, Prophesying Peace, 1944–45*, Chatto & Windus, London, 1977
—— *Diaries, 1942–1954*, abridged and introduced by Michael Bloch, John Murray, London, 2006
Lewis, Jeremy, *Cyril Connolly: A Life*, Jonathan Cape, London, 1997
Lloyd-Jones, Hugh (ed.), *Maurice Bowra: A Celebration*, Duckworth, London, 1974
Lowe, John, *Edward James: A Surrealist Life*, HarperCollins, London, 1991
Luke, Michael, *David Tennant and the Gargoyle Years*, Weidenfeld & Nicolson, London, 1991
Lycett Green, Candida (ed.), *John Betjeman: Letters, Volume I: 1926 to 1951*, Methuen, London, 1994
—— *John Betjeman: Letters, Volume II: 1951 to 1984*, Methuen, London, 1994

Malcolm, Janet, *Two Lives: Gertrude and Alice*, Yale University Press, New Haven, 2007
Marlborough, Laura, Duchess of, *Laughter From a Cloud*, Weidenfeld & Nicolson, London, 1980
Meyrick, Mrs, *Secrets of the 43: Reminiscences*, J. Long, London, 1933
Mitford, Nancy, *Love in a Cold Climate*, Penguin, London, 1954
—— *The Pursuit of Love*, Penguin, London, 1962
—— *Highland Fling*, Hamlyn, London, 1982
——, Alan S. C. Ross *et al.* (eds), *Noblesse Oblige: An Enquiry into the Identifiable Characteristics of the English Aristocracy*, Hamish Hamilton, London, 1956

Montgomery-Hyde, H., *The Love that Dared Not Speak Its Name: A Candid History of Homosexuality in Britain*, Little, Brown & Co., Boston, 1970

Mosley, Charlotte (ed.), *The Letters of Nancy Mitford*, Sceptre, London, 1994

——— *The Mitfords: Letters between Six Sisters*, Harper Perennial, London, 2007

Mosley, Diana, *Loved Ones: Pen Portraits*, Sidgwick & Jackson, London, 1985

——— *A Life of Contrasts*, Gibson Square Books, London, 2009

Mosley, Leonard, *Castlerosse*, Arthur Barker, London, 1956

Motion, Andrew, *The Lamberts: George, Constant and Kit*, Chatto & Windus, London, 1986

Muggeridge, Malcolm, *Chronicles of Wasted Time*, vol. II: *The Infernal Grove*, Collins, London, 1973

Mulvagh, Jane, *Madresfield: The Real Brideshead*, Black Swan, London, 2009

Nichols, Beverley, *Are They the Same at Home?* George H. Doran Company, London, 1927

——— *The Sweet and Twenties*, Weidenfeld & Nicolson, London, 1958

Nicolson, Adam, *The Gentry: Stories of the English*, HarperCollins, London, 2011

Nicolson, Harold, *Some People*, Constable & Co., London, 1930

Niven, David, *The Moon's a Balloon*, Hamish Hamilton, London, 1971

Olson, Stanley (ed.), *Harold Nicolson: Diaries and Letters, 1930–1964*, Collins, London, 1980

Owen, Jane, *Eccentric Gardens*, Villard Books, New York, 1990

Powers, Alan, *Eric Ravilious: Imagined Realities*, Philip Wilson, London, 2012

Prieto, Gregorio, *Paintings and Drawings*, introduced by Luis Cernuda, Falcon Press, London, 1947

Pryce-Jones, David (ed.), *Cyril Connolly: Journal and Memoir*, Ticknor & Fields, New York, 1984

Quennell, Peter, *The Wanton Chase*, Collins, London, 1980

Richardson, John, *Sacred Monsters, Sacred Masters: Beaton, Capote, Dalí, Picasso, Freud, Warhol, and More*, Pimlico, London, 2002

Rose, Francis, *Saying Life: The Memoirs of Sir Francis Rose*, Cassell, London, 1961

Ross, Alan, *Blindfold Games*, Collins Harvill, London, 1988

Rowse, A. L., *Friends and Contemporaries*, Methuen, London, 1989

Salter, Elizabeth, *Helpmann: The Authorised Biography of Sir Robert Helpmann*, HarperCollins, London, 1978

Schiaparelli, Elsa, *Shocking Life: The Autobiography of Elsa Schiaparelli*, V&A Publications, London, 2007

Sheldon, Michael, *Friends of Promise: Cyril Connolly and the World of* Horizon, Hamish Hamilton, London, 1989

Sitwell, Osbert, *Laughter in the Next Room*, Macmillan, London, 1949

Skelton, Barbara, *Tears Before Bedtime* and *Weep No More*, Pimlico, London, 1993

Stannard, Martin, *Evelyn Waugh: The Early Years, 1903–1939*, Paladin, London, 1988

Stein, Gertrude, *Everybody's Autobiography*, Vintage, New York, 1973

Stravinsky, Igor, and Robert Craft, *Conversations with Igor Stravinsky*, Faber & Faber, London, 1959

——— *Memories and Commentaries*, Faber & Faber, London, 1959

——— *Selected Correspondence: Volume II*, Faber & Faber, London, 1984

Sturgis, Matthew, *Walter Sickert*, Harper Perennial, London, 2005

Sweet, Matthew, *The West End Front: The Wartime Secrets of London's Grand Hotels*, Faber & Faber, London, 2011

Tamagne, Florence, *A History of Homosexuality in*

Europe: Berlin, London, Paris, 1919–1939, vols I and II, Algora, New York, 2006

Taylor, D. J., *Bright Young People: The Rise and Fall of a Generation: 1918–1940*, Vintage, London, 2008

Thomson, George Malcolm, *Lord Castlerosse: His Life and Times*, Weidenfeld & Nicolson, London, 1973

Thynn, Alexander, *A Plateful of Privilege*, Artnik, London, 2003

Toklas, Alice B., *The Alice B. Toklas Cook Book*, Michael Joseph, London, 1954

Treglown, Jeremy, *Romancing: The Life and Work of Henry Green*, Faber & Faber, London, 2000

Vickers, Hugo, *Cecil Beaton: The Authorised Biography*, Weidenfeld & Nicolson, London, 1985

—— Unpublished Diary, 1981

—— (ed.), *The Unexpurgated Beaton Diaries*, Phoenix, London, 2003

—— *Beaton in the Sixties: More Unexpurgated Diaries*, Weidenfeld & Nicolson, London, 2003

War Department, The, *Instructions for American Servicemen in Britain 1942*, Washington D.C.

Waugh, Evelyn, *Vile Bodies*, Penguin, London, 2012

Wellesley, Dorothy, *Far Have I Travelled*, John Barrie, London, 1952

—— *Lost Planet and Other Poems*, Hogarth Press, London, 1942

Wheen, Francis, *Tom Driberg: His Life and Indiscretions*, Chatto & Windus, London, 1990

Wilson, A. N., *Betjeman*, Hutchinson, London, 2006

Woolf, Virginia and Jeanne Schulkind (ed.), *Moments of Being: Unpublished Autobiographical Writings*, Chatto & Windus for Sussex University Press, London, 1976

Wyndham, Francis, *The Theatre of Embarrassment*, Chatto & Windus, London, 1991

Wyndham, Joan, *Love Lessons: A Wartime Diary* and *Love is Blue: A Wartime Journal*, Mandarin, London, 1995

Ziegler, Philip, *Diana Cooper: The Biography of Lady Diana Cooper*, Penguin, London, 1983

Zinovieff, Sofka, *Red Princess: A Revolutionary Life*, Granta Books, London, 2007

Acknowledgements

My mother, Victoria Zinovieff, showed great generosity of spirit while this book was being written. It was not easy for her to see what is also her story being opened up by her daughter, but she remained positive and helpful throughout. I am especially grateful.

Many people contributed to my research, but none more than Mary Gifford, Secretary of the Berners Trust. She was tireless in searching through archives and providing data from the work for her thesis on Lord Berners. Eternal thanks.

Several people explored Gerald Berners's life long before I did and much of the material we all used is now gathered in the British Library. Gavin Bryars carried out research and interviews in the 1970s and '80s, and although his biography was abandoned in favour of his work as a composer, the vital material remains. It was very useful to me, as were Mark Amory's *Lord Berners: The Last Eccentric* and Peter Dickinson's *Lord Berners: Composer, Writer, Painter*. Like Peter Dickinson, whose devotion to the music and entire Berners oeuvre has lasted many decades, Philip Lane has also done much to promote Lord Berners's music. He gave me material from his own research and was always helpful. Francis Wyndham was one of the few people who were able to tell me first-hand about my grandmother's life from when she was young. His insights were profound and I came to see him as Jennifer's guardian angel. Some others also stand out for the quality of help they gave me: Cressida Connolly, Clarissa Eden, Jack Fox, Algernon Heber-Percy.

I am enormously grateful to everyone I interviewed: Lyn Ash, Des Ball, Betty Bennett, Hamish Bowles, the late Richard Brain, Jonathan Burnham, Robert Carsen, Tessa Charlton, Sylvia Crack, Deirdre Curteis, Gordon Dowell, Charles Duff, Nell Dunn, Jonathan Gathorne-Hardy, Sarah Gibb, Barbara Gilmore, Henry Harrod, Dennis Haynes, Susan Hazel, Jocelyn Hillgarth, Samuel Horrocks, Sarah Horrocks, Nicholas Johnston, Susanna Johnston, Henry Keswick, Bill King, Candida Lycett Green, Joanna Mersey, Jeremy Newick, Benedict Nightingale, the late Don Pargeter, Janetta Parlade, Joe Pauling, Victoria Press, Anne Redmon, Jonathan Ross, James Skinner, Joy Skinner, Andrew Smith, Mario Testino, Hugo Vickers, Roger Vlitos, Judith Webb, Martin Webb, Eddie Williams, Annabelle Zinovieff, Leo Zinovieff, Peter Zinovieff.

That gratitude also goes out to those who assisted my research in various ways: Howard Bailes, Nicolas Bell, Al Cane, Bridget Dickinson, Jane Fox, Howard Friend, Katherine Freisenbruch, Fred Koch, Jeremy Lewis, Susan Maddock, Christopher Mason, Adam Nicolson, Sarah Raven, Juliet Souter, Margaret Townsend, Anthony Wallersteiner, Michael Wells, Alyosha Zinovieff, Jenny Zinovieff.

Candida Lycett Green very kindly gave permission to quote from two poems by her father John Betjeman: *The Arrest of Oscar Wilde at the Cadogan Hotel* and *Before the Anaesthetic*. Thanks to her and to Jane Ross for permission to quote from Alan Ross's poem, *JW51B*.

Thank you, Alan Hollinghurst, for reading the manuscript with amazing care and taking the art of correcting to new heights. Thanks also to Paul Johnston, Gavin Bryars and Peter Dickinson who commented on early drafts.

Thanks to my dear agent Caroline Dawnay for her marvellous support. And to Sophie Scard and United Agents.

Dan Franklin has been the most wonderful editor from the initial proposal right through to the final corrections. I am deeply grateful. Also, to everyone at Jonathan Cape who has been involved with the book, especially Clare Bullock, Neil Bradford, Penelope Goodare, James Jones, Mikaela Pedlow, Eugenie Todd and Peter Ward.

Thank you, Lara and Anna, for all your support – the best daughters that anyone could wish for.

This book is dedicated with love to my husband, Vassilis Papadimitriou.

Index

IRENES

CUPID AND PSYCHE

Le Carrosse du Saint Sacrement

Berners